THE GERMANS AND EUROPE

THE GERMANS
AND EUROPE

A Personal Frontline History

Peter Millar

A

Arcadia Books Ltd
139 Highlever Road
London W10 6PH

www.arcadiabooks.co.uk

First published in the United Kingdom 2017
Copyright © Peter Millar 2017

A catalogue record for this book is available from the British Library.

ISBN 978-1-910050-89-7

Typeset in Sabon by MacGuru Ltd
Printed and bound by TJ International, Padstow PL28 8RW

ARCADIA BOOKS DISTRIBUTORS ARE AS FOLLOWS:

in the UK and elsewhere in Europe:
BookSource
50 Cambuslang Road
Cambuslang
Glasgow G32 8NB

in Australia/New Zealand:
NewSouth Books
University of New South Wales
Sydney NSW 2052

For my much-loved grandson
William Stanley Millar
24.7.2015–14.2.2016

Even little lives shape the world

Contents

Introduction

History is not something that just happens; history is something we live. All of us. Each of our lives is a history in its own way. The wider, longer narrative that is commonly referred to as 'History' is a version of lives past and present seen by an individual (the historian) from a particular perspective, through myriad filters: social, cultural, national and linguistic, as well as that own individual's experience. To that extent, all histories are personal.

Journalists are by definition not historians to begin with, but they can become historians, if only by looking back at the events which they have experienced, usually at closer hand than the academics who will later write about them. In that respect this book is the result of 35 years' labour which began when I first arrived in East Berlin in the spring of 1981, a wet-behind-the-ears young journalist on his first full-time posting for Reuters news agency.

It was a strange, exciting and challenging experience. I had previously worked as a trainee in London, then been posted to Brussels to join a team covering what was then the European Economic Community. It had been interesting if not particularly exciting work which I found relatively easy because, unlike many British journalists in Brussels, I had been a student in Paris and spoke fluent French.

Berlin was altogether different, especially East Berlin. I was on my own in the office, save for an East German secretary, and my command of German, which I had studied only to A-level, was rusty, which meant it struggled hard with a part of Germany where few people had any English (Russian was more common) and the thick Berlin dialect was a challenge even to other Germans.

I had been allocated East Berlin at such a young age – I was 26 when I arrived – because despite its exotic status as the capital of the Cold War, scene of spy exchanges, home to the sinister Stasi secret police and symbol of Europe's partition – not much actually ever happened. But one day it might...

Eventually it did, and although I had long left Reuters, I was there when it did, and all the better prepared. My career from 1981 on took me to Warsaw, Moscow, then back to London to work first for the *Sunday Telegraph*, then the *Sunday Times* as Central Europe correspondent, in which role I followed the events that led to the collapse of Communism from Prague to Warsaw, Budapest to Bucharest, and that glorious evening in November 1989 when I staggered through Checkpoint Charlie with a beer thrust into my hand as the Berlin Wall was finally breached.

Since then I have watched and reported on the end of the Warsaw Pact, the collapse of the Soviet Union, the democratisation of the Eastern European countries and their accession to the body that came to represent a new, free and united Europe: the European Union, and seen the tests that has posed to old ideas of nationalism and its sporadic, worrying resurgence. I have watched the metamorphosis of my old home, Berlin, from a charismatic but bedraggled old lady to the dynamic, bustling, cutting-edge European capital it is today, and observed the Germans' satisfaction, occasionally laced with discomfort, at the evolution of the city into the political powerhouse of Europe.

For modern Germany has a problem. Its economic strength and geographical position make it prone to accusations that it aspires to run Europe, allegations that cut deeply because of comparisons too often drawn with the horrors of the Nazi era. Germans will, if pushed, point out that it was a catastrophe first and finally for the Germans themselves. Germans, notably German Jews and socialists, were Hitler's first victims, and German civilians in the end saw their cities reduced to rubble and old men, women and children burned alive in firestorms. They also know that in that brief 12-year period Germans started the war that all but ruined their own country, committed atrocities and attempted genocide. It is not easy being a German.

The modern world tends to forget that for most of history there was no such thing as a country called 'Germany'. The word, if used at all, referred to the geographical area of much of Central Europe, just as Iberia referred to a geographical area of southwest Europe, or indeed 'Italy' referred to a peninsula occupied by half a dozen states. The best analogy today is Scandinavia. 'German' referred primarily to the language and by extension to those who spoke it, whether their loyalties were owed to the Austrian Emperor, King of Bohemia, Duke of Saxony, Elector of Brandenburg or any other of the myriad princelings, archbishops and other nobles whose lands spread like an unfinished jigsaw across the map of Central Europe, which they knew as Mitteleuropa. Both 'Italians' and 'Germans' spoke many different dialects, any of which could have evolved into a separate language, and with it a different nationality, as Dutch did.

We will look at how attempts to reimpose some form of order on the fractured society of what used to be called the Dark Ages, but is now referred to as Late Antiquity, were focused on some form of recreation of the *pax romana*. We will see how the ghost of Rome and its ancient rulers has haunted European history from the decline of the empire in the third to fourth centuries to the French Revolution and the empire of Napoleon, which in itself was a new evocation of the Roman ideal, how the imperial concept drifted north of the Alps after the fall of Rome, and the complex relationship between states and religions, emperors and popes. Above all we shall see how the Germans' position in the heart of Europe and the fact that they have, despite war and plague, been the most numerous linguistic group, have meant their borders have for much of history been fluid. Three of the cities on which I base this history are no longer part of what is today called Germany, but they have all been German cities. The borders of what we have called Germany since 1871 have changed no fewer than half a dozen times. The map, and the country, we know today date no further back than 4 October 1990.

The format may feel strange at first because this is not a traditional linear history, not least because the history of the Germans in Europe has been anything but linear: for centuries there was no one nation, no one capital. The traditional linear history usually has more to do with the present than the past. It comes with an element of inevitability, as if the reader should take for granted that all of history was a clear and simple lead-up to the present day. This is the sort of history favoured by former British Prime Minister David Cameron and his one-time education minister Michael Gove, both of whom thought schoolchildren should be taught 'our island story', as if the forging of the United Kingdom was a glorious and inevitable process instead of a story of conquest, rebellion, forced union, secession and currently uneasy compromise.

The reality of history, as we should acknowledge in the age of fake news and alternative facts, is that it is always a fiction of sorts, a story told by an author called a historian trying to make sense of a past comprised of a vast array of possibilities, choices, conflicts, and, most frequently of all, accidents. Good examples of the last are the fall of the Berlin Wall, and the UK's decision to leave the European Union, neither of which was intended by those who set in motion the events that led to them.

This personal history begins, as it should, in Berlin, where I first arrived as a young journalist in 1981 and the complexities of the German situation and German history truly began to make their mark on me. It then moves to where Germany ends, and where to some extent it began, on its former far northeastern border, the Russian city of Kaliningrad, once the 'King's Rock', where the Teutonic Knights of the 13th century began to carve out an empire. It then goes to perhaps Germany's best-known city, 'toy town' Munich with its lederhosen, famed beer festivals and covered-up brownshirt past; to Frankfurt, home of Europe's money and embryonic 19th-century dreams of German unity; to the great port of Hamburg, Central Europe's window on the world; Dresden, the 'Florence of the Elbe' hit by a holocaust of its own; Vienna, which could and maybe should have been capital of Germany, had history taken a different fork; Cologne on the banks of the Rhine with its cathedral and carnival, the oldest city in Germany, dating back to the reign of the Roman Emperor Claudius; and finally upriver to Strasbourg, the city that has changed hands between French and Germans more times than any other, and the lands of Charlemagne, ruler of the Germanic tribe that gave its name to France. We will make brief excursions to the Spain of Charles V, the England of Henry VIII and the Romania of Nicolae Ceauşescu.

On the way we will make pit stops, to take a look at a few idiosyncratically chosen aspects of German life: beer, money, cars, music, food, sex, their rivalry with the Russians and their relationship to their fellow Europeans. Mistakes, omissions, opinions and attitude are all mine. I hope my German friends will understand, as I have tried to understand them.

1

Berlin

A special party in a special pub, the mouse that roared, from obscurity to oblivion, a tale of two cities and an unexpected resurrection

Happy Birthday

In the summer of 2013 my wife Jackie and I attended a party in a pub in Prenzlauer Berg, one of Berlin's trendiest and most sought-after residential areas. Just a few decades earlier it had been the most dilapidated district on the wrong side of the Berlin Wall. It had also been our home.

Some 32 years previously, in the late winter of 1980–81, I had arrived in East Berlin as a young and relatively inexperienced foreign correspondent for Reuters news agency. When I got married six months later my wife came out to join me, making our 'choice' of first marital home improbable enough to feature in her hometown newspaper, the *Scunthorpe Evening Telegraph*.

My posting to East Berlin, where I was the only non-German correspondent on the 'wrong' side of the Wall, was an accident that changed my life, gave me what amounted to a second family, and an umbilical cord to a city that perhaps more than any other had embodied the 20th century: seductive, scarred, ugly. And utterly magical. Even if the magic had at times been frighteningly black.

That party in the summer of 2013 was held on 1 August. A century earlier Kaiser Wilhelm II had unveiled a monument to the Battle of the Nations fought in 1813 outside Leipzig. The victory of Prussia, Austria, Sweden and Russia over Napoleon had seen 54,000 killed and another 27,000 wounded in the bloodiest battle in European history to that date. No one had any idea of the catastrophe to occur just one year later, in August 1914.

That same summer a Berlin housemaid called Clara Vahlenstein had a lucky lottery win, and she and her husband Hermann changed their lives forever by buying a pub in the bustling working class district of Prenzlauer Berg, dominated by six-storey *Mietkasernen* (rental tenements). They initially called it Vahlenstein's Destille, and sold spirits as well as beer and coffee to the hardworking locals of an inner-city suburb typical of the rapid expansion Berlin had undergone in the late 19th century as it was transformed from a medium-sized northern German provincial city into the capital of a huge new nation. In the end, however, Berlin tradition won out: the pub stood on the corner of Metzer Strasse, named for the siege of Metz, one of the battles in the Franco-Prussian war that had created the new Germany. And as most Berlin pubs stood on corners and were named for them, Clara's became Metzer Eck.

I first stumbled (literally) into Metzer Eck on a cold night in the early winter of 1981. Despite its label as capital of the Cold War; East Berlin in the early 1980s was something of a slow news city, a dull Soviet fiefdom without even the usual crop of dissidents to be found in most of Moscow's satrapies. My first story had been, ironically given my Northern Irish upbringing, a football game between Ballymena and a team from Leipzig: Reuters had a broad distribution network. An office in drab East Berlin was rare and something Reuters was determined to hold on to: one day something exciting might just happen.

To pad out my salary I was required also to cover events

in the isolated exclave of West Berlin. It was coming home via Checkpoint Charlie from a chaotic night covering riots in the student, squatter and Turkish immigrant district of Kreuzberg to the relative peace and calm of the totalitarian East, that I first found myself in Metzer Eck. I got out of the U-bahn at Senefelderplatz and, seeing a rare light in the darkened streets, ventured in, hoping for a nightcap, or at least a bit of warmth, and maybe – though I doubted it in East Berlin's cautious, mistrusting society – a bit of conversation. I found both, and a whole lot more: an open back door into the heart of real Berlin, a culture of ordinary, charming, friendly people of all classes – regulars included bakers, builders, musicians and actors – who over generations had hunkered down and taken the shit that history had thrown at them.

The night of that party in the summer of 2013, 32 years after I had first stumbled through the doors, the current landlady of Metzer Eck, Sylvia Falkner, Clara Vahlenstein's great-grand-daughter-in-law, stood on the steps before a crowd of several hundred and news cameras of unified Berlin's local television channel and declared: 'We survived two World Wars, the Wall going up and the Wall coming down, and we're still here!'

In almost any country, at any time, the survival, almost totally unchanged, of one small pub in the hands of the same family for a century is a rare thing; in the circumstances of Berlin, it is almost a miracle. During the Vahlenstein/Falkner family's tenure Germany's borders changed more than a dozen times; they had been under the rule of an emperor, a socialist democracy, the Nazi dictatorship, a Soviet-style Communist dictatorship and since 1990 once more a democracy. Five currencies had crossed the bar, from the Kaiser's *Reichsmarks* to the *Rentenmarks* invented to rescue the inflation-plagued Weimar Republic, to the East German 'Marks of the German Democratic Republic', to the D-Mark of post-1990 unified Germany, and eventually euros.

Two young men called Horst had lost their lives: Sylvia's husband, conscripted into the East German National People's Army when I first arrived in Berlin, who tragically succumbed early to cancer shortly after celebrating the fall of the Wall. And his uncle: conscripted into the Hitler Youth in his teens, then taken away by the invading Russians and left to rot of consumption in a repurposed Nazi concentration camp at Sachsenhausen, just north of the city. Berlin and Berliners have lived Europe's most terrible century close up and personal. Far from all of them deserved it.

Just Another Brick in the Wall?

Almost my first introduction to my new home had been a literal overview of Berlin's real geography thanks to the British army, who in 1981 still nominally controlled one of the three (American, French and British) sectors of West Berlin. Their forces were based near Nazi architect Albert Speer's Olympic Stadium, since transformed into the national football stadium that hosted the 2006 World Cup final.

An army helicopter took me high above the divided city – taking care never to make the potentially dangerous mistake of crossing into East German airspace. The 1971 Four Power Agreement – signed as a form of normalisation during the détente years – was so complex the Western Allies and Soviets had had problems even defining what they were referring to. Neither side admitted the division was final but neither had the faintest intention of withdrawing its troops. All that had to wait for the events that followed November 1989. Both sides insisted (relatively accurately) that it was not they but the German civilian authorities that ran things. Seen from a bird's-eye vantage point in early 1981 the grotesque artificiality of the Wall and the 'death strip' that lined it like a scar on a wound, stood out in the landscape like a crooked concrete lasso encompassing the western two-thirds of the city.

It would later amaze me how few western Europeans understood that it was West Berlin, not East Berlin that was cut off by the Wall. There were absurd anomalies. Most visible of all from the air, was the preposterous little exclave from an exclave that was Steinstücken.

The occupation zone had been delineated according to postcodes and local administrative boundaries. But this history of legal jurisdiction in Europe over the centuries has often led to obscure anomalies. There is an ancient stone in the English Cotswolds known as the Four Shires Stone because it once marked the meeting point of four shires, or counties. Today there are just three: Oxfordshire, Warwickshire and Gloucestershire, but because two adjoining fields once belonged to the bishop of otherwise distant Worcestershire, they were for centuries considered legally part of that county. Steinstücken was about the same size as one of those fields and theoretically was part of a borough of West Berlin. It consisted of nothing much more than a few dozen allotment gardens, but rather than challenge this or annex such a tiny, relatively worthless piece of land in the tense atmosphere, the East German authorities had simply built a separate wall around these few hectares, and a narrow, wire-fenced connecting corridor, a few hundred metres long, for pedestrians to access it. Every time the few dozen allotment holders wanted to tend their garden, they had to go up to the dreaded Berlin Wall and ring a bell on a little doorway set into it. The door would then be opened by an East German border guard who would escort them to their allotment. When they wished to return home with their carrots or whatever, they repeated the process in reverse.

At ground level, too, West Berlin was a curious place. After it became hermetically sealed off from its historical hinterland, accessible only by air, locked trains, or along a well-watched stretch of motorway with checkpoints at either end, its population began to plummet. In particular the well-to-do middle classes with jobs in the booming economy of

West Germany began to desert it: keeping a business running in the exclave was expensive, the future unpredictable in what was effectively an island in a hostile sea. It was not legally part of West Germany, even if its own authorities and the government in Bonn acted as if it was. West Berliners were granted West German passports, but West German driving licences were not recognised on the access roads; West Berlin issued its own.

Bonn gave financial subsidies in the form of tax relief to West Berlin residents to stop a growing drift away from an enclosed city. But one of the greatest influences on maintaining the population level of West Berlin was that young men who studied there, wherever in West Germany they came from, were exempt from military service. The result was an even more artificial city with a population inordinately dominated by the elderly and the young. The middle-aged, middle-class upped sticks to Hamburg, the new media centre, Frankfurt, the new financial centre, or Bonn, the new political centre. If Berlin had become a pair of conjoined twins, it was West Berlin that had become schizophrenic.

By the time I arrived, David Bowie had just left, after completing his 'Berlin trilogy' of albums: *Low*, *Heroes* and *Lodger*. Bowie had issued a German version of his 1977 hit, 'Heroes', as '*Helden*', recorded with Brian Eno in a studio just 200 metres from the Wall, with its references to lovers from East and West, gunshots and the 'shame' being on the 'other side'. In 1981 it was still being played, though had to some extent given way to an equally resonant Pink Floyd hit that came out two years later. Even in the East as I wandered around the half-ruined tenement blocks, patched up and still inhabited that hot summer, the 20th anniversary of the building of the Wall, I heard it echo from open windows out over the *Innenhöfe*, the grimy courtyards which served both as bin storage areas and playgrounds for children: 'All in all you're just another Brick in the Wall'.

West Berlin became an almost obligatory destination for

musicians on European tours. The stone-built poetry amphi-theatre behind the Olympic stadium – poetry declamation was still an Olympic event in 1936, as it had been in ancient Greece – had just been renamed the Waldbühne (Stage in the woods) and become a venue for concerts. I saw Simon and Garfunkel and Queen there, and relaxed while Acker Bilk and his band came to play jazz for that classic German lazy Sunday brunch institution *Frühschoppen* (literally an 'early glass').

The comparison between East and West Berlin was like Superman and Bizarro, the one an exaggerated distorting mirror of the other, although it was hard to decide which was which. East Berlin centred around Alexanderplatz, a pre-war tram terminal, now a mostly empty open space with a 1960s television tower, a state hotel, a state depart-ment store, an S-bahn overhead railway station, a vast police station and a selection of small state-run fast food stands selling sausages of dubious consistency, and *Broiler,* a pecu-liarly East German term for anaemic roast battery chickens (think KFC without the breadcrumbs). West Berlin centred on the Kurfürstendamm and Bahnhof Zoo, previously fash-ionable but outlying districts of the capital (in London terms think Sloane Square and the King's Road), where shops and cafés rubbed shoulders with video cabin arcades showing hard-core pornography, noisy bars showing football and streets awash with fashionistas, tramps, teenage junkies and prostitutes. The most buzzword film, which came out my first summer there, was *Wir Kinder vom Bahnhof Zoo* (We Kids of Zoo Station), a gritty, bleak tale of a 13-year-old girl drawn into a world of drug abuse and prostitution, giving handjobs to businessmen in flash Mercedes. Bowie wrote the music and played a cameo role as himself. For a 26-year-old, brought up in prudish Northern Ireland, it was an overdose for the brain and senses all at once, and compared with the austere, repressive, yet – as I was to find out – curiously homely atmosphere of the East. It was a tale of two cities in one that ingrained itself on my psyche and made almost anywhere else on the planet feel dull in comparison.

Metzer Eck played a huge role in my seduction by the exotic siren that was Berlin in the early 1980s. I belonged to a small, select number who were able to cross freely between the two halves of a divided city that to most Berliners were worlds apart. There were some restrictions: my access to the glitzy late-night bars and heady nightclubs of West Berlin – already beginning to lose the brassy sheen they had been designed to display in the 1960s and 70s – was restricted by the fact that at the end of an evening I had to make my way back through Checkpoint Charlie and stagger home in a darkened half-city with no late night transport or taxis. But East Berlin had charms of its own, less evident but particularly to someone with a sense of and fascination with history, more recondite and more exotic. I would wander the streets late at night, soaking up the atmosphere of a city that to my mind looked little changed since the 1930s: most of the six-storey tenement blocks that lined the main broad avenues of Prenzlauer Berg and the side streets that connected them had long been patched up enough to be inhabitable again, their traumatic existence still visible as the scars of glancing artillery shells and bullets. Street lighting was negligible, an eerie sodium glow that cast strange shadows, little if any lit shop windows, and few welcoming bars. (In reality, I would later learn, it would have been busier and brighter in the 1930s, but nothing much had changed since the bleak 1950s.)

There were few cars on the road – just a few coveted, rusting Soviet Ladas and rather more of the funny little semi-fibreglass East German Trabants – only the occasional clunking tram or the rattle of the overhead S-bahn railway. A few hundred metres north of my first-floor flat on the broad arterial Schönhauser Allee was an intersection with another broad two-lane road that had once (and is again) been called Danziger Strasse but was then officially Dimitroff Strasse, having been renamed by the East German regime in 1950 after a Bulgarian Communist leader. This might also have been arterial had it not ended just a few hundred metres to the west in a three-metre concrete wall and a 'death strip' separating it from the West Berlin district of Wedding.

But only a short walk eastwards and the next junction with two side streets was almost exactly as it had been in the early 1930s, with two bars facing one another across the wider road. These were called respectively Schusterjunge (to the north) and Hackepeter (to the south). The names themselves belonged deep in Berlin iconography. A *Schusterjunge* in most of Germany is literally a 'cobbler's boy', but in Berlin it is also the name for a dense, but very tasty small brown bread roll. These were most commonly eaten with either *Schmalz* (dripping) or *Hackepeter,* a concoction of raw pork minced and mixed with onions, salt and herbs. Together they are actually (the pork has to be fresh enough) quite delicious.

Back in the early 1930s Hackepeter and Schusterjunge on Danziger Strasse were anything but delicious: the street between them was frequently the scene of bloody battles between the hardline Communists who patronised the Schusterjunge and the Nazi brownshirts who drank in the Hackepeter. By 1981, of course, the patrons of both bars paid lip service to socialism, but there was still an uncanny feeling of lingering ghosts. Hackepeter boasted a small skiffle band most evenings, was filled with smoke and, unusually in Berlin, the normal measure for serving beer was a half-litre straight glass rather than a 25cl stemmed one. One of the waiters was a lean, narrow-faced man in his early 60s with a pinched look on his face that made me not wish to ask him what he did in the war, a feeling that was disturbingly reinforced by a print of the bar of an idyllic woodland scene entitled *Buchen Wald im Harz* (literally 'Buchen Forest in the Harz mountains', but nobody after 1945 had forgotten that Buchenwald had been the site of a Nazi death camp). Even more disturbing was the fact that of the two it had the more convivial atmosphere.

No surprise then that I was looking for a less disconcertingly engaging local that first night, when timorously
(smaller East Germans bars could be less than welcoming
in those days, all new faces looked on with suspicion as a
possible Stasi informer) I pushed open the door to Metzer
Eck. What I found was a homely local, with a chatty group
around a large table in one corner, a few blokes standing
at the bar, and another by the shoulder-height white-tiled
stove that provided heating. I ordered the standard Berlin
Bierchen – 25cl of fresh hoppy Pils – and took up my place on
the other side of the stove, pulled out a copy of *The Times*
and began reading. These were early days and I hadn't quite
realised what a controversial act this was: East Germans were
forbidden access to all Western newspapers, though this
was primarily aimed at West German publications, a fact
I had learned the hard way when Müllerchen, the mousy-
moustached, thick-accented concierge for my flat block had
come banging on my door asking if he could have the second
section of the *Frankfurter Allgemeine*; I would later learn he
wanted this not for the conservative newspaper's views on
the global financial situation, but for the TV pages. Subver-
sive enough, I supposed?

I hardly expected anybody in the bar to recognise *The
Times*, but one did, and asked, in decent English, if he might
take a look. Realising that English was my native tongue
and that I was that extremely rare thing: a foreigner in East
Berlin after nightfall, he took the opportunity to practise his
conversation skills, something that got us wary looks from
everybody else. Over the next few weeks we became friends.
After a few encounters I – perhaps unkindly – refused
to speak English regularly to him (I was in Germany for
heaven's sake and my own German needed at least as much
practice, particularly in the Berlin dialect), and got to know
the other regulars. Within a month or two, I had got into
the habit of shaking hands with everyone I knew, or if there
were more than a few seated at the table to adopt the local

time-saving habit of rapping my knuckles on it and nodding to the assembled company. The breakthrough moment came one evening when Alex, the partner of landlady Bärbel, waved me over and offered me a seat at the *Stammtisch,* that holy of holies in almost every German watering hole, the 'regulars' table'. Beer had broken borders. From that moment on, I was part of the community. Alex would become a lifelong friend: we would celebrate German unity together in October 1990 in front of the Reichstag in what was no longer 'West' Berlin. Of course my life in the early 1980s was rather more cushioned than that of my drinking companions: I could go to West Berlin whenever I wanted. So could East German pensioners but that was because their own government hoped they would stay there and cease to be a burden on the workers' and peasants' state. Most East Germans watched what they said to whom, always aware that somebody in the company they kept might be an *IM*, an *Informeller Mitarbeiter,* a stooge for the hated Stasi, secret police. They never quite knew when they might be under Stasi surveillance, but for most of the time most of the people could assume they were not, as long as they were not openly critical of the government in a public forum. The advantage of the *Stammtisch* was that it was not a public forum: you had to be invited, and that meant you had to be trusted. Over the years I gleaned many journalistically useful insights into everyday DDR life, but if I ever used them, I was very careful to conceal their source.

As a Western correspondent, I always assumed I was a regular object of the Stasi's attention. After the fall of the Wall in 1989, I gained access to my own Stasi file, some 300 pages long and full of observations, some better than others, some hopelessly wrong, about me and my wife. We would discover that there had been 29 microphones hidden in the walls of our apartment, in every room. But then we had always assumed that anyhow, all I learned from my file was the number. I also found confirmation that the next door apartment which seemed permanently empty was indeed the surveillance centre with banks of tape recorders. We found our own Stasi 'cover names': I was Streamer, my wife was Sea, visiting friends were labelled Otter, Jellyfish or other vaguely 'watery' nicknames. We were also followed occasionally for weeks at a time, including one 10-day period in which a two-man car team spent eight hours a day watching us, including on a visit to a lake where they tut-tutted when I put my jeans back on over a wet swimsuit. Bizarrely, and indicating the wastefulness of human surveillance in the pre-internet era, they never really seemed to have caught on to the Metzer Eck circle: the files reveal that the Stasi worked 9–5, and were apparently never on duty by the time I headed out to the pub around 10 p.m.

Crossing the Line

Meanwhile I collected local stories around the *Stammtisch*. Hannelore, one of the barmaids at Metzer Eck (whose thick Berlin accent has coloured my German ever since), told me a heart-rending story of her uncle, nicknamed Piek, who lived on what he had always considered the southern fringes of Berlin until the Wall went up. One evening he and three friends were sitting, perforce in a pub they had never particularly liked, grumbling about the fact that their old local – just a few hundred yards away – was now in 'another country' that they had no right to visit. A few beers later, they decided to do something about it: they staggered out down the road to where the recently erected barbed wire fence – a predecessor of the concrete wall – was loose, forced their way under it, and ran for the pub on the other side. All except Piek, who was a bit more portly, got stuck, was shot and wounded, dragged away by the guards who rushed to the scene, and was never seen again. Where you were on the night the Wall went up was the most important memory in most East Berliners' lives.

The partition of Berlin had officially taken place in the immediate years after its fall to Soviet troops. The Soviet Union, Britain and the USA divided the city into three administrative zones, with a portion carved out of the two Western Allies' sectors to give to the French (the Russians being of the opinion that France had 'lost' the war and wasn't getting anything from them). The administration was in theory divided equally, but in practice soon broke down as the Russians made clear that if all of Germany could not be turned into a neutral buffer zone, then they would use their own occupation zone, and as that included Berlin, more than 150 kilometres from what would become the frontier with 'West Germany', the city in its entirety would become the capital of their puppet state.

They made their intentions clear as early as March 1948 by restricting West Berlin's supply lifeline, stopping and checking every train or truck entering the Western Allies' occupation zones. The American commanders began flying in supplies instead. The Berlin Blockade had begun. In reality, often overlooked by Western historians, the Russians had some right to feel they were being ignored: they had been deliberately excluded from talks between the Americans, British and French as well as the western zones' other neighbours, Belgium, the Netherlands and Luxembourg, over a post-war solution for Germany. These western states were determined that the whole of the country should not fall under the Soviet umbrella as was rapidly happening to the countries of Eastern Europe the Russians had 'liberated'. In June that year a new currency, the Deutsche Mark, was introduced in the western zones; the Soviets responded by introducing their own currency for their occupation area and closing down access to West Berlin to force the whole city to use it. All surface travel was blocked. The British and Americans responded with a mammoth daily airlift. At first it seemed doomed to failure and the supply situation in West Berlin deteriorated, but within two months the necessary aircraft had been supplied and there were a remarkable 1,500 flights a day coming into Berlin's main airport, Tempelhof in the American sector, and the British military airfield, Gatow. What had seemed impossible was working.

The Soviets tried to win over West Berliners by offering free food if they registered their ration cards in the East, but it didn't work. Eventually, in May 1949, the Soviets gave up and lifted the blockade. But the tensions remained. The year 1949 saw the emergence of two German states: the Federal Republic of Germany (Bundesrepublik Deutschland) and the German Democratic Republic (Deutsche Demokratische Republik). In 1953, following the death of Stalin, East Berlin workers went on strike demanding higher wages and democratic rights. The Kremlin fired the first warning shots as to how it would treat future protests in its new eastern European satrapies: it sent in the tanks. Soviet troops used live ammunition on protestors across East Germany, killing more than 150. From then on, East Germans lived in fear of similar reprisals. The border between East and West Germany which had been relatively open until the previous year was by now effectively closed, with fortifications rapidly increasing. The Iron Curtain was becoming real. Only its greatest symbol had yet to be built. It would not take long. Berlin was the hole in the bucket: East Germans wishing to leave walked down the street into West Berlin, from where many caught a train or plane to those cites that were securely located in the new country to the West. The future of Berlin still hung in the balance.

The real division came on 13 August 1961, with the Cold War at its height after the failure of the anti-Communist, American-backed Bay of Pigs invasion of Fidel Castro's Cuba just a few months earlier. Overnight East German soldiers pulled barbed wire along the borders of the Soviet sector and brought in building workers, who began to erect a breeze block wall behind the wire. Panic spread rapidly in the East. Families on both sides of what no one had ever imagined could become a border, started worrying about what it would mean for them. One of the most poignant stories is that of Manfred (Manne) Schulz, another regular at the Metzer Eck *Stammtisch*. Manne's parents lived in Wedding, a district in the French-controlled zone, bordering the Soviet one, but for practical reasons – his friends and the school he went to – Manne lived with his grandmother, a few streets away in Prenzlauer Berg. Hearing noises on the street, he slipped out of bed and unbeknown to his grandmother, left the house and went out to see what was happening: when he came across the soldiers and the barbed wire, he dashed off to tell his parents. They had been asleep and found it hard to take him seriously. While they were discussing the situation, Manne nipped out again and went back to his granny's. Nobody stopped him, but by morning it was clear that he could not return again. It was years before he saw his mother and father again.

As it turned out, fate was bittersweet in its treatment of Manne. By his mid-30s he had become diabetic and seriously overweight. He was therefore unable to work and classed by the East German state as a pensioner, which gave him only a tiny income, but the right to travel to the West. Manne chose instead to stay in the East, and made a small fortune (by East German standards) by smuggling in (usually in his commodious underpants, which border guards were understandably reluctant to search) such sought-after items as pop music cassettes and hard-core pornography, both readily available in West Berlin but lucrative rarities in the East. In return he legitimately took from the East popular cigarette brands such as Marlboro, manufactured in Soviet fiefdoms Romania or Bulgaria, and much cheaper in East Berlin than West.

The most famous photos of East Berliners desperate to flee to the western half of their city as the Wall went up were taken in Bernauer Strasse, which was technically in the western zone but the postcode ran along the pavement, so the houses on the eastern side of the street were in the Soviet zone. Western photographers captured dramatic images of people living in the upper stories throwing luggage out of the windows and jumping out after it, while soldiers and builders bricked up the ground floor doors and windows. The houses were later demolished. Bernauer Strasse today is the scene of the sole remaining (or rather, reconstructed) section of the Wall.

Karin, a good friend of mine who worked as an engineer in a state factory, lived only a few streets away on Reichenbachstrasse, which faced the eastern side of the Wall. Every day when she opened the door onto the street, the first thing she saw was a three-metre high concrete wall, topped with barbed wire and a sign that proclaimed *Staatsgrenze: Sperrgebiet* (State frontier, forbidden zone); I knew, but she had never seen, that beyond lay 50 metres of sand, with tank traps and other obstacles, patrolled round the clock by armed border guards with dogs, and then the western face of the Wall, again three metres high and topped with a one-metre diameter rounded 'barrel' that prevented anyone trying to climb it getting a grip.

But a 20th-century city – even back in the 1960s when the Wall went up – could not be divided simply by erecting a wall at ground level. Over the coming weeks, months and years after 13 August 1961, engineers, technicians and city planners from the East were hard at work, carving up the underground infrastructure: electricity and water supplies, service tunnels, and especially, all the U-bahn underground railway. In the case of some lines it was relatively easy to do, such as the line I lived closest to in the 80s. This was primarily an east–west line: they simply severed the western section. For me to get to Checkpoint Charlie I simply got on at the nearest stop, Senefelder Platz, and got off at the final stop, which was still tellingly called Stadtmitte (city centre), even though it was now as far as anyone from the east could travel, and in an area that had become rather bleak and neglected. For me it was a short walk through Charlie to where I could get back on the U-bahn again, on what had once been the same line.

Things were not always that straightforward, however, notably on the main north–south line. The occupying forces had divided the city along postcode boundaries into three wedges as if cut from a cake (later four, when the British and Americans gave the French a share which the Russians refused). Because East Berlin included the heart of the old city, the north–south U-bahn line cut straight through it. The initial solution was simply to brick up the entrances to stations in the East and eliminate the line from the network maps. This left it an entirely West Berlin line, albeit one that ran under the centre of East Berlin. In East Berlin it was removed from the map. On West Berlin maps, the stations in the middle were marked 'closed' and trains did not stop. In reality for several years the trains passing through would slow down and open the doors automatically in case any East Berliner had managed to find a way down onto the platform in the hope of jumping aboard. The East countered by having the stations patrolled by armed guards.

Eventually, as the years became decades and there was not even the slightest indication left in the East as to where the station entrances might have been, the guards were withdrawn and the Western trains, though they still slowed down, no longer automatically opened their doors. It was a surreal feeling to take the north–south line in West Berlin, and pass through these ghost stations, the most significant of which was Unter den Linden, the old city's famed prime avenue. Looking out the window at the dimly lit platform, all that could be seen was long-unused ancient wooden benches and the tiled walls with Unter den Linden spelt out on them in the old Gothic script. I used to always try to imagine where on Unter den Linden above ground it actually was. It was only after 1989 that I found out: it was not far from the Soviet embassy. Today it is not only reopened and busy, but perfectly preserved as a historic monument, complete with the tiled Gothic script.

For most of the 28 years of partition, Berlin remained a scene for great espionage novels, such as Len Deighton's *Funeral in Berlin*, with its downbeat hero Harry Palmer, or John le Carré's *The Spy Who Came in from the Cold*, which introduced the man who would become the archetypal British spymaster of the Cold War years, the pudgy, cerebral, bespectacled cuckold, George Smiley. Even Ian Fleming, who preferred more exotic background for his spy novels, made a camouflaged reference in his first novel, *Casino Royale*, with the first 'Bond Girl', a double agent archly named Vesper Lynd (you have to say it aloud).

For most Europeans, even the Germans, and certainly for most of the rest of the world, Berlin, a city sprung from next to nowhere two centuries earlier to become the most famous, then infamous city in Europe, virtually disappeared as a real city for the best part of three decades. Only on rare occasions was their attention drawn back to the former German capital and its curious situation. One such was just two years after the building of the Wall, when in June 1963, charismatic US President John F. Kennedy visited the city and gave a soaring speech that went around the world. It also, accidentally, became the subject of an infamous urban legend that endured for years. Praised at the time, Kennedy's proclamation of solidarity with West Berlin – 'Today in the world of freedom the proudest boast is *Ich bin ein Berliner*' – was to be crassly misinterpreted by know-it-alls in the Anglosphere as 'I am a donut'.

The apparent rationale was that in most of Germany, a *Berliner* refers to a spherical, jam-filled doughnut, which happens to be one of the city's specialities. According to the anglophone would-be experts in German grammar, by using the indefinite article, rather than omitting it as Germans routinely do when stating where they come from – '*Ich bin Münchner*', '*Ich bin Dresdner*' – Kennedy had apparently confused the confectionery with the citizenship. The tale gained credence after it was circulated in respectable newspapers from the *Guardian* to the *New York Times*, and became almost as famous as the speech itself. Ha, ha, even the greatest US President can make a chump of himself abroad.

The only trouble was it was wrong. Strictly grammatically Kennedy had not made an error. The use of the article is optional, even though most Germans choose to omit it, but also its inclusion in this case had the additional connotation that Kennedy was not saying specifically that he himself was from Berlin, but that anyone could proclaim solidarity with the city's citizens. It was the concept of being a Berliner, rather than the actual fact, that mattered. There was yet another, more pertinent, flaw in the 'howler' theory: people from Hamburg or Essen might refer to a jam doughnut as a *Berliner*, but Berliners themselves did not.

In Berlin it is a *Pfannkuchen* (often wrongly translated into English as a 'pancake'). My own experience turns the legend on its head: I found it hilarious the first time I saw a *Pfannkuchen* in a pastry shop in West Germany labelled a *Berliner*. Kennedy's Berlin audience were not just being polite when they applauded his speech rapturously rather than laughing, they had never seen anything remotely funny in his wording.

But even such instances as Kennedy's visit did not linger long in the global memory as Berlin retreated from being a great capital city to a backwater of only symbolic relevance. Many people outside Germany imagined that Berlin lay on the inner-German border and that the wall that had been built through it was down the middle, rather than all around the isolated exclave of West Berlin. The reality was much more claustrophobic. West Berliners were barred from the beautiful Brandenburg countryside, could no longer venture out as they once had done into the woods and lakes that surrounded them. Perhaps the closest equivalent might be Manhattan, if nobody was allowed to leave the island, and instead of water all around there was a concrete wall. The

Wall blighted the lives of nearly everyone on either side, albeit in different ways.

East Berliners, by contrast, could jump in the car, if they were lucky enough to have one, and drive out of town for a walk in the woods or a dip in a lake, down to Dresden or Leipzig or up to the traditional Berliner holiday resorts on the Baltic coast, beautiful islands such as Rügen, where the lucky few had holiday homes inherited from pre-war parents or grandparents. My friend Alex had a little wooden bungalow up there. He managed to hold on to it until after reunification, when he sold it for what seemed to him a vast price, but was probably a bargain to the West Berlin purchaser. But in 1981, the fact that West Berliners were cut off from the rest of their own city and the countryside around them had largely faded from the comprehension of those born after the Wall went up. There was a similar gap in the world-view of those East Berliners who were under 18 when the Wall came down in 1989. They were a generation that had no actual knowledge of West Berlin, not even on a map, because the only maps you could buy in East Germany showed West Berlin as a blank white space.

An anomaly by any definition, West Berlin was still legally an occupied city, treated as part of West Germany although by international law it was not. Only in the early 1970s did the situation partially normalise. In 1971, the four former allies, the USA, UK, France and the Soviet Union signed probably the most precisely defined yet simultaneously obscurantist treaty in history: the Four-Power Agreement. It was supposed to be the Four-Power Agreement on Berlin, but as the Soviets insisted it covered only the anomalous territory of West Berlin, the defining two words were dropped. It was possibly the most complex 'agreement to differ' in history, to the extent that the areas it applied to were defined not by name but by reference to areas they abutted. At no point does the name 'Berlin' even appear, only 'relevant area': they knew what they were talking about, but didn't agree on its status, only how they were going to handle affairs relating to it. There isn't even a definitive text in German. But it was the beginning of what would come to be known by a French word: *détente*.

Just what was and wasn't 'proper' Berlin for the next nearly three decades became a moot question. The East German authorities referred exclusively to their half-city as Berlin, occasionally reluctantly tagging on, *Hauptstadt der DDR* (capital of the German Democratic Republic), and referred to the other side as *Westberlin,* as if it were some objectionable theme park declared off-limits on moral grounds. On the Western side they too referred to their half of the city as just 'Berlin', as if the bit on the other side of the Wall – the city's historic heart – was little more than a withered amputated limb waiting for future science to find some way to re-attach it.

The Mouse that Roared

The reality is that throughout much of history the average German-speaker would have laughed at the thought of Berlin becoming the capital of a united German nation, a concept which itself seemed unimaginable. It had spent centuries as a relatively obscure and largely unlovely diminutive parvenu in the company of the ancient mediaeval centres of Germanic culture such as Cologne, Dresden, Munich, Vienna and even distant Königsberg. Berlin doesn't even get a mention in written records until the 13th century, by which time Cologne was more than 1,000 years old. Indeed, the oldest part of Berlin may have been an offshoot: the earliest mentioned settlement in the heart of the modern city was called Cölln, with reference to a smaller settlement known as Bärlin a few hundred metres away. The first reference to either was in 1237, today considered (for lack of any other evidence) as the city's foundation date.

Ironically this became a date of some significance and

something of an East–West political football in 1987 just over two years before it became of no relevance whatsoever. Both Berlins had decided to mark the city's 750th anniversary, but despite overtures from the West, East Berlin – still ruled by Erich Honecker, the man who claimed he had helped build the Berlin Wall – dismissed them out of hand. The authorities in the East claimed that it contained *all* of the ancient city, implying that therefore the Western part, which they generally disliked even mentioning, as if it was some sort of cancerous growth rather than an integral part of the city since the mid-19th century.

The East German regime had a certain element of history on its side; the district known as Mitte (centre) was entirely in the East. The Brandenburg Gate, which Westerners from tourists to US presidents had stared at from 'viewing platforms' in the West, as if it were the closed gateway to a prison camp, had been built in the late 18th century as a formal entrance into Berlin, at that date still a city with – ironically enough – a wall around what would become East Berlin. The Tiergarten to the west, where the viewing platform stood, had – as the name 'animal garden' implies – been a hunting ground outside the city walls.

In reality, the heart of the city which they were celebrating had largely been razed to the ground by British and American bombers and then crushed by Russian tanks. The Adler hotel – Berlin's equivalent of London's Savoy – which would be rebuilt in grand style in the 1990s, in 1987 wasn't even a heap of rubble, just a dim memory in the minds of a few very old Berliners. Unter den Linden, Berlin's equivalent of the Champs-Élysées, and the pre-war promenade of choice for European glitterati, was now dominated by the unprepossessing slab of the Soviet embassy with a statue of Lenin glowering out of its gardens. Further east the royal palace had been demolished by the Communists and replaced with Karl-Marx-Platz, a huge expanse mainly used as a car park (and so mostly empty), dominated by a 1970s glass and steel structure known as the Palast der Republik (mainly used for political party conventions and occasional concerts by carefully vetted pop stars).

The Communist authorities had planned the celebrations for years. As early as the autumn of 1981 – four years before the anniversary – my wife and I stood out in the biting Berlin wind to watch as a giant crane hoisted two pre-assembled spires onto the twin towers of the Nikolaikirche (Church of St Nicholas), the city's oldest surviving building, dating back to the supposed foundation date. For four decades the building had been a shell without spires ever since its almost total destruction in World War II. It was one of the Communist regime's proudest moments, albeit done to reinforce that its part of Berlin alone was heir to the city's history.

For most of European history, not just Germans but anyone in Europe would have considered preposterous the idea that Berlin would one day be capital of a country with imperial pretensions – and later the political powerhouse of Europe. Throughout the Middle Ages and beyond, Berlin was a cold, northern town in a small state called Brandenburg, absurdly linked in 'personal union' of its ruler to a duchy on the eastern shores of the Baltic. Not only was it merely the capital of a rather small if ambitious state, it was not a particularly big town, let alone a city. In Shakespeare's day, at the end of the 16th century, London already had 200,000 inhabitants. Paris twice that. The largest German-speaking city was Vienna with some 50,000. In comparison Berlin was a small town of 12,000 inhabitants at most.

To make things worse, it was all about to be devastated by the Thirty Years War of 1618–48, when a third of its housing was burnt down or made uninhabitable and the same percentage of the population either died or fled. The response was a deliberate policy of encouraging immigration, which had the effect of making Berlin the most cosmopolitan and most liberal city in the German-speaking lands. Brandenburg's rulers invited people from all over Europe persecuted for their ethnic identity or religious affiliation. Among the first to be welcomed were several hundred Jewish families, but the biggest influx came after French King Louis XIV repealed the Edict of Nantes in 1685 and declared Protestant-ism illegal, forcing French Protestants (Huguenots) to flee the country. Many fled across the Channel, where most were speedily moved on to the northern counties of England's tur-bulent colony, Ireland, taking with them the weaving skills that would create a new industry: Irish linen.

Brandenburg's ruler, Friedrich Wilhelm, who would come to be known as the 'Great Elector', declared religious toler-ance and issued an open invitation to the Huguenots, who flocked to the city in vast numbers. They were welcomed with open arms as skilled migrants, given their own churches, schools and even special tax concessions. By the end of the 17th century about a third of the Brandenburg-Prussian cap-ital's population spoke French as their native language. The influence has never completely faded. Even today it is accept-able in Berlin, as in no other German-speaking city north of the Swiss border, to use *merci* for 'thank you', while *Pardon* is still used as an alternative to *Verzeihung,* as an apology.

The arrival of the Huguenots was the first big popula-tion increase and saw the city grow to more than 100,000 in the mid-1700s, but even by 1800, when London was already home to over a million, Berlin had little over 150,000. It was not until the industrialisation of the mid-19th century that population growth really took off, then accelerated with the impetus of German unification, when it overnight became the capital of a 'German Empire'. Between 1850 and 1900 Berlin's population almost quintupled from some 400,000 to just under two million. It would reach a maximum of nearly 4.5 million before the outbreak of World War II. The trauma that followed meant that even today the reunited German capital has a long way to go to return to that figure.

But while still a relatively small city in European terms, Berlin's emergence from its status as a provincial backwater to capital city of an up-and-coming power, and a centre of the Enlightenment renowned for progressive, liberal thinking, was encouraged by one particularly inspired monarch: Friedrich der Grosse (Frederick the Great). Friedrich II came to the Prussian throne in 1740, was brought up and taught by Huguenots and to the end of his life preferred speaking and writing in French rather than German. He made French the official language of the Prussian Academy of Sciences. Small in stature and considered by some effeminate in his mannerisms, Friedrich was highly intelligent, literate – he corresponded with Voltaire – and a remarkably gifted general. His 46-year rule would be taken up with near constant warfare. His father had left him one of the largest and best-drilled armies in Europe, and he made full use of it during the War of the Austrian Succession (1740–8) and the Seven Years War which followed (1756–63).

Friedrich switched alliances as it suited him for military and territorial advantage as the occasion presented. He first snatched the resources-rich province of Silesia from Austria, then wholeheartedly joined Vienna in plotting the first partition of Poland in 1772, which crucially involved the biggest step in the process of filling in Brandenburg-Prussia's patchwork quilt of territories. By seizing what had been Royal Prussia, subject to the Polish crown, Friedrich finally united his possessions on the eastern shore of the Baltic with the core lands of Brandenburg, based around Berlin. Polish Pomerania became germanised as Pommern. The Hansa city of Gdansk/Danzig was now definitively Danzig, at least for another two hundred years.

At the apex of Friedrich's rule, he was spending nearly 86 per cent of Prussia's income on the maintenance of his army, sparking the joke that Prussia was not so much a state with an army as an army with a state. It was not only Friedrich's military skill that would be his legacy to the Germans and Europe, it was his enthusiasm for the introduction of a new crop that would put an end to the occasional famines that haunted northern European realms dependent on grain: the potato. Although known in Europe for 200 years already, outside Ireland the potato was still seen more as a horticultural curiosity than a foodstuff. Friedrich realised that a tuber grown underground relatively easily was a more reliable edible crop than grain which required much more land and was subject to the ravages of the weather, birds and insects. In a series of decrees issued throughout the mid-18th century, he demanded that potatoes be planted on any bare plot of land throughout Prussia, and made a show of regularly eating them himself to promote their popularity. His great admirer, Catherine the Great of Russia, followed suit, importing bags of seed potatoes from Prussia. Ironically Friedrich had fed not only his own army, but that of the nation which would become its nemesis.

The most tangible remains of Friedrich's rule can still be seen today, happily untouched by the devastation of World War II, at Potsdam, then a small town southwest of Berlin where he built a series of palaces that would become known as Prussia's Versailles. They are, however, much smaller in scale, notably his favourite, a remarkable, elegant and understated masterpiece of rococo architecture he called, typically in French, Sanssouci, 'Carefree'. Friedrich's last wish was to be buried next to Sanssouci alongside his favourite greyhounds, but this was ignored by his successor and his body was interred in Potsdam garrison church, where it remained for 159 years, until moved to protect it from capture by the Red Army. Only in 1991, following German reunification, was his last wish finally fulfilled. Visitors today often leave a potato on his tomb.

But if it was Friedrich who made Prussia a player of note on the world stage, Berlin's debut as a European capital of note was reduced to ridicule shortly after his death when in 1806 Napoleon Bonaparte marched in triumph through the Brandenburg Gate, the city landmark erected just 15 years earlier. The king and government decamped east to

Königsberg and French troops remained on the streets of Berlin for two years, and would pass through again on their ill-fated march on Moscow in 1812. The man who would do more than any other to make Berlin one of Europe's major capitals was born just three years later, in the year Napoleon faced his Waterloo.

∈∋

Otto von Bismarck was born in the little town of Schön-hausen, not far from Berlin and after which Schönhauser Allee, the street where my East Berlin flat was located, was named. He belonged to the social class known as *Junkers*. Often considered particularly Prussian, if only because that is where they longest survived, the name originally referred to landed gentry in general as a minor honorific of nobil-ity. It survives to this day in Flanders and the Netherlands as *Jonkheer*, and undoubtedly its most famed incarnation is the President of the European Commission, the Luxem-bourger Jean-Claude Juncker. Its most notable survival in the English-speaking world is in the New York state city of Yonkers, a relic from its 17th-century Dutch foundation. The great Protestant reformer Martin Luther, when he was hiding from the Catholic powers at Wartburg Castle in the mid-16th century took the self-deprecatory alias Junker Jörg. When his contemporary, England's Henry VIII, who had written a book-length excoriation of Luther, describing the reformer as a 'venomous serpent, a pernicious plague, an infernal wolf', chose to renounce Catholicism and proclaim himself head of his own church (the Church of England) so he could divorce one wife and marry another, Luther scath-ingly remarked, 'Junker Heinz will be God and do whatever he lusts'.

By the time of Bismarck's birth, the term *Junker* was pri-marily associated with the class of Prussian landowners who possessed vast estates in the eastern lands from Königsberg to Berlin. They were often treated with contempt by those who claimed more ancient, noble status from the princedoms Prussia was rapidly assimilating in the 19th century. But it was the Prussians who were in charge of the assimilation and as a consequence the *Junkers* called the shots.

Bismarck was appointed as Prussian representative to the diet set up in Frankfurt to consider some form of German unification in the years following the European revolutions of 1848. He quickly became convinced that if there was to be any form of union, Prussia rather than Austria should lead it. Being subsequently appointed Prussian ambassador to first Russia, then France, was an excellent preparation for his future. When the man Bismarck would soon turn into the first 'emperor' of a united Germany came to the throne of Prussia in 1862, he recalled his ambassador to Paris and made him chancellor (prime minister) and foreign minister. In one of his first speeches Bismarck gave an ominous hint of how he saw Prussia's future, achieving its goals (by which he clearly meant a united German state ruled from Berlin) not by fine words but *Blut und Eisen* – blood and iron – a phrase that would be used to more pernicious purpose by the Nazi regime which came to power decades after his death in 1898.

Over the next decade Bismarck worked tirelessly to make upstart Prussia the undoubted superior to the Austrians, who had so long dominated the old order among the German states. His coup was to use the age-old argument over the disputed provinces of Schleswig and Holstein, which had been held for 400 years by Danish kings until 1864, but since had been supposed to be shared between the two greatest German states. The ridiculous solution was to give Schleswig, the northern duchy, to Prussia, while the southern duchy, Holstein, which shared a common border with Prussia, was given to distant Austria. Inevitably this led to arguments about how Schleswig in particular should be governed, separated from the rest of Prussia by a chunk of newly Austrian land. Bismarck used a technicality in Austria's attempt to have it ratified by the Frankfurt assembly to send his troops into Holstein, prompting Austria to declare war, supported by almost every other German state.

Today, among anglophone historians in particular, the conflict is usually referred to as the Austro-Prussian war or even the Unification War, but at the time, and to a certain extent even today in German historiography, it was known as the *Brüderkrieg* (the 'Brothers' War) or simply the *Deutscher Krieg* (German War), which at the time was considered a war of Prussia versus 'Germany', given that nearly all the other German-speaking states were allied with Austria. But militarily the Prussians had the upper hand and it was to be the first genuine *Blitzkrieg,* a phrase that hit global head-lines with the German onslaught on Poland in 1939, and was repeated by the Israelis' Six-Day War of 1967 against its Arab neighbours.

The Austrian-led army was outmanoeuvred and out-fought in a conflict that lasted just seven weeks. The Prussian victory was helped by Bismarck's persuasion of the new state called Italy (only established five years earlier in 1861 by a similar union of statelets) to attack from the south and claim the Austrian province of Venice, which it regarded as part of its new national identity. The decisive battle was fought near a small town called Königgrätz, then part of the Austrian empire, today a regional city of the Czech Republic called Hradec Kralové, known for its IT and food-processing indus-tries. The battle was fought on 3 July 1866, and in a single day the Prussian army all but destroyed a force more than twice its size. The war staggered on for nearly another three weeks, but in reality it was over.

The peace terms were nominally generous, with no land or reparation claimed from Austria (apart from the already lost Holstein), but a host of its minor, supposedly indepen-dent allies – including Frankfurt and Hanover – became part of Prussia, further filling in its patchwork quilt, while the Austrians yielded superiority in the German-speaking world to Prussia. If there was ever going to be a country called 'Deutschland', it was now suddenly and unexpectedly clear that its capital was not going to be Vienna but Berlin. More than a century later my East Berlin friends would regularly joke, wryly and not without some bitterness, that a little Austrian corporal who joined up in the Bavarian army in 1914, would eventually be the man responsible for Austria's revenge for Königgrätz: one Adolf Hitler.

With Vienna now sidelined, Prussia was by far the dominant power in Central Europe, with all the other German statelets little more than satrapies. The time had come to realise the dream of a German union – on Prussian terms. As so often before and since, the best way to encourage a spirit of 'national' union was another war with an old rival; what could be better than the country ruled by the nephew of the man who had humiliated the people of Berlin: Napoleon III, the new self-styled emperor of France. The claim of a German princeling to the throne of France aroused fears of encirclement in Paris. Even when it was withdrawn, it had the desired effect of arousing anti-Prussian feeling in France. Historians still dispute whether Bismarck or Napoleon III did most to engineer a war that would have disastrous consequences for a century, but there is little doubt that at the time both welcomed it for their own ends: for the French ruler it was a chance to recreate the empire of his famous uncle; for Bismarck it was the means to bring all the lesser German states together under Berlin. Bismarck won. The war lasted some nine months and at the end of it a country called Germany was born. There was a brief victory parade on the streets of Paris, but the real drama was enacted at Versailles. A few weeks after the signing of a peace treaty, in March 1871 in Louis XIV's celebrated Hall of Mirrors, Prussia's King Wilhelm I was unanimously – after some discussion – proclaimed Kaiser (Caesar), the first emperor of a truly united Deutschland. The great-great-grandfather of my friend Tatjana Dönhoff – whose family had a Versailles-style palace outside Königsberg – was standing in the back row of those acclaiming him. The same room would be used for the signing of the peace treaty in 1919 which reversed France's humiliation, but set the scene for another far more terrible war, the almost total destruction of Berlin and a brutal division that would only end in 1989.

Bismarck himself, despite the frequent foreign perception of him as a warmonger (which he was, but only when he knew in advance the aims his wars were intended to achieve) and an empire builder (which he was, but within limited boundaries), having achieved his ambitions, became a determined peacekeeper. He was long dead (1898) by the time World War I broke out, but would surely not have taken the gamble that led to it. In 1878, when war between Russia and Turkey over the Balkans threatened the overall peace in Europe, he famously remarked (often mistranslated) that his newly created Germany had no interest in a matter that *die gesunden Knochen eines einzigen pommerschen Muskatiers wert wäre* ('was barely worth the healthy bones of a single Pomeranian musketeer'). Indeed, it was his dismissal by the new, young, ambitious Kaiser Wilhelm II, who ironically was more interested in social problems than his father's old-school conservative minister, that eventually led to the destabilisation he had predicted. In the year of his death Bismarck had said, 'a great European war will break out over some damned foolish thing in the Balkans'. The assassination of Austrian Archduke Franz Ferdinand in Sarajevo happened just 16 years later.

Bismarck's rule is even today associated with more than empire-building and foreign policy, but actually some of his greatest achievements came in the social field. The centenary of the outbreak of World War I saw some lamentable recycling of the old myths that there was some sort of moral imperative to a conflict that was essentially a war between the old empires. Many politicians at the time cynically tried to suggest that it was somehow necessary to 'save'

Europe from an illiberal, undemocratic Germany. While the Germany Bismarck created was by no means perfect in any way, least of all in its democracy, it was in many aspects more socially aware than most other European countries, including Great Britain. Despite his own innate conservatism, Bismarck realised that the best way to keep radical left-wing revolutionaries in check was to take the wind out of their sails by adopting and implementing a carefully controlled degree of social reform. In 1883 and 1884 he managed to pass two pieces of legislation that were remarkable in the Europe of his day.

The first was the creation of a national health insurance service, by which employers contributed one-third and the workers two-thirds of the costs of a system that provided medical care and up to 13 weeks' sick leave a year. The following year, not without political difficulty, he managed to expand this principle with a deal that provided full insurance for workers disabled by workplace accidents, with the full costs paid by their employers. Perhaps most presciently of all, Germany in 1889 became one of the first countries in the world to introduce a state old age pension, contributed to by workers, employers and the state, and paid to all workers over the age of 70. The first similar scheme was not introduced in the UK until 1908.

There are also questions over the various levels of democracy in the late 19th and early 20th centuries. From the creation of the Reich in 1871, full universal male suffrage was instituted. The revolution that broke out in Germany in November 1918 and led to the armistice which ended the war, promised full universal suffrage, instituted for all men and women over the age of 20 in January 1919. In contrast male universal suffrage in the UK only came in at the end of World War I in 1918 (47 years after Germany), and although some women were allowed the vote from the same date, it was not until 1928 (10 years after Germany) that women under 30 and without property were granted full suffrage.

Suffrage in France is a story of good news and bad: full male suffrage for the over-25s from 1792, but not for women until 1944, granted by Charles De Gaulle's provisional government as the occupying German armies retreated.

The Brown Plague

Suffrage, however, is not the only element in democracy. It depends how much a vote is worth, especially in countries without proportional representation where the effect of an individual vote can be marginalised. And how voters can be manipulated. In the 1920s and 30s, Berlin was considered by the Nazi propaganda master Joseph Goebbels as the 'reddest' city in Europe after Moscow. It took a mammoth effort on his behalf, mainly by recruiting street thugs, organising fixed street brawls with the Communists (as in those between Hackepeter and Schusterjunge referred to earlier), plus the relentless demonising of the city's Jewish population as the root of all evil, both capitalist and Communist. He was equally adept at using cheap practical jokes. During a showing of the 1930 film adaptation of the great World War I pacifist novel *All Quiet on the Western Front,* one of the books chosen by the Nazis to be burned in the streets in 1933, Goebbels had hordes of white mice released into the cinema, sending women screaming while his storm troop thugs laughed at the ensuing panic.

Goebbels aimed his campaign squarely at both traditional right-wing supporters from the extreme nationalist front, and the impoverished poor who had traditionally voted Communist or Social Democrat, persuading them that an 'elite' who cared little for their interests ruled over them. Not for nothing was the party called the 'National Socialist German Workers' Party' – NSDAP in its German abbreviation, a combination of adjectives which pushed as many populist buttons as possible, but was soon commonly shortened to 'Nazi'. Eventually the message worked. Yet even at their highest, in the 1933 elections – the last Hitler allowed – when, after the propaganda coup of the Reichstag fire, the Nazis took 43.9 per cent of the vote nationwide, the total in Berlin did not exceed 33.1 per cent.

In the 1928 elections, the Nazi party (legalised for the first time after its failed 1924 putsch in Bavaria) got only 2.6 per cent of the vote and a paltry 12 seats in the Reichstag. But over the course of the next five years, German politics drifted to more extreme positions on the right and left, with both the Communist and Nazi parties increasing their number of seats in 1930 and July 1932, when for the first time the Nazis became the biggest party, with 230 of the total 608 seats. But no party won a majority, and divisions were so extreme it proved impossible to form a coalition. The result was a rerun election in November, in which the Communist vote again rose while that for the Nazis fell, although they were still the largest party. Crucially Franz von Papen, a former member of the Catholic centrist party, who had been an ad hoc consensus chancellor, stood back and in January 1933 persuaded the president Paul von Hindenburg, an elderly World War I general who was a constitutional figurehead, to make Hitler chancellor. 'We can control them,' he notoriously said.

Within two months, following a fire which gutted the Reichstag and was blamed on the Communists but now widely believed to have been a Nazi plot, Hitler got support from other right-wing parties to pass a 'temporary measure' which in effect made him dictator. The die had been rolled.

⋐⋑

The fall of the Berlin Wall in November 1989 was one of the pivotal moments in 20th-century history, arguably as important as the beginning or end of either World War, and certainly far more important than its erection in 1961, for it symbolised the end of Europe's 40-year division along an ideological, militarily defended fault line. Nobody in power, either east or west, expected it, even though with hindsight that now appears remarkably short-sighted. Some of us, reporters on the ground, had the vaguest inkling that the tremors which had begun to be felt at the fringes of the Soviet Empire with the rise of Solidarity in Poland in 1981, might eventually change the geopolitical landscape. But none of us expected an earthquake.

True, the ground had been shaking enough across Eastern Europe during the spring and summer of 1989: I had been in Budapest to see campaigns for free elections take to the streets, seen Austria and Hungary relax border restrictions, a 'pan-European picnic' on the frontier that provided an opportunity for hundreds of holidaying East Germans to flee to the West, Poland hold elections that gave Solidarity a genuine share of power. As the summer turned into autumn, more and more East Germans tried to turn legitimate holidays in other Soviet bloc states into escape routes to the West. The West German embassy in Prague had been turned into a refugee camps by thousands of East Germans claiming political asylum. The same was beginning to happen to the embassy in Warsaw, even though Poland had no frontier with the West. Kerstin and Andreas, daughter and husband of Bärbel, my landlady in Metzer Eck, were among them. The East German government was beginning to make plans for sealed trains to cross their territory, in order to 'expel' their reluctant citizens. East Germany was starting to feel like a pressure cooker that desperately needed to let off steam: would getting rid of the 'troublemakers' do the trick, or would it only encourage others?

There was, of course, another solution, one we didn't like to think of. We had seen a variation of it played out just that summer, at Tiananmen Square in Beijing. In the early autumn of 1989 regular protest marches began to take place in the southern East German city of Leipzig. Before long, every Monday a huge parade of people would gather in the city centre and march along the inner ring road, carrying red banners that challenged the Communist Party's supremacy, although with mild slogans, notably 'Wir sind das Volk' (We are the people). They chanted it too, the noise always loudest as they passed the local Stasi headquarters. As the weeks went by, the demonstrations got bigger, noisier. I have vivid memories of standing on the steps of the Stasi building (to get a better view) one cold Monday evening in late September, staring over the heads of tens of thousands of demonstrators illuminated by bleak white central street lighting, into a misty distance, waiting nervously for an ominous rumble of heavy engines. One of the largest Red Army bases in East Germany was little more than 30 kilometres away. At a word from Moscow, the tanks could be rumbling towards us, like they had done in East Berlin in 1953, in Budapest in 1956 and in Prague in 1968. It gave a very distinctive edge to the atmosphere of nervous enthusiasm.

The word never came. Mikhail Gorbachev, the relative new boy in the Kremlin, was not out of the same mould as his predecessors. We would later discover the hardliners in the East German politburo had begged him to send in tanks against their own people. On 6 October, East Germany celebrated its 40th 'birthday party', with its own military parades, displays of Communist Party loyalty and a meeting of Warsaw Pact leaders. The traditional 'comrades' kiss' between Honecker and Gorbachev was strained. In response to Honecker's refusal to carry out reforms, Gorbachev would reply, 'History punishes those who act too late'. Thousands of East Berliners took to the streets that night, shouting 'Gorby, Gorby!': a Soviet leader had become a popular icon. Honecker sent out the riot police and Stasi agents to infiltrate and finally crush the crowds. I was among them, cornered by police near Schönhauser Allee S-bahn station, piled into vans and driven out to suburban barracks. From the back of the vans we captives, in surprisingly ebullient form given our situation, threw the lie of 'the German Democratic Republic' in the faces of our captors, singing the Internationale and chanting, '*Volkspolizei, steht dem Volke bei!*' (People's Police stand up for the people!). More than a few of the mostly young police looked nervous, even downright embarrassed.

At the police station, where hundreds were being led off to jails, my passport just about rescued me from the fate of the crowd. I was pulled out, interrogated overnight, then taken to Checkpoint Charlie and expelled from the country. It could have been a disaster, had I not had a second passport in another nationality with which to re-enter just a few weeks later to witness the end-game. That fateful night, 11 November 1989, I had been to a demonstration at the port of Rostock on the Baltic, and was on the way back to Berlin when I heard an astonishing piece of news on West German radio: hundreds of East Berliners were being allowed to cross the Wall. In the end it would turn out to be an accident, the cock-up theory of history in action: a misinterpreted poorly drafted statement from the politburo, a lack of communication, an absence of clear orders to the border guards and sheer weight of numbers. I forced my way through the jubilant partying crowds on the Western side of Checkpoint Charlie, bumped into East Berlin friends in the heart of West Berlin and we partied, with a million others, until dawn. It had been an accident, but the genie would not go back into the bottle. The world would never be the same again. Less than a year later, on 4 October 1990, Alex Margan, my one-time pub landlord, now close friend, and I stood outside the Reichstag – on the western side of a wall that was already almost totally gone – and cracked open a bottle of sparkling *Sekt* as we watched fireworks to celebrate something neither of us had ever thought we'd live to see: a reunited Germany.

Where Are We Now?

Prussia is no more. The distant northeastern statelet on the outermost fringes of the German-speaking world, which grew and grew eventually to dominate and create the first nation-state to bear the name 'Germany', was deliberately, systematically, erased from the map of Europe. The country of Kant and Copernicus, Frederick the Great and Bismarck, was simply gone, dismembered or replaced. When I arrived in Berlin in 1981, the Martin-Gropius-Bau – a former Museum of Art, then right against the Berlin Wall on the western side – was home to a comprehensive exhibition dedicated to the history of the vanished state, entitled 'Prussia: An Attempt at Balance'. The aim was to rid the history of Prussia from the Nazi ghosts which had contaminated it. At the same time a similar reappraisal was taking place on the other side of the Wall: only the previous year the equestrian statue of Frederick the Great, which had survived the war intact, was reinstated on Unter den Linden, after 35 years of exile during which it had come close to being melted down by the Russians. But a rehabilitation of Prussia's past in no way amounted to its resurrection. Almost all its original territory had been ceded in 1945 to Poland or the Soviet Union. Those it had acquired in western Germany over the centuries had been reassigned to the new federal states created in the decade following 1945.

Today, Prussia's ghost survives in the west primarily, in its Latin form, in the names of such football teams as Borussia Dortmund and Borussia Mönchengladbach.

Berlin today is wholly changed. It is once again a flourishing European capital, arguably the most powerful. The empty heart has been given a transplant, with the shift of national institutions – parliament, chancellery ministries, civil servants – from their long-term but temporary home in the little university town of Bonn in the Rhineland. Global corporations have set up offices in the restored city centre. Potsdamer Platz, once one of the busiest traffic intersections in Europe, but for the decades that I had known it a desolate wasteland with a graffiti-covered section of the hated Wall running through it, is once again a bustling metropolitan centre. The Reichstag is now the Bundestag, the working parliament of Europe's largest democracy. Where once there were underwater mines and barbed wire under the bridges, there are now tourist boats offering sightseeing cruises along the Spree from the new chancellery offices to the museums in the old city's heart, still undergoing rapid transformation.

The underground remains of Hitler's *Führerbunker*, which had been partially destroyed in 1946, then lain for decades underneath the 'death strip' between eastern and western sides of the Berlin Wall, was after 1990 filled in or sealed up, with the street plan altered and new housing built so that the site was effectively erased. Only in 2006, after the international success of the 2004 film *Downfall*, covering the last weeks in the bunker, and to appease any morbid curiosity on the part of football fans coming to Berlin for the World Cup, was a historical information panel erected near the site. Berlin has moved on far enough for history to be buried, but not forgotten. Only a few minutes' walk away is the vast field of differently sized concrete slabs that is to me, with its silently horrific condemnation of the anonymous mass murder that is genocide, one of the most poignant memorials to the victims of the Holocaust.

Berlin today is a city of hope and enthusiasm, power and money, filled with people from other parts of Germany with their own traditions and accents, challenging the native Berliners' long exclusive right to a city that had forgotten it used to be the capital of a great nation. It has unexpectedly caused some resentment. West Berlin had got used to being a curious, mock-cosmopolitan exclave, an anomaly in every way, German in name but not really in soul. East Berlin was a relic of the old, pre-war Berlin, homogeneous, curmudgeonly, emanating *Schnauze* (attitude) and thick with its own rough idiosyncratic dialect. Both old Berlin and West Berlin are gone, and in their place is a modern, European metropolis, genuinely cosmopolitan but still with a flavour all its own.

It still bears the scars of its history, new ones as well as old: grandiose construction in areas that were once more modest, some ill-fitting structures thoughtlessly thrown up after 1990, while older buildings from the 1970s, particularly in West Berlin, now look jaded and in many cases have been torn down. The farce of its overdue Berlin-Brandenburg airport rolled on for years past its supposed opening date in 2012. Germans from other parts of the country find it a hard city to love, particularly those from Munich, arguably the prettiest of major German cities. My friend Mani, who has lived in Munich for 40 years, visited Berlin for the first time in 2011, and came back shocked: '*Das KANN NICHT die Hauptstadt sein*' – 'That just CANNOT be the capital!' The comment of another Munich resident of 10 years was more dramatic still: '*Das ist eine Katastrophe*'. And he came originally from a German community in poverty-stricken northern Romania!

But then Berlin's charm has never lain in its beauty. It is now as it was when I first arrived back in 1981, a *jolie laide*, that great French expression that means beautiful and ugly at once; its charms lie elsewhere, in its style, its attitude, its lifestyle. There is a strange symmetry with the past: when I first arrived in this city, Berliners on either side of the Wall told me how they could no longer find their way around their city – old thoroughfares were blocked, old familiar routes no longer worked. I find the same now: I still turn right or left unnecessarily on a road that today goes straight ahead.

In his penultimate album, *The Next Day*, released in 2014, that celebrated one-time Berliner, David Bowie, who had so captured the romantic tragedy of the divided city in the 1980s with *Helden/Heroes*, produced a moving elegy to the city he once lived in that was also a poignant comment on mortality and the passage of time.

Remarking on the transformation of the city since the fall of the Wall, he is moved by the simple fact that it is now possible to get a train from Potsdamer Platz, which in his time was a derelict wasteland.

He poses the perennial human question: 'Where are we now?' I share his answer, as would the former US Defense Secretary Donald Rumsfeld with his infamous but accurate reference to 'known unknowns' and 'unknown unknowns' – the moment we know we know we know.

But then Berlin has never been short of musical evocations. Perhaps the best known remains that made famous three-quarters of a century earlier by the city's most celebrated daughter, Marlene Dietrich: '*Ich hab' noch einen Koffer in Berlin...*' (I still have a suitcase in Berlin).

So do I.

The Germans and Food

It's not just sausages, stupid! Not that sausages don't play an important part in German cuisine. The *Wurst* – or its little brother, the *Würstchen* – is an integral part of German life, so commonplace that if you wish to refer to something of absolutely minimal importance, you might say, with a slight tweak to the pronunciation to make clear you're not talking literally: *das ist mir Wurscht* (that's just sausages to me!).

In reality, despite having its own hearty, meat-based character, the cuisine of the German lands draws equally heavily on influences from the surrounding countries, from the herrings of Denmark and the Netherlands, to the cabbage and beetroot of Eastern Europe, and the pasta of Italy.

For a start, Germany is not the only country in Central Europe where the humble sausage plays a large part in the diet. The German names of some of the more popular sausages reflect the fact that they are not really German at all, such as the ever popular *Schinkenkrakauer* (literally 'Krakow ham', giving away its Polish origins) or the spicy *Debrecziner* named after its origins in Hungary's second-largest city. For centuries the pig was the essential animal in Central Europe: almost every family kept one of these omnivorous, fast-growing, easy-breeding creatures. The pig would be slaughtered in the autumn to give a wealth of nourishing fatty meat that could be cured by smoking or salting, along with the various varieties of black pudding made from the blood, all a welcome alternative to the only other crop, bland root vegetables, to feed the family during the long cold winters.

It is precisely for that reason – preservation – that the vast majority of German and other Central European sausages are made from 'processed' meat. This was not the unpalatable product of industrial methods (including reclaimed meat from battery chickens) used by today's giant food companies, but more domestic methods that essentially involved some form of pre-cooking so that the finished product could be kept longer. The classic German cooking sausage such as the frankfurter (to which we shall return) was pre-cooked then preserved by bottling in brine.

This method of preservation also effectively prohibited the inclusion of more perishable products such as the 'rusk' – dried bread – often used to bulk up the traditional British banger, a raw meat product produced in a more temperate, and considerably wetter, climate for immediate cooking and eating rather than preserving. This difference is what lay behind one of the classic anti-EU scare stories about a 'Brussels threat to great British banger', which, if you believed the stories fabricated by ill-informed British tabloid journalists, was going to be banned because it contained less than 99 per cent meat. The reality was about language and labelling: nobody was suggesting – as reported – that the British product could no longer be called a *sausage* in English; they were suggesting it could not be called *Wurst*.

But the pig did not end up just as sausage meat, convenient though it was to stuff its own intestines to make an easily stored snack: it also became what in English we call ham and bacon, in German *Schinken* and *Speck*. Here again a difference between the two goes back to the need for preservation and different cultural traditions for doing so. *Speck* is not intended to be cooked, but instead is salted or dried (often both) and hung in a dry place to be cut over the long winter months. The Austrians in particular, with their often extreme Alpine climate, became specialists in producing 'mountain meat'. *Tiroler Bergspeck,* is justly renowned, as also is *Schwarzwälder Speck*, produced in the depths of the Black Forest.

Up north, in the damper climate near the Baltic, other varieties of ham evolved, softer and more reliant on salting rather than drying for preservation. Ham from Braunschweig is perhaps most comparable to the cooked hams of northern France and England, although usually more spiced. But it was in Berlin that I first encountered perhaps the most remarkable of the softer, more moist German hams: *Lachsschinken,* literally 'salmon ham'. The reason for the unusual, and not particularly appetising, name – ignored by those for whom it has long been part of everyday life – is that *Lachsschinken* looks like smoked salmon and almost has its texture. Pink and almost translucent when thinly sliced, it has a delicious light smokiness and almost melts in the mouth. Needless to say, it is one of the more expensive ham products.

Another Berlin favourite, considered a staple main meal, is the lightly smoked cooked meat known as *Kasseler,* a name that confused many Germans because they take it to apply that it comes from Kassel, a town near Frankfurt to the far southwest of Berlin. In fact the name comes from a 19th-century Berlin butcher who invented the means of marinating, brining and lightly smoking a piece of pork that could then be eaten hot or cold. Usually served sliced, it is a tasty everyday easy meal.

The classic pork dish of Berlin cuisine, however, is the *Eisbein,* a salted ham hock traditionally boiled and served with boiled potatoes and *Erbsenpuree,* uncoloured mushy peas. In my days living in East Berlin, where there was never a problem getting meat, but you had to take pot luck with whatever bit of pork the state butcher might – almost literally – throw at you, Alex Margan, my local pub landlord, would regularly curry favours to acquire a dozen or so ham hocks which he would then serve up to pre-booked selected customers at a *geschlossene Gesellschaft* (private party). Whenever it came up, Alex's *Eisbeinessenabend* (Eisbein-eating evening) went straight into my calendar.

The cut of meat is identical to that which in the rest of Germany is traditionally roasted and, particularly in Bavaria, known as a *Haxe,* common slang for an ankle and related to the English word 'hock'. Order one in a Munich beer garden and it will come glistening pinkish brown and coated with a thick layer of crackling, crunchy or tooth-threateningly impenetrable depending on how long it has sat in the oven and warming tray (you can hardly order something that requires long roasting from scratch). It is served with steak knives to cut through the crackling and rarely eaten with anything else, other than perhaps a savoury potato salad on the side.

In contrast the Berliner *Eisbein* looks like a naked infant served up pale pink and with the fat not roasted but white and wobbly. Out of instinct I would invariably slice through and discard the blubber: this was just about excusable for a foreigner, Alex told me, but considered extremely bad form for a native Berliner, particularly in the DDR, where nothing was wasted.

'You're missing the best bit,' said Dieter the barman, who, if you caught him emerging from a hot bath, might have looked not dissimilar to the meat on his plate, as he sliced through a thick hunk of white fat and forked it, still wobbling, into his mouth. I stuck to the pink, slightly salty ham underneath. It was, and still is, one of my favourite simple home-cooked dishes.

The other great Berlin classic is *Kartoffelsuppe,* potato soup, which is much more than it sounds. The potato, introduced to Prussia in the 18th century by Frederick the Great, was as huge a success in Germany as it was almost everywhere in Europe. *Petersilienkartoffel,* boiled potatoes with a dusting of chopped parsley, is a standard accompaniment to main meals and the potato fast took over from the dumpling as the starch and stodge in the national diet. Potato salad is ubiquitous, in various varieties, some primarily made with *Quark,* a type of yoghurt, but also cooked in a thin savoury broth which adds flavour and served sprinkled with chives or sliced cucumber.

Equally there are many varieties of *Kartoffelsuppe,* usually served with the sort of long thin processed sausage known around the world as frankfurter, but in Germany almost universally as a *Wiener,* its actual origins being more connected with Vienna than Frankfurt. But most of these are little better than thick potato broth; it is only in Berlin that the *Kartoffelsuppe* comes into its own.

I was introduced to this unique, cheap, savoury and nourishing dish inevitably in East Berlin – potatoes were the one item always in supply in those shops that went by the explanatory if unimaginative trade name of *Obst Gemüse* (Fruit and Veg). It was the favourite dish of Jochen Kaske, the first person I got to know in my local, Metzer Eck, the one whose mother spied on me for the Stasi. Astounded that we had not tasted this wonder of local cuisine – the few establishments in East Berlin that were entitled to call themselves restaurants aspired, in a comically bourgeois fashion for the Workers' and Farmers' State, to a version of *haute cuisine*, usually incredibly badly. A few of the few pubs served a version of *Kartoffelsuppe*, but not, Jochen proudly boasted, anything like the real home-cooked thing. He insisted on making us some.

And it was great: not overly thick, the potatoes cooked then pulverised, but not blended (where would you get a blender in East Berlin?), in a broth made from pork bones, flavoured with salt and marjoram and, in the place of the sausage – although that was an optional extra if you had some – tiny cubes of *Speck*, or whatever bits of dried pork rind you might have to hand. The important thing, he insisted, was to leave it to rest for 24 hours after making it, for the flavours to mature. It was true, too. My wife, still struggling with German in those days, found a recipe explained by a friend much easier to understand than anything in cook books, soon mastered the art and we have since tried and tested it many times.

The other soup that was practically unique to the DDR was *Soljanka*, Ukrainian in origin but a standard dish in East German bars. Essentially *Soljanka* was an improbably more exotic variant of *borshch*, beetroot-based, with slices of the vegetable along with onions and cabbage in a broth based on rough stewing beef, a few pieces of which were ideally to be found in the soup. The real exotica was the chunks of red or yellow capsicum pepper. Just the fact that such a southerly vegetable, still not overly common and relatively expensive in 1980s Britain, was to be found in East Germany astonished me – I had certainly never seen any fresh in the *Obst Gemüse* shops – until I realised that they were relatively easy to come by, imported from fraternal Communist Romania, pre-cooked to preserve them and packaged by a giant bottling cooperative outside Bucharest. *Soljanka* was a dish I came to love and still try to find when I am back in Berlin, though it is not so readily available these days: somehow the thin layer of grease that invariably floated on top has not found great popularity among the customers of the floods of restaurants that have sprung up everywhere in the now trendy eastern districts of newly cosmopolitan Berlin.

As with many things, Berlin often has its own idiosyncratic names not shared in the rest of Germany, as we have seen with the infamous 'Berliner/Pfannkuchen' story. One is the Berliner Boulette, essentially a cross between a meatball and a hamburger patty, made either of beef or pork, which can be eaten in a bread roll or on its own, usually accompanied by the ubiquitous potato salad. Similar items can be found all over Germany but they are more commonly referred to as a Frikadelle, or in Bavaria by the tongue-twisting term Fleischpflanzerl, or if made of veal by the even more challenging Kalbsfleischpflanzerl. Try ordering one after you've had a few beers.

We have already come across that other Berliner twin speciality Hackepeter and Schusterjunge in the names of the onetime warring Communist and Nazi bars in Prenzlauer Berg; the dark Schusterjunge (cobbler's boy) roll is unique to Berlin, but the raw minced pork and onion confection that is Hackepeter is common across most of northern Germany as far south as Cologne, but outside Berlin it is referred to by the less evocative and rather less attractive name of Mett.

Raw pork has such a stigma attached to it across much of the world that most people tend to react with horror to the idea of eating it spread on a roll, particularly at breakfast. But most Germans don't even blink an eye. Even in communist East Germany it was served in the better hotels (which could be sure of getting the best quality meat and having the requisite hygiene and refrigeration facilities). There are strict government-enforced rules for preparing and serving Mett, chief among them that it should never be kept at temperatures of more than three degrees Celsius. Should you be lucky to come across some, swallow your prejudices and try it. It's delicious.

The great speciality of North Germany, of course, is the herring, as it is for all the Baltic countries and the Netherlands. Only the UK, bizarrely, seems to have forgotten its fondness for what was once a national staple along the British and Irish shores. The classic way in which herrings are served throughout Germany is as *Matjes,* young herrings, only fished at a certain time of year, preserved in a mild brine, and usually served lukewarm with a variety of sauces ranging from dill-based to creamy yoghurt variations and most often with *Petersilienkartoffel.* The other classic preparation is the *Bismarckherring,* a fillet marinated in vinegar, much more like the old British rollmop. The name is alleged to have come from the great 19th-century Prussian chancellor, who was a great herring fan, apocryphally famed for having declared, 'If herrings were as rare as caviare, people would appreciate them a lot more.'

It would be wrong to omit in even the most cursory discussion of German foodstuffs, the three stalwarts that take second place to the main feature of many dishes: sauerkraut, bread and dumplings. Sauerkraut, like sausages, is one of those things that the British and other Anglophones tend to think of as typically German, whereas in fact the easily grown cabbage, pickled to preserve it, has for centuries been a staple not just of Central European diets but from the French borders via Russia, all the way through Northern Asia to the Sea of Japan.

When I lived in Moscow in the mid-1980s, it was a joy to go round the corner from our flat on Sadovo-Samotechnaya, Moscow's inner ring road, to the Tsentralny Rynok, the central market next to the Moscow State Circus, to see the old ladies offering tasters of their pickled cabbage – *shchee* in Russian – from large wooden barrels. Each one had a slightly different flavour, a 'cure' handed down from their grandmothers, they would all swear.

The pickled cabbage itself, though, is just the part-processed raw material of a good sauerkraut. The real art comes in how it is prepared, even if it has been already cooked as when bought in jars in shops rather than from a barrel. What matters, as well as how long you further cook it for, is what you add: traditional spices such as caraway seeds (*Kummel*), dill, black pepper, a dash of white wine. Again every cook has their own preference. It is true that a lot of sauerkraut served up in large commercial restaurants can be much of a muchness, but believe me, you know it when someone has worked hard at preparing their own variation. The best I have ever tasted was in the lovely old Gröninger Bräuhaus in Hamburg where I ordered roast belly pork, which came with a generous helping of slightly spiced, richly flavoured sauerkraut that had obviously been cooked in a rich broth with just possibly a dash of their extraordinary unfiltered beer tossed in. I complimented the chef-cum-waitress on it, and she just smiled the sort of satisfied smile that says, 'I know'.

German bread is a topic almost as foolish to tackle in as short a space as German music in the chapter where I have attempted to do just that. The traditional ubiquitous table bread is pale brown in colour, even though it is often described as 'white bread' from the same basic confusion between 'wheat' and 'white' that infects the beer world. The point is that a great number of delicious German breads are made with other grains or a mixture of grains. *Roggenbrot,* rye bread, is common, as is *Dreikornbrot,* made from three different grains, usually wheat, rye and barley. And then there is the most nourishing of all, *Vollkornbrot,* made with freshly threshed whole grains in the dough.

That brings us to the dumplings, the main 'filler' on German plates before the arrival of the potato. Again shared across Central Europe, there are wider differences than the outsider might think between different types of dumpling – in German either *Kloss* or *Knödel* – from the bready slices served in Prague and eastern Austria, to the spherical glutinous *Kartoffelknödel,* my favourite – though the texture initially takes some getting used to – and the equally spherical, earthy *Leberknödel,* 'liver dumpling' made of minced cow's liver blended with breadcrumbs and boiled. In Austria and Bavaria a *Leberknödelsuppe* is a thin broth with one of these in the middle of it like a dirty warm snowball tossed in, and is considered a quick, cheap and cheerful lunch.

Also with 'liver' in the name, but not in the dish, is the classic Bavarian *Leberkäse,* which literally means 'liver cheese' but contains neither, being in reality a processed pork meatloaf, served in warm slices often with mustard and potato salad on the side, and ideally washed down with a *Weissbier.* I am more a fan of 'liver cheese' than 'liver dumpling'.

The other great carbohydrate to be found on plates of German speakers either side of the Alps is a speciality known as *Spätzli,* tiny irregular dumplings, essentially a doughy pasta, made with flour, eggs and water. They are mostly served as a filling accompaniment to a meat dish, but are also popular eaten as a meal on their own, usually liberally covered with melted cheese, particularly as a weighty warming lunch in ski resorts, and a good choice for vegetarians. In the latter case they may also be known as *Kasnockerl,* the *Kas* being a dialect form of *Käse* (cheese), and the latter sharing an etymology with the Italian *gnocchi.*

When it comes to cheese, German taste – despite a

typically northern European leaning towards dairy products – is relatively bland. Alongside nondescript clones of
Franco-Swiss cheeses such as Emmental and Gruyère, the
only distinctively German cheese on supermarket shelves is
Tilsit, a mild cheese with a network of small, irregular holes,
normally eaten in thin slices. It was, as may be inferred from
its style, originally developed by Dutch immigrants encouraged in the 18th century by promises of religious tolerance to
move to East Prussia, which had been devastated by plague.
The name comes from the town of Tilsit, founded by the
Teutonic Knights in the 14th century, and since 1945 known
as Sovietsk – despite the demise of the Soviet Union itself –
on the border between Lithuania and the Russian exclave of
Kaliningrad.

That is not to say the German lands do not produce great
cheese: they do, mostly from the far south, Bavaria, Austria
and Switzerland. Hard mountain cheese – *Bergkäse* – has
much in common with the spectrum that runs between
parmesan and Gruyère. Germany is also the home of real
'cheesecake', which immigrants to the US took with them
and reinvented. A *Käsekuchen* is a great and almost essential
part of the late afternoon tradition of *Kaffee und Kuchen*,
coffee and cakes, which is as much a part of life as the siesta
in Spain.

Perhaps the most extraordinary cheese-based German
dish, however, is the exclusively Bavarian *Obatzda*, which
I freely admit has given me less pleasure than almost anything else I have ever eaten in a German-speaking country.
Varying in colour from pale pink to bright orange, *Obatzda*
is a mixture of Camembert-style soft cheese with butter and
paprika, served as a dollop on a plate to be eaten with bread
or perhaps raw radishes in a Munich beer garden in summer.
A great dish to order if you want to establish local credibility;
the only trouble comes, in my opinion, with trying to eat
it. To qualify the 'almost anything else' above, I should add
that the one thing I like less than *Obatzda* is also a southern

German dish. Variously called either Swiss or Bavarian or Munich *Wurstsalat:* sausage salad. Another beer garden favourite, it has its fans and endless minor variations in the recipe for the perfect variant, but to me there is only one easy way to describe it: thinly sliced spam with onions in vinegar. A perfect recipe for one thing only: heartburn. Avoid.

Another regional German dish which requires mention, if only because it was the favourite of Helmut Kohl, the 'unification chancellor', who was noted for being something of a trencherman, is *Saumagen.* Often wrongly described as a 'German haggis' because it literally means 'sow's stomach', the traditional casing. And like haggis, the actual thing turns out to be a lot tastier than you might think from the description. *Saumagen* is primarily popular in the Rhineland, specifically in the Pfalz (Paltinate) district, where Kohl was born. Rather than containing spiced offal, as is the case with the haggis, a *Saumagen* is made from diced lean ham, onions, diced potatoes and herbs – occasionally with chestnuts added in autumn – mixed together, cooked and forced into the stomach, or intestine, to be heated to just below boiling point before serving, usually in slices. Personally it is one of those dishes I can take or leave, and I always suspected Kohl raved about it to boost his 'man of the people' credentials, until on more than one occasion he had it served up at state banquets.

The other stalwart regional speciality that has expanded beyond the boundaries of its native home to conquer most of the German-speaking – and wider – world, is the Wiener Schnitzel. They may not eat that many frankfurters in Frankfurt or hamburgers in Hamburg, but they certainly eat Wiener Schnitzel in Wien. Almost anywhere you go in Vienna, schnitzel is on the menu, indeed occasionally, in a few bars in the city centre Altstadt, it may be the only thing on the menu. It is a simple dish which it is supremely easy to do badly. Essentially a veal cutlet hammered as flat and thin as possible, breaded and fried on both sides until it is golden brown, there are many restaurants which also – or only – offer it made of pork, primarily because it is a lot cheaper. If they do, they should tell you, because the real thing really ought to be veal. It is often served with boiled potatoes and maybe a cabbage or cucumber salad, but best of all with a generous dollop of lingonberry/cranberry sauce. Unsurprisingly, several restaurants in Vienna claim to be its home, notably the large and ancient Figlmueller in Wollzeile street, although it does little favour to its reputation by stressing how large its versions are, with photographs of them hanging over the plate, without mentioning as obviously as it should that their standard is made of pork (veal also available). Unquestionably the best I have ever eaten is at the Andechser am Dom, in Munich, just next to the great double towers of the cathedral.

One other Austrian speciality deserves a noble mention only because it is another simple dish that is rarely done as well as it can be: *Tafelspitz*, famously the favourite dish of Austria's most revered and last crowned emperor, Franz Josef. Literally, the 'top of the table', its simple description is disarmingly unimpressive: boiled beef in broth. And that's what it is, except not quite – or at least not always – as dull as it sounds, conjuring up images (and lack of tastes) of the old British working-class dish of grey meat. The key to a good *Tafelspitz* is the root vegetable broth it is cooked and served in. Even at its worst, *Tafelspitz* is nowhere near as bland or stringy as the 'boiled beef and carrots' I remember from my childhood (my mother was a nursery school cook), but it can be relatively bland and uninteresting. At its best it is superlative, a basic dish turned into a remarkable eating experience, and the one place above all others where that experience is to be enjoyed at its best is in Vienna, specifically at the small upmarket restaurant chain founded by Ewald Plachutta, who has turned his mastery of 'boiled beef' into Gault-Millau and Michelin awards. The photographs on the wall of the original restaurant on Wollzeile testify to visits from as varying a clientele as Woody Allen, John Cleese,

Omar Sharif, Mick Hucknall, Diego Maradona, John Kerry and Mikhail Gorbachev. Diners may choose their own cut of beef from those prepared in the kitchen. It is then served in a rich broth enriched by yellow carrots, onion, celeriac, leeks and parsley root, presented at table in copper pans, most importantly with a bone containing marrow which is to be scraped out and spread on crunchy toast. Almost single-handedly Plachutta has restored an old and much-loved dish that had grown dull with age to a culinary masterpiece.

But the truly unique dish in German cooking – if one can call it that – is the most unlikely, untypical of creations, a speciality of Frankfurt and all but unheard of anywhere else in Germany, so distinct from most German cuisine that I still find it the most improbable item on any menu: *grüne Sosse*, literally 'green sauce'. I first tasted it home-made by the German partner of an old Irish schoolfriend I had not seen for several years, and it was such a shock that I was convinced that the pair had done what was once the most difficult thing to do in Germany – it is much easier nowadays – and gone vegetarian.

What we were presented with was a plate of firm boiled potatoes with quartered boiled eggs and a vast tub of what I can only describe as pale lime green goo, which we were supposed to spoon over them before eating. That was it, the whole dish, no meat anywhere in sight. For someone who had known the days when a 'green salad', particularly in East Germany where fresh vegetables were rare and widely regarded with suspicion, came with chunks of fried *Speck* in it, it was a serious shock to the system, especially when Reinhold informed me proudly that it was an 'ancient' German traditional dish and his own personal favourite. I have since discovered that there are variants in other parts of north-central western Germany, but essentially this is a dish confined to Frankfurt. There's the truth of it: most Frank-furters' favourite dish is vegetarian (though they will add a dollop of *grüne Sosse* to fish or meat as well).

The traditional recipe uses seven herbs – borage, cress, parsley, chervil, burnet, sorrel and chives – supplied by the city's allotment holders, and mixed by hand, not sieved or blended, with oil, salt, pepper, lemon juice, garlic and yoghurt. And as if that were not enough, it's traditionally accompanied not by beer or wine but by cider. It's not exactly described as such – there is no native German equivalent for the French or English word – but as *Äpfelwein* (apple wine) but then again only if you're an outsider: in Frankfurt dialect, they say *Ebbelwoi*. It is brewed by small farmers in the surrounding countryside and that's what you're expected to order if you turn up at any of the little bars that specialise in it in the Frankfurt district of Sachsenhausen.

So much for the oddities, but we must also glance at the dessert menu. The ubiquitous Apfelstrudel is almost certainly the best-known dessert from the German-speaking world, with its slices of cooked, spiced apple in thin pastry dusted with icing sugar. But that is not to do justice to the other baked delights, notably those from southern Germany. The most delicious and unchallenging for the foreigner is *Kaiserschmarren,* which most Austrians would claim as their own, and many visitors to ski resorts will certainly have come across, though its popularity extends beyond the borders of the little Alpine republic. Essentially it is a sort of sweet omelette, hashed up in the pan and lightly browned, served up with icing sugar again and usually accompanied by *Apfelmus,* a sweet apple compote. Just the thing to replace your calories, washed down with a fruit schnapps, after a hard day on the slopes.

Definitely more challenging, but a must for my two children since the age of five, is the daunting-looking *Germknödel*. Shaped disconcertingly like a D-cup breast implant, this great mound of white doughy carbohydrate topped with a thick scattering of poppy seeds and swamped by a lavish dollop of pale custard has, I fear, never tempted my taste buds, even when I actually tasted it. But I have to admit its appeal to two young adolescent boys was unmistakable. I have often wondered if it was more a physiological thing: the body's automatic instinct to replace lost carbohydrates as efficiently as possible. There is also a specifically Bavarian version, shaped more like a Hovis loaf – unbaked – but it hardly attracts me any more than its semi-rotund cousin.

Perhaps the most common item on the dessert menu – after Apfelstrudel – across the whole of the German-speaking world is *rote Grütze*, a cold summer pudding based primarily on redcurrants with the addition of sugar, a splash of rosé wine, whatever other red fruits you have to hand – raspberries are common, strawberries occasionally too – boiled up and strained, then mixed with a little cornflour to make it set, and served cold with whipped or sour cream.

Which bring us back to the sausages, if only to list a few of the more unusual varieties beyond those frankfurters, which really only became a global phenomenon once German immigrants to America turned them into the hotdog. The real basic sausage in the German repertoire is actually the *Bratwurst*, intended for roasting or grilling as its name (*braten*, to grill) suggests. The standard *Bratwurst* is about 20 cm (eight inches) long, though there is no hard and fast rule, just over two cm (half an inch) thick, and is mostly made from pork but also includes veal or beef, almost always unsmoked. They are served everywhere: in pubs, restaurants, on the street. The most famed comes from the former East German state of Thuringia with a recipe dating back centuries and traditionally flavoured with caraway seed and marjoram.

Further south, Nürnberg in central Bavaria, by contrast, is famed for its distinctive tiny sausages on average the size of an adult's little finger. *Nürnberger Bratwürstchen* are traditionally served in multiples of three: either three as a snack in a roll, half a dozen on a plate with sauerkraut as a light main meal, or the full dozen for the true gourmand.

And then there is Munich, home to the most curious

– some would say infamous – German sausage of them all, the *Weisswurst*. Nothing to do with wheat here: the *Weisswurst* is simply white, or just off-white, pale, smooth and flecked with tiny bits of green. It looks like the swollen fingers of a waterlogged corpse. That is a bit harsh – tantamount to a national insult to Bavaria, a Münchener might say – but then it is widely acknowledged that the most tangible border in modern Germany is marked out by the *Weisswurstlinie,* the white sausage line. Nobody north of the line ever eats *Weisswurst,* indeed they tend to look on them with a mixture of curiosity and mild disgust. Yet for the initiate there is simply nothing better for a Munich breakfast than *Weisswurst und Weissbier.* For the morning is the time for *Weisswurst*: traditionally, though this no longer applies, they were supposed to be ordered and eaten before the bell of the Alter Peter church towering over the city's famed Viktualienmarkt (food market) chimed noon.

And the Viktualienmarkt is still one of the best places to enjoy them, sitting with your beer under the leafy shadow of the chestnut trees. The only thing is that the first-timer needs a word of warning: *Weisswurst* are served in linked pairs, floating in the water they have been heated in, in traditional grey and blue pots, every bit as disconcertingly white as ever. The pallid colour comes partly from the fact that ordinary salt rather than the pink nitrite preserving salt is used, but also from the veal that is supposed to be the chief ingredient (though nowadays cheapskates also use pork).

The historical origins of this Munich speciality are unknown, but the legend claims that on carnival Sunday in 1857, one Sepp Moser, landlord of the Zur Ewigen Licht (Eternal Light) inn on Marienplatz in the city centre, was making veal *Bratwurst,* when he realised he'd run out of sheep's intestines for skins, sent out an apprentice to fetch more only to have him come back with pigs' intestines instead, too thick and too tough to use for *Bratwurst.* With guests already waiting, Moser made the sausages, but instead of putting them on the grill, where he feared they would burst, he brought them up to simmering point in hot water, and served them like that. The skin is still not eaten: the *Weisswurst* is cut open lengthwise, the slightly sweet, parsley-flecked flesh removed and eaten with Munich's trademark sweet grain mustard. One of the world's best breakfasts, happily now to be enjoyed (in most hostelries) at any hour.

But what of the most commonly eaten sausage in Germany, particularly popular on the way home after a night out drinking? I would like to say it is a gastronomic creation of proud and ancient origins. Unfortunately it is not. Originating on the streets of West Berlin in the 1980s, the *Currywurst* is exactly what it would say on the tin if they came in tins. Quite simply it is a basic *Bratwurst,* as cooked and served on street corners all over the country, but served with the addition of a huge pile of curry powder on top of which is poured tomato ketchup. A culinary masterpiece it is not, but as a piece of innovative late night street food it is as fine as any in the world. Berlin now even has a *Currywurst* museum.

History is always in the making.

2

Kaliningrad

Where an empire began and ended, a city whose most famous inhabitants changed the way we see and understand the world

The Road to Nowhere

I first set foot in Europe's last forbidden city on an icy day in early March 1990 at a unique moment in European history when rules that had endured for half a century ceased to apply, and a timid Lithuanian taxi driver could be bribed to brave roads lined with snow and ice and trigger-happy Russian soldiers.

Early that morning we – myself and Tomas, a glum pessimist, more worried about the health of his ageing Lada than any pipe dream of democracy – pulled out of Vilnius on the frozen roads with flurries of sleet, snow and the acrid scent of cordite and revolution in the air. Our destination was Kaliningrad, the stolen red star in Stalin's tarnished crown, the sweetest prize in Russia's 'Great Patriotic War': a warm-water home for the Soviet Baltic fleet and mastery of a city that throughout its history had played a pivotal role in the creation of the German empire. It had been the final proof that not only had Stalin's empire triumphed over Hitler's, but that the successor to the tsars had triumphed over the empire of the Kaisers. Its conquest had such symbolic importance that Stalin had made it part of Russia herself, and not the adjacent puppet Soviet Republic of Lithuania that separated it from its new motherland. It never occurred to him that one day his empire too might fall apart at the seams.

I had been in Vilnius, still legally capital of Soviet Lithuania, for over a week, covering for the *Sunday Times* one of the final chapters in the story of tumbling dominoes that had begun spectacularly 16 months earlier with the fall of the Berlin Wall. Anti-Soviet riots in the streets had led to the erection of barricades and a declaration of independence by self-proclaimed parliamentary deputies. The Soviet empire was crumbling, the Kremlin was in denial. It had issued an ultimatum and was threatening to send in the troops.

But today was Sunday, publication day, which meant I had at least 48 hours before I had to concentrate on next week's story, and there was another adventure to hand. During the three years I had spent in Moscow for Reuters during the 1980s, visiting Kaliningrad had been an impossible dream; the ancient city of the kings of Prussia was a secretive destination sealed off to all foreigners, on a par with a few cities in Siberia and the Ural mountains, home to gulag camps or secret atomic weapons facilities. Even Soviet citizens needed special permission to travel there.

For me there was magic in its original name: for nearly 800 years since its foundation in the 13th-century Kaliningrad been called Königsberg, 'King's Rock'. A fortress city built by the Teutonic Knights, it was the first seat of Prussian monarchs and until 1945 one of the most important cities in German history. Without Königsberg there could have been no 'kings' in Prussia, and without a King of Prussia, no Kaiser of Germany, no 19th-century German Reich and therefore no 20th-century 'Third Reich'. The whole of German history, the whole of European history, would have been quite different.

I had flicked through old German travel books with pictures of quaint timbered houses hanging out over the banks of the river Pregel on the Fischerinsel, the 'Fishermen's Island' in the heart of the old town, and the curious, single-spired cathedral with the mausoleum of the great 18th-century philosopher Immanuel Kant.

Now, with the region in turmoil, it occurred to me that there was every chance the road west was open and we were unlikely to be stopped in a car with Soviet number plates. Tomas had allowed himself to be persuaded by a healthy fee paid in cash Deutsche Marks. In the current state of unrest he knew only two things: capitalism was coming, and the D-Mark was king.

As it turned out, Tomas was right to have been apprehensive. Our journey encountered no problems from officialdom or army, but the elements conspired against us: the Lada with its virtually treadless tyres slithered hither and thither on icy roads amid gusting showers of snow and sleet. At first, things went well: there was no sign of any checkpoint to indicate that we had left the Soviet Republic of Lithuania and entered the Russian oblast of Kaliningrad. Our passage went unnoticed save for a few cows squatting on the cold, damp grass, philosophically chewing.

Somewhere out there I knew had been the ancestral home of a friend of mine, a member of the Dönhoff family whose great-great-great-grandfather had attended the proclamation of the first German Kaiser in the Palace of Versailles in 1871. Their own home, Schloss Friedrichstein, had been a contemporary of the French Sun King's palace and almost as big. But I knew already none of it remained, burnt to the ground by the Red Army in 1945. The landscape we passed was one of dreary, scrubby farmland, obviously underworked, and rusting barns.

We were still some 40 kilometres from our destination when disaster struck: an overhanging branch weighed down by icicles fell and shattered our windscreen. Luckily even Tomas's old Lada had the sort of glass that disintegrates into little square chunks rather than spiky shards, but it still took us half an hour to clear them from the seats and dashboard, leaving us no option but to drive on with Tomas squinting through his glasses (the fact that he wore them was an advantage), while icy wind blasted in at us. It was 20 kilometres further before we found a garage where the mechanics initially suggested it would take a week or more to acquire a new windscreen, before the transfer of a hundred D-Mark note convinced them it could be found and fitted in a few hours.

That left Tomas cursing the gods, the Russians, his bad luck and the greed that had led him to agree to the folly of this expedition, while I, determined that no minor motor vehicle incident was going to abort my grand plan, took a taxi – or rather another Lada driven by one of the mechanics' mates for a price – into the centre of Kaliningrad. Within half an hour I was there, in the heart of the forbidden city, sitting in a cellar *pivnoi* (beer bar) with some boisterous sailors from the Baltic Fleet, with a head full of history only too conscious that the sign on the half-ruined redbrick archway above ground said Бранденбургские Ворота (Brandenburg-skiye Vorotá), in German Brandenburger Tor, the same as its more famous cousin in Berlin: the Brandenburg Gate. Sitting there drinking a Soviet brew that as ever tasted like tepid British home brew, I could feel a tingle not so much running down my spine as lodged in it: I was on the edge of one of Europe's political tectonic plates and the ground beneath my feet felt no longer certain.

Fortified against the cold, I emerged into a man-made wilderness. The double-towered redbrick archway of the Brandenburg Gate, which had once been the gate in the city walls that led towards Brandenburg and Berlin, was pockmarked with shell and bullet holes from its 'liberation' in 1945. Nothing else remained visible here of the once quaint, romantic, Gothic cityscape of meandering narrow mediaeval streets that I had pored over in pre-war photographs. In their stead stretched wide dual-carriageways, empty of traffic save for a few cars and battered open trucks. In all directions these wide, underused highways were lined with drab eight-storey flat blocks, dwellings that seemed deliberately designed to blend with the flat, grey wintry sky.

Apart from the scarred gatehouse with the bar in its basement, the only building of note I could see was a ruin: a great structure in redbrick with high walls and buttresses bearing shell holes and scorch marks, with no roof, and at one end, the remains of a roofless circular tower like some giant brick model of a photographer's telephoto lens, pointed at the heavens. It stood on its own, on an island of sorts, a wasteland really, crossed by a multi-lane motorway less than busy with a few Ladas and Zhigulis, but mostly rusting trucks carrying nothing from nowhere to nowhere. Around this hulking skeleton of a structure was a field of scrub with a crust of crumbling ice. This, it was obvious enough, was all that remained of Königsberg Cathedral. I walked across the dirty ice and entered the ruins. Of the original flooring little could be seen; more scrub grass had fought its way through the earth, between the high brick walls held up by iron girders to stop them collapsing. The whole resembled a derelict railway siding more than any building that might once have had a religious function.

Only at one end was there a relatively untouched structure in granite that might once have been pink and a name and date engraved on it: Immanuel Kant 1724–1804: the last resting place of Königsberg's most famous son, the man who wrote *The Critique of Pure Reason*, widely regarded as the foundation stone of much of modern philosophy. The wasteland outside, I suddenly realised, must once have been home to the Albertina University, founded in 1544 and once one of the leading universities in Europe. Kant had been educated and spent most of his long life teaching there. For a while I wandered round aimlessly, painfully aware of the passage of time, the destruction of war, the shades of the past and the bleak reality of the present outside. It was only as I noticed the darkening skies above the ruins and a chill breeze blowing through the charred brick slits of the glassless windows that I realised I too was not immune to the passage of time. In particular I had to get back to the garage where Tomas would be waiting, hopefully with a new windscreen, so that we might begin our journey back to Lithuania. In the uncertain political and military situation we could not dare even consider overnighting in Kaliningrad, or indeed drawing attention to the fact we had been there at all.

Walking out across the desolate parody of a cityscape, I remembered the story about the famous seven bridges of Königsberg, and the Swiss mathematician who had turned a popular pub puzzler into the basis of a complex theorem that laid the basis for work still done in the field of topology and graph theory today. In the mid-18th century Leonhard Euler from Basel, who also happened to be an astronomer, physicist and engineer, was working at the Imperial Russian Academy of Sciences in St Petersburg, but toying with the idea of taking up a position in Berlin. On a visit to eastern Prussia, he discovered a problem that had perplexed Königsbergers for years, usually in late night conversations in beer bars among drunks plotting their route home: whether it was possible to start off anywhere in the city and cross each of the seven bridges that united the two sides of the Pregel river, and its two islands, once, and once only, and return to the same place (as drunks often do). This, he was told, had been the subject of many a long argument among the locals.

Euler took it as a scientific challenge, and set about using the laws of geometry to tackle it. By involving abstract methods, he proved that it was impossible, and indeed that any problem which met the same preconditions would also be insoluble. He had discovered a mathematical theory of impossibility.

Five of the seven bridges should have linked from the island where the cathedral stood, and where I now found myself. What, I wondered, was left of them. Then I realised that the urban motorway that ran across one end must have taken the place of two. Of the other three, I could find only remnants of two, and not remnants I was willing to venture across in the ends of following any scientific or historic path; where there might once have been wood or even stone, all that more or less linked the island in the vicinity of the ruined cathedral with the 'mainland' on either side were a few rusted and twisted iron girders. I decided to take Euler's word for it and headed back towards the main road in search of a lift back to Tomas and his Lada.

The Crusaders of the North

The history of Königsberg/Kaliningrad, the city that defines in its own curious way the post-World War II settlement and the still uneasy relationship between Europe and Russia, goes back to the Middle Ages and the clash between Christendom and Islam.

In the aftermath of the first crusade, when the invading Arabs were pushed back and the Christian 'Kingdom of Jerusalem' established in 1099, pilgrims from all over Europe began to flock to the 'Holy Land' on a once-in-a-lifetime marathon journey that was considered a sacred duty, to Christians of the time what the haj remains to Muslims today. It was a long, arduous and dangerous journey during which, apart from the cost of food and lodging, the pilgrims faced threats from thieves and unscrupulous merchants.

The crusading knights, who had won the Holy City back from the infidel Muslims, now saw it as their duty – and a lucrative one – to protect the pilgrims. Over the decades several military–religious orders grew up to do this job, even if some tended to get their sacred and secular roles mixed up. These days the most widely known is the Order of the Knights Templar, whose fame has been fired in popular imagination by fanciful conspiracy theories from Dan Brown and other pap thriller writers. But there were many others:

the Order of the Holy Sepulchre, the Knights Hospitaller (based in Malta) and the Deutscher Orden, set up specifically to look after the needs of German-speaking pilgrims. Literally the 'German Order' it is more usually known in English by a name that somehow sounds more evocative, if slightly sinister: the Teutonic Knights. The Knights were founded along the lines of the Knights Hospitaller, from whom they took a form of their insignia known as the Maltese Cross, which would eventually become the style of the most significant German military medal, the Iron Cross. In a similar if even more bizarre transmogrification, cheap white metal replicas of the 'Iron Cross' would become a hippy icon in the 1970s: I remember buying one in London's Carnaby Street and wearing it on a chain around my neck. Nobody thought anything of it at the time. The far right and the concept of neo-Nazism were considered absurd among a youth celebrating the 'Age of Aquarius'.

The Knights Templar may have lived on longer in the popular imagination, largely due to their forced elimination in the 14th century, but the influence of the Teutonic Knights on European and world history was to be significantly greater. Their foundation was not propitious. The order was set up in Acre, the second most important city in the Kingdom of Jerusalem, while it and the Holy City itself were under siege by the great Kurdish Islamic warrior Saladin. The Teutonic Knights were recognised as a separate order by Pope Celestine in 1192. By then, however, things were not going well. Jerusalem had fallen to Saladin. Acre had withstood the siege but in an argument over ransom money the Christian commander, the francophone Richard, nicknamed *Coeur de Lion,* who also happened to be King of England, had 2,700 Muslim prisoners decapitated, provoking Saladin to do the same to his Christian captives.

The so-called 'Kingdom of Jerusalem' would last another hundred years, but without owning Jerusalem itself, which obviously reduced the number of pilgrims from Europe. Over the next 40 years, and particularly under the rule of Grand Master Hermann von Salza, the Teutonic Knights drifted away from pilgrim-protecting to become a straightforward military order, little different to well organised modern mercenaries, except that they had a basic allegiance to Christianity, manifested not so much in a tendency to turn the other cheek, as in a ground rule of not working for Muslims.

With business at an all-time low in the Holy Land, the Teutonic Knights took employment elsewhere, notably for a while in Transylvania, where they enabled widespread migration of German colonists to protect the lands claimed by the King of Hungary from potential Islamic invasion. But the trouble with the knights was that despite taking their employer's money, they tended to regard the lands they protected as their own. In 1225 the Hungarian king declared them expelled (although he was happy to keep the hardworking colonist farmers they had encouraged to populate his lands.).

By chance the Polish Duke of Masovia, the area around Warsaw now known as Masowsze, failing to heed the lesson of the Hungarians, invited the order to move north and defend his borders on the Baltic against pagan tribes known as the Prusi. They were granted a base in an eastern district called Chelmo (which they renamed Culmerland). The Holy Roman Emperor Friedrich II, the Germanic prince who saw it as his duty to protect Christendom in general, gave his fellow German speakers the right to seize the land of these northern pagans on the grounds that it would be good training for killing Saracens and regaining Jerusalem, of which he also claimed to be king. The ensuing conflict took 50 years and was one of the best documented early examples of genocide (until the conquest of North America, South America and in particular Australia showed how to do it more efficiently). In truth, neither side was keen on fair play: the native Prusi were said to roast captured knights over a fire, in their armour, 'like chestnuts'.

In the end, the defeated Prusi were either killed or assimilated (baptised and taught German), their language and culture extinguished. The knights then expanded into the other Baltic states, in particular Livonia (modern Lithuania), bringing German and Polish speakers with them. Only their attempt to expand into Russian territory failed when they suffered a crushing defeat in 1242 at the hands of the Novgorod prince Alexander Nevsky, whose sobriquet was gained from the ice of the river Neva on which he slaughtered the invaders. The event was famously celebrated 700 years later in a 1938 film by Soviet film director Sergei Eisenstein with a soundtrack by Prokofiev, neither of whom could have known that the triumph they were celebrating would be equalled just five years later at Stalingrad. Alexander Nevsky even today is Russia's most celebrated historical hero: he is at a safe distance, with fewer black marks against him than most rivals.

Secure in their captured territories, and chastened (for the moment) against thoughts of further eastward expansion, the knights founded their King's Rock: Königsberg. The king in question was Ottokar II of Bohemia, to whom they nominally owed allegiance, but the city would be synonymous with their order, and with the concept of a greater German empire, for the next 790 years. Yet at that time, 'nations' and 'nationalism' were largely unknown concepts; religion was the common bond and loyalty was paid to feudal masters. The Knights were happy to serve the King of Poland in expelling would-be settlers from German-speaking Brandenburg who had tried to make their home in the coastal province known as Pomorsze (literally the 'land beside the sea'), which would eventually be Germanicised as 'Pommern', and known in English as Pomerania. German domination of the lands they had initially been invited into as allies became apparently permanent. And not all of those who had invited them regretted German replacement of their fellow countrymen. The Slav Prince Wizlaw of Rügen, the Baltic island that in the mid-20th century would become a favourite holiday destination for East Germans forbidden to travel abroad, famously declared back in 1221: 'God forbid that the land should ever revert to its former state, that the Slavs should drive out the German settlers and again undertake its cultivation.'

The main prize on the Baltic coast was the port town which the Poles called Gdansk, and the German settlers Danzig. The Knights took it, as ordered, from the Brandenburgers, but instead of delivering it to the King of Poland, kept it for themselves. They brought in settlers of their own, German-speaking but owing strict allegiance to the brotherhood, and expanded the city into a fortress. Only reluctantly, after a further series of conflicts with the Poles, did they acknowledge that they held it as a fiefdom.

Fearing the fate of the Knights Templar, who had been turned on by their papal and secular sponsors, banned and broken up, the Teutonic Knights, who had maintained their headquarters in Venice, now moved it to a new fortress on the Baltic called Marienburg, the fortress of the Virgin Mary. I first wandered around its great redbrick battlements in 1981, during the rise of the Solidarity free trade union movement in Gdansk. It felt weird at the time to sense the ghosts of the austere Teutonic Knights looking out onto the Baltic, masters of all they surveyed and a realm they had created, at a time when once again the local population was rising against hated overlords, this time Russian.

The irony of the Knights' retention of Danzig was that because they had been forced to pay reparations to Poland, they raised taxes on both Danzig and Königsberg, leading the nobles and the citizens who lived in them to revolt. The rebels asked the Polish king for help. The Knights were defeated and the areas they had Germanised – in proof of how little the concept of 'nationhood' applied at the time – now declared themselves a separate, direct fiefdom of the King of Poland, called 'Royal Prussia'. Over the next century, as the Knights' power waned, Poland and Lithuania grew closer, eventually uniting in the Polish-Lithuanian Common-wealth, one of eastern Europe's largely forgotten empires, despite lasting for some 200 years and at its height reaching from the Baltic to the Black Sea.

The Polish-Lithuanian expansion squeezed the Teutonic Knights to a rump state centred on Königsberg. Ironically it was dealt an accidental death blow by one of its most successful rulers. Albert of Prussia, elected 37th Grand Master in 1510, became a follower of Martin Luther, changed the state religion to the new Protestant Lutheranism and founded the Albertina University. It was a successful reform in economic and secular terms, but the change in religion effectively meant the end of the Teutonic Knights as a monastic military order with its origins in expanding Catholic Christianity. The order itself was not officially disbanded, but lost all influence in Prussia, retaining only tiny scattered territories – self-governing bishoprics and monastic communities – it possessed in other parts of the German-speaking world, including today's Austria, Switzerland, Slovakia, Slovenia, Italy and the Czech Republic. The Deutscher Orden continues to exist today – I regularly walk past one of its local headquarters in a Munich backstreet – as a Catholic religious charity with no more than a thousand or so members.

Albert secularised not just the state but also his own position with the new title of Duke of Prussia, its security once again guaranteed as a fiefdom from the King of Poland, who happened to be his uncle. It was Realpolitik in light of the rise in power of Poland–Lithuania. Even Albert was not to see that his new secular duchy would not only with time become free of its fealty but during the three 18th-century partitions of Poland swallow a large chunk of its former overlords' territory and become once again a great military power that would eventually preside over the creation for the first time in history of a unified German state.

The Man Who Stopped the Sun

The university that Albert founded was still in its infancy during the lifetime of the Duke's greatest contemporary, a man who changed the way people saw the world forever. Nikolai Copernicus arguably surpassed Kant as one of the greatest minds ever produced in those lands that would change hands so often between Germans and Poles. Indeed it is still in dispute which 'nation' can properly claim him for its own, a question he himself might hardly have understood and would certainly not have considered important.

Copernicus was born in Royal Prussia, that area which had sided with the Poles against the Knights, adjacent to what towards the latter part of his life would become Albert's Ducal Prussia (the two would only become united in the 18th century). Copernicus spent most of his life between the two. Indeed the man who changed humanity's conception of the universe, was primarily known in his lifetime not for stargazing but for his successful career in diplomacy, medicine and monetary reform. The word 'polymath' might have been coined for him.

We do not even know which language Copernicus considered his native tongue. Everything he wrote was, like all educated writings of the period, in Latin. His name was written variously as Copernic, Kopernik, Kopernigk and Copernicus. Its origin, in times when people were often given surnames according to their trade – Thatcher, Archer, Fletcher, Barber are all classic English examples – may well have come from the business of his father, a wealthy merchant selling copper (*Kupfer* in modern German) from the Silesian mines to maritime traders in Danzig. The bright young man was well educated at the famed Jagellonian university in Krakow, then capital of Poland (where teaching would have been in Latin) and the independent Italian bishopric of Bologna, where he signed up to the *Natio Germanorum*, a student organisation for German speakers. It is likely – but by no means certain – therefore, that his native language may have been German, but that he spoke fluent Polish too, became competent in Italian during his time in Bologna, also learned Greek, and was fluent in Latin, the chief form of communication between scholars.

Like many well-educated, well-connected young men of the time, he acquired a sinecure from the Catholic church, first as a canon of the Church of Holy Cross in Breslau, to which we shall return shortly, and later also from Frauenberg – Frombork in Polish – although the meaning 'Hill of Our Lady' suggests the German version was the original. It is not known if he was ever ordained as a priest, but his remains are buried there. Fear of religious controversy made him insist for most of his life on keeping his life's greatest work – *De Revolutionibus Orbium Coelestium* (On the Orbits of the Heavenly Spheres) – secret from all but a few very close friends until he was almost on his deathbed.

In his public life he wrote treatises on money, its worth, its use and its value. He was one of the first to conceive of the idea of 'money supply', and to suggest that in the long run gold and silver coins would yield to 'debased' coinage, made of non-precious metals. His writings on money caught the attention of local rulers and he became an adviser on monetary reforms to both Prussian and their overlord Polish rulers. His first paid job had been given to him by his uncle who was Prince-Bishop of Warmia, yet another fiefdom of the Polish crown. When his uncle died, his successor gave Copernicus a property adjacent to the cathedral, which would be his primary residence for the rest of his life. He had already been making astronomical observations for many years, and a few of his friends were aware of his efforts to plot the movement of heavenly bodies. But in the public sphere, Copernicus was employed as a diplomat. His skills led to him being made the Prince-Bishop's economic administrator, requiring him for a time to move to Olsztyn – Allenstein in German – and while he was there he ended up commanding the city's military defence against a raid by the Knights, then subsequently negotiating the peace.

But all along his real interest remained astronomy. He had made a new series of observations of the Sun, Mars and Saturn a decade earlier, and written a draft of what would become his masterpiece. By the 1530s rumours about its content had begun to leak out, even reaching Rome, the one thing he dreaded, where to his surprise a number of cardinals expressed interest in the theory that the Earth might not after all, as had been believed since the time of Ptolemy, be the centre of the universe and the Sun's apparent daily movement across the heavens in fact the produce of the Earth's movement around the Sun.

The trouble was that to the average person such an idea seemed preposterous: you only had to look up at the sky to see that the sun moved across it and therefore around the Earth. With the Church in Rome struggling to retain its authority against the Reformation, it might easily have been assumed that the papacy would favour the accepted conservative vision of the universe while these new 'Protestants' might be more open to fresh ideas. But it was not always self-evident. Phillip Melanchthon, a theological ally of Martin Luther, wrote of rumours about a Polish astronomer who 'moves the Earth and stops the Sun'. It sounded scathing but Melachthon was seriously interested in astronomy himself and would send a pupil to Copernicus who would eventually persuade him to go public.

By 1536 Copernicus had received a letter from an archbishop in Rome asking for details of his research. Rumours were leaking all over the place. All around him friends and colleagues were advising him that it was time to publish. Even though some of his friends had become Protestants, Copernicus himself remained a loyal Catholic, but by now in his late 60s, he eventually agreed, though only after composing a cautiously worded dedication to Pope Paul III. The man he chose to take the finished opus to the printers in Nürnberg should be a close friend who was also a Catholic bishop, in concert with the Protestant pupil sent by Melanchthon.

The finished first edition was allegedly delivered to Copernicus on his deathbed in May 1543. He was suffering from an onset of apoplexy and paralysis which had struck him down over the winter. The legend is that he awoke from a coma, took one look at his book and passed away peacefully. His life's work was finally out: people would no longer see the heavens above them in the same light. They could at last claim confidently they were telling the truth when they said they felt the Earth move under their feet.

⋲⋺

Between the Prussia of Copernicus and that of Kant lie two hundred years in which the fate of the little German-speaking provinces in the fiefdom of the mighty Polish crown was transformed completely and a new state grew up which would become the basis of the country we today call Germany.

A crucial element in Albert's secularisation of his domain was that as it was no longer a monastic state, and the ruler no longer a monk: he could marry and produce heirs. Moreover, he was a member of the Hohenzollern clan. Originally from Swabia in the southwest of the German-speaking lands, they took their name from a spectacularly isolated hilltop castle which still stands today, much romantically rebuilt in the early 19th century, as a fairytale fortress. By the mid-14th century, however, the Hohenzollerns had become one of those families which elected the Holy Roman Emperor. Their territories migrated north to a substantial chunk of land around the little town of Brandenburg on the Havel river, but soon moved their seat to the east to another little town, called Cölln, which lay on the Spree and had recently been united with a hamlet on the other side known as Berlin.

Albert of Prussia's plans for a dynasty of his own were abruptly extinguished when his two sons died in infancy. His nephew, Johann Sigismund, the Prince-Elector of

Brandenburg, quickly married Albert's daughter, Anna, overnight creating a family landholding to be known as Brandenburg-Prussia, which included both territories, plus a handful of little bishoprics and minor duchies to the far west and south which had also fallen into the family's clutches. Compared to a modern state it was a ridiculous little patchwork of unconnected areas. The slow and gradual filling in of the gaps in the patchwork would over the coming centuries create a state to rival the Habsburg family's Austrian-based landholding and unite most of what would eventually be called Germany.

By now the power of the Polish–Lithuanian Commonwealth was beginning to wane under the onslaught of Russian-backed Cossacks in Ukraine in the west, Ottoman attacks in the southeast and opportunistic Swedish invasion from the north. It was the beginning of a terminal decline that would see the Commonwealth wiped from the map in stages culminating in the 18th-century partitions of Poland, in which Prussia and Austria would share the spoils with Russia. The Thirty Years War wrought devastation on Brandenburg but also won the Hohenzollerns more territory, spurring their sense of self-aggrandisement to the extent that they coveted the title of 'king'. The problem was that, although the title of Holy Roman Emperor had long been little more than one of many held by the powerful Habsburg family, under the loose rules which its members adhered to, the title of 'king' was forbidden to those who were nominally vassals to the 'emperor'. But the Habsburgs desperately needed all the help they could get in their attempt to stop the Spanish Crown being taken from their family by their French Bourbon rivals. And there was a solution: Poland's decline meant that the Hohenzollerns now held their Prussian Duchy in full title rather than as a nominal Polish fiefdom. And the duchy, like Poland, was outside the empire. There was nothing that in theory prevented the Prussian part of their territory being declared a kingdom.

On 18 January 1701, therefore, Prince Elector Friedrich III of Brandenburg-Prussia staged a scene of extraordinary extravagance that involved 30,000 horses and 1,800 carriages and borrowed ceremonial from all over Europe for his own coronation ceremony in the city where he was born: Königsberg. The King's Rock had now fulfilled its manifest destiny. Dressed in robes of scarlet and gold with diamond buttons and an ermine mantle, he placed the crown on his own head (as Napoleon would do in Paris nearly a century later) and declared himself 'King *in* Prussia'. It was a clever bit of wording as it posed no direct challenge either to the Polish monarch who still was lord of 'Royal Prussia' nor to the Habsburgs, who could say they had not allowed anyone to assume a 'royal' title within their 'empire'. They did not know that they had accidentally allowed the creation of a power that would come to challenge and eventually surpass their own.

By 1772, the Hohenzollerns joined in the first partition of the former superpower, Poland, and absorbed the territories of 'Royal Prussia'. With splendid disregard for the Habsburgs they were fast coming to see as rivals, they changed their title to Kings *of* Prussia. The stage was set, the prize was at last evident: a country called 'Germany'. The only questions were when and how.

Teaching the World to Think

Half a century before the Hohenzollerns transformed Königsberg into the coronation city of kings, a horse livery manufacturer from Memel, today the port of Klaipeda in modern Latvia, and a local girl called Anna Reuter had a child they, with more than a hint of piety, named Emanuel, which he himself, after studying Hebrew, would spell 'Immanuel'. A rather dull, studious child, he enrolled as a student at Königsberg's Albertina University at the age of 16.

Inspired by his great predecessor, Copernicus, he studied

astronomy, read Isaac Newton and concluded that the solar system and our galaxy itself were both part of spinning clouds of stars which he called *nebulae*, the Latin for clouds. As so often, he conflated cosmology and philosophy, becoming increasingly interested in the latter, eventually becoming Professor of Metaphysics and Logic. He acknowledged the influence of Scottish philosopher David Hume, whom he credited with awakening him from 'dogmatic slumber', and as a result immersed himself in his work, without publishing anything for more than a decade in his middle age.

When he finally did turn out a work of philosophy again, it was a long, often almost impenetrable tome of 800 pages that eventually came to be seen as one of the most important works ever published in the field and led to the author being recognised as the father of modern philosophy. It was entitled *Kritik der Reinen Vernunft,* The Critique of Pure Reason. It is and was intended to be an analysis of how we think, of how the human brain takes in information, processes and reacts to it.

Kant's writing is dense and challenging, yet cautiously optimistic in its long-term belief in an abjuring of religion and its diktats, along with a representative democratic form of government that was not based on the 'mob rule' of narrow majorities. For Kant, 'morality' was a central element in reason, and the two were inseparably linked, irrespective of the concept of happiness, as were morality and freedom. His concept of the *Rechtstaat*, a state based on the rule of law, is an integral part of the constitution of today's Federal Republic of Germany, first formulated in 1947, as a direct contradiction to both the Nazi and Communist states.

Given the horrors that Germans over the past century both lived through and unleashed, it is unremarkable that the first sentence of modern Germany's constitution is in my opinion the finest in the world: *Die Würde des Menschen ist unantastbar.* It is simultaneously simple, clear and forthright in German, and yet not easily translated into English. The problem is primarily with the word '*Würde*' which dictionaries translate variously as 'worth' or 'dignity'. A rather formal translation therefore might be 'Human dignity is inviolable', but to really understand it the brain needs to take in such alternatives as 'human rights are not to be challenged', 'a human life is precious beyond value', 'everyone has equal rights under the law', 'mankind is the measure of all things', and, of course, a knowledge of 20th-century German history.

That first line of the constitution is designed to ensure that the morality which Kant equated with reason and freedom are never again violated as they were for a dozen years in the middle of the last century. Immanuel Kant would have been delighted, yet horrified at what made it necessary.

Kant left a legacy of philosophical thought that would resound throughout the German-speaking world and beyond. Philosophers over the next 50 years or so are even today regularly referred to as 'post-Kantian', and there were none of value who felt they could ignore his work. To go into this in any depth would require tens of thousands of pages, which have already been written, and go beyond the intellectual effort of, if not most readers, at least this author. It will have to suffice to give a brief account of the most significant works, and their influences on later history.

Born in Danzig in the latter years of Kant's life, Arthur Schopenhauer (1788–1860) would become both a keen student of his work, and a serious critic of it. Schopenhauer insisted that our interrelation with the world around us and our perception of reality was not just dependent on our senses and understanding, but also our relationship with our own physical bodies. He believed that Kant paid too little attention to or inadequately described human will, which he characterised as the 'will to live', not about wishes but about driving desire, often futile and amoral, which fuelled human society.

He was a keen orientalist and much influenced by Buddhism, but was also, in early 21st-century terms, a misogynist and racist, believing that women were ordained to be mothers and housewives, and that only the ancient Egyptians and Hindus deserved parity with the 'white races', while the best leaders among 'dark people' were those with fairer skin. On the other hand he was a keen supporter of animal rights and tolerant of homosexuality.

Schopenhauer's *bête noire* was Georg Friedrich Hegel (1770–1831). Born in Stuttgart, Hegel is considered the champion of the 'thesis-antithesis-synthesis' concept of argument, counter-argument and conclusion, which he held was embodied in the French Revolution, where the idealistic revolution was followed by the Terror, but which would eventually end up in a republic of free citizens. He believed in the citizen's duty to the state, and the state's duty to the citizen and to that extent has as broadly optimistic an outlook as Kant while totally opposed to Schopenhauer's essential pessimism. The latter called him a 'charlatan', and he remains a controversial figure. One of those influenced by his writing was Karl Marx.

Friedrich Schlegel (1772–1829), an atheist who became a devout Catholic, was born in Hanover and became a diplomat for the Austrian Chancellor Metternich (another example of how 'nationality' and 'statehood' mattered little in Central Europe as late as the end of the 18th century). Schlegel lived and lectured in Paris, and was one of the most important discoverers of the common roots of what are now called the Indo-European languages. He compared the morphology of German, Greek, Latin, Persian and Sanskrit and discovered remarkable similarities in both vocabulary and syntax. His 1808 book *On the Language and Wisdom of India* changed the way most peoples thought about the subcontinent, and the origins of civilisation.

Friedrich Nietzsche (1844–1900) became one of the most controversial figures in German philosophy, not least because of his snappy turn of phrase (worthy of tabloid headline writers), which was open to dangerous interpretation, notably 'God is dead', his book *Beyond Good and Evil,* and the *Übermensch* or 'superman'. Nietzsche fought against an instinctive pessimism. He despaired of the 'common man', which gave him a deep dislike of democracy and mass culture. He was for a while friends with composer Richard Wagner but disliked his excessive glorification of Germanic culture and his anti-Semitism. He condemned Jewish and Christian morality equally as fostering a 'slave mentality', which with their insistence on equality denied and tried to repress those of exceptional talent. He believed a common morality was not suited to a world where inequality was evident. Like most of his calling, he was scathing about his colleagues, referring to Plato as 'boring', and called Kant and Descartes 'naïve'. He would become a serious influence on Martin Heidegger (1889–1976), whose main work on the relationship between human life and the passage of time – *Being and Time* – is a seminal work of the 20th century.

From the 18th and 19th centuries German philosophers leapt to the forefront of the European tradition to take their place alongside Descartes, Rousseau and Voltaire in France, Hobbes and Mill in England, Hume and Smith in Scotland, Kierkegaard in Denmark and Tolstoy in Russia. But the greatest slur on that reputation came in the 1930s and 1940s when the cult of Nazism tried to build an intellectual foundation out of dribs and drabs of German philosophy. Schopenhauer and Nietzsche's talk of the importance of the will was exploited in the Leni Riefenstahl propaganda masterpiece film of the 1936 Nürnberg rallies, *The Triumph of the Will,* while its introduction showing Adolf Hitler, 'descending from the heavens like a god' – airplanes were still relatively novel forms of transport – was intended to echo the 'superman' idea. Similarly Schlegel's research into Indo-European languages and Schopenhauer's concept of parity with ancient Hindu civilisation led to Goebbels's creation of the 'Aryan' myth.

Concluding this brief overview of the riches of German

philosophical thought is perhaps the most remarkable thinker of them all, a man who in early 21st-century terms might not be considered a German at all. Ludwig Wittgenstein was Austrian, born in Vienna, and briefly attended the same school as Adolf Hitler. He fought in World War I against the British and Russians, then served as a hospital porter in London during World War II, and died a British citizen.

He was born into an immensely rich and talented family – they had seven grand pianos in their house – cursed with a genetic streak of depression: three of his four brothers committed suicide and Wittgenstein considered it himself. A brilliant mathematician, dismissive of authority, he did not suffer fools gladly, especially when they were his teachers. He called Schopenhauer 'shallow' and Bertrand Russell, who had taught him at Cambridge before World War I, 'glib'. Russell initially considered him a crank before deciding he was a genius. Wittgenstein declared most other philosophers 'stupid and dishonest'. Eventually Russell would agree with him, considering his pupil's criticism of his work 'an event of first-rate importance in my life'.

In stark contrast to the voluminous works of most philosophers, Wittgenstein in his lifetime published only one brief 75-page work – the 1921 *Tractatus Logico-Philosophicus* (A Logical Philosophical Treatise) – a book review and a children's dictionary. The great bulk of Wittgenstein's work was published posthumously in 1953 as *Philosophical Investigations*.

The *Tractatus* is for me personally, as a linguist as well as someone who likes to think he has a brain but has never come to terms with Kant, about as good as philosophy gets. It argues that the limits of language are the limits of philosophy, if not of thought, because language is the only medium within which thoughts can be expressed and exchanged. In other words, every time you had a student discussion late at night when somebody put you down by saying 'that's just semantics', you could at least have claimed token support from Wittgenstein. Unfortunately at times he leaves most of us in the air with his use of mathematics to make logical equations. It is hazardous to attempt to sum up Wittgenstein in a single line, even though essentially that was at the heart of his teaching: if you can't say this in a simpler way you might not know what you are talking about. And nor might anyone else.

The 'Lost Lands'

Königsberg and its fate stand today as the greatest symbols of what some Germans still refer to as the 'lost lands' (a term officially frowned upon since Willy Brandt's legendary fall to his knees in Warsaw in atonement for the Nazis' crimes in Eastern Europe). Nobody really expects or would even dare to suggest that the territories lost in 1945 might ever become German again. There is a hope and widespread belief that Europe has evolved beyond that era. But two cities in what is now Poland still have an ineradicable resonance in German history: Danzig/Gdańsk and Breslau/Wrocław.

When I first lived in East Berlin in the early 1980s, I was very aware of the importance of street names in a city so marked by different versions of history. There was, for a start, the anomaly that the U-bahn station called Stadtmitte (city centre) was right on the edge of East Berlin, just a hundred metres from the impassible Berlin Wall. Then there was Otto-Grotewohl-Strasse, named after East Germany's first Communist prime minister: prior to 1964 it had still been known as Wilhelmstrasse, named for a Prussian king, but notorious as the site of Hitler's Reich chancellery. And then, just up the road from our apartment, at a major intersection with what had once been Berlin's inner ring road, was Dimitroffstrasse, named for a Bulgarian Communist leader; but all the locals still called it by the name it had been known by since it ceased to be a cart track: Danziger Strasse.

Danzig was one of those great emotive names in German history. I knew all about its origins as one of the merchant cities in the Hanseatic League, that German-dominated trading organisation that ran the length of the Baltic coastline; about its status as a 'Free City' in the years between 1918 and 1939 after East Prussia had been detached from the rest of Germany and the 'Polish Corridor' to the Baltic created; about its central role in Günther Grass's great wartime novel *Die Blechtrommel* (*The Tin Drum*), in which his stubborn, irascible anti-hero Oskar Matzerath refuses to grow up; and as the place where World War II began when a German battleship opened fire on a Polish garrison at the Westerplatte on the coast in the early morning of 1 September 1939.

Grass would become a symbol of Germany's contorted conscience, as in the years after 1945 Germans from Dresden to Cologne, Hamburg to Vienna tried to come to terms with what had been done in their name. *The Tin Drum*, published in 1959, was the prime factor in his being awarded the Nobel Prize for Literature 40 years later. He had always admitted being a member of the Hitler Youth and having believed in its ideals, but maintained that during the war he had been conscripted, aged 17, and served only in an anti-aircraft battery in Danzig. It was only in 2006, at the age of 78, that he admitted in fact he was conscripted into the *Waffen-SS*. The revelation stunned the world, not because it linked him to any atrocities; the *Waffen-SS* was a primarily military unit and Grass claimed he had never fired a shot, and only realised the truth about the regime at the Nürnberg trials. It was still a body blow to a united Germany which treasured Grass for having purged its historical conscience. My friend Michael Jürgs, Grass's biographer, admitted it had never even occurred to him that he might have served in the SS. Grass himself said he came clean in his old age because it had weighed on him all his life.

Within months of my arrival in East Berlin, however,

Danzig was to be forever transformed in my heart into the city it by then had already become: Polish Gdańsk, a symbol of freedom, rebellion and revolution. Like everywhere else in this northeastern corner of Central Europe, Gdańsk/Danzig has seen many variations in its name and its population, though prior to the development of nation-states, they had more or less comfortably rubbed along together, grumbling about the taxes and impositions of whoever happened to be their overlords.

But from 1945, the city had for the first time fallen under an ideology dictated from Moscow and which most people despised. The free trade union Solidarity had been set up in 1980 and a triple cross erected outside the mammoth shipyards to commemorate workers killed a decade before in brutal suppression of wildcat strikes. In 1981, as Poland seethed with revolt against the Soviet-backed dictatorship, I spent more and more time not in East Berlin but in Warsaw and Gdańsk. They were heady times as we listened to the firebrand electrician Lech Wałęsa who, in a future then still distant, would end up President of Poland, and have the city's airport named after him. I was reporting from Poland in turmoil in early December 1981, when a German–German summit obliged me to return to Berlin: East German leader Erich Honecker was meeting with West German Chancellor Helmut Schmidt outside East Berlin. It promised to have historic implications. As I drove through a night thick with falling snow, I was unaware that I was leaving the real story behind. The next morning Polish Communist Party leader General Wojciech Jaruzelski declared martial law. The border I had just crossed was sealed. In comparison the German–German summit was a non-story. Over the weeks that followed the best story I could offer was Poland by proxy: notes from Reuters' Warsaw correspondent, temporarily cut off from all external communication, scribbled in tiny writing on minute pieces of paper and smuggled out by his wife, who passed them on to me in West Berlin. It was already clear the the story begun by Lech Wałęsa and his fellow shipyard workers in Gdańsk was far from over.

For most of its history it was trade, not nationality, that dominated Gdańsk/Danzig, which had a large population of not just Poles and Germans but also Scottish and Dutch. When the city centre was restored in the 1950s and 1960s, the architects were encouraged to use Dutch rather than more historically accurate German models. Yet whatever the architectural historical accuracy, the city rebuilt from rubble acquired its own new history and its own new monuments in the 1980s, a history which it can rightly be proud of.

The biggest city that might be assumed to be schizo-phrenic over its switching of identities, yet has lived with it throughout history, is the minor metropolis that today is called Wrocław but for most of its thousand-year history was known as Breslau. The original name, by which it was known from earliest records in the 11th century until the mid-13th was Vratislava, almost identical to the capital of today's Slo-vakia, Bratislava. The name may come from a contemporary ruler possibly called Vratislav, but in all probability all three derive from variations on 'Slav Brotherhood'. The city was a major hub of the early kingdom of Poland, which was, along with the later France and England, one of the earliest 'nation-states' to emerge in Europe. The German version of its name has its origins in the disaster which struck eastern and Central Europe in the mid-13th century: the Mongol invasion. Vratislava was torched at the approach of the Asian horseman hordes. When it was resettled shortly afterwards, the great German migration eastwards, spearheaded by the Teutonic Knights, was already under way. The new name was a Germanisation of what the new inhabitants heard.

Over the coming centuries Breslau became more and more German, although it never quite lost its Polish roots and heri-tage. The first known work to be printed in Polish appeared in Breslau in 1475. Breslau's status as a recognised town was reinforced when in 1261 it adopted the Magdeburg Rights, imitating that city's compact with local rulers guaranteeing it a certain degree of autonomy: at the time the rulers of the territory (rather than the town) were still Polish. But these were days in which families, dynasties and feudal loyalty mattered more than vague concepts of 'nationality'. Breslau's rulers in turn changed between kings of Poland, kings of Bohemia, kings of Hungary and eventually the emperors of Austria. In the chaos of the Thirty Years War, it was occupied in turn by armies of Saxony and Sweden, lost nearly half its population to plague, converted to Protestantism and then had Catholicism partly restored by force. When the War of the Austrian Succession broke out in the 18th century over the accession of a woman to the throne, the peace treaty gave Breslau to the Prussians. By then the population was 98 per cent German-speaking (many of them Jewish), with the Poles just a tiny minority.

By the early 20th century the city had grown to over a million, making it the metropolis of the region, but catastrophe was on the way. The Nazi invasion of Poland in 1939 entailed mass deportations of Poles to territory 'beyond the Reich'. By then Breslau had long been considered almost 'purely' ethnically German: the SS had drawn up rulebooks as to how such nebulous things were to be worked out and categorised. At first British and American bombings in the West sent German refugees scurrying east, then Russian advances in the East sent others scurrying west. This would soon turn into an exodus on a biblical scale, a tide of refugees created by one wave of national intolerance followed by another. The Communist Polish regime given the land in 1945 used a reverse method of the Nazi ethnic code to forcibly expel any inhabitant who wasn't considered sufficiently 'ethnically Polish'.

The price of nationalism become racism in full cry is to be found at another emotionally charged site that is in the territories that adhered to the great 13th-century Germanic push eastwards, but in fact for most of its history was disputed between Poland and Austria, not Prussia.

The great and beautiful city of Krakow was at one stage

capital of the vast Polish-Lithuanian Commonwealth, but after its partitions it declined to be a provincial city under Austrian Habsburg rule. Restored to newly reborn Poland in 1918, its darkest days were to come when an Austrian-born corporal became chancellor, then dictator, in Germany. In the wake of the Nazi invasion, it was once again renamed Krakau, but the true horror was to take place not in the beautiful mediaeval city itself, but in a small town in its administrative jurisdiction, some 50 kilometres to the west, called Oswieçim, but better known to the world by its German name: Auschwitz.

Like many places we have visited in this chapter, Oswieçim has a long and varied history dating back to the early 13th century. It was over the centuries occupied by Poles, Prussians, Swedes and Austrians. But it is for the concentration camp opened on its outskirts in 1940, and the horrors that were committed there, that the town has gone down in history, something that the present-day inhabitants have perforce got used to. There is perhaps no other place name in the world that comes close in terms of evoking the depths to which inhumanity can sink.

I once, accidentally, got into a row with a fellow parish councillor in North Oxfordshire, the depths of rural England, when I described an illustration in a brochure distributed by a developer hoping to build an estate of unwanted houses on the edge of our village as 'looking like the gateway to Auschwitz'. My comment, in the mind of my fellow councillor, who I later realised had a Jewish background, was taken as an insult, a trivialisation of the Holocaust. He was right in that it was probably ill thought through on my part, but wrong in that far from intended as trivial or stupidly satirical, it was simply factual: the artist's impression of a three-storey brick gateway incorporating an archway was eerily close to an image forever etched on my retina: the bridged gateway to Birkenau, the off-site extension to Auschwitz, and the site of most of the extermination programme.

My fellow councillor had never been to Auschwitz; I have over the decades visited the site of such unspeakable horror at least half a dozen times. The city centre site has the infamous wrought iron gate with the duplicitous slogan 'Arbeit macht frei', its ambiguous translations including 'Work is liberating' and 'Work will make you free', neither of which is indisputably true and certainly not in this evil context. But whereas the inner-city Auschwitz museum is a ghoulish monument to atrocity, it is small in scale, and hardly a site for the mass murder associated with it. That is to be found at Birkenau, half a dozen kilometres away, where the infamous gate sits over a railway line leading to a terminus where the fit and able to be worked to death were separated from the sick and elderly, marked out for immediate 'termination'. Amid the rows of long low barracks, where thousands of human beings were crammed together as slaves, perhaps none is more poignant than the vast communal latrine hut where row after row of long benches each are punctured with hundreds of adjacent holes for the seated disposal of human waste. Death camps know no privacy.

I first visited Auschwitz in 1979 while covering the first pilgrimage of Pope John Paul II to his homeland and the city of Krakow where he had been archbishop. He was the first pope ever to visit the extermination camp. It was one of those occasions that evoke emotion even in cynical secular reporters. For those visiting for the first time the grim rails running from the gatehouse to where the gas chambers once stood against the background of tall, white-barked birch trees that gave the place its name (*Birke* is German for 'birch'), it became something of a cliché to write 'here no birds sing'. My fellow reporters from the UK tabloids used to love that line. It may have felt like that visiting in the depths of winter in the grey days of Communism, but for most of the year it is far from true. In the warm spring of 2007 when George W. Bush visited, the birches were in leaf and the air was full of birdsong. Nature is remarkably unmoved by human atrocities.

Humans move on too. I was only a little bemused to find there was a beer festival going on. Not at the concentration camp, but on the main square of the town. But the town too is growing. There are new bungalows not far from Birkenau's perimeter fence…

For Whom the Bell Tolls

It was a crusade to spread Christianity at whatever cost that first sent German-speakers into the far northeast of Central Europe, and the result over many centuries – though not without difficulties – was a flowering fusion of cultures and ethnicities. What brought it all to a bloody and traumatic end was an explosion of xenophobic nationalism and a lust for ethnically exclusive territory. Adolf Hitler's war began in Gdańsk/Danzig and focused on spreading one ethnic culture to the east at the expense of all others. It was from the eastern Prussian territories that in June 1941 Hitler launched his *Lebensraum* ('living space') attack on the Soviet Union that would prove to be suicidal, not just to himself, but to seven centuries of German settlement in the lands east of the Oder/Neisse rivers that just four years later became the frontiers of a divided and much-reduced country that would for decades after question the validity of the nation-state concept it had so belatedly been dragged into.

The same East Prussian territories, to be precise, a location known as the Wolfschanze (Wolf's Lair), near the town of Rastenburg, deep in the forests south of Königsberg, was to be the scene of the final attempt to halt the dictator's suicidal plans while there was still time. It was there that the closest attempt to assassinate the dictator was carried out by members of his own army, most of them from the conservative old Prussian aristocracy, who realised they had been duped into a cruel war that would lead to destruction by a plebian Austrian.

By July 1944, after the disaster of Stalingrad and the

massive loss of manpower and equipment, it was clear to almost everyone in the German command that the war was lost. The only hope was to negotiate a peace rather than unconditional surrender. And that was only possible if Hitler, who had unleashed the war and was responsible for most of its savageries, was removed. Given that he had made this impossible by any democratic means, the only answer was assassination. There had already been numerous plots against him, including volunteer suicide bombers, but none had succeeded, largely because Hitler regularly rearranged meetings at short notice. Baron Henning von Tresckow had even sent a bomb disguised as brandy bottles to a friend based at Rastenburg, but it failed to go off. Tresckow sent a message from the eastern front that read: 'The assassination must be attempted at any cost. Even should that fail, the attempt to seize power in the capital must be undertaken. We must prove to the world and to the future generations that the men of the German resistance movement dared to take the decisive step and to hazard their lives upon it. Compared with this, nothing else matters.'

The man he sent it to was Claus von Stauffenberg, an aristocratic officer recently promoted to the General Staff and therefore in regular meetings with Hitler. Von Stauffenberg took his briefcase containing a bomb into the Wolf's Lair and placed it under the table next to Hitler, before making an excuse and leaving the room to catch a plane for Berlin. Unfortunately an aide moved the briefcase to the other side of the table leg with the result that the bomb's explosive blast was deflected and Hitler suffered only minor injuries. Von Stauffenberg and the main plotters, some 40 in all, including senior officers and generals, were rounded up and shot by firing squad. They were the lucky ones. A purge to find anyone else vaguely implicated resulted in a wave of torture and executions, several of them strangled with piano wire and then hanged. In 1981 I attended the annual memorial service to those executed so brutally at Plötzensee Prison in

West Berlin, where there is now a monument to the German resistance against Hitler. The Wolfsschanze lay south of the arbitrary line drawn by Stalin through the old province of East Prussia, the southern half of which was given to Poland while the northern sector became the Russian 'oblast' of Kaliningrad. Had it remained in German hands it would no doubt have been destroyed or made inaccessible like the buried remains of the *Führerbunker* in Berlin. As it is, the Polish Communist regime simply left it to decay in the midst of the wood, but since the fall of Communism, it has been reopened as a tourist attraction and hotels and restaurants have sprung up for the visitors.

The war doomed Königsberg, as it doomed all of the German lands in eastern Central Europe, achieving the exact opposite of Adolf Hitler's plans. A German raid on Moscow inspired a retaliatory attack on the Baltic city. But it was attacks by the British Royal Air Force in August 1944 that destroyed its ancient historical centre. Lancaster bombers from a small village in Lincolnshire in one night took out two of Euler's celebrated seven bridges and reduced the cathedral to the shell I saw in 1990. The city burned for days from the incendiary bombs. A relatively few 5,000 civilians lost their lives, but 200,000 were made homeless, soon to flee west as the Red Army advanced. The surviving orphans fled to western Germany or to neighbouring Soviet Lithuania, where they became known as *Wolfskinder* (wolf children), waifs and strays living by theft, mugging and prostitution. In the end, after the Soviet onslaught on 'Fortress Königsberg' there was almost nothing of the city left.

The greatest single disaster came in January 1945 when the *Wilhelm Gustloff*, a former cruise liner which was being used to evacuate people from East Prussia and Danzig, was torpedoed by a Russian submarine with the loss of 10,000 lives, most of them children.

In the final months of the war four and a half million Germans fled their ancestral homes in the east. These included Marion Dönhoff, aunt of a friend of mine, who had been involved in the Stauffenberg plot and only narrowly escaped detection because of her family's aristocratic history. She fled their vast palace on horseback, riding all the way to Hamburg, where she would reinvent herself as a giant figure in the new democratic Germany's press.

The extent of human displacement in the decade from 1945 to 1955 was on a scale unseen since the days of Attila the Hun. A further five and a half million Germans were expelled from the new Poland – shunted westwards by the Soviet Union, which in turn forcibly moved millions of Poles from the territories it had claimed to the land taken from the Germans. Some two million were expelled from what was once again Czechoslovakia. Hundreds of thousands were also expelled from Hungary and Romania. The controversy over Chancellor Angela Merkel's decision to accept refugees from war-torn Syria was a reflected memory of the plight of German refugees half a century earlier.

For many years those displaced hankered after their former homelands and formed societies in West Germany, not so much to agitate for the impossible dream of regaining territory, but for nostalgia and ensuring their old traditions did not die out completely. While the West German government was reluctant to give any encouragement that might look like revanchism, there was still an understanding and a fear that the whole history of Germany might be rewritten to exclude the vast territories in the East, and end up as little more than 'Rhineland folk tales'. Unification with East Germany in 1990 and the move of the capital back to Berlin at least levelled the balance somewhat, as did Poland joining the European Union and the removal of border controls. Today freedom of movement and cultural interchange is once again as good as it was in the days of Copernicus. Except for Königsberg/Kaliningrad itself, of course.

Mikhail Kalinin was one of the nastier pieces of work in Stalin's regime, a revolutionary agitator of peasant origins whom Stalin used as a puppet. Unbeknown to most people – including most Russians – he was nominally Soviet head of state from 1919 until shortly before his death in 1946. His title, which came with little power, meant that he personally signed every one of Stalin's decrees, including those of the great purges of the party during the reign of terror of the 1930s. Kalinin's docility ensured his own survival, but it came at a price: in 1938 his own wife Yekatarina was accused of speaking ill of Stalin and sentenced to 15 years in a Siberian Gulag. Her eventual release in 1944 came about through no intervention of her husband but because she herself had written to Stalin confessing her 'mistakes'. She would, however, outlive Kalinin by 14 years. The man himself, on the other hand, was commemorated in a host of ways, with numerous places named after him. The only significant one where his name has survived is the former Königsberg, which became Kaliningrad after his death.

During the Soviet years it was not a name that anyone thought of arguing with. Who would have thought that Sverdlovsk would one day again be Yetkatarinburg, or that Gorky would revert to Nizhny Novgorod, let alone that Leningrad would once again be rechristened St Petersburg? Post-1990 therefore it became a serious possibility that Kaliningrad, named for such an undistinguished and dislikable flunky, would get a new name. Or revert to its old one.

But there were problems: now a Russian exclave separated from the motherland by an independent Lithuania, Kaliningrad was exposed and isolated, an unlovely concrete-covered dump of a city with little remaining of its past, and not much hope for its future. The Baltic Fleet, with its two bases in Baltiysk (fomerly Pillau in German) and Kronstadt (the original name meaning 'city of the crown' was amusingly retained), was in decline and short of funding by a country that was no longer a superpower. When Lithuania and the other former Soviet Baltic states, Latvia and Estonia joined the European Union and Nato, it felt as if the tether to Mother Russia had become tenuous indeed. There was even a rumour, widely reported but equally widely denied, that Mikhail Gorbachev and his successor Boris Yeltsin considered offering the territory to unified Germany in exchange for a write-off of Russian debts. Whatever the truth of the matter – hugely improbable in the opinion of most scholars and diplomats – there was never a way in which a German government was going to be enthusiastic about having territory on either side of Poland: sometimes history has no enthusiasm to rewrite itself.

The early 21st century, however, has turned Kaliningrad's post-Soviet anxiety on its head, with Russian involvement in eastern Ukraine making the Baltic states uneasy about having Russian territory on either side. A separate agreement between Russia and the EU has nonetheless made travel to and from Kaliningrad slightly easier than to Russia itself. Even though there remain no direct flights other than to Russia, there is discussion on opening more road borders, which remain fortified and controlled.

But Kaliningrad post-1990 has changed beyond recognition from the dismal place I first visited. Initially its economy declined dramatically with the links to Russia cut: smuggling and prostitution flourished, but with time, the injection of cash from Moscow as the Russian economy recovered, and the discovery of the potential from tourism, things have changed. Notably a series of city mayors embarked on a dramatic building and rebuilding programme, designed to restore some of the vanished city's flavour if not its ethnicity. Much of it looks more like a theme park or a Disneyland version of pseudo-mediaeval Germanic architecture amid the concrete blocks that still house most of the population. The city's inhabitants still dislike its name and alternatives pop up from time to time. Kantograd is a favourite. Significantly the web page offering advice, hotel bookings and visa advice to tourists is www.konigsberg.ru. Today's city is an anomaly of history, that perhaps begs not to be resolved.

The desolate island with its blasted ruined cathedral has changed more dramatically than anywhere else in the city. The quixotic single tower was rebuilt, complete with a spire lifted on top by helicopter, the gaping windows through which I had stared at the bleak skies were once again filled with stained glass. The restored cathedral now has two chapels, one German Lutheran, the other Russian Orthodox. In the tower above hang four bells, which every quarter hour chime the first four notes of Beethoven's Symphony No. 5: the hand of Fate knocking at the door.

It is still knocking.

The Germans and Russians

When world leaders meet, the most important thing is always how well they understand each other. It has always been assumed in the anglophone world that the Prime Minister of the United Kingdom and the President of the United States speak the same language and therefore understand one another perfectly, even if they do not always agree. It is an assumption that is as often wrong as it is right. Not just because of the often confusing differences between British English and American English, but because their family backgrounds, upbringing, traditions and ways of looking at life separate them as much if not more than their politics.

The two early 21st-century leaders who know and understand each other more than any others are Germany's Angela Merkel and Russia's Vladimir Putin. There are many things on which they disagree, but they still understand one another better than any other pair, because they know, quite literally, where the other is coming from.

They grew up on the same side of the fence: the opposite side to that of most of the other leaders they deal with on a daily basis. They soaked up the same ideology, albeit to radically different degrees, and both saw that the system they had grown up with was doomed to fail, even if their reaction to that failure was dramatically different. Apart from this shared experience, they also share a tight linguistic bond, stronger by far than that between any British and American leader: rather than imagining they are communicating in a shared single language, each speaks the other's native tongue perfectly. In other words, they really do speak the same language, twice over.

The German chancellor grew up in East Germany; she learnt Russian, not English, as her first foreign language. And learnt it rather well. She came top of her class, won a prize and spent her gap years hitchhiking around the then Soviet Union. Putin studied German as his first foreign language and in his

KGB career spent five crucial years in Dresden with an under-
cover identity as a Russian-German interpreter and translator.

Both therefore know the language and culture of where
the other grew up, experienced the convulsive collapse of
Communism – and subsequently went on to be defining
leaders of their countries.

There is a mistaken idea, particularly in Britain, that
Britain is Germany's greatest rival, and if not, then France.
The former has almost no validity at all. A German kingdom
(Hanover) supplied a new dynasty for the British monarchy
from the 18th century on. The British army at Waterloo had
a regiment called the King's German Legion, while the Allied
victory was due in large part to the arrival of the Prussians
under General Blücher. For the greater part of two centuries the British monarchy were either Germans or married
to Germans. Queen Victoria and her beloved Prince Albert
spoke German at home.

The rivalry with France is far more real, and historical,
going back to the 9th century; we shall return to it in the
concluding chapter. But it is Russia which for seven centuries
has challenged and defined Germany's far more fluid borders
in the East. From the victory won by Alexander Nevsky over
the Teutonic Knights in the Battle on the Ice in 1242, to the
surrender of General Paulus's Sixth Army at Stalingrad in
1943, Russians and Germans have fought against each other
– and occasionally, as in the partitions of Poland, connived
with each other – over the question of where Germany ends
and Russia begins. To date, by and large, the Russians have
come out better.

The great 18th-century Prussian military genius Friedrich
der Grosse, known in English as King Frederick the Great,
had a maxim which he said had been passed down to him by
his father on his deathbed: 'there would always be more to
lose than gain by going to war with Russia'. It has repeatedly
been proved true.

Not that Friedrich himself abided by it. In the Seven Years

War from 1756 to 1763, he was in such despair at the plight he had got himself into fighting multiple armies that he was prepared to cede East Prussia to the Russians merely to get rid of one enemy in order to concentrate on the war against France and Austria (Britain was virtually his sole ally). He was rescued only by the death of the Russian Empress Elizabeth and accession of her nephew, Peter III, who happened to be one of his greatest admirers.

Peter was a native German-speaker – indeed, he spoke hardly a word of Russian – having been born in Kiel, then part of the tiny independent duchy of Holstein-Gottrop, to a German father and the then only surviving daughter of the Russian Tsar Peter the Great. The childless Elizabeth had brought him to St Petersburg and declared him her heir, though not before having married him off to another minor German noble, his second cousin, Sophie Friederike Augusta, scion of yet another German mini-state, Anhalt-Zerbst-Dornburg.

Unlike her husband, this proud and ambitious young woman had made every effort to learn Russian, converted to the Russian Orthodox faith and become a firm favourite and admirer of the Empress. An admirer to the point that she considered her a role model as a ruler, unlike her husband, whom she cordially detested, considered in her own words an 'idiot', more interested in dressing up his guardsmen and playing toy soldiers than in ruling a great empire.

Having signed peace with Friedrich, this new ruler of the vast Russian Empire decided his prime foreign policy objective was to use Russian might to restore the territory of Schleswig to his dukedom of Holstein. His wife thought there might be more important matters to deal with, led a palace coup against him and assumed the crown herself, under the name she had been given on her conversion to Russian Orthodoxy, Yekaterina, or Catherine. One German had ruled Russia for 180 days. His German wife would rule it for 34 years and be dubbed 'the Great'.

During her reign Catherine would extend the boundaries of Russia to the south and west, notably creating in 1764 a vast new province which was initially going to be named in her honour but was instead called Novorossiya, New Russia. Taking in territory seized mostly from the Ottoman Turks, who in turn had succeeded the Mongol Golden Horde, it included Crimea and a huge swathe of lands to the north of the Black Sea. There are some Western commentators today who consider 'Novorossiya' a modern idea dreamed up by Putin supporters to justify expansionist aims in what in 1991 was declared part of an independent Ukraine. Whatever the rights and wrongs of the current conflict, Novorossiya is anything but a modern idea, rather a historical name for a territory that Russians consider to have been theirs since the time of Catherine. I hope when Merkel and Putin are talking, she at least takes that into account.

That is not to discount fears in other Central and Eastern European countries that Russian – and/or German – ambitions might be to their disadvantage. Catherine also connived with Frederick the Great to carry out the partitions of Poland by which three German-ruled states – Prussia, Austria and Catherine's Russia – in three successive bites effectively swallowed up what remained of the once-great Polish–Lithuanian Commonwealth, ending both nations' independence for more than a century.

This Russified German Tsarina also took it upon herself to bring in German and other Western European philosophers, to introduce German-style schools with the aim of giving Russians a more liberal education. She invited in craftsmen from all over Europe to improve the backward Russian economy, to the extent that there are still Russian words for trades today with a German origin. One notable example found in almost every Russian town is парикмахерская, transliterated as 'parikmacherskaya', a Russification of Perruquemacher, in itself a hodgepodge word, meaning 'one who makes *perruques*', French for wigs, a fashion essential in the days when Catherine imported western European hairdressers.

Catherine also brought in large numbers of settlers from all over the German-speaking lands and gave them rights to farm, mostly in the rich soil on the banks of the Volga. In 1924 the Soviet government even gave the Volga Germans a form of supposed 'home rule' within the Autonomous Soviet Socialist Republic of the Volga Germans in the south of European Russia between the old Russian province of Saratov and Tsaritsyn, which a year later would be renamed Stalingrad.

When I lived in Moscow in the early 1980s I got to know a young Soviet man from Kazakhstan who was proud of his ancient German ethnicity. His surname may have been the undoubtedly Germanic Weissenberg, but his first name was the indubitably Russian Vladimir. He spoke almost no German, except for a few words with a thick Russian accent. Indeed he had never met a 'real' German and my heavily Berlin-accented fluency in the language led him to assume, despite assurances to the contrary, that I was.

On his return to Kazakhstan he passed my contact details on widely, and before long I was receiving a flood of letters, written in patchy German, often with an uncertain grasp of the Latin alphabet and use of some old Gothic script characters, from whole families of resettled Volga Germans, asking for help and support.

Despite the general assumptions of life in a totalitarian state, especially as a foreign journalist, I have to assume none of these communications were ever intercepted by the KGB, as their contents would invariably have got the writers a one-way ticket to much further eastern parts of Soviet Russia.

On several occasions small deputations of two or three would turn up in Moscow (rail travel within the Soviet Union, even over long distances, was surprisingly easy and cheap). They would ring our number and present me with gifts of homegrown fruit – which I admit to accepting, fresh fruit being rare enough in Moscow in those days – in the hope that somehow I could secure them a route to West Germany. Or even East Germany; I am not sure they were aware of the difference.

All I could offer in return was the address and telephone numbers of the West German embassy, but they insisted they had tried that and received no response. From the wording of many of their letters this did not completely surprise me. More than a few referred to that 'brief happy time, in the summer of 1942, when our boys came so close to liberating us'. Needless to say, the outcome of the Battle of Stalingrad dashed their hopes. And referring to the Nazi troops as 'our boys' was not exactly a way to curry favour with the West German embassy. Ironically, however, many of them got their wish to emigrate to Germany after reunification in 1990 when people of German ancestry from much of Eastern Europe and beyond were offered citizenship under a 'law of return' originally designed for the estimated nine million who had been expelled from former German territories in Poland and the former Czechoslovakia. But today there are still between 500,000 and 1.5 million ethnic Germans or people of German descent living in Russia.

Whatever influence and power Germany exerted in Russia was dramatically reversed in 1945 when a Russian – albeit Soviet – flag once again flew over Berlin for the first time since the nadir of Frederick the Great's wars. The Germany that Angela Merkel grew up in was a Russian client state, the German Democratic Republic, which West Germans joked was 'neither German, nor democratic, nor a republic'.

Ironically it had been the German empire which had facilitated the collapse of imperial Russia during World War I by allowing Vladimir Lenin free passage from exile to the Russian frontier, confident that he would foment a revolution that would end the war. It worked. But it also led to the cruel regime that wreaked revenge on Germany after 1945.

With the Soviet victory, there was also a flood back into

eastern Germany of Marxists and Communists who had fled the Nazi scourge and been given sanctuary in Moscow and who were overnight transformed from political refugees into ambassadors of the new orthodoxy. Although others might have called them stooges.

One of the most interesting was Markus Wolf, member of a diehard Communist family who had fled to Moscow with his father after the Nazi takeover, returned to the Soviet zone of occupation after the war, became first a journalist (reporting on the Nürnberg trials of the leading Nazis) and later a founding member of the *Staatssicherheit*, the state security service which had gone down in notoriety as the Stasi, of which he would go on to be head of the foreign intelligence service. His greatest coup was infiltrating the office of West German Chancellor Willy Brandt with his agent Günther Guillaume. He also successfully ran agents in Africa, including one, dubbed East Germany's James Bond, whose daughter I had known in East Berlin.

Wolf was a genial, intelligent man, who could with some plausibility claim to wash his hands of the Stasi's domestic abuses, in that he was primarily concerned with foreign intelligence. He fled East Berlin after the fall of the Wall, but was denied political asylum by not just Austria, but Russia too, returned, was arrested, tried on treason charges, convicted and sentence to six years in jail. But he appealed and in a remarkable triumph of legality and the German justice system, had the verdict overturned on the grounds that he had been a citizen of the DDR (East Germany), a country recognised by the BRD (West Germany) and that therefore had never been a citizen of the country he was accused of committing treason against.

I met Wolf after his release, and over coffee and cakes in front of the Rotes Rathaus, the landmark redbrick building that had been the city hall of East Berlin and was once again that of all Berlin. He talked wittily about amusing escapades dealing with difficult foreign dignitaries, notably the notoriously whore-mongering Fidel Castro, and at the end of our chat, amenably agreed to sign a copy of my own Stasi file, '*bestätigt, als Spaß!*' – confirmed, as a piece of fun. He would go on to write a bestselling book: not an auto-biographical confession, but a cookbook of Russian recipes from his youth.

It was Russia – and its new fiefdoms in Poland and Czechoslovakia – which presided over pushing the borders of German lands in Central and Eastern Europe back to a level not seen since the 13th century. Those are the same borders which largely persist today, only now, since the collapse of the Soviet Union, codified peacefully and guaranteed by the former fiefdoms' democratisation and membership of a European Union in which borders are no longer hostile barriers.

But Kaliningrad still lurks within them.

3

Dresden

The Saxon capital, the 'Florence of the Elbe', its destruction, resurrection and my accidental 'Star Trek moment'

Hiroshima on the Elbe

Since the end of World War II, there have been few cities in the world with a name more evocative of destruction than Dresden. Hiroshima certainly. Nagasaki, Warsaw, among others, but few cause more argument than the fate of Dresden on St Valentine's Night 1945.

Dresden means a lot of things to me: it was the first East German city I got to know well outside Berlin. It was the scene of a memorable event in February 1982, more momentous with hindsight than it seemed at the time, and for which I might – just might – have been partly responsible. I adore its people's unique, idiosyncratic accent, considered the least liked by their fellow Germans, but for me forever associated with a large lady who drank in my local in East Berlin and had a thing for orange leather trousers. I am in awe of its phoenix-like resurrection, which has made it again one of the most beautiful cities in Europe.

But before diving in to any of the rich history and culture, we must get around the elephant in the room: 13–15 February 1945, when in four consecutive bombing raids, the 'Florence of the Elbe' was reduced to dust and rubble. After

1945, when consciences in the war-torn countries finally resurfaced, Dresden was the one that disturbed the British most. Why and to what purpose had one of the most beautiful baroque cities been razed to the ground in the closing months of the war? The answer was almost always one word: Coventry.

The Midlands city had one of the few almost perfectly preserved mediaeval centres in England, most having been lost to Victorian industry and 'progress'. I had never been to Coventry at this stage of my life – I was still only 26 – but I knew that the Luftwaffe had done serious damage to the city's ancient heart, reducing its great cathedral to a shell. Coventry had been bombed on numerous occasions during the first few years of the war, notably during the Battle of Britain in 1940, but also again in 1941 and 1942. The city centre suffered enormous damage; tens of thousands were made homeless, while nearly 1,500 lost their lives and thousands more were injured.

The greatest eventual victims of the raids on Coventry, however, would be German civilians. The bombing had shown the destructive power of not just high explosives but also incendiary bombs, which in concentration caused what came to be known as a 'firestorm'. It was a principle which the newly appointed head of Britain's Bomber Command, Arthur Harris, had been developing for years. On a pre-war visit to Frankfurt, he had wandered around its beautiful mediaeval heart and, rather than admiring it, noted down what an exemplary target its immense concentration of wooden architecture would make for creating a firestorm. He would later carry it out, as he would in dozens of other German cities, most notably Hamburg and Dresden.

The technique was euphemised as 'area bombing' or 'carpet bombing', and its greatest victim was almost certainly Hamburg, where in a one-week period in the summer of 1943, more than 40,000 were killed and the city virtually flattened. But there was in the case of Hamburg an arguable justification: the port city was unquestionably a major industrial centre, home to some of Germany's greatest dockyards, building the U-boats which laid waste to the transatlantic convoys on which Britain depended. The same argument had applied to Coventry which, although a smaller city, was a major hub of Britain's industry, motor-manufacturing in particular.

Dresden was no such thing. It was a baroque beauty of a city, a symbol of German humanism. Yes, it had industry, as did any sizeable city – Dresden had a population of some 600,000 at the time – but it was in no way a major contributor to the war effort. It had no major garrison beyond the minimum defences most German cities had by that stage of the war when the country was being invaded from all sides. It housed at the time tens of thousands of prisoners of war, many of whom died in the hail of bombs dropped by their own compatriots in the case of the British and Americans. A powerful account of the horror is given by one eyewitness, the American sci-fi author Kurt Vonnegut, in his book *Slaughterhouse-Five*. Vonnegut was an American prisoner of war in Dresden at the time and only survived because his guards took the prisoners with them to shelter in the reinforced camp basement.

In the aftermath of Dresden's destruction the Nazi propaganda machine went into full swing: there was little need to point out the apparent barbarity of such wanton destruction of architectural beauty, but the loss of life was dramatically exaggerated. There were claims that at least 135,000 had died. In the end, perhaps, the exaggeration was their undoing. By the time of my first visit to Dresden in 1981, the number had been reduced to some 35,000, and still squarely blamed on the 'barbarity' of the British and Americans, compared with the financial aid given by the 'fraternal Soviet Union' to rebuild some of the city's destroyed monuments. Today, the accepted number is down to 25,000, far less than died in the firestorms in Hamburg, but still the greatest number of human beings to be burnt alive in a single night before the apocalypse of the atomic bombs.

Beginning in the immediate post-war years there was a growing amount of soul-searching in both Britain and the US about what happened in Dresden, and the effectiveness versus loss of civilian lives of the entire carpet-bombing campaign. German war production, which was meant to be shattered, had risen continuously in the final months of the war. The argument that the war had ended earlier because of the destruction of Dresden was widely known to be bogus; the war ended when it did because of the relentless Russian advance on Berlin. The Russians were sufficiently unconcerned about Dresden, albeit after the bombing, that they let American forces take the city, confident that it would be handed back to them in the peace settlement.

The men who had flown the bombers were for decades not granted a campaign medal of their own, because of a vague feeling of shame among those who had given them their orders. They felt, justifiably, left out, which only increased the bitterness and a personal sense of shame that for decades haunted many of them despite the armchair warriors who sprang to their defence. Substantial numbers of Harris's own men had all along had misgivings about the orders they were following. The appellation 'Bomber Harris' may well have been an officially sanctioned euphemism to conceal his real nickname among his own men: 'Butcher Harris'.

Eventually, decades later, the 'wrong' was redressed: the men of Bomber Command got their campaign medal. There was even a statue of Harris erected on the Strand in London, though for years after, it was regularly defaced with red paint on St Valentine's night. Even Winston Churchill, who had sanctioned the Dresden bombing, as he had the rest of Harris's campaign, confessed to misgivings. But then it was Churchill himself who had famously said 'history will be kind to me, because I intend to write it'. It is not equivocation, merely a matter of fact, that Adolf Hitler, though no historian, believed exactly the same. There were plans laid down for the Holocaust to be erased from history, for all records to be destroyed and for the horrors of the extermination camps to die with those who ran them.

I firmly believe that the destruction of Dresden was a war crime, and had Britain lost the war, even a less vindictive and lawless regime than that of the Nazis would have seen Harris tried and executed. But then victors' justice has been a factor in human conflict since rival tribes started killing one another. It is often – in fact almost always – forgotten in Britain that the dreaded flying bombs which wreaked a futile but frightening mini-Blitz on London in the dying months of the war had another name besides the jokey black humour English 'doodlebugs'. To the Germans they were known as *Vergeltungswaffen*: 'revenge weapons'.

Breaching the 'First Directive'

Weapons of war are not the only destroyers of cities. Men with clipboards, blueprints and theodolites can do every bit as much damage. The soulless concrete corpse that makes up much of the centre of modern Coventry was the result not just of the Luftwaffe bombing but at least as much of the well-meant but ultimately arrogant attitude of 1960s planners, who opted for a 'modern rethink', which involved pulling down many ancient buildings that might have been preserved. There is some, if not much, reassurance to be found in the fact that the Communists in East Germany did much the same thing. On my first visit to Dresden I stayed in the Hotel Newa, named after the Neva river on which Leningrad stood, one of four almost identical drab 20-storey blocks which overlooked a dreary pedestrianised street that led into town from the station, lined with the usual DDR state shops with names such as 'House of the Book', 'Fruit and Veg' (usually just potatoes and onions), or perhaps *Uhren Schmuck* (Clocks and Jewellery), with a few tawdry trinkets on display. Its highlight was a nondescript low-level 1960s fountain, featured on black-and-white postcards surrounded by Young Pioneers, Communist kindergarten kids, leaning over to dip their hands in it.

The one thing the East German authorities, aided by generous Soviet funds, had concentrated on was the restoration of the Zwinger, a splendid rococo palace with an intricate double courtyard, already by the early 80s perfectly restored to its pre-war glory. The expenditure on the Zwinger, however, meant that much of the rest of the city centre had been thrown up, with basic shops and cafés on the ground floor.

All that changed dramatically after reunification in 1989, when large sums of federal money were invested in restoring as much as possible of the old city centre to a resemblance of its former glory. I regret to say that the Hotel Newa on Prager Strasse is still there, somewhat spruced up but no more appealing than it ever was, at least from the outside. The shops and restaurants have changed however. Prager Strasse now boasts a McDonald's and a Starbucks. I am not sure how much of an improvement that is.

At one of the restaurants in the rebuilt baroque-style buildings on the main square, Neumarkt, there is a paragraph on the menu which boasts that Dresden was the first city in the DDR to see a protest against the establishment, as early as February 1982, the 37th anniversary of the raids. It is a protest I will never forget. I recall it fondly and with just a touch of embarrassment because there is a better than evens chance that I was accidentally responsible for it.

The real blame (or praise), however, should lie with Volker, a long-haired happy-go-lucky hippy gravedigger. He lived in the basement of our block on Schönhauser Allee in Berlin, was a few years young than me, a heavy dope smoker – easier to get hold of than you might think even in East Berlin – and in a passionate relationship with a 15-year-old girl who, I would later discover, was the daughter of East Germany's closest equivalent to James Bond, a top spy working with the East German and Cuban troops in Angola, waging a proxy war against apartheid South Africa, as well as in Ethiopia and Mozambique. We knew nothing of that at the time.

What I did know was that Volker was deeply involved with 'Swords to Ploughshares', a movement of mostly young people, given official backing by the church, who sought to emulate the youth of West Germany, who at the time were protesting regularly against the planned stationing of US Pershing missiles on their soil. Their name had been chosen carefully, from a Biblical quotation, but more importantly embodied in a Soviet statue outside the United Nations building in New York. It was hard for the Communist authorities to object to anything endorsed by Moscow. The church in East Germany had commissioned cloth patches embroidered with the slogan and an image of the statue. These were beginning to appear sewn on to jeans by tacitly rebellious young people. Even that was enough to win them opprobrium from conservative (i.e. Communist) parents, and sour looks from policemen. As yet, however, wearing the patch was about as rebellious as any of them got.

One evening over a few beers and a joint in Volker's basement, we were discussing war and peace (as people in their 20s do) and the bombing of Dresden came up, unsurprisingly as the 37th anniversary was only a week or so away. Volker told me he had heard from 'some friends' that there was going to be an event of some sort down in Dresden to mark the anniversary. Nothing big obviously, he didn't know exactly – he was never a very precise sort of bloke at the best of times – just some sort of silent vigil around the ruins of the Frauenkirche to demonstrate the DDR's youth's commitment to peace.

This all sounds well and good and completely unobjectionable to Western ears now – as it did then – except for the fact that this was the German Democratic Republic, in which the idea of democracy was doing exactly what you were told to. East Germany, following the lead of the Soviet Union, which had after all donated that statue, believed that stationing more American missiles in West Germany, with a range that more or less assumed they would target sites in East Germany, was a dangerous escalation of the Cold War. It was a fair point: the tense situation in those years, as threatening as the Cuban missile crisis two decades earlier, is particularly well dramatised in the 2015 German television series *Deutschland 83* by Anna and Joerg Winner. The East German government's line was that American missiles were obviously bad, but any Soviet missiles that might be deployed were equally obviously good. And a demonstration of any sort on home ground was therefore out of the question.

The Frauenkirche was unquestionably a powerful symbol. This magnificent towering baroque church apparently survived the 650,000 incendiary bombs dropped on the city. In the city centre temperatures reached 1,000 degrees Celsius. It therefore seemed a miracle when, on the morning of 15 February 1945, after the firestorm had finally died down, the remaining inhabitants of Dresden crawled out of their hiding places to see the grand old church still standing there proudly. It was false optimism. About 10 a.m., the super-heated stone pillars that bore the bulk of the church's weight exploded, sending the whole 6,000 ton edifice crumbling into the crypt below. Ever since, the ruins had been left as they were, ostensibly deliberately, as a *momento mori*, a memorial to the horror of the firestorm, but also almost certainly because any attempt at rebuilding it would have seemed impossible and there was no money available in a Communist state to build a new, simpler modernist cathedral, as was done in Coventry.

A poignant place to stage a rally of any sort, especially one dedicated to peace, but an unannounced, unofficial rally was certain to arouse the attention of the local police, and the Stasi if they found about it. Could it really be that East

Berlin's tame hippy peaceniks were going to raise their heads above the parapet? I asked Volker how many were likely to attend. He said he didn't know, but that he was thinking of going down if he could find a way to get there. It would have been easy and inexpensive to take a train, but he would have had to find a place to stay. I had no hesitation in saying I would drive him there and back. If this actually happened, it would be a news story. A pretty good one.

I went back to the office and – not having had much of any interest to report on in the past few weeks – knocked out a few lines that said East German Swords to Ploughshares activists were planning to rally in Dresden on the anniversary of the bombing, 'according to informed sources'. The latter phrase was a sort of routine code used primarily in Soviet bloc countries where information often travelled in obscure routes which nobody was keen for the security services to trace. Better was 'dissident sources', but Volker hardly qualified as a fully fledged dissident: he was, after all, just a 20-something gravedigger. It probably wasn't the most responsible story I had ever filed, but then what did it really matter: if the demo happened, it happened. If it didn't, then either my 'sources' had been misled or the demonstrators had had second thoughts. I was only mildly surprised when West Germany's main television channel ARD gave it a brief mention 'according to Reuters' towards the end of the evening news.

That Saturday afternoon, my wife Jackie and I, along with Volker and one of his mates, also with a Swords to Ploughshares patch on his jeans, piled into my office VW Golf and set out on the three-hour drive to Dresden. We parked in a side street and made our way, through fine falling snow, to Neumarkt, where the ruins of the Frauenkirche lay. That there was something going on was unmistakable. We could make out a few dozen people milling around, and in the near distance behind them several lines of policemen. I told Volker to go and join his mates, assuming he would know several of those present. He said he didn't. Then, a few minutes later, he spotted a girl and headed off towards her, though whether it was because he knew her or just fancied her, I couldn't be sure. I got out my notebook and camera: it was important to look as if I was reporting what was going on, not taking part. Almost immediately I attracted the attention of a couple of policemen, who came over and told me to put both away: there was nothing going on. To their shock and horror I ignored them: East German policemen were used to their own domestic press doing what they were told. Then, even more to their horror, I walked into the growing crowd, now several hundred in number, who had begun placing lit candles in jam jars on the ruins. In the light snow, it was a moving symbolic scene coming to life before our eyes.

I started asking a few of them why they were there. The answers were disappointingly not dissimilar to those I might have got from a gathering of the FDJ, the official Communist Party youth movement: 'We want no more wars', 'We want no more missiles'. Then I asked, 'Including no more Soviet missiles in the DDR?' That was met with a bit of silence, until eventually one girl of about 19 nodded nervously. Obviously encouraged, one of her friends came over and said loudly, 'Of course', while another added, 'Absolutely', before both pulled their scarves up to cover their faces. I looked behind me and saw why: the police numbers had doubled and looked disconcertingly as though they were about to advance. In the end they backed off, cowed by the fact that by now several West German television teams had turned up. The demonstrators formed a big circle holding hands and sang some relatively inoffensive peace songs: a bit of badly accented Bob Dylan and Joan Baez if I remember rightly. And a few of them had their photographs taken; by the police, not the press.

As the crowd slowly began to disperse, sloping away into the sleety drizzle illuminated bleakly by the pallid white light of Dresden's sparse streetlights, I began asking how they had spread the word about tonight: their accents suggested there were quite a few Berliners here, very clearly a lot more than locals, given that the thick Saxon Dresden accent was absolutely unmistakable. The first one I asked replied, 'I heard about it on ARD.' The more people I asked, the more I got the same answer. I began to feel a chill run down my back. I was beginning to realise why there were so few locals here. Dresden was jokingly referred to by people from the rest of the DDR as the *Tal der Ahnungslosen* (Valley of the Clueless): its geographical and topological situation, situated in the Elbe Valley relatively far from the West German border, meant they could not receive West German television. Most people in the rest of the country could, including absolutely everyone in and around Berlin, where there was a huge television transmitter in the middle of West Berlin.

I realised what I had done. I had, in the terms of the *Star Trek* fan I still was, 'broken the First Directive': I had interfered in the internal affairs of the native civilisation. There was no real reason to think I had caused the demonstration, but it seemed fairly certain that a lot of those taking part were there because I had reported what Volker had told me over a couple of beers in his basement flat. On the way back I asked him how he had heard about it in the first place. He shrugged and said, 'Oh, I dunno. It was just something I heard someone say would be a good idea. Still, it was good, though, wasn't it? Lots of people turned up, and stuff.' I nearly crashed the car. To what extent I really contributed to that demonstration actually taking place is unknown, but there is no doubt that a lot of those who turned up that evening heard about it thanks to ARD's broadcast of my report of Volker's unreliable opinion. I neither know, nor these days do I care. If in any way I contributed, I am glad. By November 1989, when things began to get serious, I was wholeheartedly in favour of the revolution and, whatever Reuters might have thought, joined in the protesting crowds, to the extent of getting myself arrested. Nothing much came of the Dresden demo directly, but it did set a precedent. The state was not in total control of everything, not always, and not forever.

In December 1989, just seven years later, as the status quo was spinning out of control in Europe, I was in Dresden to watch as West German Chancellor Helmut Kohl climbed onto the lower stones of the Frauenkirche ruins for his first official visit to what was still at that moment the independent East German state, and gave what he himself said was the 'most important and difficult speech of my life'. Already, driving through the streets from the airport he had been greeted with chants of 'Helmut, Helmut', almost exactly as Germans, east and west, had chanted 'Gorby, Gorby' to welcome the Soviet leader in the month that led up to the fall of the Wall in Berlin. More significantly they also chanted *'Einheit, Einheit'* (unity, unity). He was officially a guest of the DDR's Communist prime minister Hans Modrow, but both knew their job was to chart a path to end the DDR's existence and create a new, peacefully reunified Germany.

Kohl was greeted at the Frauenkirche by a sea of black, red and yellow German flags, significantly without the hammer and compasses emblem of the DDR in the centre. Kohl grasped the spirit of the hour and addressed the crowds as *'Liebe Landesleute'* (dear compatriots). Standing among the crowd on that cold December night, the feeling was one of pure euphoria, of witnessing a historic moment when German reunification had effectively become inevitable. He ended his speech, pertinently standing on the ruins of one of Germany's greatest churches, with the words, *'Gott segne unser deutsches Vaterland'* (God bless our German fatherland). Kohl himself later recalled taking a late night drink in the quiet of his hotel room in Dresden (the Bellevue, a smart old manor house on the Elbe, rather more attractive than the Newa), and thinking to himself: 'It worked.' German unity, he believed, was unstoppable. 'It's what the people want. This regime is over for good.' Dresden poet Thomas

Rosenlöcher agreed, writing in his diary that evening, 'From today onwards the DDR has ceased to exist.'

It is hard to imagine in the early 21st century what Dresden looked like in the middle decades of the 20th. The skyline from across the Elbe looks remarkably like it does in paintings of the late-18th and 19th centuries: elegant, serene, romantic. The great dome of the Frauenkirche soars as majestically above the city as ever; it is worth mentioning that the first time it was damaged was shortly after its completion, when it was hit by Prussian artillery fire, Saxony and Prussia being on opposite sides in the Seven Years War. The decision to reconstruct the church was taken shortly after reunification and the foundation stone laid in 1994. Work began in 1996, after all the stones from the ruins had been cleared, cleaned, measured in detail and it had been ascertained, as well as could be using high-tech computer programmes, where each had been in the original building. In the end it was reckoned that the 'new' church contained some 43 per cent of the stonework from the original. Their blackened colour still marks them out from the new. The reconstruction was finished in 2004, and the building consecrated in 2005.

In a splendid gesture of reconciliation, the church was topped with an orb and cross made at London goldsmiths Grant MacDonald by Alan Smith, whose father had flown a Lancaster bomber on the night of the raid. 'My father used to tell me about the horrors and the suffering of Dresden,' Smith said. 'He did not want it to be forgotten.' The orb and cross were hoisted on top of the church in a ceremony watched by crowds, including many older inhabitants who were reduced to tears. England's Duke of Kent, president of the British Dresden Trust, took part, saying it was a symbol of hope for a 'free, peaceful and united Europe'. Coventry also presented the new church with a 'Cross of Nails', first created by Richard Howard, provost of Coventry Cathedral from three giant nails from the roof of the destroyed building, copies of which were distibuted worldwide to churches that have been damaged in warfare. Dresden's is now on the high altar.

China Town and Prison Castle

Before the trauma visited on it by the 20th century, Dresden's greatest claim to fame for most people who had never been to the grand and beautiful baroque capital of the Free State of Saxony, was its manufacture of fine porcelain. Dresden china, as it was widely known, was considered the greatest European equivalent of the real thing – that made in China itself. In fact, it wasn't made in Dresden, but in Meissen, a beautiful if relatively minor city some 25 kilometres away, which for some 40 years in the 15th century held the proud title of capital of Saxony until Dresden usurped it.

I first visited Meissen in early 1982 when, as a small town in a relatively hard-to-get-to part of the closed-off DDR, it had almost no tourists, and on a winter's day this beautiful mediaeval town, with its magnificent castle, the Albrechts-burg, dating from the early 15th century, had an almost eerily beautiful atmosphere: bare, empty, quiet and peaceful. In those days there were not even any guided tours of the porcelain works, though there was a small museum whose staff were overwhelmed at seeing a foreign reporter. Today I find it hard to remember just how isolated places like Meissen, however famous, were in the depths of the unwelcoming DDR.

Porcelain-making began in Meissen in the early 18th century in the reign of Saxony's most famous ruler, Augustus II (nicknamed 'the Strong'), who was also King of Poland. His initials, AR (Augustus Rex), were initially painted on all their products. In 1720, however, the manufactory began using a symbol of two crossed swords. Up until the opening of the Meissen factory, porcelain had been a mystery to Europeans, and the rich who favoured the fine ceramic paid small fortunes – equivalent to the price of gold or silver – to import it from China, to the extent that the name of the country became identical with the name of the product.

Augustus was determined to break the monopoly and charged Johann Friedrich Böttger, who had been an apprentice to a pharmacist in Berlin, with discovering the secret. Böttger worked out that a key ingredient was the mineral kaolin, which would come to be known as 'china clay' of which there were significant deposits in the vicinity of Meissen. When mixed with alabaster and fired at extremely high temperature in a wood kiln, this produced a material that combined translucency with strength. Overnight, the Chinese monopoly was broken and Meissen china became renowned throughout Europe and a major source of income for the Saxon crown. Unfortunately for Böttger, one of his apprentices ran off to Vienna, taking the secret with him, setting up a porcelain manufactory there, and within 20 years the secret was no longer a secret and porcelain was being made all over Europe, notably in Vienna and Berlin (Frederick the Great occupied Meissen in 1756 and took some of its experts back home with him). These were soon joined by London and Paris, where the manufactory at Sèvres would come to rival Meissen.

The birthplace of the European porcelain industry retained its cachet, and its crossed swords trademark – one of the earliest trademarks to be recognised as such in Europe – was enough to raise the price significantly. Focusing on ancient Chinese designs, Meissen developed its own distinctive onion pattern; the Chinese original had been based on a pomegranate, but as nobody in 18th-century Saxony had ever seen a pomegranate, they adopted a more familiar agricultural product. The original design was, like most Chinese porcelain, blue on white but there are also rare red, green, pink and black pieces to be found. In fact, Meissen became famed for its colours, often used in large porcelain statues of saints and animals.

During the 19th century manufacture shifted from the Albrechtsburg Castle to a purpose-built factory in the town and its production began to expand from fine tableware to intricate figurines. English collectors in particular were taken by these and with only a vague idea of where Meissen was, came to describe them as Dresden china. Arthur 'Bomber' Harris, the man responsible for the Dresden bombing, described the harsh British public reaction as linked to 'German bands and Dresden shepherdesses'.

On that first visit to Meissen in 1982 I felt obliged – no, I admit it, I was curious – to visit another resonant relic of World War II in the vicinity, one that had recently claimed national attention in the UK as the result of a nostalgic/heroic television series: *Colditz*, based on a castle which had been converted to serve as a prisoner-of-war camp. The television series had showcased the best and worst of British attitudes towards the war in the early 70s, a period when I was a young teenager. The characters were plucky Allied prisoners – all officer class, of course – who treated escaping as something between a noble duty and a public-school prank, augmented by Germans who were occasionally honest, decent, 'good chaps' just doing their jobs, and the more familiar stereotypical robotic villains.

In reality – at least the reality of a small town in Communist East German in the early 1980s – Colditz was a great bulk of a thing situated on a rocky bluff that completely dominated the surrounding countryside and the little community that clung to it. Originally built in the 11th century, the castle had been radically overhauled several times, notably in the 16th and late 17th centuries, when Augustus the Strong expanded it to include nearly 700 rooms. In the early 19th century, this vast accommodation allowed it to be used as a workhouse for the poor, before it was eventually transformed into a sanatorium for the rich, then a mental asylum.

The Nazis turned it into a prison, primarily for Communists and Jews, and then, from 1939, a high-security

POW camp which gained a reputation for repeated escape attempts. Notable inmates included Douglas Bader, a British air force pilot who had lost both legs in an air accident in 1931 but was nonetheless accepted by the RAF and flew using prosthetics. Bader was forced to bail out of his Spitfire over occupied France in 1941 and was taken prisoner. Allowed by the Germans to retain his prosthetic legs, he continued to make escape attempts, resulting in a threat to remove his prosthetics, but instead he was sent to Colditz, where he remained until 1945.

Colditz proved to be far from escape-proof, and a great number of those confined there for previous attempts combined their knowledge and experience. Perhaps the most celebrated prisoner to escape was Airey Neave, who would later become British Secretary of State for Northern Ireland, only to die from a bomb planted by the Irish National Liberation Army (INLA): his car exploded as he was driving out of the House of Commons car park in London. Neave had been the first British prisoner to successfully escape from Colditz.

The relatively liberal commandant of the prison was, in contrast to certain other POW camps, a stickler for following the rules laid down in the Geneva Convention. Inmates were allowed regular sport, language lessons (from fellow inmates), to give one another music lessons and stage concerts as well as theatrical performances, ideally to distract them from attempts to escape. Instead the stage itself became a prop to help them do so. Neave teamed up with Dutch officer Anthony Lutyens, who could speak German, which Neave could not; a hole was made under the theatre stage leading into an attic above the guardroom. Wearing home-made German uniforms, sewn by fellow prisoners and coloured with theatrical paint, the pair strolled past the guards, who came to attention at the sight of two officers, climbed over the outer wall from the castle gardens, bought train tickets south to Regensburg in Bavaria, and despite several awkward incidents eventually crossed the border into Switzerland.

In the early 1980s Colditz had reverted to its previous use as a sanatorium-cum-hospital with beds for some 400 patients, and specialised in ENT operations. I had, however, registered my desire to visit with the Foreign Ministry in East Berlin, who were clearly of the opinion that a nostalgic feature about wartime heroics against the hated Nazis was the sort of thing – rather than listening to 'unstable dissidents' – that a foreign correspondent in the DDR ought to be doing, and fixed up an official visit. I was greeted by two men, who introduced themselves as 'curators' and took me for a jovial tour of a few preserved former cells, and were more than delighted to show me the 'theatre', complete with the stage and trapdoor through which Neave and Lutyens had escaped.

In 1996 the medical facilities were moved out and the castle became a museum, concentrating as much on its ancient history as that of a POW camp. It belongs to the Free State of Saxony, which has spent large sums of money on renovation and restoration.

The Saxon Strongman

The north side of the Augustus Bridge, across the Elbe from old Dresden, is perhaps the best spot from which to catch a glimpse of the city's famous baroque skyline. A little further on, at the start of a pedestrianised street which I remember in DDR times being lined with drab, mostly empty shops, and a rather good ice cream parlour, stands one of the world's most spectacular equestrian statues. Larger than life size, on a rearing horse, man and beast totally covered in gold leaf, dressed as a Roman Caesar with a laurel wreath on his head, it is, of course, the man himself, Augustus the Strong. Saxony's equivalent of England's Henry VIII or the legendary King Arthur, Augustus was a historical giant who bestrode the stage of Europe in the early 18th century like a colossus, a man of such importance to the history of Dresden and Saxony that even the Communists regilded his statue. The very first time I saw the statue, a couple of locals made sure I knew how the people of Dresden felt about their one-time ruler with a famous rhyme: '*Lieber August, steig hier nieder und regier uns in Sachsen wieder*' (Dear Augustus, get down off your horse and rule us in Saxony once again). During the altercations in Dresden and elsewhere in East Germany in the run-up to the fall of the Berlin Wall, a placard with the famed rhyme was hung from the horse's head, with a new couplet attached: '*Lass in diesen schweren Zeiten lieber unseren Erich reiten*' (In these troubled times, let our Erich get up there instead), a less than subtle reference to the country's Communist boss.

Augustus was not particularly tall, standing 1.76 metres (5' 9"), above average for the day, but not exceptional. What *was* exceptional was his strength. He is one of the few rulers whose historical epithet refers more to physical prowess than fame and glory. Augustus's party trick was to break iron horseshoes with his bare hands. His other great hobby was a 'sport' much enjoyed by some members of the Central European aristocracy of the time: *Fuchsprellen*, fox tossing. It was a highly popular spectator sport, which involved releasing a fox or other wild animal (at one fabled contest Augustus used a total of 647 foxes, 533 hares, 34 badgers and 21 wildcats) within a courtyard in which the competitors, arranged in pairs, each held one end of a sling laid on the ground. As the animal passed over it, the pairs pulled as hard as possible, sending the unfortunate animal flying into the air. The record height was some seven metres, which was quite remarkable, not least for the animal involved, which rarely survived. Augustus made a point of showing off his strength, by partnering himself with two of the strongest men in his court holding one end of the sling, while he himself held the other with a single finger.

Born in Dresden in 1670, there were no great expectations

of him as a youth. Friedrich Augustus was the second son of Johann Georg III, Duke of Saxony and Princess Anne Sophie of Denmark and Norway. He was given an excellent education, learning the three most important languages besides German: French, Italian and Spanish, as well as theology, music and military science. His education was completed with three years on a grand tour of Germany, Italy, Spain, Portugal, Denmark and Sweden.

Unexpectedly, however, his older brother, Johann Georg IV, who had succeeded their father in 1691, contracted smallpox from his mistress during Carnival in Venice and died, leaving Friedrich Augustus as the new Duke of Saxony. A great admirer of the French Sun King, Louis XIV, he had visited Versailles on his grand tour just as Louis was expanding the palace enormously and moving his court there. Augustus decided that absolute rule was the way to go and determined also to make his mark on Dresden by enriching its buildings. His attempt to copy Versailles gave the city the Zwinger, which, as we saw earlier, was one of the first monuments in Dresden to be restored after 1945, and today remains one of the city's most impressive and treasured sites. Had Augustus had his way, it would have been vastly bigger, extending the gardens down to the Elbe, where the city's famous opera house, the Semperoper, was built in the 19th century. It was also in the reign of Augustus that work began on the Frauenkirche, though it was not completed until a decade after his death.

The circumstances of the age suited Augustus's plans for self-aggrandisement. Saxony was one of the more important states in the German-speaking world precisely at a time when the neighbouring Polish–Lithuanian Commonwealth, which had dominated Eastern Europe for more than a century, was faltering. The Commonwealth's rulers were normally elected from among the European princes by the 'nobles' democracy', the aristocratic parliaments of the two partner states. In 1697, Augustus, using bribery, pressure and a secret conversion to Catholicism to make himself eligible, managed to get elected king, a move that would inspire the rulers of Brandenburg–Prussia (the latter of which was at the time an isolated small state surrounded by Poland) also to grab a royal title by proclaiming themselves kings *in* Prussia, thus getting around the blanket ban on monarchies within the Holy Roman Empire. There was some controversy attached to his election, unsurprisingly given that his rival, the French François Louis, Prince of Conti, actually got more votes. Both were proclaimed winners by different factions, but Augustus made his point sufficiently forcefully (by marching in with a Saxon army) to win the day, his ultimate aim being to end the elections and make the throne hereditary.

Augustus's cultural legacy was unsurpassed – Meissen porcelain, the Frauenkirche, the Zwinger, and other baroque treasures in and around Dresden, notably the palace at Moritzburg – but his military adventures were less successful. He was given a false sense of his own superiority by driving back the Ottoman empire from Polish–Lithuanian territories to the south, but that was as good as it was going to get. He then allied himself with Denmark and Russia to attack and capture Sweden's territories along the Baltic coast, but this failed miserably when it turned out Sweden's King Karl XII was a better general than any of them could boast. He turned back Augustus's Polish army on the Baltic and occupied Warsaw, in an attempt to remove Augustus from the throne of Poland, on which he put a puppet of his own, tying the Polish–Lithuanian Commonwealth to Stockholm rather than Dresden. This led to civil war in Poland, during which Augustus controversially allied himself with Russia, but lost again as the Swedish army entered Saxony and forced him to abdicate formally as King of Poland. But if the Swedes had dealt with the Saxons, they had not reckoned with the Russians, who defeated them at the Battle of Poltava. The result was the dramatic retreat from Sweden's possessions in 'mainland' Europe – beyond the Baltic – and the definitive emergence of the Russian empire as a dominant force in northern and Eastern Europe.

With Russia's Peter the Great now the man to be reckoned with in Europe, the drastically weakened Polish–Lithuanian Commonwealth became in effect a Russian protectorate. Augustus was invited to reclaim his Polish throne, but under no illusions that he did so other than by the grace and goodwill of the Russian Tsar. He had not made the throne hereditary, indeed he had barely clung on to it, although his son did succeed him, but only thanks to Russian support. Given the military and political disasters that marked his career, it can be hard to understand why those Dresdeners staring up at his statue near the banks of the Elbe would ever wish he would come down off his horse and rule them again. But then you only have to turn around and look across the river at the restored Dresden skyline to think again. Wars proved to be Augustus's undoing, and two-and-a-half centuries later would be the undoing of Dresden. Peace has seen its remaking.

Call Yourself a Saxon?

The very name Sachsen – in English, Saxon – is a core part of the concept of Anglo-Saxon, today a loose (and essentially meaningless) term for the English-speaking world, even though a huge chunk of its language is based on Norman French rather than the underlying Germanic root. Ironically the word 'English' itself comes from the old German/Danish *aengelsc*. This was the adjective which signified those from the southeastern district of the mostly Danish Jutland peninsula today in the German Land of Schleswig-Holstein, just north of Kiel. It may be a matter of some amusement for 21st-century fans of the fantasy *Game of Thrones* series to note that it is likely the name Angeln derived from 'those who live by the narrow sea' ('narrow' in German is *eng*). The Roman historian Tacitus, whose *Germania* remains the oldest source of written information about the German-speaking lands, referred to the Anglii as a remote tribe living beyond the Elbe, home of the better known people he called the Langobardi, which today speakers of Germanic-based languages such as English can easily recognise as 'long beards' but who would go down in history as the 'Lombards', who migrated south rather than west and gave their name to northern Italy.

The Angles, despite the survival of their name, were almost certainly the junior partners amid those tribes of migrants who upped sticks in the period known, even in English, as the great *Völkerwanderung*. This great 'movement of peoples', which began in the middle of the fifth century, was fired in part by the collapse of the Roman empire and the spoils to be won in the sunny lands to the south, and in part by the invasions of Central Europe by nomadic horse warriors from the steppes of Asia. The Saxons, whose name would over time be used (inaccurately) for greater numbers of Germans across Europe than any other (save perhaps for the Alemani, whose name survives in Spanish and French – Alemania, Allemagne – as that of Germany), appear to have been the Angles' more numerous near-neighbours to the southwest in today's Holstein and across the Elbe through today's Niedersachsen (Lower Saxony) to the Dutch coast.

Ironically, the state known as Sachsen/Saxony, of which Dresden is capital, has next to nothing to do with the people historically known as the Saxons. The name was transferred dynastically as early as 1180 when the title Duke of Saxony was inherited by a family branch based further to the east in a castle near the town of Wettin, traditionally linked to the great mediaeval bishopric of Magdeburg. The Wettin dynasty subsequently inherited Meissen, taking the title Dukes of Saxony, with the result that it was automatically applied to the people they ruled, who historically had far greater links with adjoining Thüringen (now a German *Land* in its own right). The main industry in both Saxony and Thüringen had since time immemorial been mining (the development of the Meissen porcelain industry was an off-shoot). Iron and copper were discovered early on, followed in the Middle Ages by silver, which created a mammoth influx of population to the area. Many of those who flocked to the Erzgebirge subsequently took up the offer of land in what is now Romania, founding the *Siebenburgen* (seven cities) of Transylvania.

After the era of Augustus, Sachsen as a kingdom went into relative decline. Magdeburg and the surrounding territory had already been lost to Prussia in the slow but relentless patchwork quilt process which would eventually see the little Brandenburg town of Berlin become capital of a united Germany. As throughout Europe, the French Revolutionary and Napoleonic wars caused upheaval. With the abolition by the French emperor of the by then nominal Holy Roman Empire, Saxony took the opportunity to declare itself a kingdom. Nonetheless, in the Prussian-led War of Liberation, which saw the French driven back and Napoleon's new order abolished, Saxony, which had fought for Napoleon against Austria, was forced to yield the northern part of its territory to Prussia. (In the political reorganisation of Germany after 1945 this would become the core of the newly established *Land* of Sachsen-Anhalt, which, although occupied initially in equal measure by Russians and Americans, would be yielded to the Soviet Zone, the later DDR.) Unsurprisingly, but undoubtedly mistakenly given the result, Saxony in 1866 opted for the Austrian side in the war with Prussia. Following Austria's defeat, it was obliged to sign a military treaty with Prussia over which was the dominant German state. After-wards Saxony's inclusion in the new Reich after 1871 was automatic, even if it (like Bavaria) remained nominally an independent kingdom until the catastrophe of 1918.

Today's title *Freistaat* Sachsen (Free State of Saxony), dates back to the revolutions of 1918–19 in Germany, when the old Saxon monarchy was abolished, and a *Rat* (in English 'council', and still used in that sense today, but at the time deliberately linked to the Russian 'soviet', which essentially means the same but has since become more heavily laden), declared the *Land* a 'free republic', germanified in a new constitution as a *Freistaat*. Exactly the same occurred in Bavaria, the one other German *Land* to bear the same title today. It is one of those quirky little ironies of history that in Saxony the title, which took its origins from a Soviet institution, was abandoned when the territory came under Soviet rule in 1945.

The *Freistaat* was restored after German reunification in 1990, this time in tribute to the brave contribution made by the people of Saxony in the struggle against Communism. When sealed trains carrying East German refugees who had taken refuge in the West German embassy in Prague passed through Dresden after an inter-governmental agreement to 'deport' them to the West, crowds stormed the station attempting to jump onto the train. There could have been no clearer signal to the regime in Berlin that it had lost all support.

Saxony today, however, is still home to one of the world's most remarkable monuments to the man considered by many to have founded Communism, or at least written its economic and political bible: Karl Marx. In 1953 the East German prime minister renamed the city of Chemnitz, one of the most industrial in the DDR with a long history of campaigns for workers' rights (quashed by the Communist regime), Karl-Marx-Stadt. To complete the honour, Soviet sculptor Lev Kerbel designed a vast monument: a 40-tonne bronze depiction of Marx's head, which stands an impressive 7.1 metres high (25 ft) and together with its vast plinth reaches a total of 13 metres (42 ft), a genuinely towering memorial. After reunification in 1990, Karl-Marx-Stadt became Chemnitz once again. But despite continuing debates, the statue remains. Locals nickname the street where it is situated Nischelgasse: Skull Alley.

So what about the other Saxons, the 'real' ones? Nieder-sachsen (Lower Saxony), which takes its name from the fact that it is a vast, low-lying plain compared to the hilly lands to the southeast, was for most of mediaeval history carved up by various duchies and other minor polities, chief among them the Duchy of Brunswick and the Electorate of Hanover. The fate of the latter was to prove the more interesting. A curious train of events led to the rulers of this relatively insignificant statelet becoming rulers of the global British Empire which would overshadow even that of Spain.

Nobody, not even the participants, would have foreseen the consequences at the time, but the marriage of a Scottish king's daughter to the ruler of a relatively minor German electorate was to have long-lasting consequences. James VI's daughter Elizabeth, wisely named after the English sovereign whose throne he had hopes of inheriting, was married off to Friedrich, Elector of Pfalz (in English, the Palatinate), a minor ruler who would come to no good in the Thirty Years War. Her own daughter Sophia was in turn married off to another German princeling, the Elector of Hanover. When the Stuart line, which had indeed inherited – and nearly lost – the English crown, became extinct with the death of Queen Anne, the throne went to her son, Georg, who became King George I of England, theoretically adding in personal union, a landlocked chunk of northern Germany to the territory of the English crown, which is why a unit of the British army called the King's German Legion, mostly made up of loyalist exiles who had fled when Napoleon conquered their home-land, fought against the French uninterruptedly from 1803 until 1816. The legion played an important role in the Duke of Wellington's forces at the Battle of Waterloo. After Napoleon's defeat, King George III of England was restored to the newly elevated title of King of Hanover. The union, however, ended in 1837 on the death of William IV and accession of his niece Victoria to the English throne because Hanoverian law at the time did not allow a woman to inherit the title.

Hanover made the same fatal mistake as Dresden in 1866, lining up alongside Germany's long-term dominant power, Austria, only to be roundly defeated by a Prussian army, and incorporated as a Prussian province, before being absorbed into the new, post-1871 Reich. Today's *Land* of Lower Saxony was created in the reformation of German territory under British occupation in 1946. By far the state's largest employer is one of the giants of both German and global car manufacturing, Volkswagen, with its main factory still on the original site in Wolfsburg as well as branches in Hanover itself and Brunswick, while there are more than one hundred other firms related to the motor industry throughout the state.

One way or another, Saxons are still in the driving seat.

The Germans and Cars

In a little drawer in my wardrobe is a collection of memorabilia: press accreditation cards for European summits, tickets for the Euro 2012 football tournament in Donetsk and Kiev, entry passes to the Red Square funerals of Yuri Andropov and Konstantin Chernenko in 1984 and 1985, and a little grey booklet with a semi-rubberised cover: my first driving licence. Issued by a country that no longer exists.

Unmistakable on the cover in black on grey is a crossed hammer and compass surrounded by a wreath of wheat, the state emblem of the 'Workers and Farmers' State', officially known as the German Democratic Republic: East Germany. When I arrived in East Berlin in the spring of 1981, I had not yet passed a driving test. Having lived since the age of 18 in Oxford and London, with year-long spells in Paris and Brussels, a car had been something I did not really need. Oxford was, and is even more so today, one of the most car-hostile cities in the world, where the bicycle rules; big cities are also not great places to own a car or learn to drive, and besides there was always a friend or colleague who had one when the urge to escape struck. I was not opposed to the idea of having or driving a car; I simply hadn't got round to it.

East Berlin was turning out to be a different matter. Public transport was cheap and reasonably efficient, but there was one big drawback: there were two systems and each covered only half a city. I needed to go back and forth between the two, not only because I was also responsible for coverage of events in West Berlin – usually squatters' riots or student protests at visits by American presidents – but because there was stuff, most stuff in fact, that I could only buy in West Berlin. I at first used the disconnected public transport system, getting the U-bahn from Senefelder Platz, near my flat, down to the station still labelled Stadtmitte (city centre), even though it was now the last stop on the line, walking through

Checkpoint Charlie, and getting back on at Mohrenstrasse on the other side. It was a bit of a palaver, but at least it was possible. After several weeks I hit on a better idea: I bought a bicycle. They were cheap and easy to find: sporting equipment was one thing almost always available in a Communist state that boasted of its prowess in sports (even if it did turn out to be mostly steroid-fuelled). So far, so good, except that it turned out not to be far enough. The border guards at Checkpoint Charlie informed me sadly but firmly that it was illegal to take a bicycle across the 'state frontier', as they were obliged to refer to it. I tried to work out the reasoning behind this: perhaps that they wanted to prevent a racket smuggling cheap East German bikes to West Berlin where they might be sold for a higher price? Or that they thought secret documents could be rolled up and hidden in the hollow crossbar? Neither made much sense, but there was a lot in Berlin in those days that didn't make sense.

There was also the issue that some of the stuff I needed to transport from West Berlin to East was not exactly easy to lug on foot: notably the thick rolls of printer paper I needed for the fax machine, or bottles of wine when I wanted a change from Romanian or Hungarian – not that even they were always readily available in the East. And then, in the end most importantly of all, unlike West Berliners surrounded by an impassable wall, I had the opportunity, when city life became too much, to just get on my bike and cycle out into the Brandenburg countryside, through wheat fields and forests. That in itself was one of the few advantages of living on the 'wrong' side of the Wall. But with a car, I could drive out to the lovely lakes only a few dozen kilometres north, even up to the Baltic coast, or down to the beautiful mountains of the Erzgebirge.

In the end, I decided there was no point in putting off the inevitable: I would have to learn to drive. Why taking cars across was permissible but not bicycles I had no idea, except of course that cars could only be bought in the West, unless

I wanted to put my name down on a ten-year waiting list. In any case, there already was an office car that had been used by my predecessor, a green VW Golf with a conspicuous blue number plate to identify it as belonging to the 'foreign press' (even though nearly all my few colleagues were West German). So, on the advice of my much bemused office assistant, I applied to be put on a driving course.

The instructors had never had a foreign journalist before. The few foreigners they had contact with were mostly minor staff from embassies, usually from Africa or South America. First of all came the theory test, something which still did not exist in the UK. It was not exactly difficult, although it was of course in German: I had to identify a few road signs (even back then and despite the Iron Curtain, European road signs were fairly standard), and know the basics of the *Strassenverkehrsordnung* (STVO). This was the German equivalent of the British Highway Code, a manual of rules of the road, more or less identical to that in West Germany, save for the fact that the maximum speed limit, including on the autobahn, was 100 kph. I would later express surprise at this to an East German car owner, who dismissed it as irrelevant, saying, '*Keiner fährt 100*' ('Nobody does a hundred'), which I initially misunderstood, given that in West Germany, where there was no speed limit at all on most motorways, 100 kph was usually about as slow as you could get without being hooted at repeatedly. What he meant, of course, was that for a sizeable number of East German cars, 100 kph was more an unachievable ambition than a regular cruising speed.

The only bit of the theory test that worried me was the part which involved basic mechanics. Not only did I not know most of the German words (I was still working hard at improving my decent schoolboy German at this stage), it was that I hadn't a clue about mechanics of any sort. I doubt if by then I had ever even opened a car bonnet. Happily the instructor was well-disposed towards me, willing to chat about things in the West, notably about the quality of a cognac he had once tasted. It wasn't hard to take the hint. On my next lesson, I commented on how much I appreciated his help and goodwill in accommodating my still developing German, and how I would be ever so pleased if he would accept a bottle of the cognac he had mentioned. He tutted, made 'don't mention it' noises and put on a stern face, just about discernible behind the broad grin, and eventually, with a great show of reluctance, said thank you very much. The next week he said it was time to do the test which he conducted himself (in a Communist state where almost everybody worked for the government it never occurred to anyone it might be a good idea to make a difference between instructors and examiners). Despite my odd hesitation on the technical questions it turned out I had passed with flying colours.

The practical test a few weeks later, after many hours of practice in a Russian Lada with a different instructor, was equally interesting. This was done in the same car I had practised in, considered the height of luxury and performance in East Germany, with my instructor, another official who I was told was the actual examiner, and a charming young woman from the Ghanaian embassy who was attempting the test for the sixth time. We were to take turns in the driver's seat: her first, then me. The test took place in the streets around Prenzlauer Berg, which was where I lived and by then knew quite well. They could be busy, and were, not so much with other cars, but with industrial trucks, screeching trams and large numbers of pedestrians. The young Ghanaian woman wasn't having a good day: first of all she drove so close to the tram line that the Lada's skinny tyres got stuck in the tracks and we had to lurch to one side to pull the vehicle out of the way of a pursuing tram, then she took a corner rather too enthusiastically causing two young children to leap to safety. She made a face of resigned disappointment for the examiner and he shook his head in sympathy. There was always a seventh time.

Now it was my turn. I have no real recollection of how well I drove. I just know that I neither got stuck in the tram tracks, nor caused risk of life or limb to any schoolchildren. I passed. To this day I still have a photograph taken by the office assistant of me proudly flourishing my driving licence in front of the Neptune Fountain in the (Eastern) city centre. Over the years that followed, I used my East German *Fahrerlaubnis* to acquire a West Berlin *Führerschein* (it was apocryphally said the Communists had changed the traditional German word for 'driving licence' because it contained the word *Führer*). After German unification in 1990, I exchanged the West Berlin document (no longer necessary as West Berlin was now part of the Federal Republic), for a new 'German' licence, which eventually I was obliged to exchange for a UK licence (though in the small print it still says, 'reason for issue': exchange for German licence).

Compared with the Russian Lada, my VW Golf was a dream. I found it hard to stick to the 100 kph limit on East German autobahns, and soon relished the freedom to put my foot down when I got the opportunity to drive in the West, holding my breath in awe when a Porsche or Mercedes soared past me while I was doing 150 kph (95 mph). But unlike most purchasers of German cars today, my respect for the automobile industry that took off in the West in the post-war years and has since become, literally, a motor of German and European industry, is always tinged with my experiences in the old East. I only once, briefly, drove a Trabant, the little two-stroke, 600 cc excuse for a car that was the height of most ordinary East Germans' auto-owning ambitions and became an improbable symbol of revolution when hundreds of them passed through the holes punched in the Iron Curtain from November 1989 on. It was not a great experience, more akin to controlling a fibreglass dodgem with no bumpers than an actual road car.

The first Trabant – the word means 'fellow-traveller' in German, a direct translation of the Russian 'спутник' (sputnik) – rolled off the production line of a car factory that had previously belonged to a firm called Audi, in Zwickau, in 1957, after a decade of having design and build held up by endless problems working out what raw materials could actually be garnered for such a frivolous consumer item. Over the next 30 years very little changed. Driving it was not a fun experience. In the early months after the fall of the Wall, I witnessed what could have been an appalling accident in the centre of East Berlin, as a large, powerful Mercedes ploughed side-on into the rear of a beige Trabant that was taking more than twice as long as the Mercedes driver had imagined might be necessary to cross an intersection when the lights changed. Happily there was nobody sitting in the back; the stunned Trabi driver sat there trembling, hunched over the wheel, the entire rear section of his vehicle was severed and shunted some 25 metres up the road. At the time it reinforced my belief in the popular misapprehension that the Trabi's body was made of *papier-mâché*. It was in fact a material called Duroplast, a supposedly toughened plastic made from recycled resins from the Soviet and East German chemical industries. In that respect it could have been said to be incredibly 'green', though in practice that really only applied to one of the more popular colours: a particularly virulent apple green. In any case, the label was hardly likely to be suitable for a car that produced nearly ten times as much pollution as West German cars of the day. An emissions scandal was not something the DDR car industry ever imagined.

Up a scale from the Trabant was a car that was almost as coveted as a Lada, named after a castle near Eisenach, in fairly central modern Germany but was then in the south-west DDR, where famously Martin Luther sought sanctuary in disguise after his excommunication by the pope. I drove a Wartburg on several occasions, much to the discomfort of its owner, Viktor, one of the translators in Reuters' Warsaw office, notably when we were following Pope John Paul II on his pilgrimages around Poland. The Pope had a helicopter, we had a Wartburg. It was hard to keep up. Viktor complained that, pushing 100 kph, and occasionally just a tad more, I was damaging his prized possession's engine during its running-in period. He might have been right. Or maybe it was just divine anger at us chasing after the head of the Roman Catholic church in a vehicle named for a castle which once sheltered one of its greatest enemies.

The German infatuation with cars has roots in their long-standing love and respect for engineering of any kind. The highest-regarded title a German can have in the eyes of others is *Herr Doktor Ingenieur*: unlike in much of the Anglo-Saxon world, a doctorate in engineering is a mark of the highest social standing. Anyone claiming to be a *Herzog* or a *Gräfin* (duke or countess: such titles were officially abolished after 1945, but some old German nobility have incorporated them into their names), has no higher social status than an *Ingenieur.*

The thrust to develop a working automobile dominated the engineering world of late 19th-century Europe, with various models developed in Belgium and France. But the title 'father of the motor car' is disputed by two Germans, neither of whom to the best of our knowledge ever met the other, but whose names would end up being inextricably linked: Gottlieb Daimler and Karl Benz.

Daimler, along with his lifelong business partner Wilhelm Maybach, had been working on creating an internal combustion engine for several years, but unbeknown to either party another engineer called Karl Benz was working on the same idea, and he managed to get his patented first, in 1879. Seven years later he also managed to patent the first motor vehicle. Daimler and Maybach continued their work separately, but with Benz always seemingly a step ahead when it came to acquiring patents for a string of devices including the spark plug, carburettor, gear shift and water-cooled radiator that eventually made up what we know as the engine of a motor car. Benz's first commercial example – the *Benz Patent Motorenwagen*, essentially a tricycle with seats and a motor instead of pedals – went on show from 1886. The model 3, the first really intended for large scale production, finally went on sale in 1888, and the world's first 'driving licence' was issued that year in Mannheim to none other than Karl Benz himself.

The concept of a 'licence' was particularly German: not just the need to regulate this new concept but also to give it a format for development and marketing: over the first few years of the 20th century nearly all the German states introduced licences and competency testing. In 1904 the world's first driving instruction school was set up in Aschaffenburg in northern Bavaria. Many other countries wouldn't bother to regulate the 'craze' for years, even decades. The UK was a relatively early adopter, requiring a licence from 1903, but a test of basic skills was not introduced until 1934. Belgium was the last to require a test, which has only applied since 1977 – the results of which I witnessed when I lived in Brussels at the time.

The first marketing campaign for the *Motorenwagen* was totally impromptu and involved a stunt that even today seems as modern as could be imagined, and was a genuine shock for the late 19th century. Benz's pretty young wife Bertha, who believed fiercely in her husband's embryonic industry and had invested much of her inheritance in it, took off without telling him, and drove herself and their two teenage sons in the three-wheeled vehicle, ostensibly to visit her mother, travelling from Mannheim to Pforzheim, a distance of 106 kilometres (66 miles), making her the first person in history to drive more than a short 'test' distance in a motorised vehicle. Despite the journey taking some twelve hours with a number of breakdowns and improvised repairs, including enlisting a blacksmith to mend a chain and a cobbler to get leather fitted to the worn wooden brakes, the story – not to mention the number of people the vehicle terrified en route – became legendary and caused a huge boost in interest in this novel method of transportation, already commonly dubbed the 'horseless carriage'. She had hoped it would make motor transport popular in Germany. Little did she know!

On the competition side the first Daimler-Maybach hit the road in 1889 and the company was already making engines for boats. Allegedly Daimler was fond of doodling and created a little star with three points indicating transport by water, air and land: the potential origin of a logo as globally famed as that of Coca-Cola or the Olympic Rings: the Mercedes star. And thereby hangs another tale, that of a rabbi's son who was a part-time diplomat, tobacco trader, insurance salesman and enthusiast for the new sport of motor racing.

Emil Jellinek had been born in Leipzig, but took Austro-Hungarian citizenship and worked for a while as the empire's consul in Morocco, then Algeria and France. Fascinated with the developments in the motor industry, he soon became determined to find ever faster models. Having made a substantial sum in the insurance business, he was now living in Nice much of the year and had set up a subsidiary selling cars to Europe's wealthy for whom the French Riviera was a favourite spot to spend the winter. He got in touch with Wilhelm Maybach, and bought several of his Phaeton cars to sell from the large house he had bought and named after his first daughter. It was a common enough girl's name in Spain, meaning 'kindness' or 'mercy', but unusual enough north of the Pyrenees: Mercedes.

Jellinek did well racing in the Phaeton reaching a top speed of 35 kph (22 mph) and entered cars in every one of the growing series of races put on in Nice each year, calling them 'team Mercedes'. At the same time he kept sending back suggestions for improvements, and eventually offered a large sum of money to the Daimler company if it would design and make a sports car to his specifications. He insisted it be called the Daimler-Mercedes. Daimler agreed and invited him to join the board and help oversee its production. He did, and the car was a stupendous success reaching the then unprecedented speed of 60 kph (37 mph). The head of the French Automobile Club declared, 'We have entered the Mercedes era.' The car was a global phenomenon and its creator even changed his surname to Jellinek-Mercedes, remarking that it was probably the first time in history a father had taken his daughter's name. Jellinek would later resume his diplomatic career for the Austrians in both Monaco and Mexico, but faced difficulties in World War I when he came under suspicion of engaging in espionage. The family fled to neutral Switzerland, where he died in 1918.

In the meantime technology in the motor car business had taken vast leaps forward in terms of speed. It was not Daimler or their Mercedes which had broken the records, but a vehicle made by their competitor, Herr Benz. In 1909 at Brooklands in England a French driver in a specially aerodynamically designed Blitzen Benz racing car achieved a speed of 202.7 kph (126.7 mph), an extraordinary leap forward in just over a decade. The great success of the German automobile industry was, however, brought to a crashing halt by war, and in the depression that followed both Daimler and Benz suffered from a collapse in sales and spiralling inflation, until eventually in 1926 they signed a memorandum of understanding for a merger. One thing they included was that they would call their cars Mercedes-Benz. They still do.

One of the other two most successful German ventures into engineering that we still live with today was set up in 1913 by a young man called Karl Rapp, who began his working life as an engineer with a company called Zust in northern Italy, then briefly for Daimler-Benz before deciding that aircraft engines were the coming thing. Rapp Motorenwerke, based in Munich, pulled in large orders from the military after the outbreak of war in 1914. But over the course of the war, his heavy engines fell out of favour in preference for those of his designer Max Friz, who had joined him from Daimler. By 1917 Rapp was ousted from the company he founded, which was now renamed simply for its location as Bayerische Motorenwerke, or BMW for short.

The terms of the Versailles peace treaty imposed on Germany at the end of the war put a spanner in the works by banning all aircraft production. Undaunted, the firm switched to turning out motorcycles and eventually small cars, the earliest, known as the Dixi, based on the British 'baby' Austin 7 made in Birmingham. Austin's early cars had won admiration around the world and were copied not only in Germany but plagiarised by Nissan in Japan, and it thrived during the World War II by building engines for Lancaster bombers. BMW also went back into aircraft production during the war, but when this was again banned in defeated, occupied Germany it struggled to find a new market.

A substantial minority of shares was acquired by the Quandt family, who brought in top engineers and designers, acquiring other companies in Germany and the US and eventually the British Rover Group, the short-lived successor to the defunct semi-nationalised car giant British Leyland. BMW, which had begun by imitating Austin, now owned it and didn't know what to do with it. In the end they sold it off. The Austin trademark is now owned (though unused) by the Shanghai Motor Corporation after huge investment by BMW failed to turn the British company around. Ironically, it is BMW which perpetuates the memory of its original inspiration, producing the successor to its most fondly remembered product, the original Mini. The Munich-based firm was listed in 2012 by Forbes magazine the 'most reputable company in the world', and its cars are coveted globally, so far untainted by the emissions scandal which tarnished the reputation of the other giant of the German automotive world, Volkswagen.

VW, which by the end of the first decade of the 21st century had amassed a host of subsidiaries and become the world's third-largest car company (after the US General Motors and Toyota of Japan), was until the emissions scandal of 2015, also one of the most trusted firms on the planet, despite potentially dark roots. The company was founded in 1936 by the *Deutsche Arbeitsfront,* the Nazi umbrella organisation set up to replace the traditional trades unions which had been banned. At Hitler's instigation the organisation took up the cause of creating a small car for the average family as a counterpart to the extremely expensive luxury vehicles on the roads. The car would be available through a workers' savings scheme at a cost roughly equivalent to nine months' average salary. And they had a man ready and set to build it, a man born in the Austro-Hungarian empire in a small village called Mafferdorf, who after 1918 had opted for the new Czechoslovak citizenship, but worked in Vienna and later with Daimler-Benz, before setting up an engineering and manufacturing consultancy in Stuttgart: one Ferdinand Porsche. He would later be forced by Hitler to give up his Czechoslovak citizenship for German, the third nationality in his life. After 1945 he applied for Austrian citizenship again, but – like all 'German' citizens of the time – was turned down. The car was officially to be known as the *KdF-Wagen,* for the Nazi *Kraft durch Freude* ('Strength through Joy') social movement. By 1938, however, when the first models appeared with Dr Porsche's distinctive, economic, cheap-to-make shape, it acquired the nickname by which it would forever after be known: the *Käfer* (the Beetle).

Hundreds of thousands signed up to what was effectively a pyramid Ponzi scheme that could never have produced the goods to meet demand and price. Meeting production targets no longer counted after 1939 as the company was turned into a manufacturer of military vehicles, most famous being the *Kübelwagen* ('bucket car') light reconnaissance vehicle also available in amphibious form. Nobody who had put money into the government-sponsored saving scheme ever had a car delivered: the most famous recipient was Hitler himself, who was given an open-top version for his 55th birthday in 1944.

VW's post-war success was again ironically down to a

Brit: an army officer who persuaded the occupation forces to order several thousand of the practical, economical vehicles. Major Ivan Hirst was put in charge of the badly bombed factories and set about getting them up and running again. Despite the fact that part of the factory roof was missing and there were few windows still intact, the workers were eager and Hirst believed it could become a viable concern. His beliefs were not shared by manufacturers from the victorious powers, who were offered control of the factory but turned it down. American magnate Henry Ford, offered the business for nothing, turned it down flat, while Sir William Rootes, a British motor industry mogul, declared the car to be 'unattractive' and predicted the business would collapse within two years. Within one year VW was turning out a thousand cars a month, and reached one million a year by 1955, and nearly ten million a year today. Rootes disappeared by 1967.

What contributed as much to the success of the German car industry as anything else was that already in the 1920s under the Weimar Republic it had been recognised that this new means of transport meant better roads were needed, especially on long distance routes. Already Berlin had a protoype of what would come to be known as an autobahn: a long straight stretch of high-quality dual carriageway to the southwest of the city, built for testing new cars, as its name implied: the *Automobil-Verkehrs-und-Übungsstrecke* (automobile transport and testing strip) known universally by the acronym *AVUS*. I can still remember being daunted by its quality and capacity for speed when I first drove my office VW Golf through Checkpoint Charlie in 1981 and decided I had to try it out on the world's 'first autobahn'. I hit 180 kph, fingers holding on for dear life to the steering wheel, when I was comfortably passed by a Porsche and a Mercedes.

Creation of the German motorway network did not, however, go as quickly as initially planned. The great depression, hyperinflation and general economic troubles of the time meant the plans for a national high-quality road network rarely reached completion. The first section of this new type of smooth-surfaced road running between Cologne and Bonn was, however, opened in 1932, by one Konrad Adenauer, then mayor of Cologne and later to become first chancellor of the new West German republic in 1949. But at the time it took the Nazi regime to make real progress, seeing a nationwide road-building exercise as a way to soak up the unemployed and at the same time ensure their loyalty to the party which would be their new employers. It seemed the perfect incarnation of the party's full name, the National Socialist German Workers' Party; it is so often forgotten that this most extreme of right-wing nationalist labels concealed its real character under a 'socialist' label. It meant the same thing: seeing the people as servants of the state.

As it happened, the party already had an expert in its ranks: one Fritz Todt, an engineer whose doctoral thesis had been on the 'Causes of defects in the construction of tarmac and asphalt roads'. Todt signed up some 130,000 men into what became known as the *Organisation Todt*, involving both private and public enterprise to relieve the unemployment problem. Todt's men worked miracles, taking the total length of the autobahn network from a paltry 105 kilometres in 1935 to an astonishing 3,300 kilometres by the outbreak of war just four years later, a quarter of today's network, much of which had to be rebuilt from scratch after 1945. There were also stretches built before 1939 which after 1945 were no longer in Germany: during the Solidarity crises in Poland in the early 1980s I would regularly drive between Warsaw and Gdansk, every time just slightly thrown by a section where the route followed the old east-west Berlin-Königsberg autobahn, turning for just a few hundred metres onto a dead straight old, but still well-surfaced roadway. At either end, where the north-south Polish route carried on its way, the old autobahn stretched into the distance, overgrown with grass. It reminded me of ancient Roman roads elsewhere in Europe, silent but enduring mementoes of a vanished empire.

The first car I ever called my own, though technically of course it belonged to Reuters, was that green VW Golf, registration QA41-04, after I passed that test in East Berlin. The only car I have ever bought brand new was the first 1600 cc VW Gold to enter the UK back in 1985. I know that because I had ordered it bespoke in those days' equivalent of online: by fax, from the Reuters office in Moscow direct to VW in Wolfsburg, and subsequently went out there with a friend to collect it, new and shiny, from the factory. I knew it was the only 1600 cc model in the UK because I had immense difficulty getting insurance for it, with the standard response: 'That model's not available here yet.' In the end they had to concede that I had one when I gave them the chassis number. I have not always had German cars but I have never regretted it when I have. To this day I still drive a car designed and made by the successors of the original 'Beetle' designer. And with no regrets.

But I will leave the last word to an American lady, a symbol of the anti-capitalist counter-culture of the 1960s, who in her last song called out in that inimitable Southern Comfort-drenched blues drawl, 'Oh Lord, won't you buy me a Mercedes-Benz, my friends all have Porsches, I must make amends.' I know she was being ironic, but still...

4

Munich

The stereotype of Germany: all Lederhosen and beer: far from the whole story, very far

'Oans! Zwoa! Sufa!'

To any beer-lover it is the finest call to arms in the world. Pronounced in thick local dialect – to any other German it has to be translated as *'Eins! Zwei! Saufen!'* (One! Two! Drink!) – it is the familiar toast for all those clutching the vast litre mugs of beer, a stereotype to foreigners but unknown almost anywhere else in the country, to raise them to their lips and swallow long and deep.

The time and place where it is heard most often in the course of a single day, for some 16–18 days in succession, is, of course, the Oktoberfest. Held on Munich's Theresienwiese, it is Germany's globally renowned celebration of excess and exuberance that attracts hundreds of thousands of locals as well as beer enthusiasts from all over the world.

The Oktoberfest has a grand historical pedigree that dates back to Bavaria's heyday as what at the time was considered a nation-state in its own right. Its origins lie in the grand festivities thrown to celebrate the wedding of Crown Prince Ludwig, later to become King Ludwig I of Bavaria, to Princess Therese of Sachsen-Hildburghausen, on 12 October 1810. As a gesture of goodwill to their people, the citizens of

Munich were invited to a grand party held on the fairground then outside the city gates and subsequently christened in the honour of the bride Theresienwiese, Therese's Meadow. The celebrations lasted five days and ended with horse races that were so popular they decided to repeat them the following year. Additional attractions were added and before long an institution was born.

Just in figures alone the Oktoberfest beggars the imagination. Set on an area that for most of the year is a dusty wasteland, it covers up to 31 hectares (76 acres) north of the city's central station. It is made up of 14 main 'tents' – in reality huge steel and wood-framed prefab structures designed to look like great marquees – the largest accommodating up to 11,000 seated drinkers, and 21 'little tents', surrounded by an extravagant funfair of stomach-wrenching rides (even before you've consumed half a dozen litres of beer), and a further 35 establishments offering just food.

In 2014 alone some 7.7 million litres of Oktoberfestbier, brewed specially by the city's six major breweries who run the event, were consumed. One hundred and twelve whole oxen were roasted, along with 48 calves, and thousands of chickens.

The Oktoberfest has become Germany's largest tourist event, attracting visitors from all around the world, who in recent years have – bizarrely in the eyes of most Germans from elsewhere – enthusiastically adopted for the duration a form of the enduring traditional Bavarian dress known as *Trachten*.

During the last two weeks of September into the beginning of October (it is really more of a 'Septemberfest' and nowadays ends on or around 3 October, the date of reunification in 1990 which has become Germany's national holiday), it is not uncommon to see British, Australian or even Japanese young men parade the streets of Munich in – often unwisely short – Lederhosen. Not that the Bavarians don't do it too. Reviled by young people back in the 1980s as old-fogey wear beloved only by their parents, somewhere early in the new millennium, *Trachten* became trendy.

Young Bavarian men as well as older will preen themselves in usually longer Lederhosen, effectively knee britches, often from expensive deer hide, that can cost hundreds of euros a pair. The traditional female equivalent – the dirndl with long skirt and wired 'wonderbra' push-up corset – is still worn by serving women in the beer tents, but their local customers have evolved more daring versions, often with short, lacy skirts, skimpy tops and sometimes revealing slashed slits.

It is all too easy for the worldly-wise to mock it all as trashy, drunken kitsch, but that's only if you've never tried to get into the spirit. By the time the second litre (*Mass*) has passed your lips, the brass 'oompah' band has got into its swing in what closely resembles a boxing ring in the centre of your tent, and – if you're in the right tent – men standing on posts are cracking four-metre (18 ft) whips above your head, it becomes hard, almost literally, not to lose your head.

I attended my first Oktoberfest a long time ago, in 1982, when I was based in East Berlin for Reuters and travelled south to meet some colleagues from the Bonn office and experience the biggest annual party in Germany. We had agreed to meet at the city's main station, not far from the 'Wies'n', once, as the word literally means, a 'meadow', but now for most of the year a giant car park awaiting its annual apotheosis.

Arriving on the overnight train, which had travelled slowly until it crossed the Iron Curtain into 'West' (in reality south) Germany near Coburg, from where Queen Victoria's beloved Prince Albert came, we got in about 6.30 a.m., and with nearly an hour to wait for my colleagues, did what everyone else seemed to be doing, had a small breakfast beer at the station café.

It is so long ago that that I might be expected – not just because of the passage of the years – to have little remembrance of that first visit, yet such was its impact that I still recall certain details vividly. First, that we all laughed at the ridiculous tatty souvenirs of silly hats and badges with your photograph holding a beer printed on them, only to end up several hours later covered in them.

The second was the unnerving experience of visiting the gents' urinals, a large structure with deep stainless steel troughs running round the walls, and nearly wetting myself when a couple of large local middle-aged men on either side undid the front flaps of their Lederhosen and unleashed in stereo a torrent I had not experienced since a childhood visit to Niagara Falls.

Beer releases inhibitions. Beer loosens tongues. It was on a subsequent visit, while I was a correspondent in Moscow in the 1980s and had revealed this fact to two 30-something American men we were drinking with (the US back then still had a considerable military and intelligence presence in the Munich area), that one of them boasted that if a Russian gas pipeline to Western Europe was ever completed 'we'll just blow it up and blame it on the permafrost'. His companion suddenly froze, went dead serious and said, 'I think you'd better make clear to Peter that that was a joke.' Maybe it was.

Possibly the most remarkable thing about the Oktober-fest, given the scale of the event and the insobriety actively encouraged, is the incredibly low level of violence: almost non-existent. It will come as no surprise to cliché lovers that it is all down to an almost unbelievably high level of organisation.

For a start, there is no overcrowding. Drinking while standing up is not allowed, except in the Hofbräu tent where standers, almost exclusively anglophone, are corralled within a small area. There is no self-service. To be served you have to be seated at one of the long tables, each of which accommodates up to ten people on benches down either side.

You will get beer only when your allotted waiter or waitress visits you; it is as well to tip generously at least in the early hours. But when you do, you are encouraged to make the most of it, clink the almost unbreakable litre glasses (commonly called a Stein by Americans, probably because they were once made of stone, but universally called a *Krug* by Germans) as long and loud as your heart demands.

You are encouraged to link arms and sway back and forwards in time to the music, you are positively encouraged to stand on the benches, but you are expressly FORBIDDEN to stand on the tables. If you do, the waitress will tell you to get down, and within seconds so will two strong young men standing behind you.

If you refuse, as I have occasionally seen young men – I fear to say almost exclusively Australian – attempt to do, you will suddenly find, without blinking, that the two men have become eight men, who will forcibly bring you down from the table and carry you in a horizontal position, facing the ground, two men to each arm and two to each leg, not just out of the tent, but to the edge of the festival area, where they will leave you sitting on the ground. They will suggest you do not come back in again that evening but will do nothing to prevent you trying, if you can, to find your mates again. It is short, sharp and quick, allows no possibility for resistance and involves no other penalty. It rarely needs to.

In 2014 there were a total of 36 instances in which young men armed with *Krüge* fought one another over the 16-day period, which is really a quite remarkable figure when you consider 6.5 million people were there.

The Oktoberfest has grown and grown, seemingly in keeping with the population of the world, although the Germans themselves remain by far the most numerous group. It is now not uncommon on the opening day, when the festival master declares, again in broad dialect, '*O'zapft is!*' (in English, 'the beer is tapped') for there to be in excess of a million people on the Wies'n.

It is this, plus the city's physical factors – its tightly knit Altstadt (old town), with those landmarks that survived World War II lovingly preserved; its legendary Hofbräuhaus, a sort of year-round indoor version of the Oktoberfest; the wide Italianesque 18th- and 19th-century avenues, built in imitation of ancient Rome; and its beautiful, extensive parks, with icy Alpine streams and shady summer beer gardens – that make Munich Germany's most attractive city.

Americans in particular, for whom it was, with Frankfurt, a major centre of their administration during the post-war occupation, are almost excessively fond of it. Until the end of the Cold War, the CIA-funded American propaganda radio station, Radio Liberty, was based in Munich, in a former Wehrmacht barracks not far from one of the city's favourite beer gardens.

The world's stereotypical German still derives from customs that belong almost exclusively to Munich and Bavaria, to the disgruntled bemusement of most other Germans. Lederhosen in Berlin are only ever worn skin-tight and usually black (though occasionally pink).

Toytown Germany? Not quite

Bavaria itself is classic material for a coffee-table picture book, from the foothills of the Alps to the meandering Danube and the fairytale palace, Neuschwanstein, built by the delusional romantic 19th-century Bavarian monarch Ludwig II, and on which Walt Disney based his pale shadow of a 'magic castle'. Pretty little towns such as Bad Tölz and Garmisch nestle beneath snow-capped mountains amid rich meadows of grazing cows.

There is even a magazine and website for Munich-based expats which caters for the large anglophone community, and calls itself, tellingly, *Toytown Germany*. Yet for all the gingerbread house beauty, of the capital and the country, Munich has a dark side that until very recently it has tried assiduously to brush under the carpet.

The capital of Toytown Germany was also the *Hauptstadt der Bewegung*, Capital of the Movement, and at the time proud of it. Unfortunately the movement in question was National Socialism. It was in Munich in 1920 that a group of disgruntled nationalists founded the National Socialist German Workers's Party, or NSDAP (*Nationalsozialistische Deutsche Arbeiterpartei*), soon to be commonly known as Nazi (from the German pronunciation of the first two syllables).

Renowned German political scientist Martin Hecht, analysing the complex and difficult question of why the Nazis were born in Bavaria has written, 'There is just a hint of that aggressive mix of demonstrative local patriotism, overweening self-confidence and beer-fuelled joviality to be gleaned at the May strong beer festival opening in the Hofbräuhaus... It was exactly this sort of biosphere of beer, party atmosphere and relaxed inhibitions that got the first Nazi hordes in the mood to get on their feet and march out of the beer halls to the Feldherrnhalle.'

This is a reference to the Beer Hall Putsch of November 1923, where a young Adolf Hitler took over a political meeting, turned it into a revolutionary march on the Bavarian Defence Ministry which was stopped at the Feldherrnhalle, a monument to past Bavarian generals, by a local government detachment of 130 troops. Shots were exchanged, and four soldiers and 16 Nazi protesters were killed. Shortly afterwards, Hitler was arrested and accused of treason in a 24-day trial, which he cleverly turned into an opportunity to broadcast his own propaganda.

He feared being deported to his native Austria, but instead was sentenced to five years' imprisonment in Landsberg outside Munich. In fact, he served only nine months and used the time to produce *Mein Kampf* (My Struggle), which became his political manifesto. After the Nazis took power in 1933, the Feldherrnhalle became a place of pilgrimage, adorned with a stone swastika (long gone), where the party's 16 dead were honoured as martyrs and a celebration was held every year on the anniversary.

From 1933 until 1945 it was obligatory for citizens who

passed the memorial to give the raised arm 'Hitler salute'.
Viscardigasse, the little street which ran behind it, was
regularly used by those who did not care to be put in that
situation. In the local parlance, it became known as Aus-
weichergasse ('Dodger's Alley').

∈∋

The history of Munich, and Bavaria, neither begins nor ends
with the fact that it was the city where Nazism was born
and for a while flourished. Alone of all the German *Länder*
today, it has retained its 1918 borders, and maintains the
sense that it might even be a country in its own right, every
bit as much as neighbouring Austria, with which, if one plan
discussed by the victorious powers in 1945 had come true,
it might have been joined, excluded from the rest of what
we today call Germany. In population and economic prowess
even today, Bavaria would be as viable a separate country as
the US state of California.

The origins of the word Bavaria, *Bayern,* go back to the
Celtic tribe known as Boier. Their lands – the southern part
of what is today Bavaria – were part of the Roman province
of Rhaetia. A local overlordship was recognised from about
the sixth century, although the city of Munich was first mentioned in 1158, a monastic settlement as easily deduced from
its name, München (monks in modern German are *Mönche*).
The oldest significant princely family were the Welfs whose
dominance, notably under Henry the Lion, came to an end in
1180 when a rival family, the Wittelsbachs, gained the ascen-
dancy, which they were to keep until all monarchic, princely
and aristocratic titles were legally abolished after the revolution of 1918.

That does not mean the Bavarians or their overlords had a
peaceful and prosperous eight centuries. The dukes who held
fealty to the Wittelsbachs quarrelled and split their lands on
numerous occasions. In the Thirty Years War, which followed

the 16th-century Reformation and saw the largely Germanic-speaking Catholic and Protestant duchies and princedoms in Central Europe in conflict (including territories from the Netherlands to today's Czech Republic and not at all cognate with what we today call Germany), Bavarian was strongly on the Catholic side, as it still is today.

The Bavarian lands themselves were on occasion occupied by troops of the Habsburg dynasty, soldiers from an empire which included what we now call Austria as well as Hungary and most of the Balkans. But on numerous occasions throughout history the Bavarians also flirted with the French, most disastrously in the War of the Spanish Succession, fought over whether a scion of the 'Austrian' Habsburg dynasty or the 'French' Bourbon family should succeed to the throne of Spain, which then was still the greatest global power thanks to its control of Latin America, though already failing faster than anyone at the time realised.

That came to an end with disastrous defeat in 1704 at a battle on Bavarian soil, today remembered there as the Battle of Hochstetten, but in the Anglo-Saxon world as the Battle of Blenheim, in which the English general John Churchill, distant ancestor of Winston, played a prominent part (fighting on the side of the Habsburgs), for which he was awarded a dukedom (of Marlborough) and a palace near Oxford named after the battle.

The fight to regain independence began with a meeting in a little town called Braunau-am-Inn, which then belonged to Bavaria, but would later be taken by the Habsburgs and become a border town, where in the 1880s customs control was in the hands of a grumpy old man called Alois Hitler, whose son would go on to be the most notorious Austrian in history.

The Bavarians won independence for a while but by the mid-18th century were again under Habsburg–Austrian control. It was only with the rise to power of a previously relatively unimportant German state called Prussia, which was beginning to challenge the Austrians for balance of power in Central Europe that it was agreed, reluctantly, that Bavaria should remain an independent state.

It is at this time that one of the most eccentric, fascinating and inspired characters in Bavarian history takes the stage. There is a statue to him on Maximilianstrasse in Munich, the road that leads up to the Bavarian parliament. It shows a classic depiction of a bewigged, cloaked 18th-century European gentleman. Only the inscription makes the curious passer-by stop and wonder at his provenance.

The Yankee Refusenik Who Became a Bavarian Polymath

The inscription on that statue in Maximilianstrasse reads: *Benjamin Thompson, Graf von Rumford, geboren zu Woburn, Massachusetts.* Benjamin Thompson, Count Rumford, Born in Woburn, Massachusetts.

Yes, one of the most fascinating figures in Bavarian history was an American. Or rather, I should say, he was born in America. Benjamin Thompson considered himself, as did most of those around him at the time of his birth in New England in 1753, an Englishman, yet he would attain greatness as a Bavarian and die outside Paris. In the meantime, in the course of an extraordinary life, he would make a name for himself as a womaniser, linguist, scientist, landscape gardener, military quartermaster, officer in both the British and Bavarian armies, in the end venerated even by a president of the country he abandoned, the United States of America.

Born to a farmer called Ebenezer in the small town of Woburn, 15 kilometres (just under 10 miles) northwest of Boston, in what is now Massachusetts, Thompson trained at nearby Harvard for a life in business, but ended up as a teacher in a town called Rumford – from which he would later take his title – but is now Concord, New Hampshire. At the age of just 17 he married a well-connected widow 13 years his senior and through her got to know the local colonial governor, who named him a major in the New Hampshire militia at the age of 19.

As local resentment against the British grew, Thompson made clear whose side he was on, which resulted in a local mob attacking his house. He responded by fleeing, abandoning his wife and their two-month-old daughter, to take up a position with the British army in Boston. On a visit back to Woburn in 1775 the rebellion erupted in earnest with skirmishes even in Rumford/Concord; he was put on trial as a suspected British spy, but got off. He immediately cashed in all he had and the following year took a Royal Navy ship to England, found a job in the Colonial Ministry and began conducting scientific experiments with gunpowder, developing an improved method of ship-to-ship communication and better cannons, endeavours which were rewarded in 1779 with membership of the prestigious Royal Society.

The following year he was given the less than promising job of Secretary of State for the American Colonies, by then in full rebellion, and in 1781 crossed the Atlantic again, set up a cavalry regiment called the King's American Dragoons, and as its commander took charge of Fort Huntingdon on Long Island.

But by 1783, with the British on the verge of surrender, he returned again to England, where he was promoted to colonel, but chose instead to travel to the continent where, in Strasbourg, he bumped into the nephew of the Bavarian-Palatinate elector, who offered him employment. After a brief return to England to say farewell to George III, who gave him a knighthood as a parting gift, he moved to Munich and began a reorganisation of the Bavarian army. One of his main achievements was the invention of a cheap but hearty soup of potatoes and peas, which solved the problems of undernourishment among the troops, whom he ordered to set up a vegetable garden in every garrison.

At the same time he began planning what remains his most lasting achievement, the layout of a vast tract of land outside

Munich's city walls in the English style – as developed by Capability Brown at Blenheim, north of Oxford – which to this day is called the Englischer Garten. The park was opened to the public in 1792, and remains a great green lung of some 4.17 square kilometres (1.6 square miles) among the world's great urban parks, bigger than either Hyde Park in London or Central Park in New York.

The Englischer Garten, despite being bombed by the British in the 1940s, remains one of Munich's glories, with several chestnut tree-shaded beer gardens, of which perhaps best is the Chinesischer Turm, a mock Chinese pagoda (rebuilt after being burned to the ground by British bombing raids in 1945), the first floor of which on sunny holidays hosts an 'oompah' band. At the garden's southern end, where a tributary of the river Isar gushes out from underground, there is a virtually year-round queue of surfers waiting to take their turn on the 'standing wave'.

The Isar tributary's icy grey-green waters provide another daredevil entertainment in summer: jumping into the water from the bank and then fighting the fast flowing current to get to the edge and climb out. Popular among Munich teenagers is to travel several hundred metres, swept along by the icy flow, from the entrance to the park to the bridge near Tivolistrasse. It is standard for drinkers coming back into the centre of town from the Chinesischer Turm beer garden on the No. 18 tram to find themselves squeezed against a gaggle of teenage girls in bikinis or teenage boys in swim shorts, dripping wet. They are rarely asked for their tickets, not least because in the less conservative 1970s, the girls wore nothing at all. Rumford would almost certainly have approved.

Ever the polymath, at the same time as mastering garden layout, he was also working on scientific investigations into the nature of heat-generation and preservation. Using practical experiments in the cannon-boring process, he discovered one of the basic principles of thermodynamics: that heat was a form of energy and could be produced by movement. He invented several types of devices for heating food (including an early coffee machine) and accidentally discovered the – nowadays extremely trendy – principle of cooking at very low temperatures, by leaving a mutton shoulder overnight in a box designed for drying out potatoes, returning the next morning to find it perfectly cooked through.

His proficiency in almost everything he touched led to promotions through the ranks of the Bavarian army from Major General to Commander-in-Chief and eventually Minister for War and Chief of Police. He was made a count of the Holy Roman Empire, taking the title Graf von Rumford and endowed two scientific prizes, one to be awarded by the Royal Society in London, the other by the American Academy of Arts and Sciences.

In 1796, with the Bavarian elector on the run after defeat in yet another war with Habsburg Austria, Rumford negotiated a peace treaty which prevented the destruction of Munich, at the same time writing a book *On Chimney Fireplaces* as a means of improving domestic heating. From 1799 he served effectively as Bavarian ambassador to London.

It is a measure of the respect he earned, even from the country he had abandoned, that as early as 1789 he had been elected a member of the Academy of American Arts and Sciences, and received – but rejected – an invitation from US President John Adams to set up an American military academy, the institution that later became West Point.

He visited Paris in 1801 and met the man who would cause more commotion in his adopted homeland of Bavaria – indeed throughout Europe – than he or anyone else could have imagined: Napoleon Bonaparte. When the French armies that same year forced Bavaria to renounce its Palatinate territory west of the Rhine, Rumford was entrusted with evacuating important cultural treasures back to Munich. He moved to Paris in 1802, was elected to the Institut National des Sciences et des Arts and and settled there, living on his Bavarian state pension, and briefly married to the widow of the guillotined chemist Antoine Lavoisier. He died in 1814, leaving the equivalent of $50,000 to Harvard University, which set up a fellowship in his name.

Meanwhile, after an attempt at neutrality in the Napoleonic wars, which saw it invaded by the French, Bavaria had in 1805 become an ally of Napoleon, its troops taking part in the war against Habsburg Austria, which was roundly defeated at Austerlitz. Napoleon abolished the by now little more than theoretical institution of the Holy Roman Empire, which the Habsburgs had long regarded as a family gift, and as a reward elevated Bavaria to the title of kingdom, which, as we have seen, the Prussians had long since adopted by stealth.

Duke Maximilian V became King Maximilian I – known familiarly to his subjects as King Max – and with his highly talented minister Maximilian Montgelas (a Münchener born and bred, despite his French-sounding name) began the process of modernising Bavaria, reforming the state and declaring himself a constitutional monarch with a two-chamber parliament.

The alliance with Napoleon had gains and costs: Bavaria gained territories that made it roughly the size and shape it is today, but out of 33,000 Bavarian troops obliged to march on Moscow with the French emperor in 1812, only 4,000 returned. Seeing how the tide was turning, Bavaria switched sides just before the Battle of the Nations at Leipzig in 1813. This cynical decision meant that when Napoleon was finally defeated, it was allowed to retain most of its territorial gains, with the notable exception of those taken from the old enemy, Austria.

When Maximilian I died in 1825, his son Ludwig, whose wedding had been so notably celebrated back in 1810 with the first Oktoberfest, finally ascended the throne. But despite his elaborately staged wedding, there was to be another woman in Ludwig I's life, a foreigner almost as remarkable, in terms of ambition and self-promotion, as Benjamin Thompson.

L-O-L-A, Lola

To all appearances the exotic figure of Lola Montez was a talented Spanish flamenco dancer from Seville who came to fame among the European nobility when she danced *Los Boleros de Cadiz* in front of King Friedrich Wilhelm I of Prussia and Tsar Nicholas I of Russia in Berlin and followed up with a tumultuous appearance in Warsaw. But a succession of torrid affairs saw her rejected by polite society. A run at the Paris Opera increased her fame, as did flirtations with the best-selling novelist Alexandre Dumas (author of *The Man in the Iron Mask*) and the composer Franz Liszt, but ended in scandal when another lover, the renowned editor Alexandre Dujarrier, was killed in a duel.

By the time she arrived in Munich in October 1846, the exuberant 25-year-old was running from a notorious recent past, while still concealing her real origins. The woman who gave her full name as Maria de los Dolores Porrys y Montez, was actually Eliza Rosanna Gilbert, daughter of a Scottish father and Irish mother, who had spent her early childhood in Calcutta, mostly grown up in the home of her step-uncle in Scotland and then gone to school in the southern English spa town of Bath, before marrying a British army officer at the age of 16 and going back to India with him. But Eliza got bored and by 1842, at 21, she was back in England, learning Spanish and reinventing herself as a flamenco dancer, despite having made only one short trip to Spain.

Whether or not the chief of the Bavarian court theatre saw through her, he would not allow her on stage until she managed to wangle an audience with King Ludwig. The 60-year-old was so besotted with this apparently exotic young woman that he insisted she be allowed to dance at the court and Bavarian National Theatre, put her up in a hotel and then in a private apartment in the city centre. The fact that His Majesty's government thought he was being played for a fool was reflected in the fact that her housemaid was a police spy who would later accuse her of taking students into her rooms for sex at night. The accusation came to nothing, although the reality was that she did see other men, mostly careerists wanting a good word put in the royal ear.

Ludwig, who spent most evenings between 5 p.m. and 10 p.m. with her, had her portrait painted for his Schönheits-gallerie (Gallery of Beauty) in the royal summer palace of Nymphenburg, then on the outskirts of the city. In 1847 he gave her a grand house of her own on Bauerstrasse in central Munich. Given that her only identity papers consisted of a travel document issued by the tiny Thuringian principality of Reuss-Ebersdorf, where she had first found her feet in Central Europe, Ludwig insisted that she be granted Bavarian citizenship. The whole of the king's cabinet refused and demanded her dismissal; instead they were dismissed, and Lola was made not only a citizen, but a countess, a series of events that unleashed popular riots.

She seemed to seek out scandals, although for a young woman still in her 20s who had a kingdom to play with, perhaps nowadays it is not so hard to understand. She would lead her dog Turk through the streets of Munich, smoking, and soon assembled a 'bodyguard' of young students, nicknamed *die Lolamannen* (Lola's lads), drawn from the university's *Alemania* fraternity, which thereby incurred the enmity of all the others. Lola soon became involved in a sexual relationship with their leader.

Before long she was sacking professors and lecturers at will, which led to a riot when she was recognised in the street near the university and had to flee for her life. The king ordered the university closed for a term and all students to leave the city within three days. They responded with a mass protest, backed up by the landlords who rented them their rooms. Crucially, the anger at Lola's behaviour in the early months of 1848 corresponded with the wave of popular revolution sweeping the rest of Europe's capitals, including those of the maze of Germany dukedoms, archbishoprics, principalities and kingdoms.

Whether from Ludwig realising his folly or yielding to his ministers, who feared popular revolution and used the 'Spanish dancer' as a pretext, a spectacular U-turn took place: the university reopened the following day, and Lola did a midnight flit to Switzerland. It was not, however, such a clandestine escape that the crowds on the streets of Munich did not turn out to cheer. One of them, Count Maximilian von Arco-Zinneberg, even managed to pick one of her cigar stubs from the gutter, which remains in the Munich City Museum to this day.

A month later on 16 March, Ludwig declared in royal council that she was no longer a Bavarian citizen. A warrant was issued for her arrest. But it was alleged she had secretly returned to the royal boudoir while revolution was stalking the streets, and Ludwig was forced to abdicate in favour of his son, declared Maximilian II.

For the next year Lola lived in Switzerland, writing regularly to the ex-king and receiving regular sums of money in return. In 1849 she moved back to London and married another British officer, only to be charged with bigamy because her first husband, whom she had not bothered to divorce, was still alive. True to form, she fled again. By now the elderly and still besotted Ludwig finally wised up and severed all contact. Lola had still done well out of it. Shortly after her first performance in Munich he had changed his will to grant her a bequest of 100,000 guilders if she remained single after his death, and an annual stipend of a further 2,400 guilders. By 1850 when the relationship came to an end, she had acquired from the royal purse some 158,000 guilders (equivalent to £1.5m today).

Lola made a few brief efforts to revive her Spanish dancing career in France, wrote up her memoirs and finally, in 1855, moved to the USA where she set up a theatre review entitled 'Lola Montez in Bavaria', playing herself, an early example of the principle of being famous for being famous. The review toured the east coast, before being taken west to San

Francisco, where she married again (no awkward questions asked). But within two years she was off again, this time taking her review to Australia. In 1857 she came back to New York, living off her wealth, which she had taken surprisingly good care of, and earned more by reading from her memoirs and writing beauty tips in magazines, even – with remarkable hypocrisy – declaring her self a born-again Christian determined to save the souls of 'fallen women'. But before she could complete a total role reversal, she fell victim to a lung infection and died in 1860 at the age of just 39. She is buried in Green-Wood Cemetery in New York's Brooklyn.

A colourful cameo in Bavarian history, Lola was in her way a leitmotiv for a Central European monarcho-aristocracy that had lost its way, very nearly lost its kingdoms in 1848, and tottered on the brink of irrelevancy. In Bavaria, what came next would confirm that.

The Mad King and His Fairy Palace

The most celebrated – if most ineffectual – ruler in Bavarian history was without doubt King Ludwig II, popularly known as the *Märchenkönig*, 'the fairytale king', whose popularity today, at least as far as the tourist industry goes, exceeds anything in his own lifetime. Ludwig had been given the same name as his grandfather, and the old man, dismayed by the outcome of his ridiculous affair with Montez, doted on his grandchild, showering him with presents. Those loved most by the dreamy little boy, still just a toddler when his grandfather was forced to abdicate, were a set of building blocks, a sort of mid-19th-century German Lego. Being of noble birth, he didn't so much build small houses as grand palaces and monasteries. It was an indication of things to come.

His nanny until the age of seven was one Sybille Meilhaus, to whom he would bear a life-long devotion, far beyond anything he felt for his aloof parents. It turned out to be a classic example of the Jesuit motto, 'give me the child until the age of seven, and I will give you the man'. He and his younger brother Otto would spend much of their time in the chateau at Hohenschwangau, south of Munich, immersed in a world of myths about the deeds of knights of the Middle Ages, all depicted gloriously in the romantic paintings and tapestries with which the castle was decorated. At the age of twelve, he was introduced to Richard Wagner's operas, with their fantastic realms of mythical Germanic history, and the pure knights of *Lohengrin*, *Tannhäuser* and *Parsifal*, and was also a fan of Friedrich Schiller's romantic poetry.

When his father died unexpectedly in 1864, the young, tall, relatively good-looking 18-year-old, with his high forehead and swept back dark curly hair, was immediately proclaimed Ludwig II, by the Grace of God, King of Bavaria, Count Palatinate of the Rhein, Duke of Bavaria, Franconia and in Swabia.

His devotion to the arts was immediately made manifest in the promotion of his beloved Wagner, whose debts he wrote off, and to whom he provided finance for his *Nibelungen* saga. Ludwig did not share Wagner's instinctive anti-Semitism nor did he approve of the composer's attempts to meddle in politics. In 1865 he reluctantly was persuaded to exile his favourite at least temporarily, providing comfortable accommodation for him in Switzerland on Lake Lucerne.

In 1866, the long-foreseen war broke out between Austria and Prussia over which should have pre-eminence among the German states. Bavaria was the third largest state, and alone among the multitude of German statelets to be remotely on a par in size or military strength with the big two. Ludwig's response was to straddle the fence, declaring for neighbouring Austria, but denying them use of the crucial railway that ran through Bavaria to Prague, the Austrian empire's most strategic city in the fight against its northern enemy. Ludwig then left the conduct of the war to his ministers and went off to Switzerland to visit Wagner.

He blamed the defeat, which was to have enormous consequences for any state that called itself 'German' – most
significantly Austria – on his ministers, grumbled about the
reparations he was forced to pay to Prussia, but let his army
from then on be subordinate to the victors, a substantial
renunciation of an independent foreign policy. As if to keep
the balance – which it in no way did – he got engaged in 1867
to Princess Sophie of Austria. He was never to marry her and
throughout his life there were rumours that he suppressed
strong homosexual urges, which he found ran contrary to his
strict Catholic faith.

But Ludwig's head was in the clouds. Literally. All over
Europe at the time, from Balmoral in Scotland to the Pena
Palace towering over Lisbon in Portugal, nobility and monarchy were turning ancient buildings into fairytale versions of
what they thought mediaeval buildings ought to have looked
like. Ludwig chose as the site of his folly a rocky pinnacle
that towered above Hohenschwangau, where he had spent
so much of his childhood listening to his nanny's romantic
tales.

In 1867 he and his brother Otto had been to visit the
recently restored Wartburg Castle near Eisenach, where
Martin Luther had taken shelter from the storm of the religious Reformation he had unleashed. Later that same year
the pair visited Château Pierrefonds in France, which was
being transformed into an imperial palace in mediaeval style
for the Emperor Napoleon III.

Drawings for the palace he envisaged were done by Munich
theatrical artist Christian Jank, guided all along the way by
the young monarch. Together they envisaged a huge mountain-top fortress-cum-fairytale palace, based in its bulk on
the mighty Wartburg, but adorned with towers and turrets,
from which any latter-day Rapunzel might have let down her
hair for some besotted knightly suitor to climb, a tale among
those collected by the Grimm Brothers in 1812 and with
which Ludwig would have been intimately acquainted. The

private living quarters were designed as a replica of the scene setting for Act II of Wagner's *Lohengrin*. Indeed much of the building is a homage to Wagner. Jank had done the drawings and the construction was overseen by architect Eduard Riedel, but in reality the king himself had the last word on every aspect.

Ludwig's choice of location for his fantastical masterpiece of faux-historical architectural eccentricity was well known to him. He and his brother had regularly climbed the paths that led steeply uphill from Hohenschwangau to a ruined fort that dated back to the 15th century, when it had been used as an overnight lodge by his ancestors when out hunting bears.

The steady uphill trek that Ludwig and his brother were so fond of is still the best way to arrive at Neuschwanstein, even if for much of the year it can be something of a route march among the hordes. The alternative is to take one of the horse-drawn carriages, though even they can get packed.

Construction began in 1869 and was supposed to be finished by 1872. But like all *folies de grandeur,* its budget overran terribly, though it was the king's own private pocket that suffered rather than the state's. The last thing Ludwig ever wanted for his fantasy was the future that awaited it: that it would become Germany's biggest tourist destination, visited by over a million tourists a year.

The crowds can be unbearable in high season, and the queues to file through its throne room endless. The interior is splendid, in a mixture of romantic and high baroque style, but there is not a great deal to see, much less than suggested by the vast exterior. The castle was designed not as a building of state, but as a purely private residence, intended for occupation by just the monarch and his retinue. Of the 200 internal rooms, only 15 were ever comprehensively fitted out, and not all of those are permanently open to the public.

The most rewarding vista is to be gained from walking even further up the path to where a little bridge across the ravine provides a literally breathtaking – and, for the queasy, stomach-churning – view of what became Ludwig's monument to himself. He would not long survive his fantasy's completion.

He had never understood Realpolitik. Four years after the debacle of the Austrian–Prussian war, he had, with the other minor German states, joined the victors in conflict with France. With the Prussian-led victory, the future of a 'greater German state' – and the inclusion of all the principalities and minor monarchies except Austria – was a foregone conclusion. The Prussian King Wilhelm I and his powerful chancellor, the East Prussian landowner Otto von Bismarck, knew what they wanted and how to get it.

When Ludwig suggested the imperial crown of the new German Empire might shuffle back and forth between the two larger kingdoms, Bismarck must have spluttered into his moustache. The idea was not preposterous from Ludwig's point of view as it might even have been seen as a return to the idea of a largely symbolic imperial role switching between a loose empire's highest-ranked leaders. But Bismarck was defining a new identity for his Germany along the model of the nation state so beloved of the English and French, and now also being espoused by those equally recently unified city-states and principalities south of the Alps which had begun to call themselves Italian. The Iron Chancellor had not gone to the trouble of expelling the Austrians from the Germanic world in order to share the spoils with the unreliable Bavarians, particularly led by a king with his head in the clouds.

In November 1870, instead of opposing the idea of a single German Kaiser, Ludwig did exactly what Bismarck told him to do: in his position as highest in rank of the remaining non-Prussian German states, he wrote formally to Wilhelm I and offered him on their behalf the imperial crown, a document known to German historians as the *Kaiserbrief* (Emperor letter). Essentially he had been bought. Bismarck used Swiss bank accounts to transfer to Ludwig substantial sums of money, made worse in the eyes of those who knew by the fact that it had largely come from the treasury of George V of Hanover, when his kingdom was seized by Prussia after the war with Austria.

But to Ludwig it was just more money for his private fantasies. In 1873 he bought the Herreninsel on Chiemsee, an island in a lake east of Munich, and in 1878 began the construction of what would be an almost exact, albeit smaller, copy of the Château de Versailles, built for France's Louis XIV, albeit with toilets and running water.

When I first visited Herrenchiemsee two decades ago, I was astounded to see how much it resembled Versailles, including an even larger glittering Hall of Mirrors, a bitter irony given that it was in the original that Wilhelm I had been proclaimed emperor, allegedly at Ludwig's behest. It was indicative of the reluctance with which he had signed the *Kaiserbrief* that he himself had not attended the ceremony. His uncle Luitpold had, more wisely as it was to turn out.

It was not until 1884 that the king was able to set foot in his mock-mediaeval fantasy palace of Neuschwanstein. In the remaining two years of his life, he would spend just 172 days there. In 1886 when he demanded more money from the government, his ministers, well aware that he had lost popular sympathy, commissioned a group of doctors, headed by Bernhard von Gudden of Munich Asylum, who on 8 June, on the basis of second-hand reports of the king's behaviour and without examining him personally, declared him 'mentally disturbed' and unfit to rule. The fact that his younger brother Otto had a dozen years earlier suffered badly from depression and been diagnosed as 'of unsound mind' provided a supposed genetic basis for their decision. The opinion of Ludwig's personal physician, who had looked after his health from childhood and declared their opinion invalid, was ignored. Ludwig was the next day declared deposed. With Otto officially equally unfit to ascend the throne, it was declared that his uncle Luitpold would rule as Prince Regent in his stead. Police were sent to replace the royal guard at Neuschwanstein.

A few days later Ludwig was spirited away from his dream castle in the early hours of the morning and taken to a more modest estate next to Lake Starnberg where he was to be confined. On 13 June, just one day later, Dr Gudden and he went out for an early evening walk in the grounds, unusually without bodyguards or carers. When they had not returned after several hours, a few police were sent out to look for them, and before long there was a whole posse out with flaming torches. Around 10 p.m. the bodies of both men were found floating in the lake some two dozen paces from the shore. Word was put around that the deposed king had drowned, possibly committing suicide, and that his doctor had died trying to prevent him. But the findings of the autopsy were never fully revealed to the public.

Ludwig had never intended nor wanted his palaces to go on show, let alone open their doors to the public, but just six weeks after his death that was exactly what happened. They have since become a prime source of tourist income for Bavaria, a genuine financial legacy left by their most ineffective king.

Whatever part Ludwig's uncle might have played in his downfall, he was certainly the prime benefactor. His regency was confirmed after Ludwig's death by a statement from the chief medical officer that Otto remained seriously mentally ill. Whereas Ludwig and Otto had disliked the austere Prussians, Luitpold had approved of their assumption of the leading role among the German states. Not for nothing had he gone to Versailles for the Kaiser's acclamation while the king and his heir apparent stayed away. He proved to be a stable if rather boring ruler, probably as a result of which his reign was long remembered by many Bavarians as the 'good old days'. Today, however, it is the 'fairytale monarch' he replaced who is the face of the long-gone Bavarian monarchy.

And if Prinzregent Luitpold means anything to most Bavarians it is the fact that his name automatically conjures up the image of a bottle of *dunkles Weissbier*, the dark wheat beer named after him.

Don't Mention the War

Luitpold died in 1912 and was replaced as regent by his son, Ludwig, who also happened to be Otto's cousin and therefore heir to the throne. The following year he proclaimed that as the regency had lasted so long, it was now at an end and assumed the throne himself as Ludwig III. Otto would remain in comfortable seclusion until his death in 1916.

None of it really mattered. The real power had long been in Berlin, the dukes, archdukes, princes and even kings little more than a historical anomaly, with little more power than the aristocracy had in other European countries. And in any case, it was all about to end in tears. The alliance with Prussia's old enemy, Austria, which the new young Kaiser Wilhelm II thought would either expand the power of both, or at worse, if the ramshackle Austro-Hungarian Empire fell apart, would allow him to absorb what he called 'Austria's German provinces', led instead to war and disaster.

By 1917 in Munich and Bavaria, as throughout Germany, opposition to the war was growing. The Social Democrats proposed changing the constitution to that of a purely parliamentary state. On 7 November – just as Berlin was on the verge of signing an armistice which the French and British would turn into an instrument of abject surrender – revolution broke out, and the monarchy was toppled. Bavaria was declared a *Freistaat*, a 'free state', a title it jealously retains to this day.

Throughout Bavaria, workers' councils were set up to run local government. The so-called *Räterepublik* (republic of councils) was widely interpreted as a 'soviet republic' ('soviet' is Russian for 'council'), and foundered on the

Bavarian people's natural conservatism. There was even a fanciful right-wing suggestion that Bavaria leave the German Reich and reinstate a monarchy. The streets of Munich were given over to fights between Communists and right-wing nationalists, many of whom were returned soldiers, horrified to find they had been treated as losers in a war which had effectively ended in stalemate. Some of these joined the paramilitary *Freikorps*. Others were attracted to a small but growing populist party that claimed to espouse both nationalism and the wishes of the working classes, the National Socialist German Workers' Party.

In the summer of 2015 a new building opened in the heart of Munich next to the classical 19th-century folly of the Königsplatz. The new structure is a stylised white cube four storeys high, with windows that are straight panels of glass, horizontal or vertical, letting light in through dark glass. It is both quietly and conspicuously modern, its entrance hall light and airy, its upper galleries uncluttered, the light coming from the windows, the illuminated display cases and the clips of black-and-white newsreel projected onto the internal walls. A building that is and is not of its time.

Simply called the 'NS-Documentation Centre, Munich, centre for learning and remembrance of the history of National Socialism', it is to Germans elsewhere a very belated apology for the scar on Munich's conscience. For, as its founding director Professor Winfried Nerdinger says, 'Munich is linked to the rise of National Socialism as is no other city.'

The location of this brilliant white cube is important: it sits on the site of a relatively unremarkable 19th-century building that once belonged to an English businessman called Richard Barlow, until, in 1930, his son Willy's widow, Elizabeth, sold it to an organisation known as the National Socialist German Workers' Club. Over the course of the following year, the club turned the building into the headquarters of what was now widely known as the Nazi Party, providing offices for Rudolf Hess, Hans Frank and Adolf Hitler among others. It quickly acquired the nickname 'the Brown House'.

The Königsplatz (King's Square) was initially laid out in that early period of artistic flowering under the first King Ludwig. Architect Karl von Fischer was commissioned to create an ensemble that would reflect the heritage of classical culture from the ancient Greeks and Romans, combined with the values of Catholic monarchy, administration and defence – the royal garrison was stationed just a block away – all embedded in green parkland. At its heart was the Propylaea, inspired by the gateway to the Acropolis in Athens and dedicated to Greece's victory in the war of independence, with the names of Greek heroes in that war inscribed inside. The columned temples on either side diverge slightly from 90 degrees to give the impression of greater space and distance. There was no real purpose to the buildings other than a display of architectural prowess and homage to Europe's classical past.

The Nazis decided to give the Königsplatz a purpose. With Hitler's declaration of Munich as the *Hauptstadt der Bewegung* (Capital of the Movement), a title even added to signs at the entrance to the city, the area around the Königsplatz was transformed in 1934 into the national headquarters of the Party, the grand classical buildings a backdrop for militaristic totalitarian propaganda theatre on the grandest scale.

Facing the Propylaea, on either side of the road where Brienner Strasse heads into the city centre, a matching pair of semi-classical temples was erected, in which the bodies of the 16 'martyrs' of the failed 1923 Putsch were interred. These were to become the scene of an almost religious cult where on 9 November every year, the anniversary of the Putsch, vast parades were held and the 'blood of the party' supposedly renewed by all those present as the roll call of the deceased was read out.

The grass that the mock-Greek temples had stood on

– supposed to echo the Athenian idyll of majestic marble structures amid greenery – was replaced with slabs of granite from every corner of the German Reich. What was supposed to have been idyllic became a parade ground.

Two crudely neoclassical buildings were erected, one the national administration office of the Nazi Party, the other Hitler's official residence and office in Munich, the so-called Führerhaus, where the 1938 Munich Declaration, Czechoslovakia's death sentence, was signed by Hitler, British Prime Minister Neville Chamberlain, French President Édouard Daladier and Italian Prime Minister Benito Mussolini. In the documentation centre today, flickering black-and-white film footage of the French and British leaders arriving is projected on the walls, beyond which you can look out the windows at the scene of the crime. One of the bitterest ironies of that desperate, wrong-headed deal which emerged only in 1945 and has latterly been (deliberately?) overlooked was that, had Chamberlain and Daladier not capitulated, the Bavarian-born chief of staff Franz Halder, believing a war with Czechoslovakia at that stage would be disastrous for Germany, had set up a plot to stage a coup against the Nazis and kill Hitler. The Anglo-French concession left him in tears. Halder would argue with Hitler about the conduct of the war he had tried to avoid on numerous occasions and in 1945 he ended up in Dachau concentration camp, but survived and went on to be awarded a medal by the US army for his work as a war historian.

Until the opening of the new museum, Munich's sole significant commemoration of the horrors wrought by the political movement born here was the Platz der Opfer des Nationalsozialismus (Square of the Victims of National Socialism), but in reality not so much a square – and certainly nothing like the vast monument near the Brandenburg Gate in Berlin – as an overlooked grassy corner on the inner ring road, with a small commemorative plaque.

The new documentation centre redresses the balance.

Pride in Bavaria's status as an economic powerhouse in modern Germany – and Europe – is tempered with details of the amount made by the local Munich motorbike manufacturer, BMW, in supplying engines for Luftwaffe aircraft. I looked differently at the label inside my smart wool and sheepskin coat purchased from upmarket Munich retailer Loden-Frey set against their 1938 advertisement proudly proclaiming themselves to be 'official suppliers to the brown soldiers and Hitler Youth', along with another Nazi uniform supplier that has outlived its uncomfortable past: Hugo Boss.

But if there is a new determination to come to terms with the dark side of Munich's past, there is also a recognition that even in its darkest days, the city had its heroes. In particular the Scholl siblings. Hans Scholl joined the Hitler Youth in 1933, but was disillusioned by the experience. Called up to the army, he was allowed leave to pursue his studies at Munich University but was summoned in the holidays to serve as a medical orderly on the eastern front. His experience of the atrocities he witnessed marked him profoundly and when he returned to Munich, he and his sister Sophie founded a resistance group called *Die weisse Rose* (The White Rose). Together with other students they produced leaflets detailing the regime's crimes, including the murder of 300,000 Jews: 'a most dreadful crime against humanity, a crime incomparable with anything else in human history'. They labelled Hitler a 'liar and betrayer of Europe's youth', called for sabotage and a general uprising against the Nazi regime. It was when distributing the last of their six leaflets, following the catastrophic defeat at Stalingrad, which most of the public knew little about, that they were caught red-handed, arrested and summarily executed. He was 25 years old, his sister 22.

The Königsplatz today is still a regular scene of mass rallies, but instead of brown-shirted party members or armed troops it is more likely to see giant stages raised for opera, jazz or blues concerts, giant screens for outdoor movie-watching or football matches. The slabs of granite are gone, the grass has been restored and on lazy sunny summer afternoons it is littered with sunbathing students from Hans and Sophia Scholl's university. There is a memorial to the pair outside the university's main building in the form of a white rose, made up of the flysheets they died for distributing. One of the halls of residence is named after them.

The 'temples to the martyrs' were blown up by the American occupation forces, who curiously, however, chose to preserve the Führerhaus, renaming it the Amerika-Haus, and turning it into a centre for German-American cultural links. It is today a music school.

Bavaria's relics of the Nazi regime include at least two other notable sites. One is the so-called Eagle's Nest, in reality a mountain-top tea house above Hitler's Berghof country house near the spa town of Badgodesberg on the border with Austria. It was built for the Führer for his 50th birthday by his aide Martin Bormann, who had purchased an area of 10,000 square metres in the area and expelled all residents save for himself, Hitler, a few other senior Nazis and a private army of 2,000 soldiers. British Prime Minister Neville Chamberlain visited in 1938 while in Munich for the fateful agreement which dismembered Czechoslovakia.

The little tea house sits atop the Obersalzberg mountain, itself 1,834 metres (6,017 ft) above sea level, with majestic sweeping views over the beautiful Alpine landscape. Hitler himself, to Bormann's chagrin, only visited the tea house a couple of times, being both claustrophobic – he didn't like the lift up – and averse to the rarified air at the summit. His mistress and eventual wife Eva Braun, however, was extremely fond of it. It is today owned by an Alpine charity, open to the public in the summer months, and home to a restaurant and shop. There is little reference to its past save for a photograph of Eva Braun sunbathing and a slightly damaged fireplace donated by Mussolini. But it is well worth visiting if only for the spectacular views and the experience of getting there up a mountain road and finally in a 124-metre (380 ft) burnished golden brass elevator worthy of Donald Trump.

The other is a city just a few hours up the autobahn. Nürnberg may not have been the birthplace of Nazism, nor its headquarters, but it became its party city, and its burial ground. This is where they sentenced the criminals to death in the war crimes trials of 1945–6. Nürnberg had been one of the prettiest cities in Germany: the real 'toytown', with wooden-beamed houses along narrow streets, and a towering castle, a treasure of mediaeval and Renaissance architecture. The Nazis besmirched its name forever. After Hitler came to power in 1933, the decision was taken to hold mammoth rallies each year at a central location in Germany. Nürnberg fitted the bill and also had a suitable venue, a great exhibition area named after the late Prinzregent Luitpold. Under the charge of Hitler's favourite architect Albert Speer, the whole area was paved and turned into a vast parade ground.

Leni Riefenstahl's momentous masterpiece, *Triumph des Willens* (Triumph of the Will) – beginning as it does with Adolf Hitler 'descending, like a god, from the heavens', perhaps the most successful ever political advertisement for air travel – documented the 1934 Nazi Party Congress in an overlong but majestic paean of propaganda for the Führer's evil empire. My late friend Bob Tilley, the *Daily Telegraph* Munich correspondent, knew Riefenstahl and admired her all his life, insisting she was just an artist who did what she did with raw material without even thinking about the content.

Nürnberg paid for its fame, first by the hail of bombs that destroyed most of its ancient heart, secondly as the fitting scene of the trial that saw the worst Nazi criminals sentenced to death. The parade grounds, where those colossal, impressive and terrifying rallies took place, today look like nothing so much as an abandoned concrete wasteland with no vestiges of grandeur and barely a suggestion of what it must have been like when filled with regimented masses. It reminds me most of a swathe of downtown Buffalo, Ohio, where there were once buildings but is now a bleak, under-used car park.

The Godfather

Post-war Bavaria came with its own saviour all but ready-made. Franz-Josef Strauss was a man of remarkable charisma, born in 1915 during the famine of World War I and who in World War II served in both a tank regiment in Ukraine and anti-aircraft battery south of Munich, but with his military career frequently interrupted by academia.

Taken prisoner of war in 1945, he was declared free of Nazi links and at the age of 29 first installed by the American occupation as a local politician, then confirmed by election. He rapidly became involved in the founding of the new Christian Social Union (CSU), set up as a moderate, right-of-centre democratic party at a time when similar new parties were being established all across a Germany in shocked recovery from the dictatorship and defeat. By 1950 all the other parties based on 'Christian conservative' principles had come together as the Christian Democratic Union (CDU) to campaign nationally. The CSU did not. There is a saying in the rest of Germany that '*In Bayern gehen die Uhren anders*' (In Bavaria the clocks work differently) and the natives do not deny it, to the extent that the public clock on the Isartor (Isar Gate) in Munich's old town has hands which revolve backwards. The CSU to this day, while allied to the CDU, campaigns only in Bavaria.

Strauss quickly rose through the ranks, was elected to the new national parliament, the Bundestag, and in 1953 became a minister in post-war leader Konrad Adenauer's government, and over his career would be put in charge of nuclear power, defence and finance. In opposition he opposed Social Democrat Chancellor Willy Brandt's policy of reconciliation with the Soviet bloc, angry at the enduring partition of Germany.

He bestrode German politics for four decades, was prime minister of Bavaria for ten years, and despite being implicated in several scandals involving defence procurement and relations with the East German regime, and an unsuccessful bid for the West German chancellorship, when he died in 1988 he was given a state funeral. I recall watching the crowds of thousands who filed past his body laid in state in Munich's Marstall, the former royal riding school. As his funeral procession passed along Ludwigstrasse, the city's grand ceremonial avenue, the peculiar nature of Bavaria's history as an independent country and a state within a state was on full view. Mass was said by Cardinal Joseph Ratzinger, later Pope Benedict XVI. The 100,000 mourners came not just from Germany and Austria but in particular the Italian province of Alto Adige, also known as Südtirol (South Tyrol), the once Bavarian and then Austrian chunk of the Alps where more than two-thirds of the population speak German, with a Bavarian-Tyrollean accent, and who had looked to Strauss as their protector. They turned up in droves in traditional *Trachten* and doffed their feathered hats as Strauss's body passed by. Munich's airport, Germany's second biggest transport hub after Frankfurt, is named after him.

The other great totem of post-war Munich is the ascent of its most famous football team, Bayern München – the Manchester United of Germany, the country's continuously most successful team, an almost permanent fixture in Europe's top ten clubs. But then the German love of football and success in playing it deserves a chapter all of its own.

Apart from beer and football there is, of course, one huge industry that keeps Bavaria on the global stage in the 21st century: motor vehicles. Halfway between Munich and Nürnberg is the ancient city of Ingolstadt, where Mary Shelley set the laboratory in which her fictional Dr Frankenstein created his monster, but which today is home to a manufacturing monster of another sort: Audi. In common with all upmarket German car makers today, BMW has its own museum of the company's history, showing off the giant robotic machines used to manufacture their vehicles.

But undoubtedly the prime motoring museum/exhibition is the colossal BMW-World next to the four-cylinder sky-scraper of the company's headquarters which towers above the Olympiapark in northern Munich, which thanks to the logic of modern business takeovers also has a fine collection of Rolls-Royces.

Not always known to purchasers, the pale blue and white diamonds on the BMW logo are taken from the 'national' flag, the one followed down the centuries by Bavarian troops whether at war with French, Prussians, Austrians or others, but also on napkins spread out on picnic tables and rosettes sold at the Oktoberfest. In the minds of the people it reflects the summer skies over the beer gardens of Munich, with fleecy clouds in a bright blue sky: *ein bayrischer Himmel,* Bavarian heaven. With somewhere up there, a genial white-bearded God. Wearing Lederhosen.

The Germans and Beer

In Munich they quip that if beer is the national religion, then the city's beer gardens are places of worship. Bavaria has almost a monopoly on the global image of German beers, but in fact, the Oktoberfest notwithstanding, Germany has a vast array of beers, differing beer styles and beer drinkers: some regional, some national, some just plain quirky, and the same goes for the places they are drunk and the people who drink them.

In Germany, as in Britain, the 'pub' is the place where people go to relax, to chat to their friends, to meet new friends, to hold celebrations and on occasion to carouse late into the night (certainly later than is possible in most of Britain).

The most formal word is *Gaststätte*, which means basically any establishment serving food and drink to paying guests. It might also be called, particularly in the south, a *Wirtshaus,* literally a 'landlord's house', which invariably means its prime purpose is the purveyance of alcohol, but also a *Kneipe,* a 'boozer', in Berlin almost invariably a corner bar.

It was thanks to the institution of the corner bar in the dark days of the DDR, when everybody mistrusted everybody else unless they were a lifelong friend, that I managed to get beneath the thick skin of East Berlin society in the bar that would become my local and source of much first-hand information about life under Communism, eventually gaining access to the holy of holies, the *Stammtisch*.

The *Stammtisch*, regular's table, is a feature of every German pub, even if only in Munich they wear Lederhosen. But drinking beer in Germany is not just a social thing, it is an intrinsic part of the culture, indeed almost literally part of religion, given that the earliest recorded brewers were monks, with a history of beer production that dates back to at least the eleventh century. Not that there weren't brewers before. Tacitus, writing in the first century AD, noted that 'their drink is a liquor prepared from barley or wheat brought by fermentation to a certain resemblance of wine' and that they were fond of 'convivial parties, in which it is no disgrace to pass days and nights, without intermission, in drinking'. His contemporary Pliny noted 'the western nations have their intoxicating liquor, made of steeped grain. The Egyptians also invented drinks of the same kind. Thus drunkenness is a stranger in no part of the world; for these liquors are taken pure, and not diluted as wine is.'

Throughout Germany, although particularly in Bavaria, beer is virtually considered a foodstuff rather than a luxury. In contrast to the British fondness for going out of an evening with the deliberate aim of drinking to excess, many male Müncheners consider it normal to have a *kleines Helles* from time to time throughout the day just to ease life along a bit. The fact that this may continue into the evening is neither here not there.

Although the legal age for drinking spirits in Germany is 18, for beer it is 16. I remember fondly the look of amazement on my son's face when not long after his 16th birthday, sitting at the Chinesischer Turm beer garden in Munich, I asked him if he'd like a *Mass* of his own, rather than sipping shyly from mine. He nodded, surreptitiously, as if we were keeping a secret, then stared at me with a look of classic teenage sceptical incredulity when I told him it was legal to go and buy one. I had to give him the money, of course, but I still savour the look of proud proto-adulthood on his face when he came back clutching two one-litre *Krüge* of foaming *Helles*.

The dominance of Bavaria in the history of German beer is not just down to the Oktoberfest, but to one of the world's most famous and oldest consumer protection laws, the Purity Law (sometimes with the adjective 'German' or 'Bavarian' attached to it). The *Reinheitsgebot* was an edict of Bavaria's Duke Wilhelm IV at a meeting of the *Landtag* (state parliament) in Ingolstadt on 23 April 1516, declaring that beer could consist only of malted barley, hops and water, later amended to allow wheat. People often ask why there is no mention in the original of yeast, without which beer would hardly become beer. The answer is simply that back in 1516, the brewers had little idea how yeast worked, seldom added it themselves but simply allowed natural yeasts from the air to do the magic for them (as indeed is still the tradition among Belgian brewers of such speciality beers as *gueuze* and *lambic*).

The title made clear its purpose: 'How beer is to be brewed and served in summer and winter in the country.' The rules were clear: 'We desire in particular that nothing other than barley, hops and water should be included and used.' It added that 'anyone who deliberately breaches this ordnance or fails to obey it should have every relevant barrel of beer confiscated by a magistrate.'

It also laid down a strict codes of weights and measures, albeit with allowance for seasonal variation: a *Mass,* a measure remarkably close to one litre today, was to be served for 'not more than one Pfennig in summer and two Pfennigs in winter'.

The most common mistake made by non-germanophone beer-drinkers is to think that what they produce is all – or even mostly – 'lager'. True, the word *Lager* is of German origin, meaning 'storage area', but its use as a form of beer is of purely English origin. To a German-speaker *Lagerbier* is beer that has been *gelagert,* in other words stored by the brewery until it is ready to be drunk.

The standard Munich beer is a *Helles,* meaning 'light' in colour, although there is also a *Dunkles,* meaning 'dark'. Both have an average alcohol content of 5 per cent ABV and are served in either half-litre or, particularly *Helles* in summer in the beer gardens, in litre tankards known as a *Masskrug* (*Mass* being the litre measure, *Krug* being the container). In

Bavaria this beer is consumed with nearly all meals, and often in between. This is the beer quaffed in quantity at the world's most famous orgy of beer consumption, the Munich Oktoberfest – where it comes in a strong 6.7 per cent ABV variety – but it is in no way the most popular beer drunk in Germany.

It may be no surprise that Germany is one of the world's largest beer-consuming countries with an average of 106.1 litres per year for every man, woman and child (though I suspect some of them are not doing their share). But this puts it only in third place, marginally behind the neighbouring Austrians (107.8) and far behind the Czechs (148.6).

Not surprising then, that the most widely drunk beer style in Germany is one that has its origins in what is now the Czech Republic, but a century and a half ago was the partly Czech- and partly German-speaking province of Bohemia in the Austro-Hungarian empire. Beer from the town of Plzen (Pilsen in German) had acquired such a bad reputation that in 1842 a German brewer called Josef Groll was brought in to fix it. Groll devised a method of long, slow bottom-fermented brewing whereby the beer was stored (*gelagert*) in cool caves and cellars. The new beer, known as Pilsner Urquell (literally: 'from the original source') had more hops than the widely drunk Bavarian beers and as a result a drier, bitter taste. It quickly caught on and when mechanical cooling equipment became common in the 1870s, slowly began the process of winning over most German tastebuds.

A Pils can be drunk in many measures, although the most common are 25 cl or 33 cl and the largest is 0.5 l (which the litre-loving Bavarians, who still prefer large quantities of their traditional *Helles*, call *eine Halbe*, 'a half'). The prime difference between *Helles* and Pils is still that the Bavarian tipple lacks that telltale bitterness. For those of us whose cultural home in Germany is Berlin, a *Mass* of *Helles* in a summer Munich beer garden is a great thirst-quencher, but after a while we begin to hanker after the distinctive hoppiness of a Berliner Pilsner.

Berlin, however, has a particular curiosity all of its own, *Berliner Weisse*, at one stage in danger of vanishing all together until reunification in 1990 reawakened interest in all things to do with the once and future capital. Quite frankly, it is like no other beer you've ever tasted, or was until eager experimenters began to produce imitations on the London craft beer scene around 2012. It is also served unlike any other beer you've ever ordered.

First of all, it is sour. Not the sour that's just 'gone off', but deliberately, jarringly, eye-wateringly sour – like a Haribo sour gummy candy – for which reason it is often served with a *Schuss* (shot) of sweet syrup, traditionally either *rot*, red, flavoured with raspberry (*Himbeer*) or *grün*, green, flavoured with the herb called *Waldmeister* (sweet woodruff). Those of us who consider ourselves purists savour the unadulterated sour bitterness for itself (in my case because I first came across it in East Berlin in the 1980s, and due to the inefficiency of the Communist market, the sweet syrups were almost never available).

Berliner Weisse is served in a large – almost preposterously so – stemmed bowl of a glass, more like a fruit bowl than something to drink beer out of. The syrup, if used, is poured in first and then the beer poured in after to create a foamy crown that fills the glass to the brim. It is officially labelled a *Schankbier*, 'not a full beer', much weaker than the German 5 per cent average. It usually comes in at around 2.8 per cent ABV and is at its very best drunk on a hot summer's day. Berliners will often knock back a Schnapps with it, just to keep the alcohol level up.

It is crucial not to confuse *Berliner Weisse* with a much more common drink usually referred to in Bavaria as *Weissbier*, which literally means 'white beer' even though a deep brown *dunkles Weissbier* (dark white beer!) is also available. *Weissbier* is a *Vollbier* (full beer), which means that it has the relatively standard alcohol content of around 5 per cent. In fact the 'white' (*weiss*) has nothing to do with the colour, but is a corruption of *Weizen* (wheat), which is what it is made with, rather than barley. And almost everywhere else in Germany it is referred to as *Weizenbier.*

But despite the efforts of new craft brewers coming onto the scene as far away as Hamburg, where you now enjoy a 'Hanseatic *Weizen*', there is no realistic denying that *Weizenbier* is Bavarian in origin, though the brewing of it has travelled widely (including to Flanders and the Netherlands, where – bizarrely – they brought the Bavarian confusion with the beer, continuing to call it *Witbier,* white beer). The popularity of Alpine skiing holidays has also spread a taste for this effervescent brew more widely across Europe.

Wheat beer's history in Bavaria is as old as barley-based beers, ancient indeed given that Bavaria's Weihenstephan brewery – which produces an excellent *Weissbier* – claims a thousand-year tradition. Situated on the outskirts of the town of Freising, near Munich airport, and now owned by the Bavarian state, beer has been brewed continuously on the site since monks there were granted a licence in 1040.

The popularity of *Weizenbier* over the centuries has been such that in 1567 the Duke of Bavaria banned it because so much wheat was being used, there was not enough left to make bread. The ban was gradually lifted, though initially just for the court brewery, which until the mid-18th century reserved the profitable business for itself.

Today *Weizenbier* can be had on draught, a very recent innovation since the mid-1990s. It was originally available only in bottles because of its high effervescence. Pouring it is an art in itself. Ideally the tall glass, tapering towards the bottom, and bottle should both be tilted towards one another, the beer poured slowly to prevent too rapid a build-up of froth – it is acceptable to set it down for a bit to let the froth settle, though practised barmen and fans can do it in one – before tipping the rest of the bottle in to form a rich white head.

Weizenbier is naturally cloudy, which is why it is sometimes referred to as *Hefeweizen* (yeast wheat beer). Some breweries do also produce a clear (*Kristall*) version, but among connoisseurs it is considered to be not quite the proper thing. The fad for putting a slice of lemon in is also regarded as anathema.

The undisputed heavyweight champion in the world of *Weissbier/Weizenbier* is the delicious but intimidating Aventinus brewed by Schneiders Weisses Bräuhaus in Tal, a street in central Munich, which has a knockout strength of 8.5 per cent ABV. Schneiders is possibly the only brewery to make nothing but *Weissbier*. I was introduced to Aventinus back in the 1980s by my Somerset-born *Daily Telegraph* colleague Bob Tilley, who suggested we had a few one autumn afternoon, without telling me how strong it was. I remember little more about that afternoon, except thinking how very apt it was that Bob spoke German with an English West Country accent, which was rather how the Austrian-born Adolf Hitler sounded to 1930s Berliners, who as a result only took him seriously when it was too late.

Apart from the legendary Aventinus, the more common strong beer is known as *Bockbier*, the name given to beers of around 7 per cent ABV, traditionally brewed around the middle of March. *Bockbier* too is mostly produced in Bavaria, but strangely its name comes from somewhere else altogether: the small town of Einbeck near Hanover in Lower Saxony. As early as the 16th century a strong beer from there was being imported regularly into its southern neighbour, where it soon found favour with the great and good, including the holy: monks in particular, already masters of brewing, took to the strong beer as a supplement to their spartan diets, and particularly during fasting periods when they were denied all sorts of protein-containing nourishment but could drink as much beer as they could brew.

Over time and under the influence of the strong Bavarian accent, Einbeck-style beer became known as *Einpockiges Bier* which eventually mutated and shortened to *Bockbier*.

The origin became further lost when, to indicate that their beer was in this style, many brewers decided to illustrate bottle labels with a picture of a male goat, which in German is *ein Bock*.

The Munich *Bockbiers* have names that traditionally end in *-ator*, a custom with a curious history of its own. Back in the 17th century, with Germany and most of Central Europe in the throes of the Thirty Years War, the monks of the order of St Francis of Paola brewed a beer in honour of their founder and called it *Sankt-Vaters-Bier* (Holy Father's Beer). Over time this got shortened to *Salvator*, still brewed by Paulaner today, and other breweries who had jumped on the popular *Starkbier* bandwagon decided to copy it, designating their own strong brews with names such as *Triumphator, Optimator*, and, inevitably, *Terminator*.

The Bavarian *Starkbierzeit* traditionally kicks off with a launch party, nowadays often including satirical political sketches at the Paulaner beer garden at Nockherberg in the Munich district of Au. The beers are brewed and drunk over a two-week period, but also make a return at the end of May, when they are known as *Maibock*. Most of these early year *Bockbiers* are pale in colour, but towards Christmas the style makes a return in wintry guise as a *Festbock,* nearly always dark and warming, not unlike the English tradition of the dark, strong 'winter warmer'.

Germany's great Rhineland metropolis, Cologne, home of the country's Karneval, a party fit to rival those in Venice or Rio, obviously has a beer of its own. *Kölsch,* from the German name for the city, Köln, is a light-coloured beer with a fine aroma, exclusively served in – by Bavarian standards – tiny 0.2 l straight, narrow glasses. No need for the thirsty to panic too much for in most *Gaststätten* there is usually a waiter to hand with a round tray hanging from a central handle, ready to replace empty glasses with full ones.

It is drunk ubiquitously in the city and surrounding area, the only parts of Germany in which is is brewed, but not much anywhere else. I used to find it the least attractive of beer styles, a tad too thin in taste, a beer made to be drunk in the Rhineland, where the main tipple is wine. But I would not say that readily to a Rhinelander. And I would not say it myself after attending Karneval for the first time in 2016, when the custom of having a fresh beer every few minutes soon grows on you, like Karneval spirit. I also came to appreciate the subtle differences in the hopping of the 20 varieties made in the city and nowhere else.

Its counterpart, from just up the Rhine, is *Alt*. Literally 'old', this is to Düsseldorf what *Kölsch* is to Cologne. *Alt* is served in the same glasses as *Kölsch,* but easy to distinguish because it is exclusively dark. The toasted malt gives it a rather herby bitterness, and it is much loved locally, again being brewed almost exclusively in the Lower Rhineland, and is popular in many towns in the area, with the exception of Cologne, where the locals affect to dislike it, explicitly because it comes from Düsseldorf.

In Germany of late there has been concern that beer consumption is dropping in favour of wine, not just the excellent and internationally underrated whites from the vineyards of the Rhine and Mosel, but a widespread and growing appreciation of fine French, Spanish and Italian reds which, despite a few brave efforts, Germany's own northern vineyards are incapable of approaching.

But there is also blame to attach to the very success of German beers internationally, the corrupting influence of globalisation and the huge sums to be made from selling worldwide. Bigger brewers almost invariably become blander brewers.

The worst villain is beyond question Beck's, which has built up an international reputation on the back of probably Germany's most insipid and tasteless beer. Beck's is Germany's equivalent of the Dutch Heineken: it owes its global success to marketing, takeovers and the dumbed down tastebuds of people who drink beer out of bottles, usually for the alcohol rather than the flavour. Other large brewers, such as Warsteiner and Radeberger, the latter a once rare and sought-after beer that was the pride of old East Germany, despite having masses more flavour and style, are in danger of going the same way as the demands of globalisation dull their individuality.

At the other end of the spectrum, the small but beautiful town of Bamberg in Franconia, north Bavaria, is a prime example of local brewers who continue to prefer to brew local beer in local style for local customers, and if they sell their wares elsewhere do so almost out of embarrassment rather than greed. There are at least a dozen independent brewers thriving in Bamberg, the most famous of them the town centre brewpub which produces the highly individual, almost idiosyncratic – and unpronounceable to non-German-speakers – *Schlenkerla Rauchbier*, a dark, rich, smoky, porter-style beer, which might best, though poorly, be described as a pint of Guinness smoked gently for several hours alongside an aged Spanish ham.

Elsewhere there are also signs that, as in the USA and the UK – and with more than a nod to what has become known as the 'craft beer' movement – small independent brewers are springing up and challenging the establishment, forcing it to respond.

In Hamburg, once home to more than 600 breweries and known as the 'brewhouse of the Hanseatic League', the number dwindled dramatically until in the past few decades most of the local breweries not only in the harbour city itself but in nearby Bremen, Braunschweig, Lübz and as far afield as Duisburg, were being bought up by local giant Holsten which in turn succumbed to that other giant of tasteless international lager, Carlsberg, based just across the border in Denmark. In response, a handful of bright new entrepreneurs have begun turning out individual beers that owe little to the Bud-Beck's-Carlsberg-Heineken blandness. Down by the quayside, in the midst of the Sunday morning fish market, entrepreneur Eugen Block set up a new brewery in a landmark harbour building, renamed it the Blockhaus, and began turning out a delicious pale, unfiltered version of Pils, and a Hanseatic *Weizen*.

On the Adolphus Bridge between the inner and outer Alster lakes, the Johannes Albrecht Bräuhaus turns out its own, again unfiltered style called Messing, along with a copper-coloured hoppy ale unsurprisingly called *Kupfer* (copper).

The Altes Mädchen in the heart of the trade fair district is home to an extremely successful and growing micro-brewery called Ratsherrn, which produces a fruity, hoppy Anglo-American style Pale Ale and India Pale Ale, as well as a 'Hamburg *Weissbier*' and a *Zwick'l*, an old German term for an unfiltered beer, as still produced in small quantities by the Munich giant Paulaner as well as the Austrian mega-brewer Stiegel.

Meanwhile, the Gröninger Bräuhaus, in superb cellars stretching underneath probably Hamburg's best preserved early 18th-century houses, turns out a delicious medium-dark beer oozing with toasty flavour. They insist on calling it a Pils, for no discernible reason that I can deduce other than the public familiarity with the name – and perhaps the lack of an alternative – that is surely ancient in both style and flavour.

Even cosmopolitan Frankfurt, with its high-rise business towers and dedication to the bland world of global finance, has its own craft beer growth industry showcased by the bar NAIV, which cooperates with an independent brewer to produce and sell an organic *Landbier*, an American-style Pale Ale, and a dark rich *Kellerbier*.

Meanwhile in Munich itself, the ancient Schneider's Weisse Bräuhaus, the self-styled home of *Weizenbier*, and producer of Aventinus, now regularly serves up half a dozen variants, including a low-alcohol version, a high-hopped version and an organic version. But the most high-flying recent arrival – now nearly a decade ago – on the Munich scene is the resourceful Airbräu micro, which sits, with its brewpub and beer garden, elegantly and usefully between terminals one and two at Munich's Franz Josef Strauss international airport. Initially it produced just its own versions of Munich's specialities: an unfiltered *Helles*, called *Fliegerquelle* (flyer's source) and, of course, its own *Weissbier*, called *Kumulus* (it is after all suitably cloudy). Now it has developed its own seasonal specialities, each of course given their own air travel related names, from *Aviator* for its Easter Bockbier and a late spring wheat beer called *Mayday*, not perhaps the last thing you want to knock back before stepping on a plane. As Dieter, long-time barman at my old East Berlin local, would always say when it got to the philosphical hour of the night, staring admiringly at his perfectly poured little 25 cl glass of pale golden Pils: '*Nix geht über ein Bierchen.*' You just can't beat a beer. I'll drink to that. *Prost*!

5

Vienna

How one family nearly took over the world and lost Germany as a result

The Last Empress

One dark, wet, dreary afternoon in the spring of 1989, as the world we had known for more than four decades was beginning to fall apart, I attended a funeral in the heart of Vienna that marked the final death rattle of an even earlier epoch and was in its own way every bit as historic as the events about to rock Europe.

The funeral service was attended by 8,000, a further 20,000 braved the frightful weather to line the Vienna streets, and in the days beforehand some 200,000 had filed past the coffin. The mourners included princes of Belgium, Monaco, Morocco and Jordan.

The deceased was an old lady of 96, a widow for most of her long life, who had lived for many years in the clement climate of the Portuguese island of Madeira. Born to a Portuguese mother and an Italian father, she had been christened Zita Maria delle Grazie Adelgonda Micaela Raffaela Gabriela Giuseppina Antonia Luisa Agnese. The 17th child of the Duke of Parma, already dispossessed of his dukedom during the unification of Italy, she would grow up to become Empress of Austria, Queen of Hungary and of Bohemia,

Dalmatia and Croatia, Grand Duchess of Cracow and Tuscany, and at least nominally, Queen of Jerusalem, before losing the man she loved, who had bestowed the titles on her.

Her future had seemed less imperial and ultimately less tragic, if grand enough, on her marriage to the Archduke Karl of Austria in 1911. It was only with the assassination of his uncle, the Archduke Franz Ferdinand in Sarajevo in 1914, that her husband became heir to the vast but crumbling Habsburg empire. In 1916, when the old emperor Franz Josef died, Karl inherited his multiple thrones. But in the midst of a war that was already going the wrong way he only managed one coronation ceremony, as King of Hungary, photographed for posterity with his wife at his side and their three-year-old, blond, curly-haired son Otto dressed in ermine between them. Two years later, the empire was no more; the imperial family, including their eight children, became refugees overnight, first in Switzerland before finding their way to Madeira in 1921. Karl died a year later, after contracting bronchitis while out buying toys for his children.

The weather on the day of the old empress's funeral was foul, yet spectacularly suited to the macabre theatre of the event. During the service itself I sat in a hotel overlooking the Stephansdom, Vienna's great 14th-century Gothic cathedral, with its soaring spire and extraordinary blue, white, yellow and green zigzag-tiled roof slick with rain. Water flowed like Hollywood tears down the mosaic of the Habsburg dynasty's double-headed eagles as the amplified voices from inside the cathedral sang the 1854 version of the old imperial anthem: *Gott erhalte, Gott beschütze unser'n Kaiser, unser Land* (God save, God protect our emperor, our country). The melody, originally composed by Joseph Haydn in 1797 in honour of Emperor Franz II and used until 1918, confused more than a few of the watching press, given that since 1922 it has been that of the German national anthem, still known to the unenlightened as *Deutschland, Deutschland über Alles*, a song originally dedicated not to global superiority but to the basic idea of having any sort of country called 'Germany' rather then more than a hundred tiny statelets.

In the cobbled streets round about, standing stiffly to attention in the pouring rain, were troops of armed men. Their weapons were muskets, halberds and swords, their headgear drooping feathered hats, the antiquated uniform of members of the *Burschenschaften,* semi-paramilitary organisations with their origins in university societies, a romantic Germanic equivalent of Oxford's Bullingdon Club or American fraternity boys. Alongside them lined up groups of hunting society members in knee britches with broad-brimmed hats and capes – unexpectedly practical given the weather.

It seemed to a cynical journalist's eye as if anyone with a fancy dress costume in the back of their wardrobe and a feasible excuse for carrying a weapon in public had got them out and come to stand guard in the rain in honour of an old lady and a lost world. Some wore the black-and-yellow colours of the old empire, lapels embroidered with the letters 'KuK' (*Kaiserlich und Königlich* – 'imperial and royal', for the Habsburg dual monarchs were emperors of Austria but kings in Hungary). Others wore the colours of neighbouring Bavaria, and more than a few those of Austria's long-lost province of South Tyrol, handed by Britain and France to Italy in 1918 as a reward for switching sides in a betrayal of its former ally.

As the mourners emerged from the cathedral and lined up behind the hearse I had the surreal impression of watching a cross between Disney's 1937 cartoon *Snow White* and a 1970s Hammer Horror Film. I was all too aware that, in accordance with her wishes and family tradition, the empress's heart had already been cut out of her corpse and interred at a monastery in Switzerland next to that of her husband. The procession moved slowly over the rain-soaked cobbles towards the ancient family crypt beneath the Kapuzinerkirche, Church of the Capuchin Friars, the body carried in a black hearse, the same carriage that had carried the

body of Emperor Franz Josef in 1916, pulled by black horses
with black plumes on their heads. All of a sudden, the iron-
rimmed wheels slipped. Behind the glass windows, the coffin
slid backwards. For one moment of exquisite tragi-comic
horror I feared it would hurtle out, hit the chief mourner,
Otto, the curly-haired toddler, by then an old man of 79,
and crash onto the cobbles spilling the ex-empress's mortal
remains onto the slick stones of Vienna.

It was, after all, April Fool's Day.

But the horses were up to the occasion, and found their
footing. Zita – or at least most of her – was interred in
the tomb of her husband's ancestors. It was a strange but
somehow fitting farewell to an old world order. Just a few
months later her elderly son, Otto, a member of the European Parliament for a German constituency, would mark
the beginning of the end of a new version of the old European order, hosting a 'Pan-European Picnic' at the frontier
between Austria and Hungary. To mark a moment of nostalgia, and a symbol of rapprochement between two small
nations that had once jointly ruled a huge empire, but had for
decades been on opposite sides of an Iron Curtain, the frontier was opened. The opportunity was immediately seized
by hundreds of East Germans holidaying in their repressive
government's supposedly loyal Communist ally to flee to the
west, the beginning of a flood that would end with the fall of
the Berlin Wall and the end of the Cold War.

Happy Families: the Rise of the Habsburgs

Including Austria in a history of Germany is nowadays
seen as less than politically correct, as if trying to recreate the Nazi *Anschluss,* by linking a little Alpine republic
with a complex and confusing history on the world stage
to the larger, modern nation-state to the north, even if for
the few years between 1938 and 1945 they were united. Austrians themselves, in particular the Viennese, so close to

the Hungarian border and with a long history of Central European multiculturalism, insist on the difference, and even joke that some foreigners are surprised to find they speak German. After 1945 the new rulers of the revived republic made a big thing of having been 'Nazi Germany's first victim', overlooking the crowds who lined the streets to welcome the 'German invaders', encouraging an act of voluntary collective amnesia.

Prior to 1871 there had never been such a thing as a pan-German nation-state. Germany was just a geographical expression. Were it not for the result of a battle only five years earlier, the nation-state that emerged might have been upside-down, with Vienna rather than Berlin its capital. Prussia with its far northeastern borderlands could have been the state excluded from what people would come to call Germany. The country we describe with that name today has seen its borders changed time and again from 1871. The 'Germany' that people refer to as if it has existed from time immemorial goes no further back than 3 October 1990.

For centuries, during which allegiances of those who spoke Germanic languages – or almost any language in Europe – were owed not to nations but to princes, dukes and archdukes, the Habsburg family had been predominant among those families. The Habsburg capital, Vienna, was as important – if not more so – in the constellation of German cities as Munich, Cologne, Frankfurt and certainly vastly more than tiny, insignificant Berlin. Vienna's position, in the southeast corner of the German-speaking world, was – and is – no more out on a limb than that of Berlin in the northeast of Germany today. In contrast to the Habsburgs, the Hohenzollerns, the dynasty who would eventually create the 'Reich' which even when it came into being in 1871 was considered to be a 'small Germany' solution – *Kleindeutschland* – minus Austria.

Austria's eventual exclusion from the late 19th-century

nation-state that would call itself the *Deutsches Reich* and, a tempestuous century later, become the Federal Republic of Germany we are familiar with in the early 21st, was not caused by a lack of ambition or success in Europe's game of thrones. It came rather from too much, too soon. Austria's dramatic rise and fall would result from the ambition of one family, who would come to rule nearly half a continent and at one stage half the world, before their realm was reduced to a tiny mountain republic and they themselves to wandering exiles. It was one of the Habsburgs' earliest rivals, Matthias Corvinus, the 15th-century King of Hungary, who coined the expression by which the family's success would be seen by the rest of the world: *Bella gerant allii; tu, felix Austria, nube* – Let others wage war; you, happy Austria, marry!

Matthias himself had created a Central European multi-ethnic state which at one stage threatened to seize the German-speaking lands the Habsburgs called home, a region that since the days of Charlemagne had been known as the 'eastern march' of his Frankish empire: *Ostarrichi,* in the oldest reference dating from the tenth century, not so very different from today's *Österreich.* As so often, its Latinisation as 'Austria' concealed its origins. Within less than 80 years of Matthias's death, his own realm had been swallowed up by his rivals and the Habsburgs would sit upon the throne of Hungary for most of the rest of the millennium until Zita's husband Karl became the last in 1916.

The Habsburgs' origins date back to the 12th century and a small clan with a castle in what is now Switzerland. By the end of the 13th they had seized control of lands further to the east. The Habsburgs made this territory (effectively the 'fat part' of the modern, post-1945 Austrian republic) their 'hereditary lands'. They then proceeded to acquire more, rapidly, and most often, as the envious Matthias had noted, by tying the knot. Over the next half dozen centuries, their scions would go on to rule almost every territory in central, southern and western Europe, including Spain, the

Netherlands, Portugal, Sicily, Hungary, Croatia and even – legally but relatively briefly – England and Ireland.

The man who started the ball rolling was Friedrich, inheritor of the southern half of the family's 'hereditary lands', who in the mid-15th century became the first Habsburg to persuade a handful of other German-speaking potentates to elect him as Holy Roman Emperor. The title that dated back to Charlemagne in the year 800 and ultimately, highly indirectly to the Caesars themselves (*Kaiser* is the German spelling, and its pronunciation is far closer to the Latin original than the English version). By the Middle Ages the title bestowed more prestige than power. That didn't stop the Habsburgs from using the prestige to their advantage. Friedrich had himself crowned emperor by the pope in Rome. He was the last to bother. From then on, the Habsburgs would ensure that a title which had passed from one German potentate to another – and was in theory open to any Christian European who could muster the votes – was effectively theirs for keeps. From 1452 until the title was abolished by Napoleon Bonaparte in 1806, the Habsburgs would hand it down in the family for three and half centuries, arguably save for one three-year glitch during the War of the Austrian Succession (1740–8) when it was briefly held by a rebellious, relatively distant relative from next-door Bavaria.

The Habsburg march towards European and eventually global expansion began when Friedrich inherited the remainder of the hereditary lands in today's Austria from his cousin, then had his son Maximilian married to the only child of his rival, Charles of Burgundy, in those days a powerful political and dynastic entity in its own right. Much of today's understanding of mediaeval and later Europe is hampered by the use of modern names of relatively recent nation-states for geographical regions. What we now call France was in the 15th century divided between three families. The two main rivals had long been the Valois clan, based in Paris, and the Plantagenets, heirs of the Norman conquerors, equally francophone but based in London, who had long ruled much of the southwest and bits of the north. The Valois had only recently seen off the Plantagenets in a long struggle which had ended with their possessions reduced to the coastal town of Calais. What we today call the Hundred Years War between England and France had really been a turf war between two originally francophone families, even if it did result in a greater sense of 'nationality' in the territories both ended up with. Henry V, the victor of Agincourt in 1415, was the first Plantagenet to make English the official language of court and government in England. The third family were a divergent branch of the Valois clan who had run the Duchy of Burgundy independently.

The marriage to Maximilian was not exactly Charles's first choice for his daughter. He only agreed after Friedrich marched on his army, which was unsuccessfully laying siege to the Rhineland city of Neuss, hampered by his mercenary English archers threatening to strike over wages. The pair were not married until six months after her father's death, by which time Mary had inherited his lands. This was no small matter: far from being the medium-sized French province which it is today, the possessions of the Dukes of Burgundy in the 15th century were a large patchwork of more or less contiguous interlinked territories reaching from the North Sea to the western Alps.

Maximilian Habsburg was left with the northern lands, including a large chunk of today's eastern France, Netherlands and Belgium. His father meanwhile had persuaded the potentates who had elected him to the imperial throne to name his son as his successor, both of them to rule jointly until his own death. Maximilian was already busy playing the wedding game in his own right, making well-connected matches for his children and eventually his grandchildren. Whereas both Friedrich and Maximilian were definitely German-speakers, both born in Austria, the former in Innsbruck, the latter in Wiener Neustadt, south of Vienna, their family's rapidly spreading ambitions quickly meant that the Habsburgs' links with their German-speaking homeland were already becoming diluted. In an age when family meant everything and nationality was scarcely a concept, nobody either cared or noticed.

Maximilian secured for his older son, known as Philip the Handsome, born in Bruges, a marriage with Joanna, the third child of the Catholic monarchs, Ferdinand of Aragon and Isabella of Castile. Their marriage had merged the two largest Christian kingdoms on the Iberian peninsula, their armies had expelled the remaining Moors, uniting in their dual monarchy in 1492 almost all of what we today call Spain. That same year a seaman in their pay, one Christopher Columbus, 'discovered' an unknown continent and 'gave' it to them. Maximilian's match turned out better than might have been expected when, after the deaths of her elder siblings, Joanna became heir to both crowns (still legally separate entities). But her mother died before her father, meaning she and Philip initially inherited only Castile.

Nonetheless, it seemed the Habsburg family had, as ever, landed on its feet. But then Philip died of typhoid fever aged just 28, having ruled for only a few months. Joanna's father declared his daughter mad, imprisoned her in a nunnery and claimed Castile and Aragon under his sole rule. Only when he died in 1516 was Joanna restored to the throne. Her son, Charles Habsburg, born in Ghent and a French speaker with little German and no Spanish, hastened to his mother's side, but his intentions were dubious. He lost no time in getting his mother to declare him co-ruler, after which he sent her back into confinement. A Spanish revolt against this outsider was quickly quashed, and with Joanna's mental condition deteriorating – understandably after multiple betrayals by members of her own family – Charles had her detained for the rest of her life.

Charles had much more coming to him. His grandfather Maximilian had been terrified that the imperial title would be lost to the Habsburgs and go to his arch rival Francis I of upstart France, or the other, rather less likely would-be challenger, Henry VIII of England. Either would have been the first non-German-speaker to hold the imperial title since the partition of the old Carolingian empire half a millennium earlier. To avoid such a scenario, he had acquired a substantial loan from the Fuggers, a rich family from Augsburg, one of the family fiefdoms, who had turned a fortune made in the cloth-weaving trade into a money-lending business. The money was used to bribe enough electors to ensure that the vote went in favour of Philip's son and Maximilian's own grandson. In 1519, the same year that the young Charles of Ghent consolidated his reign as Carlos I of Spain, now for the first time a nation-state as well as a geographical area – though it is doubtful whether the king would have recognised the concept as having anything to do with his subjects rather than his own family possessions – he added the title of 'Holy Roman Emperor', and became overnight the most powerful man in the world.

Interlude: The English Connection

Most British schoolchildren, if they have heard of Charles V at all, know him only as the obliquely defined 'emperor', who, as the nephew of Catherine of Aragon, used his control over the papacy to prevent Henry VIII getting an annulment from the wife who had given him a daughter but not a son. It is one of the quirks of history that the man who did more than anyone else to hinder the spread of Protestantism and keep much of Europe Catholic, was indirectly responsible for Henry's break with Rome, and England eventually becoming Protestant.

The links between the originally Germanic dynasty that provided Spain's first and most powerful king, who in the early 16th century was by far the most powerful man on the planet, and England's most notorious and still best-known monarch were multiple and intricate. The reality of course is that Henry VIII was a minnow, with a tiny kingdom covering just half of one European island, compared to Charles's global empire. Given the Habsburg tactic of expanding their family empire by marriage, however, it was no surprise that England also featured in their plans to dominate Europe.

The 19th and 20th centuries and the rise of global transport curiously corrupted the British attitude to the rest of their continent as if they were somehow separate. The English Channel, known in both French and German as 'the sleeve', with no suggestion that this narrow strait off the coast of Europe in any way belongs to the country on one side of it, was not so much a barrier as a highway in days when travel by sea was easier and faster than by land. In the 16th century, when 'British' was a meaningless term all but unheard of other than in reference to Roman times, and the English royal family had until recently spoken French and ruled over large parts of what is today France, Henry's main concern (apart from providing an heir) was to build his influence on the European mainland. This was partly why he commissioned grand portraits of himself by the famed Bavarian painter Hans Holbein, who was persuaded to come to England, where he remained for eight years working primarily on royal commissions.

Henry VIII had himself been an outside contender against both Charles and Francis I of Spain in the competition to become Holy Roman Emperor. When Henry and Francis met at the celebrated Field of the Cloth of Gold on English soil outside Calais in 1520, the year after both had lost out to Charles, it was an attempt to feel his way as to which of his erstwhile rivals would prove more important to him. Only a fortnight earlier he and Queen Catherine had entertained Charles/Karl/Carlos at Dover and Canterbury, a meeting organised by his canny counsellor Cardinal Wolsey, and made a great deal of showing him around England's then still Catholic Canterbury Cathedral, the queen fawning on the nephew who would subsequently refuse to grant her husband a divorce.

The soon-to-be-challenged links were then already long established, although Charles was nine years younger than Henry. His mother Joanna, older sister of Henry's wife Catherine, had been on her way back to Castile with her husband, Philip, Charles's father, in 1506, when their ships had been wrecked off the English coast. For several weeks the pair were guests of the then still Prince and Princess of Wales at Windsor Castle.

Not altogether surprising, then – particularly given the Habsburg preference for dynastic empire building, not to mention marrying their own relatives – that their son Charles was subsequently engaged to marry his first cousin, Henry and Catherine's daughter, when he was 22 and she just six. That engagement was subsequently replaced with Mary's betrothal instead to Charles's son, Felipe, 11 years her junior.

It is routinely overlooked in the teaching of popular English history that when Mary Tudor was on the throne, she legally shared it with Charles's son Prince Felipe of Spain, the son of the man who had tried so hard to get her father not to abandon her mother. For the five years that Mary sat on the English throne (and therefore that of Ireland), parliament was summoned in the name of 'King Philip and Queen Mary' and all official documents issued in both their names.

The 'Spanish Armada', seen as a pivotal moment in the British national myth – though it was an English-only affair and did not in any way involve the kingdom of Scotland – was arguably, indeed was argued by Philip/Felipe, an attempt to regain his marital inheritance and incorporate England in the global Habsburg empire. He had little legal justification in English terms; there had been prescriptive clauses in the marriage agreement. But in terms of international custom, he was well within his expectations. One way or the other, the Armada foundered and it didn't work out like that. But it is worth remembering that just half a century earlier both royal houses would most devoutly have wished it had done.

The Man Who Ruled the World

The Habsburg family's adventure on the world stage was leading them further and further from their Germanic roots. It made no sense to call Charles V/Carlos I, a francophone born in Burgundian Flanders, either 'Austrian' or 'German'; what mattered was family, the fact that he was a Habsburg. The German-speaking hereditary homelands in Austria were now just part of a package of inherited goods to be handed down the family line.

And it was quite a package. The family's domains in Europe now included, as well as Spain, most of (in modern terms) Austria, Slovenia, Belgium and the southern Netherlands, chunks of eastern and northern France, Italy south of Rome, including Sicily and Sardinia, and within a few years he would restore the 'lost' territories of Bohemia (effectively today's Czech Republic), Hungary, Silesia and northern Croatia. To these add Spain's vast and expanding territories in the New World and in Charles's lifetime his overseas empire would grow to include (again in modern terms) Mexico, Venezuela, Peru, Chile, Colombia, Cuba, Guatemala, Honduras, Nicaragua, Panama, Costa Rica, Belize, Florida, southern California, southern Texas, and southern Louisiana. Charles V was a global colossus who bestrode two continents and reached out towards a third when Spanish traders based on Mexico's Pacific coast sailed further west until it became east and founded a colony on the group of southeast Asian islands that would eventually be named after his son as *las islas Felipinas*, the Philippines.

Charles V's reign was one of the most important in European history, not only because he was the most powerful man in the world. The fact that he also became the richest had a huge impact of the continent's development. The colossal hordes of silver that the Spanish brought back from their newly discovered mines in South America changed Europe's economy, providing such great supplies of the precious metal (which as a result was eventually devalued) that everyday people could use it as coinage. Money – particularly silver – for the first time replaced land as a measure of wealth. And because Charles was not just King of Spain but also ruled vast territories all across the continent, the silver that arrived in Seville quickly spread to his other possessions throughout the German-speaking world as well as to Hungary, Bohemia and Flanders. In just 60 years the port of Antwerp's population rose fivefold, making it one of the most important trading centres in Europe. Capitalism had arrived.

If it seems we have wandered far from a history of the Germans in Europe, it is because at this particular stage of European history, the most important dynasty in the German-speaking world had wandered so far. The mid-16th century was a time of great change, great challenges, when a 'New World' across the Atlantic beckoned Europeans and the 'Old World', the 'Christendom' which was the term used by most people when they thought of what we today call Europe, was being plunged into crisis by the Reformation. Over the centuries that followed, Europe would come to dominate the world, and the question of who or what dominated Europe would eventually take on a global dimension.

In the few decades during which Charles ruled a substantial proportion of the world, his Habsburg empire was not just unwieldy but unworkable in days of such slow communication. His role as King of Spain, and nominal military leader of Christendom, was challenging enough. He spent much of his reign fighting Francis I of France, who tried to claim his Burgundian territories. The French monarch's defeat led him to an alliance considered treason by most of Europe: with the Muslim Ottoman Sultan Suleiman the Magnificent, who rewarded his French ally by attacking the Habsburgs' rear, the empire's southern and eastern fronts in Italy and Hungary. In 1529 the forces of Islam laid siege to Vienna itself, and were only defeated by his brother Ferdinand at the head of a typical 16th-century Habsburg force: Austrian pikemen standing alongside Spanish musketeers.

With Charles as Holy Roman Emperor, champion of European Christianity, and most powerful man in the world, the Habsburgs original home, Vienna, was the equivalent of Washington DC today, or more accurately, Rome after the Empire's move to Constantinople, its fall considered equivalent to the collapse of Western civilisation. The loss of Constantinople itself in 1453 and the Ottoman Muslim breakthrough into the Balkans had been bad enough. Now, the Gates of Vienna became in the popular mind synonymous with floodgates holding back an Islamic tide. The siege of 1529 was the first great attempt, following on the seizure of the Hungarian capital Buda (Pest would not be joined to it until the 19th-century Danube bridges were built), leaving the Habsburgs with just the western provinces. The Ottomans were repulsed, their invincibility dented. But it was only a first attempt. They would be back.

The demands of rule in Spain, fending off the Turks in the Mediterranean and suppressing the rise of Protestantism, meant that Charles had devolved the government of his Central European lands to Ferdinand, victor of the siege. In 1556, exhausted by the endless strife forced on a ruler who had sought peace above all else, Charles abdicated and retired to a monastery. His Spanish realm he left to his son Felipe, while Ferdinand officially inherited the territories he had long ruled in Charles's name.

In 1558, when Charles died, Ferdinand also inherited – more or less by default – his title of Holy Roman Emperor. It had long been more symbolic than powerful, but now that it seemed it had become a matter of course that it be simply passed down through the Habsburg family, it became just another title that barely conferred any meaningful dominion over the lands the empire nominally included. In fact, the main importance of the empire over the next century was to provide an overall aegis to keep the traditional hereditary lands together, despite being divided between various Habsburg sons. It was no longer imperial expansion on the dynasty's mind but fighting off the twin threats of the Ottoman Turks pressing from the southeast, and the religious schism of Lutheran Protestantism versus traditional Catholicism wreaking havoc to the north and west.

When the Ottomans came back, a century and a half after their first attempt to burst through the Gates of Vienna, and again laid siege to the city in the summer of 1683, it finally looked like Christian Europe faced being overrun. The tables only turned when the forces of the other great European empire – the Polish–Lithuanian Commonwealth – led by Polish King Jan Sobielski crossed the Danube in September, by which time Vienna's food supplies were all but exhausted. The great battle that broke the siege was a catastrophic defeat for the Ottomans and arguably the most important pre-20th century battle in the history of Europe. Not only did it limit the spread of Islam in Europe, but it opened the door for the Austrian branch of the Habsburgs to extend their empire once again, this time to the east and south, taking or reclaiming Hungary, much of modern Romania and the Balkans. The outcome secured Austrian power for another two centuries, but once again distracted the biggest power in the German-speaking world from what might otherwise have been its manifest destiny.

∈∋

It is not unfair to say that if the Habsburgs made Austria, they also ruined it. As will have been obvious from the above, their interest was purely familial: in other words, tribal at the lowest (or highest) level. When the family line ran into difficulties, so did Austria, and Europe. Already weakened by the inbreeding that kept the diverse parts of the empire together – the elongated 'Habsburg chin' had become a distinguishing feature of members of the clan – family fertility also began to suffer. With the death of Carlos II of Spain, it looked as if the Habsburgs might be about to recreate a global dominion with the Austrian Charles VI asserting a claim to the throne. This inevitably inspired the other rival European powers to intervene, notably the French Bourbon royal family, who eyed the throne for themselves and persuaded the Austrian lands' nearest neighbour and closest rival, Bavaria, to join them.

The Habsburgs for their part managed to cobble together an alliance of several other Germanic states, their former fiefdom of the Dutch Republic and an up-and-coming would-be nation-state that was itself born of a patched-up failed dynastic union: the recently formed Kingdom of Great Britain created by the political union of England and Scotland under an imported Germanic monarch. The War of the Spanish Succession effectively ended in a score draw with the Bourbons winning the grand prize of Spain and its vast New World possessions, but saw the Habsburgs take as compensation all the Spanish branch of the family's domains in Europe. This meant the southern 'Spanish' Netherlands became the 'Austrian' Netherlands, a fact which had little impact on the natives other than that they, unlike their Protestant cousins in the Dutch Republic to the north, remained Catholic, the main fact that ensured they would one day become Belgium.

It also meant the passing of control from Spain to Austria for the Italian kingdoms of Naples and Sicily and the duchy of Milan, 'Italy' at the time being still a geographical term rather than the name of a country, as was 'Germany' or 'Iberia' or indeed 'Great Britain' prior to the recent 1707 Anglo-Scottish Act of Union. (The war also saw the new British kingdom steal a rocky Spanish outpost called Gibraltar.)

But the Habsburgs' succession problems weren't over. Charles VI himself had only daughters and had to pass a law, known as the 'pragmatic sanction' to allow them to rule. Inevitably, once again, the other powers saw an opportunity to profit from a dynastic disagreement. The War of the Austrian

Succession saw the game of thrones recommence with more or less the same cast. Perhaps its most significant outcome, and most ominous for Austria and the House of Habsburg, was the emergence of yet another embryonic power on the European stage: the uppity northeastern German kingdom of Prussia, with its twin power bases in Berlin and distant Königsberg. Under its ambitious new leader, Frederick the Great, it opportunistically saw a chance to seize valuable territory from the Habsburgs. Maria Theresia won her case in the peace treaty, significantly signed at Charlemagne's ancient capital, the nominally 'free city' of Aix-la-Chapelle/Aachen in 1748, confirming her as ruler of the Habsburg lands, but only at the price of conceding the loss of the mineral-rich province of Silesia to her Prussian neighbour.

She kept a hold on the by now almost meaningless 'imperial' title through her husband Franz/Francis, yet another cousin, who had been brought to Vienna from his native Lorraine at an early age and groomed to be her consort. He could take the 'imperial' title which she, as a woman, could not, but there was never any doubt that Maria Theresia was in charge. Nonetheless, with his death and the eventual succession of their son Joseph to both titles, it was nominally the end of the Habsburg dynasty and the beginning of the 'new' Habsburg–Lorraines (though to all but the most hidebound paternalists, who somehow imagine there is less validity in passing a line through the male rather than female blood – particularly given that the latter is more certain – it was a question of *plus ça change*).

Perhaps the most sombre site to visit in Vienna today is still the Kapuzinergruft, the crypt of the Capuchins, where the body of the Empress Zita was laid to rest that drab April day in 1989. But it is not her tomb that evokes the most abiding sorrow, nor those of the other great and grand of the House of Habsburg. It is the rows of black sarcophagi of some of the youngest to be interred here, the bones of Maria Theresia's children, three of whom died in infancy and another three in their teens. The second to last of her brood also had a less than happy fate, despite promising beginnings. Married by proxy at the age of 15 to the future King of France, Maria Antonia would be better known to history as Marie Antoinette, who, nine months after her husband's overthrow and execution, was dragged through the streets of Paris in a cart.

The first and last woman to rule the Habsburg lands reinvigorated an empire in slow decline, gave it a legal code, a more efficient bureaucracy and expanded its territories, notably through the partition of Poland with Russian and Prussia, which gave it the province of Galicia, among other lesser territories. The greatest survival of Maria Theresia's reign to this day are the silver coins minted in her lifetime. The Maria Theresia silver *Thaler* were such pure silver that they became an accepted form of payment all over Europe and beyond, and could still be used for payment in Ethiopia and parts of Arabia into the early 20th century. First minted in 1741, they were so popular as an internationally accepted form of silver bullion that they continued to be produced long after her death in 1780, but always bore that date.

The name '*Thaler*' comes from a valley in what is today the Czech Republic, and known as Jáchymov Valley, but for most of its long history more commonly called Joachimsthal, the valley of St Joachim (*Thal*, now usually written *Tal*, being 'valley' in German). The coins minted from the silver mined in this valley took its name and became known as *Joachimsthaler*. Over time this was commonly abbreviated to *thaler*, *taler* or in the Low German dialect spoken in the great trading port of Hamburg and the nearby Netherlands, *daler*. The English took it across the seas to their New World colonies, a journey that was the beginning of a global odyssey which saw what came to be known as the 'dollar' become the name for some two dozen currencies worldwide.

Historically the inhabitants of Joachimstal and the surrounding areas were largely, but by no means exclusively,

German-speaking, living more or less happily with their Slavic-speaking neighbours. The question of nationality only arose – to catastrophic effect – in the early decades of the 20th century. They both belonged to the Kingdom of Bohemia, ruled over for a time by the Polish Jagiellonian dynasty before passing to the Habsburgs in 1526. The borderland between Slavic- and German-speaking populations was a pair of natural mountainous ridges, to the east known in Czech and Polish as the Sudety (a name that would briefly take on immense significance in the mid-20th century) and to the west in German as the Erzgebirge, literally 'ore mountains'. The Erzgebirge is probably the oldest mining area in Europe, in use for mining tin as far back as 2,500 BC, but later and through the mediaeval period for silver.

These are not high mountains, but they are nonetheless forbidding enough, particularly in winter. Driving through them in the snowy early spring of 1990, just after the collapse of the Iron Curtain, testing out whether the borders between the former Soviet bloc countries – which had been often almost as forbidding as those between East and West – had really gone, I found the driving snow and the narrow twisting roads as formidable a frontier as anything erected by man. But hills that contained ore were attractive to the cultures on either side of them from the dawn of civilisation, and settled by both Slavs and Germans. Saxon and Bavarian settlers were welcomed by Slavic rulers for their relatively advanced industrial skills, notably the production of cheap but plentiful glass made by mixing wood ash from the abundant forests with sand, the typical green tinge still found in everyday German wine glasses until very recently.

When the Kingdom of Bohemia came into the hands of the Austrian-based Habsburgs, they regarded it as only natural there should be a substantial element of German-speakers in their ever-expanding realm. But prior to the 20th century they took it briefly too far: Maria Theresia's successor, the Emperor Joseph II, tried briefly and unsuccessfully to force through German as the sole official language in all the Habsburg lands, including the Slavic provinces of Bohemia and Moravia as well as Hungary.

The German-speakers were not restricted to the border regions of Bohemia but drawn to its famed and cosmopolitan capital, Prague, which by the 14th century was one of the largest and most famed cities in Europe, a popular centre for the new trade of banking, dominated by families from the Italian and German city-states, as well as a large Jewish community, some of whom had fled from Spain after their expulsion in 1492. Prague's religious diversity, its ethnic mix of Czechs and Germans and its fame as an intellectual hub did not make for a tranquil city. In 1402 Jan Hus, a Czech theologian inspired by the reformist teaching of Yorkshireman John Wycliffe, had begun preaching for reform of a corrupt Catholic church. He was summoned to the imperial city of Constance, now in Bavaria, and burned at the stake in 1415. A series of revolts by his supporters came to be known as the Hussite wars, and proved a prequel to the Protestant Reformation a century later and the Thirty Years War of the 17th century.

Embellished by its opulent merchant class and the fact that several Holy Roman Emperors chose it for their residence, Prague became one of the most beautiful cities in Central Europe (and one of the few to survive the horrors of the 20th century almost intact) with a famed and flourishing university, attracting students from across the continent. German, the language of the court in Vienna, was the most commonly used language in the streets, although it vied constantly with Czech, and most people had some of both, while Latin was the language of the university. From the mid-1400s Prague would be a majority German-speaking city, but for most of that time nobody thought it mattered. It was only from the latter years of the 19th century that German rapidly began to lose its dominant status to a flood of Czechs pouring in from the countryside and it shrank to a minority language by the end of the century. Ironically it was in that period that it produced two of its greatest, and certainly most German, literary figures, the close contemporaries Rainer Maria Rilke and Franz Kafka.

The most widely known globally today, Franz Kafka, was a German Jew – though he also spoke Czech – born into a middle-class family living in central Prague in 1883. Trained as a lawyer, he worked in succession for several insurance companies, usually as a loss adjuster, which he treated as a necessary evil to sustain his love for writing, but it almost certainly informed his attitude towards life as a labyrinthine struggle with the incomprehensibility of existence and bureaucracy. The most influential of his works include the novella *Die Verwandlung* (Metamorphosis), in which a travelling salesman finds himself inexplicably transformed into a giant insect, *Der Prozess* (The Trial) about a man arrested and put on trial by an unknown authority for an unknown crime which is never explained to him, and *Das Schloss* (The Castle) which relates the story of a rural surveyor trying to get details from the castle to which his village belongs and which disputes his legal right to live there, only granting it to him on his deathbed.

Kafka was a self-conscious, insecure figure, ferociously heterosexual but who never married, relying on a string of relationships, brothels and pornography. He never finished any of his full-length novels, was little known in his lifetime, burnt much of his work while living briefly in Berlin, died of tuberculosis in 1924 at the age of 40 and left instructions that everything he had ever written should be destroyed after his death. Fortunately his executor ignored the request and published his collected works between 1925 and 1935, making the world belatedly aware of one of the most remarkable founders of modernist writing, the genres of dystopia and subliminal surrealism – and, of course, a new adjective in the language of literature: Kafkaesque.

Rainer Maria Rilke – born in 1875, also to a middle-class Prague family – remains much less famed outside the

German-speaking world. His birth name was the French 'René', but he changed it to 'Rainer' in his 20s after falling in love with the glamorous cosmopolitan Russian, Lou Andreas-Salomé, married and 14 years his senior, because she thought it sounded more 'masculine'. Rilke himself became a true European cosmopolitan, travelling to Moscow and Salomé's home city, St Petersburg. He would become particularly fond of Paris and Switzerland, but also made a pilgrimage to Toledo in Spain to see the paintings of El Greco. During World War I he spent time in Trieste, then still an Austrian city, and later in Munich. He was called up for active service in 1916, but discharged thanks to the influence of well-connected friends. Rilke's poetry is largely impressionistic in style, often mystical with religious references, particularly to angels, and often with a strong sense of location, and an undertone of quiet despair.

∈∋

A society – and an empire – that had thrived as a multicultural state, was brought to an end in the horrors of the mid-20th century, ironically inspired by those who thought nation-states were permanent. Woodrow Wilson's idea of giving ethnic groups their own countries was well-intentioned, despite it coming from the leader of one of the least ethnically homogeneous nations on earth. But it was music to the ears of the young Hitler, whose annexation of the Sudetenland and Austria (he would not have seen any real difference) could have been seen as furthering the ethnic solution that had been frustrated by other European powers' Realpolitik. It ended in tears. Floods of them. Even after the war, when over three years, more than three million 'Germans' – whose families prior to 1938 had only ever lived in 'Austria' – were forced from their homes and became refugees fleeing to yet another German state – West Germany – that was already itself only half a country.

The Transylvanian Connection

It was not just the northern fringes of the Austrian Empire abutting modern Germany that had substantial German-speaking populations. I first travelled to Romania as a reporter for the *Sunday Telegraph* in 1987 at a time when foreign journalists were banned by the totalitarian regime of dictator Nicolae Ceauşescu. I stumbled on board the train at Budapest station in the hour before dawn, and crawled into a lower bunk in a six-person sleeper car, which turned out to be occupied by a group of young Czech students, then was woken at the border an hour or two later by grim-faced Romanian border guards. They stared blankly at my Irish passport with the occupation given as 'translator' (in those days it was required that passports carry professions).

My mission was to investigate reports of growing tension between the increasingly repressive regime in Bucharest and the substantial Hungarian minority in the northern part of the country, known in Hungary as Erdély, but globally better known by its ancient Latin (and modern Romanian) name of Transylvania (in both languages literally the 'land beyond the woods'). Part of the Habsburg family empire since the Ottomans were repulsed in 1683, Transylvania had nonetheless been considered – especially since the *Ausgleich* of 1867, in which the empire was saved from internal conflict by declaring Austria and Hungary 'equal partners' – as belonging to the Hungarian crown. It had – and still has – a substantial ethnic Hungarian population (some 1.3 million, just under one in five Transylvanians).

Transylvania's rich and colourful multi-ethnic character, superbly celebrated in Miklós Bánffy's Transylvanian trilogy, is still evident today: most major towns have three names – one Romanian, one Hungarian and one German. The German names have little to do with the fact that they were once under 'Austrian' control and more to do with the fact that in the 12th and 13th centuries the local Hungarian overlords (much like the Polish bishop of Rügen mentioned earlier) had actively encouraged settlement by industrious German farmers, to not only work the land but defend it. The threat they faced was an invasion of Christendom by non-Christians from the depths of central Asia; at first the pagan Mongol hordes, then their heirs, the Tatars, and eventually the Islamicised Ottoman Turks. Transylvania also has a German name: Siebenbürgen, reflecting the seven cities founded by the 'Saxon' settlers.

Commonly referred to as 'Saxons', these German-speaking settlers were actually mostly *Franken* (from Franconia in northern Bavaria today) – or even *Schwaben* (from Swabia, what is now Baden-Württemburg). But over the centuries the word 'Saxon' had come to refer loosely to almost any German from the central plains. Outside the immediate lands of the German-speaking tribes, 'Saxon' became a sort of catch-all nickname.

The settlers proved to be good farmers and valiant frontiersmen. They even resorted to a new, unique form of stamping and defending their Christian Germanic identity on their new frontier: they built *Wehrkirchen,* literally 'defensive churches', putting high walls with ramparts around their holy place so that the community could shelter within when under attack. An image of these God-fearing farmer folk survived into the 20th century in vivid caricature as the pitchfork-wielding peasants in old black-and-white Hollywood horror movies, always ready to storm the hideaway of a monster or bloodsucker, forever incarnated in the global imagination by a fictional character invented by a Dubliner: Bram Stoker's Dracula.

There is an irony that the embodiment of evil passed down most effectively over the centuries was not some Mongol or Turk but a local who fought against them, impaling them on stakes as a warning to other would-be invaders. This gruesome habit adhered to his name and he became knowns as Vlad (a Slav name traditionally meaning 'victor') the Impaler. His father, ruler of Wallachia, today's southern Romania and at the time a much-contested buffer zone between Hungarians and Turks, had been inaugurated into a knightly order of the Holy Roman Empire called the Order of the Dragon – *drago* in Latin. In Romanian dialect, which favoured patronymics, his son became *dragwlya,* 'little dragon', or, in local spelling, *dracula.* As a child he and his brother Radu had been given over to the Ottomans as hostages to assure his father's right to rule, and they learned Arabic and to read the Koran. Assuring the sultan that he would be a loyal vassal, Vlad was allowed to return on his father's death, but revolted and led a bloody crusade against them, impaling his captives' bodies – dead or alive – on wooden stakes. Allegedly, the Ottoman sultan Mehmet II, conqueror of Constantinople, turned back in horror on encountering a forest of 20,000 impaled bodies.

Undoubtedly a cruel ruler, but in a cruel age, his reputation was largely blackened by the Saxons, whose loyalty he obviously distrusted and who were persecuted during his reign. If we owe the modern vampire story to a Victorian Irishman, we owe the arguably more gruesome supposedly historical reality to Jobst Gutknecht, a Bavarian printer who in 1521, in between copies of Lutheran hymnals, produced the original Dracula horror story, a pot-boiler of its time, which includes the lines: (in late mediaeval German): *Er liess kinder braten, die mussten ire mutter essen. dann schneyd den frauen die brust ab, die mussten ihre man essen. danach liess er die alle spissen* ('He had children roasted and their mothers forced to eat them, then he cut off the women's breasts and their men had to eat them. Then he had them all stuck on spits.') Whatever the grim truth, Vlad the Impaler left a mark on Germanic demonology. There are woodcuts of him from the 15th century, but the oldest surviving painting dates from about a century after his death, and hangs even today in pride of place in the former Habsburg castle Schloss Ambrass outside Innsbruck.

Back in 1987, I found myself accidentally thrust back

into that era when arriving in Sighişoara – Schässburg to the Germans who lived there, Segesvar to its Hungarian residents – late one evening. I discovered the only place able to serve up a meal was a restaurant in the ancient house where Vlad Dracula was born in 1431. It was without a flicker of irony that the bored waiter, annoyed by being interrupted by a customer, told me that the only thing available was calves' brains on toast. And all they had to wash it down with was Bull's Blood (a strong Hungarian red wine). Today it sounds like a joke menu that might be served up in a vampire theme park; in starving Ceauşescu's Romania, it was was bread, meat and wine: luxury.

The next morning, keen to interview the local peasantry about ravages of the 20th-century bloodsucker in his palace in Bucharest, I set off down a small road in autumnal rain and mist, my thumb stuck out in an over-optimistic hope of cadging a lift, in a country with few taxis outside cities, and fewer private cars. Within half an hour I got a lift – on a horse-drawn cart – which took me to the next village, where I encountered a scene that might have come from one of those early 20th-century black-and-white movies if they'd ever had anyone to do their historical research. I was staring at a real *Wehrkirche,* a little church peeping out over the top of a high defensive wall with arrow slits. As I stood looking up at it, a man in a dog-collar asked if he could help, then invited me in to the *Pfarrhaus*, the vicarage or manse, itself as old as the 15th-century church. His native language was German.

For the next several hours, I sat with him and his wife, my own age, early 30s, in old armchairs around a fireplace with a bubbling cauldron hanging over embers kept continuously but frugally alight. They were more than charming, intrigued to have the first foreigner they had ever known in their village, and a German to boot (they were so thrilled that I was 'one of them', I could not find it in my heart to disillusion them). They told me of the decline in the village population, of people moving to work in factories in the cities, of the Communist Party's distrust of 'the Saxons', even though they had lived there nearly a thousand years. They told of harassment by the Securitate, Romania's Communist secret police, of a fall in already low attendance at their historic Lutheran church, in a country where religion was actively discouraged.

They offered me lunch, always a guest's problem in impoverished countries where hospitality is a byword, but supplies are barely adequate for the hosts' own needs. I accepted of course – anything else would have been an insult – and to my delight was served probably the most excellent soup I have ever eaten, from the cauldron hanging over the fire. 'We top it up every day, with root vegetables, some chicken bones if we have been lucky enough to get some, and boil it up again.' It was exquisite. I left them reluctantly, not wanting to force them into offering me a bed, and set off into the drizzle to the village hostelry. As we said goodbye in the doorway of the *Pfarrhaus,* their sole underpowered light bulb glowing dimly in the parlour, I asked them what they hoped for in the future. They shrugged and said that they knew people, fellow 'Saxons', who had 'escaped' to West Germany. 'Maybe,' they said, more in forlorn hope than expectation, 'just maybe.'

Only two years later, 'maybe' happened. After the fall of the Berlin Wall and German reunification in 1990 there was effectively a door opened for anyone of German ethnicity or extraction to 'come home'. It had been meant as yet another move to putting behind a redefined German nation-state the traumatic events of the mid-20th century – the brutal expansion in the Nazi eastern drive for *Lebensraum* and the subsequent brutal expulsion of Germans from the lost eastern lands after 1945. But it also opened a Pandora's box: effectively undoing centuries of history in Eastern Europe. Over the space of a few years, the Romanian 'Saxons' all but disappeared, packing up and leaving what had been their ancestral homeland for seven centuries for a perceived more affluent existence in the 'West'. People whose ancestors migrated here from early mediaeval duchies and fiefdoms and whose only 'German' overlords were for centuries Austrians, have ended up 'returning' to a nation-state they know of only from television but have never been part of.

The *Wehrkirchen* remain, but few are anything more than historic relics today with neither pastor nor congregation. A few have been placed on the UNESCO World Heritage register, as have the old 'seven cities'. The German population of Romania which in the 19th century was around three-quarters of a million, has shrunk today to little over 30,000. The whereabouts of the pastor and his wife I met in their little village outside Schässburg nearly thirty years ago is sadly unknown to me, though I suspect they fetched up somewhere on the distant Rhine. But I have retained – or rather regained – a link to the last of those ethnic German Romanians for whom home is still home, no matter what it is called or what nation-state currently claims to own it.

The tiny town of Oberwischau as it has been known locally since the mid-14th century, is today officially referred to on maps as Viseu de Sus, but a sizeable proportion of its population (total 14,000) still speak German and preserve the traditions that have come down to them over the centuries. They perform 'Saxon' folk dances on festive occasions but are proud to think of themselves as both German and Romanian. They are particularly proud – in a very German fashion – of a little steam railway, preserved in the same way the English preserve and dote over relics of bygone industrial years. Known in Romanian as 'la Mocanita', it winds up from Viseu into the thick woods near the Ukrainian frontier along what maps call the Vaser valley, its very name a nod to its heritage, referred to by locals as Wassertal, valley of the water. It is the last survival of the once numerous Carpathian logging trains that ran on the old Austro-Hungarian narrow-gauge tracks. Many of these little railroads survived in Romania's backward economy until the late 20th century, only facing decimation with the economic and industrial boost that came with the fall of Communism. Today, it is owned by a private Romanian concern – with a German name, RG Holz (wood) – and still runs a logging business as well as catering for tourists.

I know it, as I know charming little Oberwischau, however, because of the transformation that has come over Europe in the last three decades: through my friend Vasi (short for Vasile, a classic example of the racial-cultural mix in Central Europe: a Slav-influenced name for a German-speaking Romanian). Born just as the changes were sweeping our continent with the collapse of Communism, he has for the past five years been a regular barman at my Munich local, Liebig-hof, in the Bavarian capital's central Lehel district. When I first met him, I considered him merely another Roma-nian come to work in Western Europe, with an excellent command of German but a notable accent. Only gradually did I discover that he was a native speaker, bilingual in both German and Romanian, from a solidly German family, the accent developed over centuries. He introduced me to Ober-wischau and his family, many of whom would never dream of living anywhere else. As for Vasi, where is home? Ober-wischau of course. Would he ever go back? I go regularly, all the time. But forever? A wry smile, and a doubtful shake of the head. 'Who knows what the future may bring,' he says. 'In any case, we are all Europeans now.' It is a fact, of sorts: the opening of borders across Europe caused most of the Transylvanian 'Saxons' to leave, but for now at least, it is also a reason why many of them remain. But at the time of writing (early 2017) there is no guarantee the borders will not return, nor where they might be drawn if they do.

There is a salutary lesson in the story of the most cel-ebrated, tragic, German-speaking Romanian of modern times, Paul Celan. Celan was born in 1920, just after Tran-sylvania and the adjacent Bukovina region had been ceded by the defunct Austro-Hungarian empire to the Kingdom of Romania. By the time he was 20, and a budding poet, his home town of Cernauti had been forcibly yielded by Romania to the Soviet Union following the Molotov–Ribbentrop pact (it is now in Ukraine and called Chernivtsi), then a year later invaded by the Nazis and their Romanian allies. Not good news if you were, as Celan was, not just German but also Jewish. He survived the war, first in a ghetto, where he began work on translations into German of Shakespeare's sonnets and continued to write his own poetry, then working in forced labour camps. After the war he moved briefly to Vienna, then to Paris. His poetic oeuvre was defined by the Holocaust, in which both his parents died in a concentration camp. He was catapulted to fame in 1948 with the bleak, chilling poem he wrote in the last years of the war, entitled 'Todesfuge' (Death Fugue). His work was much celebrated in post-war West Germany, where he went on reading tours, and 'Todesfuge' was included in most school anthologies. He continued, however, to live in Paris, and committed suicide by throwing himself into the Seine in 1970.

Downfall

Following the calamitous defeat of the Central European powers in World War I and the subsequent implosion of the Habsburg lands, their empire splintered into its ethnic component parts, much encouraged by US president Woodrow Wilson, who disapproved of 'colonialism', but appeared unaware of the nationalist demons he was unleashing by unravelling it overnight. The big question that remained was what to do with the territories that on 'ethnic' grounds were predominantly German. Within days of the armistice Zita's husband Karl, the Austrian Emperor and King of Hungary who had been crowned in Budapest in 1916 but not yet in Vienna, withdrew from all state affairs. (He never officially abdicated, with the result that the family were banned from the new republic of Austria until 1966.) A hastily convened national assembly chose the Social Democrat Karl Renner, a

German-speaker from northern Bohemia, as the leader. The
new assembly included representatives of parts of Bohemia
and Moravia who objected to the new state of Czechoslovakia in which German speakers would be a minority on the
fringes, and declared the democratic republic of Deutschös-
terreich (German Austria), the old way of referring to all the
lands where the population spoke German.

The German-speaking areas within the toppled empire
had never been contiguous: there were large numbers of
ethnic Germans in Hungary and Transylvania but in particular in the provinces of Bohemia and Moravia, along the
north and west frontiers of the new Czechoslovak republic.
The assembly insisted that it had been the Habsburg dynasty,
not their German-speaking subjects, that had brought catastrophe, and that they alone should not be made bear the
blame simply because of their language. The state's borders,
particularly in Bohemia and Moravia, were not viable and
the clear intention of the assembly was that all the German-
speaking areas of the former Habsburg empire adjacent to
the former 'German Reich' should be ceded to the new, democratic Weimar Republic. Their wording even included a term
that would eventually become notorious: *Anschluss.* In the
context of the time, it seemed logical, indeed fully in accord
with Wilson's principles of national self-determination. Pleb-
iscites in several regions clearly supported it. The *reductio ad
absurdum* of the German-speaking rump of a once global
empire seemed an absurdity indeed. If the Habsburgs' scattered German-speaking lands were not united with the larger,
and still relatively new, ethnic polity next door (in 1918 there
had only been a state bearing the name 'Germany' for a mere
47 years), it would leave once mighty Austria as a tiny rump
while the new nation-states carved out of the old empire
would have substantial disconsolate minorities within their
frontiers. So does one peace sow the seeds of the next war.

But there was no way the victorious allies, who, playing on
the revolutions in the German states, had turned an armistice

into a surrender, were going to allow the 'losing' country – i.e. imperial Germany, even reconstituted as a democratic republic – to acquire rather than cede land. It would have weighed on their minds that when Kaiser Wilhelm II had decided to uphold his alliance with Vienna, despite his scorn for the moribund empire's imperial posturing in the Balkans, he had always calculated that in the event of failure 'Austria's German provinces will fall into my hands'. The treaty of Saint-Germain-en-Laye, which settled the fate of Austria, and the Treaty of Versailles, which would settle that of Germany, decided otherwise.

The result of British and French intransigence was an insistence on an emasculated Austrian republic made up of the contiguous bulk of German-speaking lands but minus the Südtirol, heedless of Wilson's pretensions and demographics thrown as a piece of war booty to the Italians (hence the huge numbers of South Tyroleans at the funerals of the Empress Zita and their great supporter and Bavarian Prime Minister Franz Josef Strauss), as well as the German-speaking territories in the new Czechoslovak republic.

This arbitrary severing of certain German lands from others within the Habsburgs' multicultural empire was particularly cruel on the rump republic's new, Social Democrat leader, who signed the treaty enforcing it. Renner was obliged to give up all rights to his ancestral family farmlands now ceded to the new Slav-dominated republic. That alone was enough for even Renner, despite the fact that his party had been banned by the pro-Nazi fascists in 1934, to approve the *Anschluss* of 1938, in the hope that Nazism was just a passing fad. He was right, of course: it did pass, but only under the most painful of circumstances. During the period of union, the grand old imperial city of Vienna was reduced in status to a provincial capital, the Austrian republic itself returned to its roots and was rebranded as the *Ostmark*, the 'eastern March', the southeastern border land of a new – if extremely short-lived – greater German empire that aimed to be the very reverse of the multicultural realm of the Habsburgs, stretching ever eastwards.

The new Reich was the brainchild of an Austrian, born in what had been the little border town of Braunau-am-Inn, who believed, as many of his fellow countrymen did, that the little rump state was a barely viable casualty of war. He could see no point, historically, practically or ethnically in the new world of nation-states rather than supranational empires of a nationality called 'Austrian'. It had been valid to be an Austrian as opposed to a Prussian or a Bavarian or Württemberger, but when all the others were now German, what was the point in being something else? He joined the German army in World War I, moved to Munich and became active in German politics. The young Adolf Hitler had enthusiastically adopted the concept of nation-state. And meant to expand it to its limits.

Hitler himself had struggled to obtain German citizenship. He had moved to Munich in 1913 and with the outbreak of war requested permission to join the Bavarian rather than Austrian army (he allegedly disliked the racial mix in the Habsburg empire's forces). But following his failed coup, two attempts to gain Bavarian (and therefore German, the Republic being theoretically a confederation) citizenship in the 1920s and one by pretending to be a police sergeant in Thuringia in 1930 were rejected, meaning he could not run for public office. This technical difficulty was only solved in 1932 when he was about to challenge retired general Paul von Hindenburg for the presidency, which he could not do if he was not a German citizen. The Nazi party, which had a coalition role in the government of the state of Braunschweig (Brunswick), appointed its leader to a minor administrative job at their provincial mission to Berlin, and subsequently gave him Braunschweig citizenship. And that meant he was a German. It was no accident that it was Hitler who made the question of citizenship one for the central government in Berlin rather than the *Länder*.

Pilgrimage to the Hitler birth house is not encouraged by the municipal authorities of Braunau today, or anyone else for that matter. So it is with no little bemusement that I have to admit to being one of the few to have gone there deliberately to visit it. I was not alone, however, not there as a historian, and certainly not as a pilgrim, but as a journalist. It was in the April of that fateful year of 1989 that I turned up for the centenary of the Führer's birth, sent by a British newspaper eager for photographs of neo-Nazis giving Hitler salutes or goose-stepping. They did neither. In fact there were more foreign correspondents than neo-Nazis from either side of the border between German-speaking states. The house itself is a nondescript three-storey building on a street corner, unmarked and unobtrusive, save for a small stone on the pavement remembering Hitler's victims.

Hitler's vision of empire was already no more than a nightmare from which Europe was about to awake when Austria reappeared on the map. In April 1945, just weeks before the fall of Berlin, Renner with the other political parties banned under the Nazis declared the *Anschluss* null and void and set up a provisional government. It was a stroke of brilliance which, in political if not moral terms, allowed the Austrian Germans overnight to claim victim rather than co-aggressor status, a coup which would allow many skeletons to linger unrattled in Viennese closets. Austria refused to pay compensation and many former Nazis escaped the investigation they would have faced on the other side of a reinstated border.

The figure that burst the bubble of Austrian innocence was Kurt Waldheim (1918–2007), who became United Nations Secretary-General in the 1970s and was subsequently elected Austrian president. In 1941 Waldheim had been conscripted into the Wehrmacht, as were all Austrian males of military age, their nationality considered no different to that of a citizen of Bavaria, Brandenburg or Bremen, and served in what was then Yugoslavia and Greece. In the run-up to his election and during his presidency, allegations that he had feigned ignorance of war crimes damaged his and Austria's reputation, although he fiercely denied any wrongdoing and no evidence of any – other than selective editing in his autobiography – was ever produced. The main result of the otherwise inconclusive 'Waldheim affair' was that Austria finally acknowledged its role in the war and the Holocaust and that its 'clean sheet' had a few grubby marks. Stolen Jewish art which had been retained as property of the state began to be returned to those who could provide evidence of pre-war ownership. Austria faced up to being 'German'. Up to a point.

The border vanished again in 1986 with the Schengen agreement on free travel throughout the EU (with the exception of recalcitrant, insular Britain and Ireland, the latter a reluctant hostage to its shared land border). For three decades only a gold-on-blue twelve-starred road sign, a toll on motorway usage and the price of diesel told the traveller in Central Europe that they had crossed from one EU nation to another: money, language and even accent remained the same.

The refugee crisis cause by the Syrian civil war after 2011 changed some of that, to the confusion and astonishment of citizens on either side, who had come to take the absence of frontiers for granted. Crossing from Austria to Germany in early 2016 I was, for the first time in 40 years, asked to show a passport. The Austrians, who had once again become used to being the little brother in their relationship with the larger German state to the north, have persistently irritated Berlin by refusing to agree policy on accepting refugees. In this there is greater accord with the similarly conservative government in adjacent Bavaria. In the curious faux-English country house of Cecilienhof outside Potsdam, back in 1982 when it was still East Germany and looked likely to remain so, I found a curious map on display. Cecilienhof had hosted the 1945 conference at which Josef Stalin, Harry Truman and Clement Attlee (Churchill having been thrown out of

Downing Street by the British electorate a week after it began) redrew the map of Europe in a few weeks. This particular map showed a European state that had never existed but oh so often, oh so nearly might have done: a 'South Germany' with the twin capitals of Munich and Vienna, and the territory of Austria and Bavaria combined.

I suspect that it had been put on display by the East German Communist regime primarily to show that there was no inevitability to the idea of just one, or even just two, German states. But it made a curious sense and to some extent still does; Müncheners even today are not overly fond of Berlin, a city they regard as a 'catastrophe', while 'Prussian' is almost a dirty word, and each finds the other's dialect somewhere between hilarious and incomprehensible. The folk from across the border in Salzburg or Innsbruck by comparison they consider kindred Alpine spirits with similar values who, in every sense, speak the same language. Since 1945 any idea of Austria again becoming part of Germany has been banished. Its new identity has been cultivated to the extent that even variant spellings of a few German words are officially tolerated – the most notable being *Kassa* instead of *Kasse* for a cash desk – but then most of Germany's regional dialects appear in writing somewhere or other, usually on pub menus. That is most noticeable of all in Bavaria where the dialect is virtually identical to that of neighbouring Tyrol.

One of my good friends with whom I regularly share a glass of wine in our local in Munich is a resident Austrian, but there is no way that he has ever considered himself a 'foreigner'. But then the same goes for Vasi, my 'Romanian Saxon' and Mani (who can nowadays hardly remember her native Slovenian).

The Remains of Empire

Vienna today is a strange city, an imperial capital without an empire. It is home to a quarter of Austria's population, nearly two million in a nation of eight, the second biggest German-speaking city in the world (it was overtaken by Berlin in the early 20th century).

The Ringstrasse inner city ring road that replaced the old mediaeval walls when they were bulldozed in 1857 to allow for the expected massive expansion befitting the capital of one of the world's great empires, is lined with baroque churches, the parliament buildings and the opera house. But dominating it all is the colossal mass of the Hofburg, the Habsburgs' imperial palace, expanded over half a dozen centuries, with its grand residential apartments, museums, library, church, stables and Spanish Riding School, where the proud Lipizzaner horses, descended from just a handful of stallions originating from the small town of Lipiça in modern Slovenia, are regularly put through their paces for the paying public. Threatened by extinction several times in two world wars, these magnificent horses survive today in the heart of the Habsburg ancestral lands – Austria, Slovenia, Hungary and Croatia – and can still be witnessed performing their prancing feats of classical dressage, at best in the riding school itself.

The demolition of the ancient city walls left Vienna's Altstadt curiously defenceless, while the Ringstrasse did not so much link it as separate it from the rapidly spreading suburbs. Relatively undamaged by World War II (in comparison to other cities in the Germanic world), it retains its mediaeval network of winding alleyways, here and there interspersed with grand squares boasting impressive imperial columns and statues. Schönbrunn, the Versailles of Austria, with more than 1,400 rooms, and favoured residence of the Empress Maria Theresia, was once half a day's ride from the Hofburg, but now sits in splendid irrelevance amid the city suburbs.

It even has its own relatively diminutive but much older version of the London Eye, the Wiener Riesenrad (built in 1897 by an engineer from Devon), which became a global icon in a much bleaker period of Viennese history: during the Allied occupation following World War II. It was from one of its cabins at the apex of the wheel that Orson Welles as Harry Lime cynically used the view of the ground far below to muse on the insignificance of an individual human life in the 1949 thriller *The Third Man*. I first climbed into one of its archaic wooden, railway carriage-style cabins in 1986, not quite 40 years after the iconic British movie scripted by Graham Greene first hit cinema screens, on a cold wintry day when the cityscape below me might as well have been a screenshot in black and white. Three decades later, in April 2016, the Prater funfair it inhabits – and which might have died without the continued presence of its cinematic celebrity – has been refurbished as a minor inner-city theme park, in full colour, but somehow stripped of the appropriate bleak atmosphere it conveyed when I first visited it. True aficionados of director Carol Reed's noir masterpiece can take a themed tour of the sewers that were Harry Lime's underground highway.

The heart of the city – the Altstadt inside where the old walls once were – is today a largely pedestrianised mix of the mediaeval and baroque, overlaid with a veneer of modernity. Along with the formal squares and busy shopping streets, the stunning spire and fabulous tiled roof of St Stephen's towering above, are quirky winding alleyways virtually unchanged since the Middle Ages. Amid Vienna's splendid art galleries, most notable is the Leopold Museum, which concentrates on the work of the remarkable artists of the late 19th and early 20th centuries, Gustav Klimt and Egon Schiele.

Again in the late 1980s and early 1990s, when Vienna was an important transport hub for correspondents covering the wave of revolutionary democratisation in its old empire from Prague to Budapest and beyond, along with a colleague from the Spanish daily *El País*, I virtually commandeered (at the *Sunday Times*' expense) a room in perhaps the city's most famous hotel, the Sacher. On chilly winter afternoons elderly dowagers, who might once have been baronesses from Transylvania or Bohemian countesses, would sit in its large-windowed café to see and be seen as they sipped coffee and nibbled the eponymous Sachertorte, that delicious cake of rich chocolate sponge and apricot jam, allegedly invented in the early 19th century for Prince Wenzel von Metternich, the last of the great Austrian foreign ministers.

⋶⋺

But what of the Habsburgs, that most extraordinary of European dynasties, whose trail of glory had led them to mastery of half a continent (if not half the world), who had taken Austria from the status of a minor German state to a global power, but in the end had reduced it to a little mountain state hanging on to the coat tails of a much greater German power?

Bizarrely, as it seemed at the time, though perhaps not as much as it seems with a long view of history, a Habsburg, Otto, son of the last King and Emperor, and almost certainly the last to aspire to the revival of the family fortunes on the scale of his ancestors, was to play a significant role in the collapse of Communism and the aspiration towards European unity.

Born in 1912 in Reichenau an der Rax, southwest of Vienna, Otto was the golden-haired cherubic three-year-old dressed in silk and ermine photographed on the steps inside Budapest's Matthias church at his father's coronation as King of Hungary in 1916. He was to live most of his life abroad, only being granted an Austrian passport for the first time in 1964, when the concept of a restored monarchy no longer seemed a serious option.

Not that his mother, Zita, had ever dismissed the option. From his earliest childhood in Madeira and later in Spain, Otto had been groomed for an upturn in the family fortunes. He was taught and became fluent in German, Hungarian,

Croatian, Spanish, French, English and Latin, enough to have had him pass for a native of most of the lands his great ancestor Charles V once ruled. His mother's aspirations came to naught, and he could have been forgiven for imagining a divine conspiracy against the family when his first five children were girls.

In his early years Otto had aspired himself to regain the throne of Hungary, which was supposedly still a monarchy under the control of self-declared regent Miklós Horthy, who amusingly, given the new state's landlocked situation, held the rank of admiral and was more concerned with holding onto the levers of power than yielding to the rightful king. Otto fearlessly opposed Nazism, in particular the *Anschluss*, and was sentenced to death *in absentia* by the regime. From the 1930s on he despised the new nationalism in Europe, foreseeing the tragedies it would lead to, and espoused the idea of a wider European unity. Still banned from Austria, he moved to Germany, took German citizenship and won a seat in the European Parliament representing Bavaria, a position he held for 20 years, famously setting up an empty chair in the chamber to represent the countries on the other side of the Iron Curtain.

I first met him in 1986 in his home on the shores of the Starnbergersee, south of Munich, and found myself both bemused and impressed by this old man (he was already 74) who wore his learning, his languages and his family heritage so apparently lightly, yet so seriously. Sitting in the elegant drawing room of his 19th-century *grande bourgeoisie* villa overlooking the lake, he showed me a family photograph album unlike any other, including the original of that famous photo of him at his father's coronation, and among other mementos, a splendid crystal glass engraved with his name, or at least one version of it: Otto Austria. 'It was a present,' he said, with an approving smile, 'from the pope.'

In August 1989, with the currents of history swirling in unexpected eddies across the continent, Otto was the sponsor of a so-called Pan-European Picnic, in a meadow not far from the Hungarian border town of Sopron, and persuaded the Hungarian government to open the borders to Austria for three hours. The picnic, well advertised with an accompanying map, unsurprisingly attracted not just Austrians and Hungarians but also thousands of East Germans used to holidaying on the shores of Lake Balaton, where they could meet relatives from West Germany. When the borders opened, with the Hungarian guards given orders to facilitate border crossing in each direction rather than shoot those attempting it, some 600 East Germans fled to Austria, where they were at liberty to claim West German citizenship. Chastised by East Berlin, the Hungarians briefly tried to reimpose border controls, but in the end gave up. The Iron Curtain had been ripped open. Within months it would be torn down.

Otto remained active to the end of his life, feted even in London. I last saw him deliver a speech on the need for Europe to come together and for Britain to play its part at the Banqueting Hall in Whitehall after he had been given the Freedom of the City in 2007. In Munich, in the summer of 2011, I accidentally stumbled across a sombre procession leaving the Theatinerkirche in the city centre. They were bearing the body of Otto, who had died peacefully at his home at the age of 98, two years older than his late mother. His funeral, like hers, was held in St Stephen's in Vienna, his heart interred in a monastery in Hungary. It was with a lump in my throat that in April 2016 I stood once again in the crypt of the Habsburgs underneath Vienna's Kapuzinerkirche by the coffin of the sole individual of this ancient dynasty whom I had personally known and could almost have called a friend.

He had been born an Austrian, lived most of his life as a German and died a European. Charles V would have approved.

The Germans and Music

It was one of those cold evenings towards the end of the Cold War, with wind whistling off Vienna's Ringstrasse and down the alleyways of the Altstadt. From a building on my right came the warm glow of a concert hall with people taking their seats. It seemed less formal than such things can often be in Vienna, and for once they had tickets for sale at reasonable prices. The music had just started and I recognised a Mozart melody, so I coughed up and took my place towards the back of the hall.

I was drifting off into the ease of the maestro's elegant, scintillating and occasionally unexpected little leaps and turns of the imagination, enjoying every moment, when it dawned on me that every so often the rest of the audience would break into something between a titter and an outright guffaw. This is not normal for concert audiences in Vienna, where austere decorum – verging on the downright stuffy – is more the norm.

I glanced around to see if there was something I was missing, when it happened again: but this time it was a collective murmur of appreciative amusement. Only then did I glance down at the programme and realise that what the orchestra was playing was not some concerto I had not heard before, or some little operatic passage, but a 'tribute to Mozart's ingenuity'. It was a deliberate joke piece, a sort of musical equivalent of the Reduced Shakespeare Company's 'all-in-one' renditions of the collective works of the Bard of Avon in all the quotes you can remember strung together in a one-hour show. The Viennese know these things. And know when to laugh out loud, and when to titter knowledgeably.

I did not, I fear, and found myself bemused even trying to spot when one familiar melody melded into another from a totally different work, except on the odd occasion when it was signalled by a sudden musical flounce in the opposite direction. But then with Mozart, with his vast output, sense of mischief and lack of respect for too many traditions, you could never be sure he hadn't at some time somewhere done something almost identical, on purpose.

By this stage I hope there is no need to go back into the 'Austrian or German' argument, which Mozart himself would not remotely have recognised: Salzburg, the now Austrian city where he was born in 1756, was at the time an independent archbishopric, had once been Bavarian, and would oscillate between Austria and Bavaria in the century after his death.

Mozart was among the most prolific of the string of German-speaking composers who would over three centuries play an astonishing, almost totally dominant role in the European tradition of formal or courtly written music – as opposed to folk or popular music, which was passed on orally or by tradition – which we have come to call 'classical'. He was a child prodigy of the most extraordinary nature. Born to a minor composer and music teacher, his interest in music began at the latest from the age of three when he watched his older sister being instructed on the clavier, and tried to copy her. Within two years he was competent on both the violin and keyboard and had already begun composing. By the age of eight, he had composed his first symphony, which, it is widely assumed, his father wrote down for him.

The Mozart family and their astonishingly gifted children became overnight celebrities and for four years toured the courts of Europe from Munich to Mannheim, Prague to Vienna, The Hague, London and Paris. It was in London, aged nine, that he met Johann Christian Bach, son of Johann Sebastian, both of whom were to become great influences on his work. After a return break in Salzburg, his father, Leopold, took the 13-year-old to Italy for a two-year tour.

As a young adult Mozart initially took a job as court musician in Salzburg but graduated, as anyone with ambition did at the time, to Vienna, capital of the German cultural world. In Vienna he met and became friends with Joseph Haydn, who spent much of his life in the employ of the wealthy Esterházy family on a remote rural estate. Haydn was more than 20 years his senior, but there was an immediate affinity between the two. Haydn told Mozart's father, 'I tell you as an honest man and before God that your son is the greatest composer known to me.' Mozart would in turn dedicate six string quartets to him.

Perhaps most significantly, it was in Vienna that Mozart really became acquainted with the work of his great predecessor, Johann Sebastian Bach, who half a century earlier had brought the baroque style of Antonio Vivaldi north of the Alps. During his own lifetime Bach received recognition primarily as an organist rather than a composer, though he has since become widely rated as one of the greatest ever. In his mastery of the baroque he was only equalled by Georg Frideric Händel, court musician to the Elector of Hanover, who would later move to London to be with his master when he inherited the English throne.

It would be hard even to begin to pick out any particular masterpiece among the vast array of Bach's productive life, though in our family it is a long-standing tradition, appreciated more by some than others, particularly when the children were teenagers, that on Christmas morning the wake-up call is the opening to his *Christmas Oratorio* with its rousing drum roll and horns accompanying the magisterial command '*Jauchzet, frohlocket*' (Rejoice and be merry). I find it gets the day off to a good start. Not everyone agrees.

Bach and Händel were both born in the same year in cities not very far apart, Halle and Eisenach, which would later become part of Communist East Germany, which was ironically keen to claim these court musicians as their own. Sadly, and despite one or two attempts, the two never met.

It was partly Mozart's discovery of and enthusiasm for Bach senior's work, augmented by his meeting with his son Johann Christian, a formidable musician and composer in his own right, that prevented the baroque wonders being totally supplanted by the new romantic '*galant*' style fashionable at the time. Mozart took themes and styles from both Bachs, senior and junior, and wrote them into some of his own myriad compositions. It is hard to believe, despite his early start, that Mozart managed some 600 compositions in almost every style: choral, symphonic, operatic, chamber music. He was master of them all by the time he died, aged just 35, only two months after conducting the premiere of *The Magic Flute* and while still in the process of composing a requiem.

The legend that he was buried in a pauper's grave has been greatly exaggerated: he was buried in a 'common' grave, because he was a commoner, not a nobleman. It was normal practice in the Vienna of the day. That said, his funeral was remarkably under-attended given his status in Viennese society. His Requiem, finished posthumously by a lesser hand, would be played at the funeral of his friend Joseph Haydn when he died, 18 years later, at the age of 77. Haydn's most enduring melody was the tune that became the national anthem of the Austrian empire, and then, in an obscure turn of fate, that of the new German empire and the Federal Republic, which claims it still today, and which caused that confusion among the press at the 1989 funeral of the last Austrian Empress. The enduring popularity of Mozart's music has encouraged the mythologising of his short but spectacular life, notably in Peter Schaffer's stage play and a subsequent film, *Amadeus*, which celebrated not only his music but also his well-documented love of practical jokes and scatological humour, what we would today call 'bottom jokes'. His least known, least recorded musical compositions are the 'dirty' songs he wrote and sang with his mates. In some ways he never ceased being a precocious child even as he surpassed in genius every adult of his era.

The phenomenon that was Mozart had a profound influence on another budding musician whose father had touted him too as a child prodigy: a lad born in a little university town far to the north on the banks of the Rhine: Ludwig van Beethoven of Bonn. Inspired by the success of the Mozart family, Beethoven's parents tried to promote their gifted child as a similar prodigy to the extent that when he gave his first public performance on the violin at the age of eight, his parents tried to claim he was only six. Beethoven himself was in awe of Mozart, some 15 years his senior and in 1787, at the age of 17, he travelled to Vienna in the hope of meeting him and studying with him, though it is unknown whether they even met. Beethoven was forced to return to Bonn after little more than two weeks to look after his sick mother and ailing brothers, his father by then having become a hopeless alcoholic.

By 1792 when he returned to Vienna to settle, his father had died. Unfortunately so had Mozart. Beethoven spent several years imagining himself as his successor and composing in Mozart's style, also under the influence of Haydn. Much of his early work was unpublished at the time, but his reputation grew rapidly and so did his own individual style, characterised by the emotion he poured into his music. He was hugely inspired by the French Revolution and dedicated his third symphony, subtitled 'Eroica', to the great general he saw as an embodiment of the Enlightenment, Napoleon Bonaparte, whose 'liberating' troops were cheered when they entered his homeland of Cologne/Bonn. When Bonaparte declared himself emperor, he was so disgusted he scratched out his name from the manuscript so ferociously he tore a hole in the paper.

Beethoven's great tragedy was the hearing loss which began to afflict him from his late 20s, possibly due to physiological damage incurred when he fell over in a fit of rage at being interrupted while working. The malady distressed him to the point of considering suicide at one stage. His hearing deteriorated gradually so that, while he could still hear some speech and music up until 1812, two years later, at the age of 44, he was completely deaf. From then on he retired from public performance but continued composing. A series of late commissions enabled him to complete what many now regard as his greatest masterpiece, the Ninth Symphony with its unprecedented and totally unexpected choral movement at the end, setting the poet Schiller's 'Ode to Joy' to music. Beethoven himself emerged to direct the first performance in the imperial theatres in Vienna in 1824, giving cues to the conductor. When it ended to tumultuous applause the composer had to be turned around to see the audience on their feet. One of the most optimistic and rousing pieces of classical music ever written, it is now the anthem of the European Union.

Beethoven in turn, primarily through the grandiose orchestration and emotional content of his work, proved to be a prime influence on a young composer of the next generation whose legacy would take the power of music into the more nefarious realms of secular power. And the abuses of which it, as with so-called 'spiritual power', is so often guilty. Beethoven wrote only one opera, *Fidelio*, but the man who would see himself as continuing his tradition of sweeping, emotional music devoted his entire life to little else.

Richard Wagner, born in Leipzig and some 43 years Beethoven's junior, was also inspired by Mozart, though more in the drama of his operas than his musical style, but expanded the sweeping Beethoven style into the world of opera. Wagner took for his inspiration both an idealised version of the early Middle Ages and the old Nordic–Germanic myths, in particular *Nibelungenlied,* an ancient saga about a ring forged from Rhine gold, and the legends of water sprites known as Rhine Maidens, the warrior Siegfried and his doomed obsession with his beautiful lover, Brunnhilde. More than any other opera composer before him, Wagner sought to fuse the on-stage drama and libretto with the music to create a new all-inclusive art form, usually referred to by its German name, the *Gesamtkunstwerk.* Wagner's aim was to fuse music, drama, poetry and stage design into one vast immersive creation. Wagner would create and make much use of leitmotivs, musical phrases linked to a particular character which would herald or mark their arrival on stage and signal or even create psychological moods.

Unusually for operatic composers, he wrote his own libretto, and even had his own opera house built in Bayreuth, northern Bavaria, with the financial help of King Ludwig II, who was already on his way to near bankruptcy with his fantastical Neuschwanstein Castle outside Munich. To this day Wagner's descendants still run an annual Bayreuth Festival to celebrate his work, notably the vast *Ring* cycle, consisting of four operas, *Das Rheingold*, *Die Walküre*, *Siegfried* and *Götterdämmerung* ('Rhine Gold', 'The Valkyries', 'Siegfried' and 'Twilight of the Gods'). A complete cycle is usually performed over four days and takes up some 15 hours. There is a sort of Tolkienesque element to this great epic story about a struggle between gods and men over a magic ring forged by a dwarf, which gives the power to rule the world.

The first ever performance was held at the opening of the Bayreuth opera house in August 1876. Over the course of his lifetime, Wagner lived and worked in Leipzig, Riga (then part of the Russian empire), Dresden, Zurich, Bayreuth, Paris and Venice, where he died in 1883 on a winter holiday. Fittingly, given his love of grand staged events, his coffin was taken down the Grand Canal on a funerary gondola before being transported to Bayreuth for burial. His widow Cosima, his second wife, 24 years younger than him, and the daughter of his contemporary, close friend and fellow composer Franz Liszt, did much to foster the preservation of his work.

Apart from *The Ring*, Wagner's operas include *Tristan und Isolde*, which yet again features doomed romantic love, *Parisfal*, a heavily Christian celebration of mediaeval knighthood, and *Die Meistersinger von Nürnberg*, which celebrates the oldest traditions of German choral singing by groups known as Master Singers, mostly aristocrats. This had emerged in the Middle Ages, derived in turn from a choral folk song tradition among the common people. Known as the *Minnesinger*, they feature in another Wagner opera, *Tannhäuser*.

It was Wagner's enthusiasm for popularising ancient Germanic traditions, and particularly the noble fantasy of *The Ring* cycle, that attracted Adolf Hitler to his work though the composer's infamous anti-Semitism probably also helped. His works also found favour with his close friend philosopher Friedrich Nietzsche, who would become another flavour in the pot-pourri of the warped ideology of Nazism, even though Wagner himself had been an ardent socialist. Nietzsche would in the end consider Wagner had 'given in' to Christianity, which he regarded as 'weakening'.

Wagner's virulent anti-Semitism and the Nazis' enthusiasm for his work made his music for many years after 1945 controversial, but eventually the splendour and magnificence of his theatrical vision has come back into repute, overshadowing his prejudices. His influence has pervaded modern stage and cinema, most notably in Francis Ford Coppola's *Apocalypse Now*, where Wagner's 'Ride of the Valkyries' accompanies an American helicopter onslaught on a North Vietnamese beach.

Among the great German pantheon of musical genius, which in the 19th century alone included such figures as Felix Mendelssohn and Johannes Brahms, both regarded as rather conservative by their more innovative contemporaries, specific mention needs to be made of two men whose legacy has since been claimed by other nations. One is Wagner's contemporary and close friend, Franz Liszt, born near Sopron in what was then part of the Austro-Hungarian empire, ruled from Vienna with German as its main language and Liszt's mother tongue. In today's Hungary, still, despite – or because of – its membership of the European Union, struggling to redefine its national identity, he is claimed as a national treasure and known as Liszt Ferenc. The truth is that he never really mastered Hungarian, indeed spoke better French and

Italian. Liszt died in Bayreuth, attending one of the festivals now hosted by Wagner's widow, his daughter Cosima, and, according to his own wishes, was buried there.

The other is, of course, Georg Fridrich Händel, who, as we have discussed, moved to England in anticipation of his former employer in Hanover becoming king and wrote pieces which have become mainstays of British classical music, including the *Water Music* and *Fireworks Music* composed to order for royal entertainments on the Thames as well as *The Messiah*, and the superb, soaring *Zadok the Priest*, written for George I's coronation and played at every English coronation since. Following his patron's coronation, Händel took British citizenship and therefore can legitimately be called an English (if German-born) composer. Amusingly, rather than a complication as it might be today, the umlaut over the first syllable in his name made it supremely pronounceable in the effete patois of the London upper crust, who correctly pronounced his name as 'Mr Hendel'. (Only in the 20th century would the 'handle' pronunciation take precedence.) He died in England in 1759, having lived most of his life in Brook Street, Mayfair, in a house which has become a museum to his memory, run from a knocked-through flat in the adjoining building which at one date housed another foreign musician who made London his home: Jimi Hendrix.

ᴄᴈ

That brings me (handily) to German popular music of the 20th and 21st centuries, from the great Marlene Dietrich, whose popularity as both singer and Hollywood film star, almost as much her long life (1901–92), spanned the century. Post-unification Berlin, the city where she was born and which her early songs most vibrantly evoke, dedicated a new square to her, despite some disgruntlement about her having taken US citizenship in 1939. She died in Paris, but in accordance with her last will was buried next to her mother and near the house where she was born, in Berlin's Städtischer Friedhof (city cemetery).

When I first arrived in East Berlin, it was Dietrich's music that still spoke to me of the old magic of a city that had been a talisman before living through successive nightmares, but had still kept the core of its identity, particularly in the East. The dilapidated eastern half of the city, with its working-class *Mietkasernen* tenements, heated by foul-smelling brown coal as it had been before the war, still resounded with the broad Berlin accent she used in some of her more down-to-earth recordings, notably 'Nach meene Beene is ja janz Berlin verrückt' (All Berlin is Going Crazy for my Legs), a song appropriated from a rival cabarettist.

Unsurprisingly the middle decades of the 20th century, after the apocalypse of 1945 and the decade of stultifying repression that preceded it, did not exactly see an immediate flourishing of new culture. What Germans – as initially most Britons and French – wanted in the 1950s was comfort music: trios, quartets and solo singers largely carrying on as before. In West Germany this took the form of sentimental Alpine folk songs – the norm in Austria and Bavaria – and cheesy pop music known as *Schlager* (literally, 'hits'). East Germany saw something similar, except that stars still needed a stamp of political reliability.

The big exception was Kraftwerk, an avant-garde techno band with a driving robotic beat formed in Düsseldorf in 1970, who only came to real prominence in the middle of the decade after the release of their iconic album *Autobahn*. But they were a major exception to the rule of bland, processed pop. It was in the early 1980s that a new German rock music began to emerge alongside the still-flourishing Kraftwerk phenomenon.

It was upbeat, rock rather than pop, without the cheesy sentimentality or romanticism of the *Schlager,* and it got the name *Neue Deutsche Welle* (New German Wave), an oblique play on words in the popular imagination on *Deutsche Welle,* the rather staid government-sponsored radio station that was the equivalent of BBC World Service.

NDW hit the road with a bang in 1981 with a high-energy rock classic from Munich band Spider Murphy Gang, entitled 'Skandal im Sperrbezirk'. The lyrics initially caused outrage with their reference to a popular call-girl and use of the word *Nutten* ('whore') in what radio stations still thought of as a pop song. With its sarcastic nod to Munich's Hofbräuhaus beer hall, it became an instant classic at the Oktoberfest, where it has now become a venerable anthem played every year in almost every tent.

Hard on their heels came Nena, the only *NDW* star ever to gain any significant international success with her big hit '99 Luftballons' (translated into English as '99 Red Balloons', giving them a colour the original did not mention). It would become a defining motif of the 80s Zeitgeist, featuring prominently as background music in the globally successful 2015 East-West German spy drama *Deutschland 83*.

The East had its own quirky pop music too, carefully apolitical. Kurtl, a cheeky chap at what I then thought was the advanced age of 50-plus, with outsize glasses and twinkling eyes, was a musician of the old school: an accordion player and singer who had had a string of minor hits in the 1960s, when the East German Communist government were keen to foster folksy songs with a heavy hint of home-town nostalgia. His favourite was entitled 'Liebes Fräulein Fernamt' (Dear Long Distance Operator Lady), a chatty little number about a nostalgic Berliner (almost certainly not further away than Dresden or Leipzig, given the travel possibilities for East Germans at the time) trying to persuade a telephone operator to put him through to home. As a song it is little more than a jolly curiosity, as an evocative period piece, unsurpassed.

One of the lasting favourites from DDR days, was a bar room song by a relatively run-of-the-mill rock band initially called called Silly, who had started out as Familie Silly, because the East German culture minister didn't like a standalone Anglicism. With their charismatic singer Tamara Danz, they quickly established a following not just in East Germany but across the Warsaw Pact countries, becoming big stars in Romania and Czechoslovakia. Silly would go on to become one of East Germany's few rock exports, lasting beyond the fall of the Wall until 1996 when Danz died of breast cancer. But with nostalgia for the East on the rise again in the early years of the new millennium, the band reformed, adopting actress Anna Loos as their front woman. The song that defined them, however, was not one of their classic rock hits, but a jokey rhythmic song called 'Der Letzte Kunde', the lament of a typical East Berlin barfly stuck to his stool at closing time with the last tram and his last female company long gone as the *Klofrau* (slang for the woman in charge of the toilets) cleans up and the barman prepares to leave. It is a whimsical, infectious and entertaining ditty that still has a place on my playlists today.

In its own way 'Der Letzte Kunde' has become one of those iconic songs that the Germans call *Kultklassiker*, cult hits, that whatever their musical merit are so distinctive they acquire a life of their own. Some of them, like 'Skandal' are closely associated with events, the Oktoberfest in that case, and none more than the vast sea of jokey, usually rude and occasionally verging on the obscene, singalongs produced annually in huge quantity for the carnival season. They are invariably beat-driven, intended to be sung as much as heard and originate almost exclusively in Austria, Bavaria and the Rhineland. Over the pre-Lent weeks they blare forth incessantly from loudspeakers in pubs, bars, streets and from every Alpine ski hut where the locals speak German.

The best known become almost immortal, even if they are only resurrected once a year. I first heard Gottlieb Wendehals's boppy 'Polonäse Blankenese' at a *Fasching* disco hosted by the volunteer fire brigade of the tiny Austrian village of Rauris on my first skiing holiday back in 1982. The same song with its bouncy *Karnewal* lyrics inciting listeners to a conga *von Blankense* (a suburb of Hamburg) *bis hinter Wuppertal* (a Rhineland town south of Cologne). They were still playing it, and the crowds singing the lyrics they know by heart, at *Karnewal* in 2016.

Musically, most *Karnewal* songs are almost totally devoid of any merit other than their tendency to get people if not exactly dancing, then pumping their fists in the air, swaying from side to side and singing along. Perhaps the most widely exported variant of the genre was the global hit attained by an improbable rockstar from the Alpine ski village of St Johann in Tirol, who was born Gerhard Friedle, but is better known as DJ Ötzi, after the 5,300-year-old 'iceman' found mummified in the Ötztal valley. He leapt to global fame in 2001 with an unlikely cover version of a 40-year-old American hit, given a disco beat and a large helping of Alpine Austrian attitude. 'Hey Baby (Oooh, Aah)' became an overnight international success and launched a career that has seen this unlikeliest of superstars selling some 15 million records, even if his continuing success did remain primarily based in the German language zone.

Mozart and Beethoven needn't start worrying just yet.

Division of Charlemagne's
Frankish Empire 843AD

Emperor Lothar's Realm
(Lothari Regnum)

Papal States

West Francia

East Francia

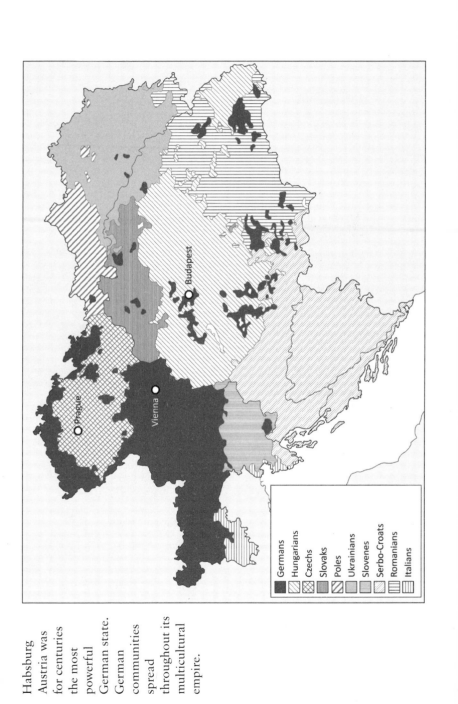

Habsburg Austria was for centuries the most powerful German state. German communities spread throughout its multicultural empire.

Germans
Hungarians
Czechs
Slovaks
Poles
Ukrainians
Slovenes
Serbo-Croats
Romanians
Italians

Prague

Vienna

Budapest

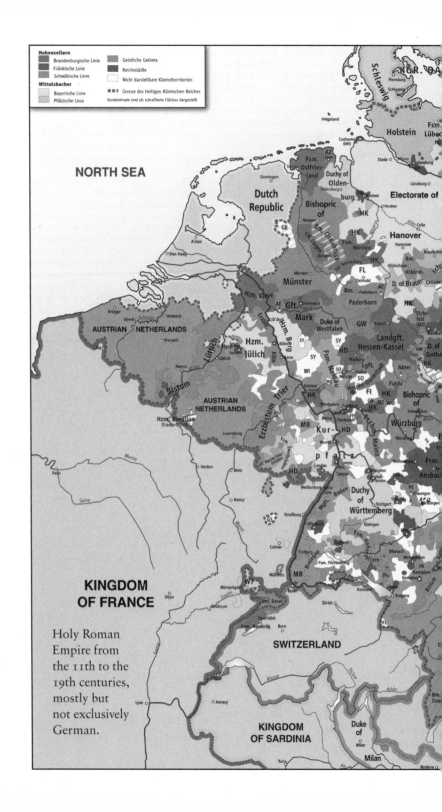

Holy Roman
Empire from
the 11th to the
19th centuries,
mostly but
not exclusively
German.

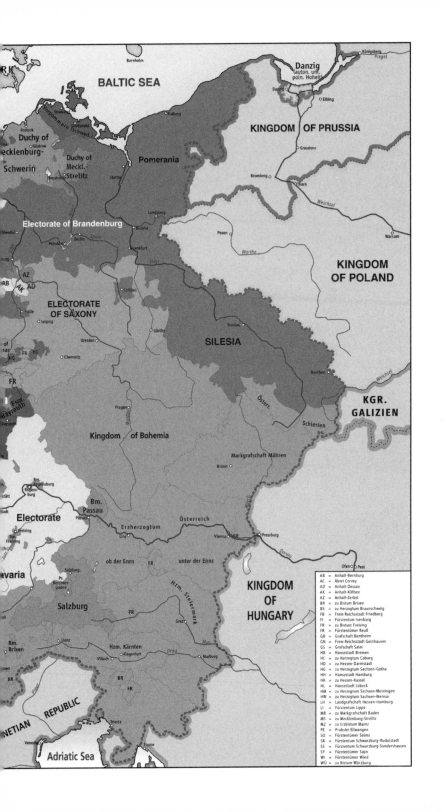

BALTIC SEA

Bornholm

Danzig
(auton. unt.
poln. Hoheit)

○ Königsberg

Pregel

KINGDOM OF PRUSSIA

Rostock

Stralsund

Duchy of
ecklenburg-
Schwerin

Duchy of
Meckl.-
Strelitz

Neustrelitz

Pomerania

Kolberg

Graudenz

Electorate of Brandenburg

Potsdam
Berlin
Frankfurt

Spree

Bromberg ○
○ Thorn

Weichsel

Posen ○

Warsaw

AB
AZ
AK
AD

Halle ○

ELECTORATE
OF SAXONY

Leipzig ○

○ Dresden

Chemnitz ○

HG

FR

Fsm.
Bayreuth

Kingdom of Bohemia

Prague ○

Cottbus ○

Görlitz ○

Breslau ○

SILESIA

Beuthen ○

Österr.

Weichsel

KGR.
GALIZIEN

Schlesien

KINGDOM
OF POLAND

Warthe
Oder

Landsberg
Küstrin

Stettin

Markgrafschaft Mähren

Brünn ○

Bm.
Regensburg
burg

Bm.
Passau

Electorate

Freising
Bm.
Freising

avaria

Salzburg
Pr.
Berchtes-
gaden

Salzburg

Bm.
Brixen

Lienz

Passau

Erzherzogtum

Linz ○

ob der Enns

FR

Österreich

unter der Enns

Vienna ○

Pressburg

Donau

Ofen ○ ○ Pest

KINGDOM
OF
HUNGARY

Hzm. Steiermark

Graz ○

Hzm. Kärnten

Villach ○ ○ Klagenfurt

BR

FR

Drau

Marburg ○

Mur

NETIAN

REPUBLIC

Venedig ○

Adriatic Sea

Trieste ○

Fiume ○

AB	= Anhalt-Bernburg
AC	= Abtei Corvey
AD	= Anhalt-Dessau
AK	= Anhalt-Köthen
AZ	= Anhalt-Zerbst
BR	= zu Bistum Brixen
BS	= zu Herzogtum Braunschweig
FB	= Freie Reichsstadt Friedberg
FI	= Fürstentum Isenburg
FR	= zu Bistum Freising
FR	= Fürstentümer Reuß
GB	= Grafschaft Bentheim
GN	= Freie Reichsstadt Gelnhausen
GS	= Grafschaft Salm
HB	= Hansestadt Bremen
HC	= zu Herzogtum Coburg
HD	= zu Hessen-Darmstadt
HG	= zu Herzogtum Sachsen-Gotha
HH	= Hansestadt Hamburg
HK	= zu Hessen-Kassel
HL	= Hansestadt Lübeck
HM	= zu Herzogtum Sachsen-Meiningen
HW	= zu Herzogtum Sachsen-Weimar
LH	= Landgrafschaft Hessen-Homburg
LI	= Fürstentum Lippe
MB	= zu Markgrafschaft Baden
MS	= zu Mecklenburg-Strelitz
MZ	= zu Erzbistum Mainz
PE	= Probstei Ellwangen
SO	= Fürstentümer Solms
SR	= Fürstentum Schwarzburg-Rudolstadt
SS	= Fürstentum Schwarzburg-Sondershausen
SY	= Fürstentümer Sayn
WI	= Fürstentümer Wied
WÜ	= zu Bistum Würzburg

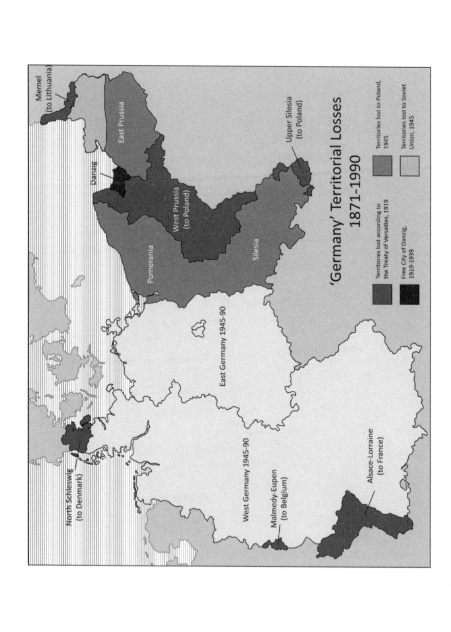

'Germany' Territorial Losses
1871-1990

Memel
(to Lithuania)

East Prussia

Danzig

West Prussia
(to Poland)

Upper Silesia
(to Poland)

Pomerania

Silesia

East Germany 1945-90

North Schleswig
(to Denmark)

West Germany 1945-90

Malmedy-Eupen
(to Belgium)

Alsace-Lorraine
(to France)

Territories lost according to
the Treaty of Versailles, 1919

Free City of Danzig,
1919-1939

Territories lost to Poland,
1945

Territories lost to Soviet
Union, 1945

6

Hamburg

Germany's Gateway to the World

Kippers, Hookers and Beatles

It is 7.30 a.m. on a bleak Sunday morning in early November with seagulls wheeling and cawing above the grey waters of the Elbe while a determined drizzle falls from the banks of clouds massing above the forest of cranes that line the horizon. I pull down the peak of my Hamburg sailor's cap, so beloved by former chancellor Helmut Schmidt, and join the crowds jostling amid the stalls where what was once the day's catch from the North Sea, but now is largely brought in by plane, is offered for sale by burly lads boasting the merits of their wares in thick Plattdeutsch dialect, rich with words and terms easily confused with Dutch or even English. I buy myself the traditional breakfast of a roll filled with a glistening, marinated herring, complete with tail sticking out beyond the rings of raw red onion, and hurry into the relative warmth and irrepressible jollity of the Fischauktionshalle to find a glass of Holsten lager to wash down my deliciously slippery oily fish, and join in the contagious merriment of Germany's earliest Sunday morning *Frühschoppen*.

Taking a hair of the Saturday night dog – *Frühschoppen* means literally 'an early glass' – is a practice widely indulged in by sociable Germans up and down the country, but it is usually a late morning affair that drags on into mid-afternoon, over copies of the Sunday newspapers and ideally a jazz band playing in the background. Hamburg's Sunday morning fish market is different, however: a national legend that starts up as early as 5.30 a.m. When the sun has only been down a few hours and is suddenly rising again, the late night revellers from the Reeperbahn who haven't bothered to follow suit flock to the Fischmarkt, which becomes a hedonistic dawn orgy of raw herring and onion, schnapps and beer.

In winter, when there is Hamburg's famously damp and drizzly weather to deal with, it is a more restrained affair, starting no earlier than 7.30. In both cases the market finishes religiously on the dot of 9.30, heralded by a loud hooter like a ship's foghorn. Its fame – for the freshness and variety of the seafood on offer, and the enthusiasm of its participants (these days it is a consumer market rather than wholesale) – attracts up to 70,000 on sunny summer Sundays and is celebrated in anecdote throughout the country. Germany has a relatively small coastline for the size of its population and hinterland, a ratio that was even more exaggerated for West Germany in the days when most of the Baltic coast was on the other side of the Iron Curtain. In those days, while East Berliners – and other East Germans – flocked to Rügen, the large holiday island off their coast, the most chic domestic summer destination for West Germans was the little island of Sylt in the North Sea, which was the place to be seen for the glitterati of Hamburg and beyond.

In 1985 a pair of semi-comic songsters from the *Schlager* tradition called Klaus and Klaus made a national name for themselves with a number titled 'An der Nordseeküste', celebrating their little bit of coastline, which became effectively the anthem of the Hamburg fish market. Disconcertingly for me, the first time I heard it belted out gustily by a load of early morning drunks, it was sung to the melody of a pub song I had known all my life growing up on another cold coast: 'The Wild Rover'. It works rather well. Try it. Replace:

And it's no, nay, never,
No, nay never, no more,
Will I play the Wild Rover,
No never, no more

with:

Auf der Nordseeküste,
Auf dem plattdeutschen Strand
Sind die Fische im Wasser
Und selten am Land

(On the North Sea coast,
On the Low German strand
You find fish in the water,
But seldom on land)

Hamburg is a long way from the sea it serves: nearly 130 kilometres (80 miles) from the North Sea coast. Its maritime history and its atmosphere as a city perched on the edge of an ocean rather than a riverbank are both due to the vast, impressive and at times intimidating splendour of the Elbe, the great river partly tamed by the city, though partial inundations are not uncommon. The Elbe has a tidal swell that can easily induce seasickness and in places it is up to ten times the width of the Thames as it passes through London.

This huge river which made the city easily accessible for ocean-going vessels yet relatively sheltered inland gave Hamburg the title of Germany's 'Gateway to the World' and made it in the late 19th and early 20th centuries one of the chief ports for transatlantic liners. Yet it was much earlier that trade shaped Hamburg's destiny: already by the 13th century it was the de facto capital of an early European Economic Community whose influence stretched from London to St Petersburg, and was to the North and Baltic Seas what the Venetian trading empire was to the Mediterranean. If the Venetians' main appeal was the spices and other exotica brought from Alexandria, the gateway to the Orient, then the glory of the Hansa, the trading league of which Hamburg was the doyenne, consisted of the rich furs and precious metals to be traded from Russia and its Siberian hinterland.

For more than three centuries, a period in which the German coastline was seemingly endless – including ports either directly in German territories or where Germans controlled the trade – stretching from Rotterdam to Riga, the ports of the Hanseatic League were among Europe's richest and most stable cities, often independent city-states in their own right, notably Hamburg and its two closest rivals, Bremen and Lübeck. Like all great ports, they evolved rules and rights of their own, as well as rough on-shore districts to service the wants and needs of men whose lives were lived mostly at sea among other male company: bars and brothels. In Hamburg this grew up over the centuries along a few streets a short walk inland from the harbour, the largest of which became known as the Reeperbahn, derived from the Plattdeutsch (Low German) word for 'ropemakers', who once inhabited the area, providing their wares to ships' chandlers. It soon attracted other traders with goods and services to offer to their crews. The area is also referred to with reference to the local church as St Pauli. Hamburgers are on matey terms with their saints, so that Paulskirche becomes Pauli, the Michaelskirche (the city's landmark famed as is the city hall for its depiction of St Michael slaying the devil) is Micheli, and St Peter's cathedral is Petri. St Pauli has however always referred to the district for its houses of ill repute rather than houses of God, and is nowadays mostly referred to by locals as *der Kiez*, a slang term that probably is best translated into American English by the US 'hood, short for neighbourhood.

Amid the early risers at the Sunday morning fish market, many of them easily identifiable by their preference for coffee over beer, there is no shortage of those whose heads have not yet hit the pillow, at least not to sleep. Watch for the weary, leery eyes and less than steady footsteps of those who have followed the infectious logic of 'one more then, lads?' until dawn has gone and a final, final one with a fish sandwich acquires a compelling logic all of its own.

The Reeperbahn today survives, in what some locals would call a dulled-down and 'Disneyfied' form of its once notorious past, as the adult entertainment centre of Northern Europe. It is the sort of district the British fondly imagine London's Soho once to have been but never really was. Even at its most disreputable, Soho was a poor shadow of even the watered-down St Pauli of today. In Soho, then as today, prostitutes plied their trade semi-legally and unregulated at the doorways of upstairs rooms usually at the mercy of pimps; in Hamburg it was, and still is, in the street and in your face. The multi-channel porno video cabins may have mostly gone, victims of ubiquitous online porn, and the 'live-sex' shows mostly dissipated, but there is no shortage of *Läufhauser*, literally 'running houses': walk-up, walk-in brothels, advertised in neon on the streets, where the 'girls' – as long as they are over 21, at least claim to be self-employed, agree to regular health checks and are certified income tax payers submitting details of rent for their 'business property room rental and turnover' – stand scantily clad at the doors, willing to discuss services and prices to the regular passing trade of embarrassed single men in overcoats, and the occasional British stag party.

One of the city's most celebrated, short-term residents, a certain John Lennon, famously declared, 'I was born in Liverpool, but grew up in Hamburg.' George Harrison, who was only 17 when he went there with Lennon and his mate Paul McCartney to play a few nightclub gigs back in 1960, is on record as saying they thought it the best thing they had ever seen: 'The whole area was full of transvestites, prostitutes and gangsters.' He said it was where they, along with Pete Best and Stuart Sutcliffe, the two Beatles members who didn't make it to the big time, first learned to play in front of an audience. They would go on to perform three more stints in Hamburg's dodgy Reeperbahn clubs, in 1961 and 1962. It was undoubtedly the place that made them into a professional outfit: Paul McCartney bought a Höfner bass guitar at the Steinway-Haus Music Store. It was also where Lennon, McCartney and Harrison first encountered Ringo Starr, who left another English band performing there to replace their original drummer Pete Best. They also met local girl Astrid Kirchner who supplied them with Preludin, an amphetamine-style drug that stimulated euphoria, but also persuaded them to get the British Brylcreem out of their hair and adopt the floppy style of a few Hamburg students at the time, the 'mop-top' haircuts which would become part of their global image.

The Indra club at the top of Grosse Freiheit, the pedestrianised strip that runs off the main drag of the Reeperbahn, today looks very much like it did when the Fab Four rolled up at its doorstep during the morning when it was closed, and had to be let in to sleep on sofas before being allocated semi-permanent accommodation next to the ladies' toilets. The exterior is still painted pink, it still has late-night music into the small hours and the toilets are only a little better than they were back then. The main difference, as for the Kaiserkeller (which these days prefers to be known simply by its street address as Grosse Freiheit 36), is that to a large extent both still live off the reputation of a then little-known English band who played at each for a few weeks more than half a century ago.

At the end of the Grosse Freiheit, where it meets the Reeperbahn, the intersection has been repaved in a circular pattern, adorned with some aluminium silhouette figures – the ensemble supposed to resemble a vinyl disc – and renamed Beatles Platz: 'the only one in the world!!!' scream the posters. It may get pilgrims, but I can't say I've ever seen any, and I wouldn't recommend it.

The young Beatles had come from Liverpool, a port city that might have been Hamburg's twin, but was languishing in post-war depression and still in the grip of hypocritical, puritanical attitudes towards sexual morality. The German city in contrast, having been bombed to within an inch of its life by the Royal Air Force, was determined to celebrate survival in any way possible. There is a remnant of what they must have felt still to be seen in the gangs of British stag parties roaming the streets around St Pauli in the early 21st century, gawping at the neon-lit legal brothels and the all-night bars like jailbird lifers on day release.

A lot of locals, however, feel with more than a touch of regret that St Pauli is, like so many districts in increasingly affluent Northern European cities, losing its sleazy identity to gentrification. Amid the hookers and the hollow-eyed druggies in and around the Reeperbahn, and the neon and the nightclubs, neither of which have much glamour left in cold damp daylight, there are today smart apartment blocks growing up, fetching high rents and profiting rather than suffering from the area's louche reputation. Partly that is possible because there are now more nightclubs and late-night drinking dens than live sex shows or even walk-in bordellos. St Pauli is in danger of becoming what London's Soho has long been: a restaurant district living on the seductive reputation of an ill-spent youth.

On a midweek evening in 2015 I poked my head around the door of the Silbersack, one of the district's legendary bars: legendary primarily for the tobacco-brown walls, their coating renewed on a nightly basis (the smoking ban is conspicuous by its absence in St Pauli where there are well-used ashtrays on every table), the faded décor, drab tables and line of cigarette-puffing blokes leaning on a basic bar necking bottles of the indifferent local Astra beer, pulled out of a cool tray on demand by a barman barely willing to acknowledge new arrivals other than to point out there is (unlike most German bars) 'NO table service'.

I managed momentary acceptance by replying in kind to the curious '*Moin*' (pronounced Mo-In) greeting common to Hamburgers and a few other northwest Germans, but incomprehensible anywhere else in the country, then blew it completely by ordering a Ratsherrn beer, from one of Hamburg's new micro-breweries, and then committing the unmistakable middle-class sin of asking for a glass to drink it from. It says all you need to know about the Silbersack today though, that he was able to reach into the cool tray and produce one. The survival of this ancient pub, determinedly glued to the working-class, no-nonsense atmosphere and attitude of the days when the Reeperbahn's clientele comprised port workers, pimps, hookers and hardened seamen, is ironically due to a handful of entrepreneurial property developers who contributed to save it as an 'intrinsic part of the community atmosphere'. It is the old story: however grimy a family heirloom might be, clean it up too much and you remove the patina that gave it value.

The Original Common Market

The origins of the Hansa lie not with Hamburg itself but with the much smaller Lübeck, the earliest known German city foundation on the Baltic which had opened up a link between the raw material riches of northern Russia – wood, furs, animal skins in general – and the manufactured products of Western Europe, from woollen clothing to wine and beer. The link to northern Russia also gave access to its great rivers, the Volga and Dniepr, to the depths of far Eastern Europe, including the old Viking-explored river trade that reached as far as Constantinople.

The money to be made inspired local traders to get together in something between a cooperative society and a military alliance with the aim of protecting and controlling trade in the region. Even London played an important role as a focus – in an age when transport was safer, faster and cheaper by ship than overland – for the north–south exchange on which their profit was based. The first record of a 'league of German businessmen' in London dates from 1157, and the Hansa maintained a base, known as the *Stalhof* in the English capital right up until the middle of the 19th century, by which time the Hansa itself had long been extinct.

Initially the Germans faced stiff competition from the Vikings' Scandinavian descendants, who had long dominated the waterways of northeast Europe and Russia, but this gradually yielded before the expansion of German influence along the southern Baltic shore and the foundation of new cities, notably with the crusades of the Teutonic Knights and the foundation of Königsberg. The traders had a common interest in establishing and maintaining stability along the coast and safety at sea: cooperation was clearly better than unfettered competition. If London was the western pole of their operations – though there were also Hansa facilities in Yarmouth, York, Bordeaux and Lisbon – then the Russian city of Novgorod was the eastern.

In theory, merchants were guaranteed the same protection as they had been under the Roman empire. The Hansa's founding city, Lübeck, was hailed alongside Rome, Florence, Pisa, Venice and Cologne as one of the jewels of the 'empire', which had, of course, long ceased to exist even though the increasingly shaky survival of the Holy Roman Empire purported to perpetuate it. The 'empire's' power to protect the Hansa and other 'free cities' which sought its support rather than succumbing to the rule of the princelings who dominated the lands around them, lay in its theoretical power to summon all the other 'member states' to declare war on anyone – including one of their own number – who challenged their freedom. It was an unwritten agreement which worked primarily because it worked: it facilitated trade by keeping the larger market centres free from the tariffs imposed from time to time on the whim of princelings ever jostling against one another for greater power and territory.

The main reason the system worked for so long was that the ultimate power any of the princelings could imagine for centuries was the title and role of 'emperor', effectively head of a largely but not exclusively German 'commonwealth', and hence the guarantor of the system. It was only in the 19th century when even the nominal office of 'emperor' had been abolished by Napoleon that the system fell apart, as the princelings aspired to kingship and the concept of 'nationalism' and eventually the 'nation-state' took hold in the German lands.

In the Middle Ages, most merchants, particularly in the Hansa, came to identify with the cities in which their warehouses were based, and these cities in turn forged alliances with others along the Baltic coast involved in similar trade. The date commonly accepted for the beginning of the formal arrangement, though almost certainly it evolved gradually, is the 1241 agreement between Lübeck and Hamburg, its close neighbour dominating the all-important Elbe and its access to the North Sea without the tedious necessity of navigating around the Danish peninsula. Hamburg began as a small settlement founded in the ninth century as a base for Christian missionaries to the still pagan Saxons, Danes and Slavs. It had been granted the status of 'free city' by the Holy Roman Emperor Friedrich I, known because of his red beard as 'Barbarossa', in exchange for supporting his crusade in the Holy Land, just one more indication – as with the Teutonic Knights – as to how the destinies of northern and Central Europe were tied up with what we now call the Middle East.

This bilateral agreement between Hamburg and Lübeck gradually attracted other cities, which in exchange for agreeing to a communal set of rules were granted undisputed access to the growing trade market. It is not hard to see a parallel with the post-1945 Coal and Steel Community between Germany and France, originally designed to prevent conflict by merging strategic industries but which evolved into a wider free trade community and eventually developed more ambitious political aspirations. The Hansa remained primarily a trading community, though it was not unknown for them to cooperate politically. Over the decades it evolved into a confederation of city-states which for the sake of mutual profit agreed to uphold security and fair trade rules, at its peak reaching not just along the Baltic coast but into the interior. One of the members furthest from the sea was Cologne which remained a member until the last *Hansetag* meeting in 1669. At its height the Hansa included some 72 member cities and a further 130 affiliates. It was, in effect, a 'common market' dominated by German traders but based not so much on nationality as mutual benefit. It is a concept that in many circles in Europe has never gone away.

This great north European trading community stretched from Flanders, in modern Belgium, to Reval, today the Lithuanian capital Tallinn. All along the Baltic coast cities joined the Hansa, with Danzig in particular rising to become as important as Lübeck or Hamburg. Their greatest enemy was, for obvious reasons, Denmark, which felt it was being cut out of the market: the short overland route between the Baltic port of Lübeck and the North Sea port of Hamburg effectively ended the need for the long maritime trek up the Kattegat and down the Skagerrak.

This confederation, which had been created by merchants but taken over by the cities where they had their bases, set up its own parliament, the *Hansetag*, which initially dealt only with the market, but over time acquired other competences. This body regularly changed meeting place between member cities. Its prime functions were to decree common trading standards, impose sanctions on those who broke them as well as non-members, to decide on acceptance or rejection of candidate members, and to undertake diplomatic missions on behalf of the membership in common. A further competence was soon added with the need to coordinate military action against the Danes and the more westerly 'Low German' (what we now refer to as Dutch, the

English word itself being a corruption of *deutsch*) cities that threatened what was in effect a German monopoly on Baltic trade. Already by the middle of the 15th century, however, the Hansa was obliged to recognise the rights of both Brügge (bizarrely known by the English primarily by its French name of Bruges) and Antwerp, where the confederation had important bases. A further conflict with the English also diminished the Hansa's dominance, made worse by the closure of its base in Novgorod when the city was first eclipsed and then conquered by Muscovy, a growing power which had at last thrown off the yoke of its Mongolian invaders.

Over the following two centuries the power and influence of the Hansa cities, as well as the membership numbers, went into slow but steady decline, partly due to a revival of land routes across Europe, but primarily, as directly mirrored by the fate of Venice, through the discovery of the New World and the resultant rise of transatlantic trade, dominated initially by Spain, Portugal and, increasingly, England.

The Hansa saw a brief resurgence as their old allies in the Netherlands fought for independence from their now Spanish-based Habsburg overlords. But with that conflict over, the Netherlanders did not resume their trade with the Baltic to the same level as before but joined the English as an emerging maritime power in their own right, looking outwards across the oceans to their new colonies of Dutch Guyana on the north coast of South America and Indonesia in the far east.

The first sitting of the *Hansetag* had been called in 1346; the last, after the Hansa had not only lost much of its market relevance but been split asunder by the religious conflicts of the Thirty Years War, was in 1669. Representatives of only nine cities turned up, and they took no decisions, not even to declare the Hansa extinct; it simply faded away. The last thing the organisation did, was to sell the London *Stalhof* premises in 1853. But the memory has never died and the people of Hamburg today still pride themselves on their Hanseatic legacy to the extent that the city is officially known as the

Freie und Hansestadt Hamburg, a reference to its ancient rights of self-government (preserved in the fact that it, alone with fellow Hanseatic city Bremen, is a city-state given equal rights as one of modern Germany's 18 autonomous *Länder*). Most visibly the city's legacy as Hansestadt Hamburg is commemorated in local car number plates, which begin with the letter 'HH', pronounced, to the mild amusement of their fellow countrymen and -women, as 'Ha, Ha'.

The demise of the Hansa diminished but did not end Hamburg's role as Germany's most important maritime trading centre. The most visible remains of Hamburg's glory as a trading city are preserved in a district built long after the Baltic Hansa had dissolved, the Speicherstadt (Warehouse City), which dates from the late 19th and early 20th century. The district is one of the islands in the Elbe, part natural, part created by canals, that was largely unused until the mid-19th century, when the first gas production facility was located there. Damaged by the firestorms of 1943, but painstakingly restored in the two decades that followed, it is today cherished as one of the more intact, coherent districts of pre-war Hamburg.

Its origins lay in an attempt to preserve Hamburg's free trade port status after the German states were united in 1871, at a time when economic growth meant that more than ever the old port facilities needed expanding. By far the biggest port in the new *Deutsches Reich*, Hamburg was now rapidly becoming one of the major ports in the world. The new Reich under the dominance of Prussia and with its king recognised as Kaiser and 'national' laws now made in the new parliament in Berlin, nonetheless allowed the constituent states to retain their nominal status to a certain extent. Kings (notably that of Bavaria), as well as dukes, archdukes and princes, kept their titles and their territories' administrative boundaries, as did the formerly 'free cities', whose relative independence dated back to the Middle Ages. But for a port which had based its historic success on free trade without tolls or tariffs, there were distinct problems in suddenly becoming part of this new-fangled nation-state.

As Prussia had pressed its dominance over Austria, so it had gathered its allies into a customs union. In the 18th and early 19th centuries there had been some 1,800 different customs and excise entities between the German-speaking territories, a state of affairs that riled in particular the great cultural icon of the growing aspiration towards some form of unification, Johann Wolfgang von Goethe. Prussia alone at one stage had more than 50 different customs areas, as it inexorably absorbed other territories. In their drive towards unity under their hegemony, the Prussians began by simplifying their own taxes and tariffs into a single system. At the same time the southwest state of Württemberg was involved in a similar campaign to bring into line the customs and excise regulations of the medium-sized German states, the so-called 'Third Germany', essentially all those that mattered but with the important exception of the 'two giants', Prussia and Austria. It was a proposal that had the support of most other European trading states, including France, Great Britain and the Netherlands, who found the paperwork and payments involved in trading with the Germans endlessly frustrating.

The initial proposals failed however, and in the meantime the Prussians had either absorbed or won over enough states to dictate developments. In 1834 a customs union was formed between Prussia and the southern German states, including Bavaria, Hessen, Saxony and Württemberg. Over the next two decades more of the smaller states joined and, with the membership of Hanover in 1854, it covered much of what would later become the Reich, leaving Austria, to Prussian delight, very much beyond the Pale. The customs union not only made it easier for foreign traders, but also – by breaking down internal barriers – hugely facilitated the growth of industry and agriculture on a much larger scale than before: as in today's European Union, farmers and manufacturers no longer had to worry about their goods passing through half a dozen customs barriers within a relatively small distance.

This was also helped by the unification of weights and measures used by the different states within the customs union. Already by 1833 they had agreed to a common measure of weight called the *Zollpfund*, or 'customs pound' (some Germans today still use the word *Pfund* for half a kilo). The term *Pfund* had been used for nearly a thousand years, but had never meant the same thing across borders: a Prussian 'pound' was only 467 grammes, while in Bavaria a *Pfund* got you 560 grammes, some 20 per cent more. The closest to the new measure was to be found in Frankfurt, where a 'pound' weighed 505 grammes. To make things easier all round, it was agreed that the common pound should be set at 500 grammes, a major first step towards metrication. The rule came into effect in 1854 and was a huge success, even if ever-conservative Bavaria held on to its 'super-pound' until the national unification under Prussia in 1871, after which the metric system based on the kilogram was used throughout the new state.

The customs union also implied some form of unification of means of payment (not unlike the creation of the euro: yet again the development of the European Union to date has a lot of prehistory in the development of German unity throughout the 19th century). South of the Main river, most of the states – all of which issued their own coinage bearing the head of their own ruler or arms of their own city-state – had used the guilder as their main coin, while to the north, most used the taler, as did Austria, which had effectively invented it. Gradually, and not without difficulties and arguments, a form of union emerged, initially by making the taler and guilder of equal weight in silver.

But for the large sums involved with the development of commerce throughout the new, vastly larger common trading area, banknotes rather than coins were increasingly needed, despite those conservatives who distrusted a currency based on a promise rather than a precious metal. Banks, almost all privately owned at that time, were already allowed to issue their own notes, provided these 'promissory notes' were genuinely convertible into silver on demand. As a result, notes issued by Prussia's partly state-owned Preussische Bank, gradually became accepted throughout the customs area and would become the only notes accepted after 1871, when the new nation-state was created and a new currency, the Mark, introduced.

The Mark had been a long-standing currency in the Hanseatic cities, but although they accepted the new currency, Hamburg and Bremen had other problems. Both had declined to join the customs union for fear it would damage their ancient status as tax-free trade centres. Although they became part of the new Germany, they remained city-states within it (as they still do in the Germany of today) and their opt-out from the customs union was allowed to continue until a mutually acceptable compromise could be found. By 1881, they had found one, although it would not come into effect until seven years later, primarily because there was a lot of building work to be done. The solution was to create in both cities, but most importantly in Hamburg, which was by far the bigger, a special tax-free zone, very similar to those created in China since the late 1970s. This required tearing down a part of the old city wall and using the territory outside for a new harbour district: a warehouse city, the Speicherstadt, which would be separated from the rest of Hamburg by a border with entry and exit controls from the tax-free port into Germany proper.

Conveniently there was a large island in the Elbe ripe for redevelopment and only narrowly separated from the city itself. Creating this new warehouse district however was not as easy as just declaring the island a free-trade district and inviting merchants to build on it. There was a reason the city hadn't expanded naturally in that direction; the area was marshy and notoriously prone to flooding. Only the very poor and those employed by a nearby gasworks lived there. As the project progressed, some 20,000 of them were compulsorily displaced and relocated. To stabilise the land, 3.5 million great oak piles were sunk deep into the Elbe, a technique similar to that used in the construction of Venice almost a thousand years earlier. These made up the under-pinning for row after row of ornate Gothic-gabled six-storey warehouses built in the typical northern German redbrick. Opened by the Kaiser himself in 1888, the Speicherstadt was a great success and enabled Hamburg to continue as one of the world's great ports – a European Hong Kong of its day – and the work went on much longer than anticipated, building new warehouses right up until 1927 with some 300,000 square metres of storage space created, for its time the largest warehouse complex on the planet.

As in so many global ports, container traffic did for the Speicherstadt in the end and from 2003 plans were drawn up to integrate the surviving historic district into the city proper. On 1 January 2013 the customs-free zone was declared obsolete once and for all, and the last remaining fences torn down. Since 2015 it has been a UNESCO World Heritage Site. As in so many other ports of the past, notably London, the ware-houses are becoming trendy apartments and the artefacts of history relocated to museums.

The last major warehouse to be built was erected as late as 1963, on the site of one that had fallen victim to the firestorms of the war. Within just 40 years it was already obsolete and disused, and in 2007 a hugely ambitious project was launched to turn it not just into an apartment building with restaurants but also Europe's most advanced concert hall, which would be a new city landmark. The idea was to retain the warehouse façade intact and build on top of it a striking glass structure resembling the prow of a ship jutting into the Elbe. The architects were Swiss firm Herzog & de Meuron, famed for the Allianz Arena football stadium, home to Bayern Munich, and Tate Modern in London, converted from an old power station. Rising to 26 storeys, a height of 108 metres (354 ft), the Elbphilharmonie was to be as distinctive a part of the Hamburg skyline as the city's great church towers and as much a cultural landmark as Sydney Opera House in Australia. Inevitably the project encountered one difficulty after another, major overruns in both spending and speed of construction, at one stage being temporarily halted altogether. It is seen by some as a sign of the city's ambitious self-renewal, by others as a definition of vainglorious self-promotion. It finally opened its doors seven years late, in January 2017, to literally rapturous applause, and was hailed as one of the most acoustically sophisticated concert venues in the world.

From Trading Ships to Warships

Whereas Prussia's Wilhelm I, under whom the very concept of 'Germany' had for the first time been made a reality, albeit with the exclusion of Austria, was largely content with his achievement, his grandson Kaiser Wilhelm II, son of Britain's Queen Victoria's daughter, also called Victoria, and thereby cousin to the British monarch George V and Russian Tsar Nicholas, took his nation-state for granted, and felt it left out among the other European powers' scramble for overseas colonies. He had a coastline, he had a major European port; why should he not have a major navy to match, and as a result acquire substantial overseas colonies?

The resultant naval race between Germany and Britain was in essence an insane extrapolation of a spat between two cousins of similar age as to who had the better toys. The main difference was that Britain was essentially a naval power, its strength at sea the main weapon in defence of its frontiers, with a relatively small land army, whereas Germany had become Germany through military strength on land, where most of its borders lay. But the Kaiser was all for expansion in this brave new world of naval power: in the significantly named *International* Maritime Museum, today housed in the Speicherstadt district, you can see the Kaiser's admiral's uniform standing stiffly to attention, empty of its erstwhile inhabitant, who in 1918 reluctantly exiled himself to first the German army HQ at Spa in occupied Belgium, then eventually to Doorn in the Netherlands where he died in 1941.

The arms race at sea between Britain and Germany had from the beginning been an absurdity which the Germans could never win: overtaking Britain's head start in what was the country's main line of defence was never going to be possible. In addition, the race was more a matter of pride than serious preparation for a war which, when it did happen, caught many people by surprise. The futility of the naval arms race was only emphasised by the one major encounter of any significance, the Battle of Jutland, a largely inconclusive spat after which the German fleet retired from the scene, only to re-emerge at the last gasp and scuttle itself in the Scottish inlet of Scapa Flow.

The colonial dream proved a fantasy too. Over a 20-year period Germany had relentlessly and belatedly followed in the tracks of the British, French, Dutch and even Belgians, colonising far parts of the globe, particularly in Africa, with Hamburg the gateway to these new overseas German territories. By the end of World War I, they had all been snatched by Germany's rivals, notably Britain and France. Britain saw the years immediately after 1918 as the occasion for the biggest land grab in British imperial history. The German territories divided up included today's Rwanda and Burundi, given to Belgium after World War I, Cameroon, seized and divided by Britain and France at the start of the war in 1914, as was Togoland, the French bit of which became today's Togo, while the British portion went to what would eventually become Ghana. Of the Kaiser's two biggest colonies, German East Africa became the League of Nations mandate territory of Tanganyika under British supervision – effectively a British colony – while German Southwest Africa was put in the less than tender care of the British dominion of South Africa. It finally gained independence in November 1989, curiously in the same week as the Berlin Wall came down.

Hamburg's original role as a trading port in the heyday of the Hansa had only latterly evolved into shipbuilding on a large scale, although particularly after the building and widening of the Kiel Canal, naval construction largely centred on the other port which, tucked away in the Baltic beyond Denmark, was considered safer from attacks from the open North Sea to which the canal still gave it access.

Hamburg's own history in the shipbuilding business has always been dominated by one company, Blohm & Voss (the ampersand was superseded by a plus sign in 1955 to become Blohm + Voss). Founded in 1877, this upstart shipyard was a novelty, given that the idea of a 'German navy' had until 1871 seemed incongruous, hardly needed by an agglomeration of mostly tiny, mainly landlocked fiefdoms. The major exception – odd though it may sound – was Austria, which prior to defeat by Napoleon's army had a long Adriatic coastline that for decades prior to Napoleon's arrival even counted Venice among its territories.

The local new boys quickly began courting trade from the Hamburg merchant fleets, which until then had mostly ordered their ships from dockyards in England and used the same for their repairs. During World War I the company was forced by the government to undertake large-scale construction of a type of vessel that was relatively new and with which it had absolutely no experience: submarines. Over the four years of war just under 100 U-boats were turned out, compared to a handful of freighters, a few torpedo boats and a single light cruiser.

The company only just survived the inter-war economic crisis and its owners – understandably for commercial reasons – welcomed the rise to power of the Nazi party and its emphasis on rearmament. The 1930s and early 1940s were boom times for the shipyard as it received a flow of orders for both military and freight ships. Among the most famous was the battleship *Bismarck*, launched in 1939 amid a huge national public relations campaign. (It would go on to be the subject of a ferocious British naval hunt across the Atlantic, which ended when it sank off the French coast, possibly scuttled by its captain, but more likely after being hit by British torpedoes.)

Its other ship of note was the passenger ship *Wilhelm Gustloff*, delivered to the Nazi trades union leisure organisation, Kraft durch Freude (Strength through Joy), which used it as a holiday cruise liner for its members. When war broke out, it was commandeered by the navy for use as a hospital ship, then later as a floating barracks in the port of Gdynia in occupied Poland. In 1945 as the eastern front collapsed, it was sent to evacuate civilians from East Prussia. On 30 January the vessel set sail on its way back, heavily overloaded with more than 10,000 people, mainly refugees, on board. Shortly after 9 p.m. on a bitterly cold evening the *Wilhelm Gustloff* was sighted by a Soviet submarine, which torpedoed it. The ship went down within 40 minutes, causing the deaths of some 9,400 people, nearly all of them civilian refugees, and some 5,000 of them children. It remains the greatest ever recorded loss of life at sea.

During the war itself Blohm & Voss concentrated on turning out U-boats once again, producing 224 of them during the six-year period, although over 30 remained unfinished by the end of the war. The company also turned its engineering expertise to making aircraft. It was no surprise to anyone that Hamburg docks therefore became the target of 38 Allied air raids, though by the latter stages of the war most of the casualties were prisoners of war brought in to work in place of Germans sent to the front.

With the end of World War II and the British occupation of Hamburg, the city's new masters took their revenge for the damage done to Atlantic convoys by U-boats built by

Blohm & Voss and at the same time got even for the loss of business more than half a century earlier. The tiny remaining workforce – employment had shrunk from a pre-war high of 14,000 to just a few hundred – were ordered to dismantle their own docks and hand over their tools for delivery to UK shipyards in the case of the more valuable material, while the rest went to the Soviet Union. The clear aim was to prevent Hamburg ever being in a position to once again make Germany a power on the seas. It succeeded militarily, but not commercially, as Hamburg has since grown again to be Europe's second largest port after Rotterdam.

Despite the part it played in two world wars, Hamburg's role was never entirely, or even mainly, as a naval base; that fell to Kiel on the Baltic. For decades before and between the wars, Hamburg had established itself as the chief mainland European port for the transatlantic shipping trade. Great liners regularly set sail for New York, and many tens of thousands of Europeans used Hamburg as the departure point for emigration to the New World, in particular Swedes and Poles as well as Germans. After the Nazi takeover, Hamburg was increasingly seen by those with most to fear from the new regime as an important escape route. The 'Gateway to the World' had become the 'Gateway to the Free World'.

Down by the main city centre embarkation point on the Elbe, two plaques tell poignant stories:

On the 13th of May 1939 more than 900 refugees, mostly German Jews, left Hamburg harbour aboard the German ship *St Louis*, which was supposed to take them to Cuba to escape the persecution of the National Socialist regime. Their hopes were dashed when the Cuban government withdrew permission for them to enter the country. After several days of uncertainty only 33 passengers were allowed to disembark in Havana. Captain Gustave Schneider set sail on a journey of several days in search of a country willing to take the remaining refugees, thereby drawing the attention of the world to their plight. The *St Louis*'s odyssey eventually came to an end in Antwerp harbour on the 17th of June, after the Netherlands, Great Britain, France and Belgium agreed to take them in. Two-thirds ended up in the hands of the National Socialists, who murdered hundreds of them.

The second relates a similar tale eight years later, with the war over:

> In the summer of 1947 more than 4,500 Jewish Holocaust survivors attempted to flee France on board the ship *Exodus* to reach the then under British mandate territory of Palestine. In international waters off the coast of Haifa the vessel was rammed by British warships and after serious fighting was towed into the port of Haifa. The British forcibly loaded the refugees onto three other ships and sent them back to France. They refused to disembark, as a result of which the British continued to Hamburg where, against their will, they were taken off the vessels by British occupation forces and interned in two camps outside Lübeck.
>
> *Exodus* 1947 drew the attention of the world and prompted the United Nations resolution which led to the foundation of the state of Israel.

Rain of Fire

In the story of the rise, fall and rise again of Hamburg, and its relationship with the rest of the German lands, one incident in particular cannot be overlooked: the vast firestorm that engulfed most of the city in 1943, a 'holocaust' if one may dare use that word in reference to a German city as opposed to its usual context referring to the mass murder of Europe's Jews. The rain of fire that fell on Hamburg in the course of one single week – though the attacks continued throughout the war – surpassed even the destruction of Dresden, which has somehow found more grip on the global imagination.

On my most recent visit to Hamburg in the autumn of 2015, it felt as if life was imitating art, or rather making me relive it. I was walking with a local friend on a cold, rainy evening along the banks of the Alster, the great inner-city lake formed some 800 years ago, at the city's foundation, by damming a tributary of the massive Elbe. We were there primarily to exercise her dog on the great expanses of greenery alongside the lake, which in summer provide the city with a magnificent recreational area. In winter, however, it is dark and dank, and, still recovering from an Achilles tendon rupture several months previously, my mind went automatically to the fictional character of Frank Stave, the limping detective hero in Cay Rademacher's *Der Trümmermörder*, which I had been translating into English. It is a remarkably well-written *Krimi,* as Germans call detective novels, particularly poignant for being set in Hamburg in the immediate post-war period when the city lay mostly in ruins and was under British occupation. Stave's job is to track down murderers and other villains in his home city, obliged to work under the supervision of an officer from the army of the nation that destroyed his city and killed his wife, burnt to death in the firestorm of 1943.

On our melancholy walk along the Alster, my friend Tatjana nodded out over the dark, calm waters and said, 'You know what they did in 1943? They boarded over the whole of the Alster and painted the outlines of house roofs on it. To disorientate the bombers who'd been told to use it as a landmark for targeting the port. Not altogether stupid, those bloody Nazis.' Not that it was enough.

In one week, in July 1943, the British Royal Air Force, backed up by the USA, used incendiary bombs to create the biggest firestorm ever seen. In just eight days of non-stop bombing some 42,700 people were killed, nearly all of them civilians, including an alarmingly high number of children, a figure similar to the total of British civilians killed by Luftwaffe bombing during the entire war. A million people fled the city and over half its housing stock was destroyed, yet only one-tenth of the workforce (the prime target alongside factories) were put out of action.

There can be no doubt that those who ordered the attacks knew what they were doing: the so-called Battle of Hamburg – though battle is a euphemism for an overwhelming display of aerial destructive capability – had been codenamed Operation Gomorrah (presumably because British sensibilities would have been offended by the word 'Sodom'). Afterwards, when a still greater force for destruction had been demonstrated, RAF officers referred to it as 'Hamburg's Hiroshima'. In fact, one US Air Force surgeon reporting from occupied Hamburg in 1946 declared that the fire effects of the atomic bomb dropped on Nagasaki 'were not nearly as bad'.

It is perhaps unsurprising, therefore, that Hamburg produced one of the most eloquent authors of what has come to be known as *Trümmerliteratur* – literature written amid the rubble – created in the immediate post-war years when most of Germany's cities lay in ruins. Wolfgang Borchert was born in Hamburg in 1921; his father was a school teacher and his mother wrote poems in the local *plaat* dialect. Wolfgang began writing poetry in his youth. He hated being forced, as almost all children were, to join the Hitler Youth. He was eventually released for repeated non-attendance, briefly arrested by the Gestapo and accused of homosexuality. The following year, 1941, he was conscripted into the Wehrmacht, and after training with a panzer division was sent to Smolensk on the eastern front. His grim experiences on the front line in the winter of 1941–2 would inform much of his work. In the spring of 1942 he was sent home with a wound to his hand from his own gun, according to him incurred by accident when he was surprised by a Soviet soldier. His commander accused him of deliberate self-harm, but by then Borchert was hospitalised with diphtheria; on his recovery he was put on trial in Nürnberg – the charge carried the death penalty – but was acquitted, and sent back to the front.

He returned to Hamburg on medical leave, suffering from acute frostbite and hepatitis, in August 1943, just a few weeks after the worst bombing raids, to find his home city in smouldering ruins. On return to active service he was arrested again, this time for parodying Joseph Goebbels. He served his time in a jail in Berlin, which herded up to six men into a single cell, some of them suspected of involvement in the July 1944 plot against Hitler. The time in jail further seriously damaged his health. By the time he was released, the war was on its last legs. His unit surrendered to the French near Frankfurt-am-Main. On the way to a prisoner-of-war camp, Borchert managed to escape and walked several hundred kilometres home to Hamburg.

The remainder of his short life was a flurry of creativity. He poured forth poetry, short stories and the work for which he is most remembered *Draussen vor der Tür* (usually translated as *The Man Outside*), an unremittingly bleak play about a man returned from the front to find he has lost everything and even the Elbe will not accept his suicide. Borchert himself called it a 'play no theatre wants to perform and no audience wants to see'. It was first performed as a radio drama in February 1947 and had its first theatrical performance that November, one day after Borchert's death. He was just 26 years old.

I first came across Borchert's work as an A-level German student in Northern Ireland in the early 1970s, scarcely aware of how relatively recent it was – that gap of barely 25 years is now less than that between the time of writing and the fall of the Berlin Wall – but it made an enormous impact on a young mind growing up in a society where armed conflict was still common. I was particularly struck by the pure passion of his militant manifesto against war, *Dann gibt es nur eins!* (Then there is only one thing!), with its powerful entreaty to the everyday man and woman in every aspect of society to refuse to cooperate, to '*sag NEIN*' (say no). This is followed by a gruesomely vivid litany of the horrors of war. In many ways Borchert can be considered a German riposte to the equally bleak poetry of Paul Celan, a testimony to the oft-neglected fact that Germans too were victims of Nazism. His output is relatively small, alarmingly readable, particularly the short stories, which form the bulk of his work beyond the poetry. Poignant and human, they do not make happy reading, but they are remarkably powerful works of literature from a young man who suffered the horrors of wartime, death and destruction, sacrifice and treachery, at first hand. And knew how to express it.

⋴⋺

Unquestionably the part of Hamburg that suffered most was the Hammersbrook district, where most of the city's dock workers lived. The large working-class housing area was totally annihilated, and has – out of respect for the victims – never been rebuilt as an area for domestic housing, but instead turned over to commercial development. The hills in Öjendorf park are, like so many in Berlin and other German cities, *Trümmerberge*, literally mountains of rubble, grassed over and made into areas for recreation. And remembrance.

One such *Trümmerberg* in Berlin, in the district of Wedding, which to my mind will always be 'just west of the Wall' from my days living in Prenzlauer Berg, has never managed to look even remotely like a genuine hill but more like the remains of some prehistoric fortress reclaimed imperfectly by nature: not the ruins of civilians housing but of one of the great *Flakbunker* (anti-aircraft bunkers) built to serve as both platforms for anti-aircraft batteries and simultaneously as air-raid bunkers for the populace. It might seen incongruous, even unwise, to have thrown up build-ings designed to serve as shelters yet simultaneously marking them as obvious targets. But the architects knew what they were doing. Back in 1981 a friend who had lived through the war as a child recalled with wry amusement standing among crowds beneath it in 1947 as Allied demolition men tried to bring it down from within using high explosives: 'There were great muffled bangs and clouds of smoke and dust, but nothing else happened. They tried three or four times, over several days, but in the end the best they could do was to knock a few bits down, exposing the iron roads reinforcing the layer upon layer of poured concrete. The adults all stood around, with wry smiles on their faces muttering to one another: '*deutsche Wertarbeit*' (German quality workmanship). No surprise that buildings which proved almost indestructible to high explosives placed within were largely invulnerable to attack from the air.

In the northwest of central Hamburg, not far from where the trades fair exhibition halls are today, there still stands a grim monument to war and pragmatism: the almost totally undamaged bulk of the Hochbunker, the largest of the city's wartime refuges and defences. Six storeys high, topped with the jutting platforms at each corner for the anti-aircraft batteries, it forms an imposing bleak silhouette against the skyline, even when surrounded – as it is twice a year, in late spring and just before Christmas – with sideshow stalls and carnival amusements for children. It is the sort of building which was always going to be easier to 'recycle' than destroy, yet still presents a stark reminder of an uncomfortable past.

They have done their best to dispel the ghosts: its six floors house graphic artists, a music school, even a specialist shop for drummers, a very sensible use of a building with two-metre thick walls. Every outlet on every floor is filled with bright lights, noise and affluent commerce. But walking up the painted concrete steps, and glancing into the dark alcoves that were once guardrooms, is an uncomfortable experience. Access to the roof is strictly off limits.

Telling it like it is...

The destruction of the fabric of old Hamburg – it is a miracle that many of its most important landmarks were not damaged beyond rebuilding – left a long and brutal scar on the national psyche. But equally miraculously, it did not manifest itself in outright hatred for the occupying army. There was a grim recognition among ordinary Germans in the *Stunde Null* (zero hour) of 1945, as the stories of the concentration camps were made public, that they had had no right to clemency. There was resentment at the British takeover of the finest undamaged houses for their garrison officials – even speculation that they had deliberately spared the richer districts so they could live in them after the war – but a general sense that things could have been worse and the only way to make them better was to work hard, and turn the occupiers into future allies. One of the prime British contributions to Hamburg in the years of occupation was the creation of a free press.

Germany's evolution from a multiplicity of states into one was reflected in the evolution of the press, with almost all newspapers and periodicals starting out with small local readerships, growing alongside literacy which soared from just 10 per cent to nearly 90 per cent between the late 18th and late 19th centuries. At the same time, the multiplicity of small princedoms and archduchies meant hugely varying degrees of press freedom. It was only in 1848, as revolution once again swept Europe, and the first assembly claiming to represent all Germans came together in the 'free city' of Frankfurt-am-Main, that censorship was theoretically banned in all the states making up the German federation. The result was a mushrooming in the number of newspapers, both those based on popularity and advertisement-paid circulation, and those dedicated to one or other party political grouping.

By 1914, the unified Germany had more newspapers than many other European powers, with approximately 4,000 printed regularly. But the number collapsed during

World War I and the left-liberal Weimar Republic, despite its guarantees of freedom of expression, did not tolerate all political views and several newspapers were banned. When the National Socialists took over in 1933, they continued the practice, but with a literal vengeance: all newspapers were forced to submit to strict censorship. Socialist and Communist newspapers were banned, and immense pressure put on any that professed a token independence. When the Dortmund *General-Anzeiger*, the largest paper outside Berlin, published a less than flattering picture of Hitler (in effect a rough caricature) on his first birthday after taking power, the entire newspaper was closed down, its name changed and reopened as an organ of the party; the artist, one Emil Stumpp, was banned from ever publishing again. Effectively the entire media became a tool of Joseph Goebbels' propaganda machine.

From a liberal German point of view, things did not immediately improve with the end of the war and occupation. The Allies closed down all newspapers and only gradually began to allow carefully controlled means of information to be circulated, after allied inspection. In the east, inevitably this led to a Soviet-style media with several newspapers published, allegedly supposed to appeal to various sections of the population, but all strictly under the control of the Socialist Unity Party (the Soviet-controlled fusion of the old Communist and Social Democratic parties).

In the Western zones the American, British and French occupation forces began to issue licences for new newspapers in late 1945/46, and although these could only publish once or twice a week initially due to shortage of paper, their number and circulation grew quickly. *Tagesspiegel* in West Berlin was one of the first. In 1946 one of the future giants of German 20th-century press, Axel Springer, set up the *Hamburger Abendblatt*, and the popular *Hörzu* (Listen) magazine giving details of the new radio programmes being licensed to broadcast by the Allies. He would follow on with the conservative broadsheet *Die Welt*, and the unashamedly populist tabloid *Bild*, which would become one of Europe's most commercially successful newspapers.

On a more elevated level, one of the most significant events in the evolution of the new media was the foundation in February 1946 of the weekly *Die Zeit*, to this day one of Germany's most respected, thoughtful and serious organs, which makes no bones about considering itself to be unabashedly intellectual.

Shortly after its launch, *Die Zeit* was edited by Richard Tüngel, who began to move the paper in a centre-right direction and advocated the then controversial creation of a new army to serve the new Federal Republic. All German armed forces had been disbanded at the end of the war, but armed police had been allowed. There were also some 145,000 men, mostly former prisoners of war, under the control of the British occupation forces in organisations such as the *Deutscher Minenräumendienst* (the German mine-clearing service). Gradually it was accepted that officials on the borders, particularly the disputed frontier with the Soviet zone (later East Germany) had a need to bear arms. It was not, however, until 1955, with the inclusion and the foundation of Nato, that West Germany was allowed its own army, today's Bundeswehr.

Tüngel's regime, however, came to an end in 1955 with his decision to print an article by Carl Schmitt, a known anti-Semitic lawyer who had supported the Nazis, even to the extent of publishing a justification of Hitler's seizure of absolute power. This led to the immediate resignation of Marion Gräfin Dönhoff (she who had been linked to the Hitler assassination plot and fled her chateau near Königsberg on horseback as the Russians approached), who had been the most prominent female journalist at *Die Zeit* since its foundation. Tüngel then made his right-wing sympathies even more evident when he tried to sack his news editor for allowing a piece attacking US senator Joseph McCarthy for his witch-hunt of alleged Communist sympathisers.

As a result, Dönhoff came back to the paper and was to become its leading light for some four decades, as editor from 1968 to 1972, and then as *Herausgeberin*, literally 'publisher' but effectively editor-in-chief, a role she exercised until her death in 2002. From 1983 she shared the role with another leading light of German centre-left thinking, the former chancellor Helmut Schmidt, Hamburg's favourite political son, who rarely appeared in public without his trademark Hamburg sailor's peaked cap. Under Dönhoff–Schmidt steering, *Die Zeit* became a byword for a politics that was not so much left-of-centre but liberal in the tradition of humanitarianism and independent-mindedness. Unlike many other newspapers in the world, *Die Zeit* can be relied on to take an intellectually coherent view on any issue with no fear of controversy.

I fondly recall interviewing the grand old lady of German journalism in the mid-1980s, before she had the opportunity to make a return journey to what was still her off-limits home. Intrepid, daunting and fearless – even then in her late 70s she drove her BMW sportscar at high speed on her daily commute to the office – she told me with penetrating, bright eyes about a habit she had maintained since childhood. 'It's called the handshake game,' she said, with a glint of pride. 'Every time I shake the hand of someone interesting, I work out whose hand they have taken, and whose hand *that* person in turn has taken. It is like genealogy but more fun, and leads in a lot more unexpected directions. I like to see how far back I can go, and where I end up. It can be surprising.' Her own proudest boast was that she was a mere seven handshakes from the great Prussian monarch Frederick the Great, which made her just eight from Voltaire. I am sure the venerable Marion could have tied together many more knots in the web of time, but it set me thinking. And put me at just one more leap from her heroes, as well as making me peruse my own chain of second-hand links.

I since advise friends that in shaking my hand they put

themselves at just one remove from Princess Diana, but also three from Stalin and the same from Hitler. In Moscow I worked with a Soviet photographer who had previously been the official snapper for Andrei Gromyko, Stalin's long-serving photographer. Over several weeks in 1982 standing outside Spandau prison in West Berlin, I shook hands with and chatted to the son of its only inmate, Wolf-Rüdiger Hess, as he waited for a chance to visit his elderly, ailing father, Rudolf Hess, the Führer's one-time lieutenant, brought back to Berlin after his quixotic flight to Scotland apparently seeking a peace agreement, and jailed in Spandau from 1947. Reuters, for whom I was working at the time, memorably asked me to update his profile, adding, in language which was a bit of a fetish among the older generation of desk men who remembered when telex costs were charged per word: 'admittedly he ungotaboutalot recently'. He died, allegedly through suicide by strangulation with a telephone cord, on 17 August 1987. I was in Spain on a family holiday at the time and extremely upset, not by his death, but at having missed the story.

Although the American zone of occupation produced its own newspapers, notably the *Frankfurter Allgemeine*, and Munich's *Süddeutsche Zeitung*, and other media would spring up all over West Germany, the relative isolation of Berlin from 1945 and particularly 1961–89, with the national capital in the relative backwater of Rhineland Bonn, the country's former capital did not automatically become a media magnet. But although the media world is changing fast in Germany as all over the world, Hamburg still has a relative domination of the weekly read, with *Die Zeit* competing with the glossy but gritty *Der Spiegel* – a fusion of the US *Time* magazine and Britain's *Economist* – as well as the more populist *Stern*.

Despite the devastation wreaked upon it in World War II, Hamburg has recovered to the extent that, with a population of 1.77m, it is Germany's second largest city after

Berlin. From the *Landungsbrücken*, today used mainly by cross-harbour ferries and river tour vessels, the skyline is dominated by just a few of the 77 cranes in operation. Some 260,000 people work either in the port or in related businesses, while on average some 440,000 people embark or disembark from cruise liners each year.

In the 1960s Hamburg's conservative city senate was reluctant to take on the new concept of containers, developed by Scots-American Malcolm Maclean, who allegedly got the idea from looking at a cigarette machine. Ernst Plate, the senator responsible for the harbour, is alleged to have declared: 'I'm not having one of those boxes in my port.' But eventually the Senate recognised the inevitability of change and invested DM35m (€17.5m) in a new container terminal. The investment has paid off and continued to the extent that Hamburg Port has developed its own software technology linked to a train turntable in Prague so that it can automatically overnight control movements of container goods trains to and from the Czech Republic, Hungary and the rest of Central Europe. Some 200 goods trains a day come into the port of Hamburg.

By far the best way to grasp just how the city and port are umbilically linked is to take a sightseeing cruise on the Elbe. It is only as the waves begin to lift and rock the boat as if you were at sea that you really understand what a vast river the Elbe really is. From its source deep in the mountains of the Czech Republic it flows for more than a thousand kilometres (over 600 miles) to the sea, but more importantly drains an area of nearly 150,000 square kilometres (nearly 60,000 square miles), including much of Germany as well as parts of Poland, the Czech Republic and even Austria.

The jaunty tars with their peaked caps, weatherproof jackets and sturdy rubberised boots who take tourists out into their domain like to make it as rough and alien as possible for their passengers, the vast majority of whom are German and the only sea they've ever seen is the Mediterranean, cutting into the waves and steering under the overhanging hulls of the great vessels awaiting repair at Blohm + Voss or docked at one of the container terminals. They also make the most of the local dialect, thick as it is with nautical terms, many sharing origins with Dutch and English words: the High German for 'ship' – *Schiff* – becomes *schipp*, and its master the *Schipper*; a smaller river is a *Fleet* and a four-masted ship a *Veermaster*.

It is important to choose one of the smaller boats, not just for the adrenalin-charged excitement of cresting the waves, but so that it can get below the low bridges of the Speicherstadt. It is often called a North European Venice, but the real comparison is with Amsterdam, with which its high-gabled warehouses share so much in terms of architecture. It is not hard to imagine what it must have been like in the late 19th and early 20th centuries, bustling with loading and unloading, workers hurrying back and forth between the Kontorhaus (where the books were kept) and the imposing industrial fairytale castle of the Wasserschloss, which housed the winch guards responsible for maintaining and repairing the hydraulic lifting equipment.

The Elbphilharmonie looks out from the Speicherstadt as a symbolic link to the entire new district emerging over its shoulder, the so-called Hafen-City (with the absurd need Germans today feel to throw in an English word here and there to seem modern). The subject of much local controversy along with a bid to host the 2024 Olympics, the Hafen-City is a 'post-industrial' development on one of the last pieces of port territory laid waste by the bombers and not brought back into use until now. The idea mooted as of 2016 is a mixed-use residential and commercial district, that currently resembles London's former dockland Canary Wharf in the mid-1980s: the infrastructure is already there in terms of underground lines and some of the planned buildings – apartment blocks, business and shopping complexes – have begun to rise. The names of the newly created thoroughfares are deliberately evocatively maritime and international: Marco Polo Terrace, Magellan Terrace, Vasco da Gama Platz, Buenos Aires Quay, Osaka Avenue, Shanghai Avenue and Chicago Quay, which, with a nod to Hamburg's past as a transatlantic liner port, will be the mooring point for all cruise ships, their nearest successor. There has been a deliberate attempt to build where possible in traditional red clinker brick. But most importantly – and possibly uniquely – nothing that was still standing in 1945 has been torn down, however outdated or ugly: there is clearly a feeling that it would be little short of criminal to destroy anything that survived. As far as possible those few structures are being incorporated into the brave new world arising around them.

It is a bold vision, and not without its detractors and a few pertinent warnings, such as those signs on all bridges leading into the Speicherstadt, that 'this area is subject to flooding at short notice'. Whether or not global warming is to blame, the frequency of floods has increased over the past two decades, an important reminder that, for a city whose life blood has been the mighty Elbe, the river is still in control. Germany's 'Gateway to the World' is open and flourishing. There may be choppy waters ahead, but it has come through them before.

The Germans and Sex

It was one of those awkward moments when cultural attitudes clash, epitomised in an expression not normally used in polite English society, least of all at a polite dinner party in London's well-to-do Kensington.

Somehow the conversation at one end of the table with more females than males had come around to men and their sometimes odd preferences, one of which was that of an ex-boyfriend for, you know, nudge, nudge, furrowed brows, eyes glancing at her own cleavage and making a strange gesture with one hand.

My German friend, whose aunt happened to own half the next street, was clearly puzzled by this secret semaphore, until suddenly the penny dropped. 'Oh,' she said, lightening up and smiling broadly, 'you mean titty-fuck? I get that all the time.' There was a silence, suppressed giggles and bitten lips, until a man butted in with an earthy grin, nodded to my amply endowed friend and said, 'Yes, I'm sure you do.' She nodded back and only a rapid change of subject by one of the girls stopped her giving detailed examples.

If the English may be among the most prudish in the world when it comes to discussing sex, the Germans are the opposite: as a rule of thumb they are more than happy to talk about sexual preference, fetishes and techniques, and not just with close friends. It is not that they are any more obsessed with sex than any other nation, just that as the European nation most fond of naturism, health and hedonism, they regard it as a normal part of life with absolutely no need for embarrassment when discussing it. Germans are happy to discuss their bodies – and bodily needs – at any time in any place. German saunas, whether mixed or single sex, insist on nudity and anyone entering in a swimsuit will be told to remove it. Naturism is hugely popular and most large cities have public park areas where nude sun bathing is allowed.

But, as any German will tell you, that is because your body is nothing to be ashamed of. And being naked has nothing to do with sex except for the incidental factor that sex is usually, though not necessarily, performed in the nude. Many people find nudism highly unerotic; many Germans do too. They are fond of eroticism but that is something different, as they will tell you in detail if you ask.

For the vast majority of Germans, as in most of the world, sex is usually part of a normal, loving relationship. The distinguishing thing about the German attitude is that there is very little taboo attached to the topic. But nor are they as a nation particularly sexually voracious. According to a survey for Bavaria-based *Focus* magazine, most German couples have sex once or twice a week. In the word of Munich sex therapist Diana Lüchern, 'I compare good sex with food. It should be tasty, satisfy my hunger and then I don't need anything more… you don't want a five-course meal every day.' She stresses the fact that sex is healthy but that people don't need to have sex 'just for health-related reasons'. '*Lust statt Frust*' is one of her mottos, slightly hard to translate because, whereas *Frust* is unquestionably 'frustration', the German word *Lust* has not just the English sense but can also mean simply 'pleasure, delight, happiness' or even a good appetite. The adjective *lustig* means 'good fun'. Sex therapy classes in Germany are more expensive than in many other European countries, notably the UK, but they are also in most cases substantially more detailed.

The focus on detail without any sense of awkwardness or embarrassment has been something of an issue since the recent vast influx of migrants from mainly Muslim countries. The enthusiastic welcome given to many seeking asylum from war and unrest was severely jolted by incidents in the centre of Cologne on New Year's Eve 2015, during which hundreds of women were sexually assaulted. Most of the men involved were wholly unaccustomed not only to women dressing in tight-fitting or skimpy clothing but also failed to realise that dress style or even physical contact was not an invitation to sex.

One of the results was a website set up in February 2016 by the government's Federal Centre for Health Education, offering a comprehensive variety of 'lessons' on sexuality for 'migrants and immigrants who have not lived in Germany long', available in Arabic, Albanian, Turkish, as well as German, English and six other languages. As well as information about the illegality of any form of violence in or out of marriage, or within families, the site offers extensive details about sexual practice and positions, homosexuality and Germany's complicated age of consent rules (see below), all with graphics that would certainly not be allowed in most of the migrants' home countries. It has come under criticism, with commentators split between those who see it as patronising and insulting to adult migrants and those who assert that migrants will not understand it (even the pictures) and in any case have no interest in conforming to Germany's liberal and permissive culture.

One figure in particular stands out in the evolution of modern Germany's liberal attitude to sex: a former stunt pilot called Beate Uhse. Barred from flying after 1945 because she had also worked as a (non-combatant) transport pilot for the Luftwaffe, the young unemployed widow began selling information on birth control via the 'rhythm method', then supplying condoms by mail order. The business grew. In 1962 she opened an Institute for Marital Hygiene store in her home town of Flensburg near the Danish border, effectively the world's first sex shop, expanded the mail order service 'in discreet packaging' to sex manuals and began stocking erotic lingerie. Gradually the line extended to include 'love toys' and eventually vibrators, handcuffs, dominatrix and schoolgirl outfits.

The chain took off nationally and is now a major listed company, selling among other things some hundred thousand vibrators a year (primarily in rose pink or candy blue

colours and 'normal sizes'). According to Heinrich Brug-
gemann, head of the company that supplies most of them,
'Today's woman wants to know what she's inserting into
her body.' His latest line became the first to receive a cer-
tificate of approval from TÜV, the national product testing
agency: the equivalent of the UK's 'kite mark'. It is a sign of
Beate Uhse company's integration into mainstream German
life that the other things it sells include bath towels, sheets,
pillow and diet pills.

But the Germans' always relatively liberal attitude
towards sex had been radically transformed in the aftermath
of World War II. Historically, prostitution had never been
illegal in the German-speaking lands of Europe. The Holy
Roman Emperor, nominally supreme leader of the German
states, even wrote a letter to the city of Konstanz to thank
them for providing 1,500 prostitutes for the ecumenical
council which met there from 1414 to 1418 (noted for con-
demning the Czech reformer Jan Hus to be burnt at the stake
for heresy). Prostitution was considered a necessary evil to
contain male sexuality. Even in the late 19th century, when
attitudes throughout most of Europe became more puritanical, the chief concern in the newly created German Empire,
as hypocritical as most of Europe in its differing attitudes to
sexual conduct for men and women, was for health checks
to stop the spread of venereal diseases. Berlin's reputation as
the *laissez-faire* capital of Europe in the 1920s is legendary,
as immortalised by English writer Christopher Isherwood's
Sally Bowles.

The devastation of war left the majority of German
cities in ruins, with scant food rations, little coal or wood
for heating, and with cigarettes as the main currency of any
value. With the male population severely depleted, and a vast
number of war widows as well as young women without
partners, the arrival of relatively rich, healthy, young and
attractive soldiers in the armies of occupation, particularly in the American zone, was welcomed. An attractive

girl or woman could get herself a lot of Lucky Strikes for an hour of her time. Open prostitution was frowned upon by the middle classes, with street hookers scathingly called *Amizonen* (a play on 'Amazons' out of the Ami-zone) or *Veronika-Dankeschön*, a satirical reference to most of the soldiers' command of German.

According to Sybille Steinbacher's authoritative 2011 book *Wie der Sex nach Deutschland kam* (How sex came to Germany), which looks back at the evolution of attitudes and behaviour in the late 1940s and 1950s, Germany in the post-war years had over seven million more women than men between the ages of 25 and 45, a figure which even by 1955 had only fallen to 2.8 million. The war itself had already had a marked effect on sexual relations in German society, a result of the decimation of the male population and the destruction of conventional family life by the mass bombing and destruction of cities, which created widows and orphans in large number and threw them onto the streets often homeless and starving. Even when the war ended, food and housing supplies took many years to get back to anything like normal. Keeping body and soul together very quickly became accepted as more important than what the body did to earn a living. Again according to Steinbacher, the sexual health authorities in the state of Northrhine-Westphalia noted that in 1950 large numbers of women 'regularly were involved in the sex trade'. The new federal authorities in West Germany responded to the growing risk of an epidemic of sexually transmitted diseases by providing regular health and hygiene checks.

∈∋

In the immediate post-war period and up until the 1970s, two cities in particular became famous for their 'girls' for predictable reasons. The first was Hamburg, which as all port cities across the world throughout history, offered a huge market catering for sailors passing through. But whereas in some port cities the market was kept out of public view, in Hamburg it was on the streets in neon lights. Hence the comment by the Beatles' John Lennon that despite having been born in Liverpool it was only in Hamburg that they really grew up. The second was Frankfurt, which in the late 1940s and 1950s was heaving with US occupation forces, who were officially forbidden to 'fraternise with the natives', though it was tacitly acknowledged that it wasn't a feeling of brotherhood they were looking for.

The years since have seen prostitution emerge from even the shadow of public deprecation. In 1999 an opinion poll of both sexes aged between 18 and 59 produced a 70 per cent majority in favour of prostitution being declared an acceptable profession subject to tax and national insurance. A law passed in 2001 formally declared prostitution to be 'an acceptable freelance business,' as long as those who practise it do so of their own accord, pay their taxes and are tested regularly for infection.

Coincidentally, as the sex trade has become regulated, business has tailed off somewhat, even in Frankfurt and Hamburg, for a variety of reasons, largely internet pornography and the expansion of more upmarket bordellos. But both are still home to several *Laufhäuser*, literally 'walk-in houses', usually multi-storey apartment blocks with each floor converted into a series of corridors lined with small rooms where each girl, usually scantily clad at the doorway, plies her business. The girls rent their rooms from the landlord, who supervises cleanliness in the public areas and provides (often minimal) security. Prices and services are negotiated one-to-one between client and provider, in a typically matter-of-fact discussion, where the default menu is *'Blasen und Ficken'* (blow job and fuck). It is essentially a self-employed business and socially accepted as such.

The difference to other less liberal countries in Europe is striking. In famously straight-laced – some would say hypocritical – Britain where prostitution is not illegal but kerb-crawling and running a brothel are, police carried out hundreds of raids in 2011–12 before the London Olympics, to protect 'the country's reputation'. Their targets were the tacky, euphemistically labelled 'massage parlours' of the East End and the seedy 'walk-up' rooms rented in central London's comparatively tame and tacky Soho.

In stark contrast, before the 2006 football World Cup in Germany, Berlin saw the opening of what was then Europe's biggest brothel, on a 3,000 square metre (32,000 square ft) site close to the city's newly revamped stadium where the final was played. Much different to the often seedy *Laufhäuser*, Artemis is a vast luxurious three-storey 'club' which boasts a swimming pool, restaurant, bar and rooftop terrace where barbecues are held twice a week. During the championship one of its two 'sex cinemas' showed more conventional 'live games' from the stadiums around the country. The owners boasted it offered football fans from around the world an 'all-in-one experience'. Artemis charges a hefty €80 entrance fee, which is only for the use of the facilities, including free lockers, changing rooms, buffet meals in the restaurant and free soft drinks. Any other services from the women, who also pay to use the facilities, must be negotiated separately.

It is far from an exception. There are now luxury brothels in most large German cities, often describing themselves as 'Wellness centres', a description once reserved for health clubs and spas. Some even organise regular golf and poker tournaments. It is not unusual for a bordello to offer half price on certain days to taxi-drivers, as an incentive to bring clients to the door, and also, more socially-minded, to the over-65s. Working girls get cut-price 'employee rates' at the in-house beauty salon, hairdressers, restaurant and boutique selling lingerie, toys and hygiene items. The girls are also allowed to post their own adverts on the brothel website. Legal prostitution in Germany is worth about €14.5bn (£13.5bn) per annum to the economy. In comparison, figures compiled by the European Union in 2015 showed that sex work in the UK generated some £5.3bn, but because, like drugs, it came under the 'black economy', no tax was paid on any of it.

In April 2016, a new coalition between the Social Democrats and more conservative Christian Democrats passed amendments to the law, intended to regularise the trade beyond previous standards. Significantly, for the first time it made condoms compulsory. 'Working girls' are now obliged to pay not just tax and contributions to health insurance, but also pensions and unemployment benefit, but also have the right to a living wage if they are working in a licensed brothel. Pimping is not only illegal but punishable by a five-year jail sentence. Given the cash nature of the business, taxation is flat rate, charge per daily use of a rented brothel room. Berlin police raided Artemis in April 2016, not because of any moral breach of the law, but because it was believed the owners had not paid some €1.5m in social security contributions on behalf of their employees.

The one concession to traditional propriety is that most of the big brothels are confined to the outer suburbs. Particularly in Munich, capital of ultra-conservative Bavaria, this was true as far back as the early 1980s when I first visited the city for the Oktoberfest. The city centre brothel ban became the inspiration for a hit song played constantly in the giant tents. Twenty-five years on, Spider Murphy Gang's 'Skandal im Sperrbezirk' (Scandal in the no-go zone) remains one of the world's biggest beer festival's best-loved anthems. A key verse is as follows:

Na, jeder ist gut informiert,
weil Rosie täglich inseriert,
Und wenn Dich Deine Frau nicht liebt,
wie gut, dass es die Rosie gibt

Roughly translated (by me) as:

Every guy knows what to do
If your wife doesn't fancy you
Rosie advertises in the papers every day
Just call Rosie and you're on your way

Perhaps the best story about German attitudes towards commercial sex emerged in the normally staid *Handelsblatt* newspaper (Germany's equivalent of the *Financial Times*) back in 2011. It was in fact a report of an incident that had occurred four years earlier at the Hotel Gellert in Budapest involving one of the country's leading insurance companies, Hamburg Mannheimer International. The company, which had prided itself on its human interface in selling insurance, turned out to have been rewarding its most successful employees with human intercourse of the most intimate kind but in relatively public surroundings. *Handelsblatt* had got its hands on an internal company report which revealed that in 2007 it had rewarded its top salesmen with a trip to Budapest, during which it privately booked the splendid old thermal baths adjoining one of the city's grandest hotels, the Gellert, at the base of Buda hill. For an orgy.

In the pool and all around it (rather splendid – I have stayed at the hotel and used the pool, though needless to say, not that particular night) were dozens of young women, all of whom had particular armbands, marking them out as either 'flirt partners' or 'full sex partners'. Or in the words of a senior company official, 'women you could chat with' and 'women you didn't need to chat with'. The less restrained Hamburg-based news magazine used a headline inspired by the parties of former Italian prime minister Silvio Berlusconi: 'Bunga-bunga in Budapest.' For added entertainment there was a television celebrity chef in charge of the menu and a fiddler (if you'll pardon the expression), who just happened to be the brother-in-law of Budapest's chief of police, the man who had given permission for the baths to stay open until 4 a.m.

The company's internal investigation concluded that the party 'overstepped moral guidelines' and noted that hiring the services of prostitutes 'went against the company's values', before adding that there was no legal problem in setting the costs against tax. *Handelsblatt* agreed.

∈∋

In East Germany, as in all Soviet-dominated states in Eastern Europe, prostitution was officially banned but socially tolerated. When I first arrived in Berlin, having been brought up in prudish Northern Ireland, I was initially shocked by the open public attitude towards sex, from the grimy hardcore video cabins on the streets of West Berlin, with their boxes of free tissues and telltale scent of disinfectant, to the high-class, immaculately turned out whores parading up and down the Kurfürstendamm. A hangout for hookers at the lower end of the market was the wooded alleyways of the Tiergarten, the great park to the west of the Brandenburg Gate, where cars frequently stopped to pick up 'passengers' in the little-used roads that wound around what had once been the embassy quarter when Berlin was the capital. Today, of course, it has been scrupulously sanitised and most of the old embassies reopened.

East Germany, by comparison, was a model of morality, almost all of it hypocritical. The closest it came to outright pornography was *Das Magazin*, a supposedly cultural and literary glossy monthly intended to show that Communism had an intellectual human face, but whose circulation was primarily based on the fact that it regularly featured 'artistic' photographs of naked young women. Even then, with no restrictions on 'full frontal', as long as it could be classified as 'artistic', it was more daring than almost anything to be bought other than from the most daring of so-called 'sex shops' in Britain.

Not that the East German regime had anything against

sex: in fact, given that the aim of most adults was, if possible, to escape their country, the regime positively encouraged as much sex as possible, merely as a means of maintaining the population. The FDJ (*Freie Deutsche Jugend* – Free German Youth), a Communist Party organisation for young people, a body intended to infuse the next generation with the values of their elders, was surprisingly popular among teenagers who might have been expected to be at the rebellious phase. The prime reason was that beyond lip service to Communist values and outdoor sports, it was also keen on another popular outdoor communal activity: mixed camping trips. Think of a mixed Boy Scout and Girl Guide camp or US summer camp with, for over-16s, no restrictions on cigarettes and beer and a lax attitude towards sex in the tents. After FDJ parades on Unter den Linden, it was not uncommon to see the placards proclaiming undying devotion to the Socialist Unity Party and the beliefs of Marx and Engels lying trampled over on the street, while their erstwhile bearers were groping and snogging in the alleyways.

The rules on homosexuality were different, but, curiously, arguably more lenient in the East. As in many countries, homosexuality had been considered a serious crime from the Middle Ages until the latter half of the 20th century. During the liberal 1920s homosexuality, though nominally illegal, was widely tolerated, especially in Berlin, where bars for openly gay men were opened. That came to a brutal end with the Nazi era, when many homosexuals were thrown into concentration camps and made to wear a pink triangle on their prison uniforms. Thousands died.

Attitudes towards gay sex, as indeed to almost everything, changed dramatically from 1945 on. In West Germany gay sex was legalised in 1969 with the age of consent set at 21, reduced to 18 four years later. In East Germany homosexual acts were legalised from 1968, but in reality the regulations had been even more liberal than they appeared, albeit in a particularly idiosyncratic way: from 1957 homosexuality was decriminalised as long as no 'harm had been done to socialist society'. I have always wondered precisely what sort of act could have fallen foul of that proscription.

West Berlin, that idiosyncratic semi-anarchist anomaly that existed between 1961 and 1989, has always probably been one of the most gay-friendly cities in Europe. It might have been expected to go the other way once the reunited city became capital and home to a more straight-laced community of politicians and civil servants. In fact, of course, the opposite has been true. Berlin has always revelled in being liberal, even to the extent, if needs be, of being outrageous. My son and a few friends went to a gay stag party in Berlin in the summer of 2015, only to find themselves refused admittance to most of the clubs they tried to go to because they were apparently too respectably dressed. Leather with strategic cut-outs or very short shorts were the height of respectability allowed: anything more daring was welcomed.

At first glance the age of consent in both Germany and Austria today appears low at 14, for both homosexual and heterosexual relationships, but in reality it is more complicated. There is a 'border zone' of 14 to 16, where a sexual relationship is permissible only as long as there is no evidence that the younger partner's lack of capacity for sexual self-determination has not been abused. Effectively this means that in a case where the younger individual has lodged a complaint an investigation will take place. Unlike in the UK, where the decades of paedophile crimes by the now notorious disc jockey Jimmy Savile were only exposed after his death, leading to a national soul-searching that at times approximated to a witch-hunt, in Germany there is a statute of limitations. The rule is that charges can no longer be brought if a complainant has reached the age of 28; it may seem unfair, but the argument goes that if it was worthy of complaint surely the young adult, if not the child, should have got round to it a lot earlier.

The huge influx of immigrants, mostly from the Muslim

world, has challenged Germany's liberalism, although possibly more in attitudes towards the immigrants than towards sex. There remains a steadfast refusal to let another culture contaminate a consensus arrived at over decades. I think that would be difficult. There is a strong sense of hedonism in Germanic culture that goes back a very long way.

As a way out of this chapter, I will risk giving you two German jokes on the topic. The first has an angry father shouting at his daughter's boyfriend: 'You've taken my daughter's virginity!' to which he replies, 'I promise never to do it again.'

The second is more – or arguably less – risqué depending on your own morality:

'What is the difference between eroticism and perversion?'

'Eroticism is when a man takes a duck feather and strokes a woman's breasts and mount of Venus with it... Perversion is when the feather is still attached to the duck.'

7

Frankfurt

An alternative capital, in every sense of the word

Wall Street on Main

Even the Germans call it 'Bankfurt', and make jokes about the supposedly soulless metropolis on the majestic river Main, a city of suits and skyscrapers, home to Europe's common currency and a very strange green sauce.

Yet Germans also hold Frankfurt-am-Main in respect, because not only does it still boast Germany's biggest and busiest international airport, host one of its oldest and biggest trade fairs, but it was for centuries the coronation site of would-be emperors, the focus of the first serious attempt at creating a unified German nation and on at least two occasions could have ended up that nation's capital.

Arriving in Frankfurt by train can give a curious impression of continental Europe's banking nexus. The station itself is a grand piece of 19th-century railway architecture, lovingly restored, high-arched and imposing and opening, as stations should, onto a wide square, with straight avenues leading into the heart of the city.

Except that it also has that other attribute of station districts: a fair amount of sleazy lowlife and dodgy bars. In particular the little cluster of streets named after German rivers – the Mosel, Elbe and Weser to be specific – houses a large number of walk-in brothels, mainly a hangover from the post-war days when this was the headquarters of the American occupation and filled with overpaid and over-sexed GIs. The Americans left, but the hookers didn't.

Then there is the fact that stations as a rule attract the lower echelons of society, the poor and the beggars, where large interchanges offer opportunities for holding out a paper cup, or filching a wallet. Not that the area around Frankfurt station is particularly a high-risk area or frequent crime scene, it is just not the best part of town and certainly not where you stay if you have flown in your Learjet to do a major refinancing deal or trade at the top end of the bourse. Frankfurt has one of the larger foreign populations of any German city with nearly a third of its 771,000 inhabitants being non-German by birth, and only a relatively small proportion of these belong to the international banking community.

Yet the Rhein-Main Metropolis, as it likes to style itself, has played a vastly more significant role in German history since its origins in the eighth century. The probably apocryphal but far from implausible legend of Frankfurt's foundation holds that the Frankish King Karl der Grosse (Charles the Great, or as we bizarrely call him by his French name, Charlemagne), was pursuing an army of Saxons who had retreated to the other side of the broad Main. Uncertain how to cross to continue his pursuit, he spotted a herd of deer crossing the river and realising there had to be a passable ford at that point, took his army across and defeated them. Afterwards he sensibly decreed that this vulnerable part of the river had to be defended and ordered his Frankish soldiers to build a fort: Frankenfort. The name is first recorded as Francofurdum, in a document from the year 794 preserved in a monastery in Regensburg, Bavaria. The first mention of a trade fair – the city's economic mainstay throughout its history down to the present day – is to be found in a Jewish mercantile document from 1150 referring to a market on the

Main, which was a major centre of trade between the Baltic and the Mediterranean.

The legend has the ring of truth not just because it makes sense but also because the area on the opposite bank, now an inner city suburb, is still called Sachsenhausen (the houses of the Saxons). In fact, Sachsenhausen is now in many ways the heart of 'real' Frankfurt. The only major area of the inner city to survive the bombing raids of 1945 – though it never had the mediaeval splendour of the destroyed city centre – it still has winding alleyways and houses dating from the 18th and 19th centuries. It is the key place to come if you want to taste Frankfurt's unique culinary speciality, 'green sauce' with boiled eggs and potatoes, washed down with a local cider which the locals in their own particular dialect call *Ebbelwoi* (apple wine). Little hostelries along the back streets serve their own or a particular brewer's *Ebbelwoi* out of traditional blue and grey jugs, and on a warm spring evening or summer's day they teem with students knocking it back in leafy gardens.

It is unlikely however that Charlemagne was the first to note the strategic location of the site. There is evidence of settlement at a much earlier date and possibly a Roman garrison on the spot. But from the early ninth century it became a meeting place for the East Frankish 'parliaments' – meetings of chieftains – and by 1220 was granted the status of a 'free city' in what remained of Charlemagne's attempts to recreate a unified Christian empire.

After Friedrich I was chosen as Holy Roman Emperor in Frankfurt in 1152, it would become custom to hold the vote for his successors there, elevating the city's status. In 1220 that was made official when it became a 'free city', meaning that it was independent of any of the surrounding princes or dukes who might have laid claim to it. A 'free city', like those in the Hansa, nominally answered only to the emperor, which as time went on and the office came to have little more than symbolic value, effectively meant they were independent city-states.

In 1356 the pope issued a papal bull declaring Frankfurt to be the permanent site of coronation for whichever prince was elected to the imperial title, prior to formal confirmation by the pope himself in Rome. Because of the complicated evolution of the imperial title, its supposed direct derivation from Charlemagne and purported descent from the Caesars themselves, a prince elected by his peers could only formally become emperor by coronation in Rome, which happened increasingly rarely. The title conferred in Frankfurt was the intermediate step of 'King of Rome', widely interpreted in much of Europe as 'King of the Germans', although in practice there was nothing of the sort and the title-bearer was no such thing. But he was at the very least first among equals, a definition that Caesar Augustus himself would have appreciated.

The city's magnificent, towering 14th-century St Bartholomäus church, almost universally referred to as the Frankfurter Dom (Frankfurt Cathedral), although it has never actually attained cathedral status or been the seat of an archbishop, was decreed as the venue for the coronations. A small chapel to the right of the altar was set aside for the electors, theoretically to hold their deliberations, although in fact these things were always agreed long in advance, before one of them emerged to be crowned. Coronations in Frankfurt continued until 1792, by which time the emperor genuinely had no clothes, at least as far as power went: the imperial title had become little more than another in the long string of titles handed down within the Austrian Habsburg family. It had meant very little for centuries by the time Francis II took the title, and would be abolished by Napoleon for dynastic reasons of his own 14 years later.

Germany's Shakespeare

Unquestionably, Frankfurt's most famous son was Johann Wolfgang von Goethe, arguably the Shakespeare of German literature, the man whose works are essential reading for all schoolchildren. A true Enlightenment man, Goethe was not just a playwright, novelist and poet, but a more than competent scientist, artist and statesman, who sprang to public notice in his mid-20s and would dominate German cultural life and letters for more than half a century.

His most influential work – which in later life he came to regret having written – was written at the tender age of just 24: *Die Leiden des Jungen Werthers* has an even more unprepossessing title in the English translations, *The Sorrows of Young Werther*. The book was one of the leading examples of the artistic movement that came to be known as *Sturm und Drang* (usually translated as 'Storm and Stress', though if it weren't for the unfortunate rhyming slang connotation, a better translation might be 'Trouble and Strife'), a youth-led literary rebellion against the discipline and formality of the previous generations.

Although the term didn't really come into use until the early 1820s, by which time the movement was on its way out, it originally comes from a 1776 play written by a friend of Goethe's, Friedrich von Klinger, also a Frankfurter, but from a lower social class than the relatively well-to-do Goethes: his father was a junior officer in the city guard. In fact it was his friendship with Goethe that helped him get a place at university to study to be a clerk. But Klinger had higher ambitions. He was a fan of both Shakespeare's dramatic style and Jean-Jacques Rousseau's philosophy. He was the author of several plays, including a comedy of sorts entitled *Sturm und Drang*. The young dramatist's *succès d'estime* was not, however, matched by financial recompense. As a result he opted to join the army as a lieutenant, then took advantage of there being a German woman on the Russian throne (Catherine the Great) to transfer his allegiances and ended up as a general in charge of the Russian cadet corps in the province of Estonia. Throughout his life – he died in 1833 – he maintained a close correspondence with Goethe.

The main thrust of the *Sturm und Drang* movement was to break free of the rigid rules of classical literature, particularly on stage, handed down from the 17th-century French dramatists Corneille and Racine. But it soon became synonymous with any form of literature that challenged the audience, championing emotion rather than reason.

Werther is an epistolary novel, a series of letters written by the eponymous hero to his friend Wilhelm detailing the ups and downs – mostly downs – of his obsession with a beautiful young orphan called Charlotte, who is already engaged to a much older man. His love is reciprocated but only in sentiment as the object of his affection is loyal to her fiancé, whom she marries, and eventually tells Werther that he must stop trying to see her. As a result Werther decides that one of the three in this cursed triangle must do the decent thing. He writes to the girl's husband asking to borrow two pistols as he is going on a journey. Charlotte sends them to him on her husband's behalf, only to have Werther use one of them to shoot himself in the head. The book ends with his sparsely attended funeral and the suggestion that Charlotte may die of a broken heart.

For something that sounds to modern ears so trite, if not downright ridiculous, it is hard to grasp the impact that it had on the young generation of late 18th-century Europe. Goethe himself, who had written the novel in just four weeks, would later effectively disown it, even while admitting he had 'fed it with the blood of my own heart'. He regretted that it had been too near to the knuckle in reflecting his own youthful obsession with one Charlotte Buff, a young lady from Hanover who had rejected his advances in favour of an older diplomat. Bizarrely, Goethe had bought them their wedding ring in Frankfurt.

But the book's runaway success was almost certainly due to the fact that it was written by a member of the younger generation and aimed at them rather than the more formal literary world inhabited by their parents. Young Werther and his tragic world represented everything that their parents did not: it is not too far-fetched to see a parallel in *The Fault in Our Stars*, young-teen tragedy by John Green, *Time* Magazine's 2012 Book of the Year, about two young lovers dying of cancer, lambasted by Britain's *Daily Mail* as an example of 'sick-lit'. A less schmaltzy equivalent might be the iconic 1955 James Dean film, *Rebel Without a Cause*, which also centres on the clash between generational attitudes. Goethe, previously unknown, became an overnight celebrity. *Werther* is widely considered to be the first example of a modern phenomenon in literature, the 'best-seller'.

Werther was such a sensation that, centuries before social media, it created a cult. All over Europe young men began donning blue jackets and yellow breeches in imitation of the doomed hero's dress. You could buy miniature figurines of Werther and even a scent named after him. It caused the emergence of a phenomenon we might think restricted to the internet age: copycat suicides, which worried the authorities as much as such instances do today. Mary Shelley, writing nearly 50 years later, had Frankenstein's monster discover the book in a leather portmanteau, only to find himself sympathising with Werther as a fellow creature rejected by those he loves.

Perhaps most significantly – arguably scarily – of all, one of the book's greatest fans was a young Frenchman who had only been five years old when it was published. General Napoleon Bonaparte, aged just 29, chose it as just one of three books to take with him on his expedition to Egypt. He would go on to read it seven times and acclaim it as one of the greatest works of world literature. In 1808, anxious to stave off a new war with Austria, he called together all the German princes in what was then the French-dominated Confederation of the Rhine for a show of strength and unanimity at Erfurt in Thuringia. To general surprise he summoned Goethe to attend also, produced his copy of *Werther* and told him he carried it with him everywhere.

Another, very different, young man who became a lifelong devotee of Goethe's works was the polyglot British right-wing politician, Enoch Powell. My one and only encounter with him was standing next to the fireplace of one of Pall Mall's gentlemen's clubs (I can no longer remember which) in the late 1980s as, realising I was a German-speaker, he recited verses from Goethe's 'Gesang der Geister über den Wassern' (The Singing of Ghosts across the Water, more commonly known in English as 'The Song of Spirits over the Waters', but I first read it in German, in Lauterbrunnen, Switzerland, source of Goethe's inspiration, watching the torrential waterfall so high that it rarely reaches the ground as more than spray, and to me the sense has never been quite the same) declaring how 'dangerous', meaning seductive, the German language could be 'to a young man'. A fervent British nationalist who campaigned fiercely against appeasement of Nazi Germany and later against non-white immigration into Britain, Powell gave me a sense that night how this remarkably intelligent, educated man had understood, and almost yielded to, the artificial romance of fascist nationalism.

In Goethe's own day *Werther* became the book 'that defined a generation' and would haunt him most of his life as an inspiration to what became known as Weimar Classicism, which he himself grew to dismiss as 'sick'. But literature was never going to be his only concern. His father had insisted that he should train as a lawyer at Leipzig University (Frankfurt had none of its own in those days) and then in what he would still have called Strassburg, the city on the Rhine that had been ceded to France at the Peace of Westphalia in 1743, but where teaching was still carried out in German. While still a young man in his mid-20s he became a minister and member of the privy council of the Duchy of Saxony-Weimar, where his campaign against corruption earned him promotion to the role of finance minister, while at the same time he instituted reforms at Jena University, helped with the planning of Weimar's botanical gardens and rebuilding of the duke's palace. He took an interest in geology and mineralogy and oversaw the reopening of copper and silver mines in the duchy.

It was Goethe who founded the Weimar art competition which saw the rise to fame of young painter Caspar David Friedrich, whose haunting pictures, from his homeland in Pomerania on the bleak Baltic coast, to his later home in Dresden, where he specialised in churchyards, forever changed the nature of German landscape painting.

By the age of 33 Goethe seemed to have no worlds left to conquer: he was a famed best-selling author and the most important man in Weimar after the duke himself. After a trip to Rome, much later written up and published from diaries kept at the time, he wrote a botanical treatise entitled *The Metamorphosis of Plants,* but the journey was most marked by the production of his *Roman Elegies,* a series of erotic poems inspired by the trip and his own love life with Christiane Vulpius, a woman 15 years his junior, which caused something of a scandal in conservative Weimar society. Vulpius would bear him his only child to survive infancy, August Walter. Although he would spend the rest of his life in the relationship with Vulpius, it did not prevent him having a fling with a noblewoman half his age. The relationship, however, continued to scandalise Weimar's aristocratic society, not so much because of their unmarried status but because of Christiane's impoverished family background. On his return, and perhaps partly to do with the public reaction to his private life and erotic writing, he asked to be relieved of his formal official duties, remaining in close contact with the duke as 'minister without portfolio'.

Throughout all this time he continued to produce literary work, including the verse epic *Hermann und Dorothea*, his second novel, *Wilhelm Meisters Lehrjahre*, and much, much more. He reacted with horror to the atrocities of the French Revolution, which he labelled 'the most awful event ever', by producing a series of satirical anti-revolutionary comedies.

In 1792, he experienced the consequences first hand and saw the misery of warfare when he was asked by the duke to accompany him on his military campaign as part of the coalition fighting revolutionary France.

In 1788 he had met and formed a lifelong friendship with the other colossus of late 18th-century German literature, Friedrich Schiller, whose plays he would put on regularly at Weimar theatre. The two worked tirelessly together, collaborating and influencing one another's work, with Schiller moving his family to Weimar in 1789. His death in 1805 devastated Goethe, and he was unable even to attend the funeral, saying he had lost 'half of myself'.

Eventually in 1806, shortly after Christiane's intervention had saved his life when French soldiers burst into their home after the Battle of Jena, Goethe eased the situation by marrying the woman he had always called his '*kleine Eroticon*'.

He met Napoleon a second time in 1808 at a court ball in Weimar, and would later describe him as 'one of the most productive men of all time', who 'bestrode the world like a demigod from battle to battle, victory to victory'. It was perhaps a coincidence that 1808 was also the year he published the work that, along with *Werther,* was to become his greatest legacy: *Faust*, his theatrical account of a man who sold his soul to the devil. It did not prevent him accepting with delight the honour of being made a knight of the Légion d'Honneur by the French emperor.

Thomas Mann, one of the great German literary figures of the 20th century, speaking in the Library of Congress in Washington on 29 May 1945, just after the collapse of the Nazi regime, compared what had happened to Germany with Goethe's Faust selling his soul to the devil. Mann, who had emigrated to the United States in 1939 and become a US citizen, said of Goethe himself: 'With him, Germany took a great leap forward in human culture,' only to add poignantly, 'or should have done.' Mann had been born and grown up in the Hanseatic city of Lübeck near the Baltic coast, where much of his massive novel *Buddenbrooks* is set, even though by its publication in 1901 he had moved to Munich, where he also wrote his other magnum opus, *Der Zauberberg* (The Magic Mountain). Both are challenging works, heavily based in realism, but with dense layers and leitmotivs. They won him the Nobel Prize for literature in 1929. Mann recognised Goethe as his great inspiration with *Doktor Faustus* a recasting of Goethe's play as a novel amid the chaos of the mid-20th century. In *Lotte in Weimar*, Mann also revisited Goethe's own inspiration for *Werther*, putting words into the author's mouth in old age, apparently foreseeing the rise of Hitler. (In the Nürnberg war crimes trials in 1946 they were mistakenly attributed by a British prosecutor to Goethe himself.)

Throughout his life and beyond it, many of Goethe's poems were set to music by the great composers of the era, including Mozart, Schubert, Wagner, Berlioz and Beethoven, whom he bumped into at a spa resort in Bohemia in 1812. They met several times and Beethoven played the piano for him, astounding him with his ability, although Goethe found him 'a very undisciplined individual'. The death of his wife in 1816 left him once again stricken with grief but so unable to cope with mortality that he failed to be at her deathbed or even attend her funeral. The final years of his own remarkably long life – he died apparently of a heart attack in 1832 at the age of 82 – were spent producing the second part of *Faust* and autobiographical works.

Goethe had been no struggling author before his rapid rise to fame. His family were upper middle class, his grandfather a judge, his father a lawyer and his sister a private tutor. They had even done the classic middle-class domestic thing, knocking together two small houses in an alleyway in the centre of Frankfurt and erecting a much grander structure over their cellars. His mother sold the house in 1795, after the death of his father, by which time Goethe himself had long since moved on and was running a theatre in Weimar. It then went through a series of hands until in 1859, just before it was to be sold to a purchaser keen to alter the property unrecognisably, it was bought up by the Freies Deutsches Hochstift, a newly founded, Frankfurt-based organisation, inspired by the 1848 moves towards some form of German unity and dedicated to the preservation of artistic and scientific heritage. Over the years that followed, they collected together artefacts from the Goethe family and put together one of the first major domestic memorials to an author and his times.

In one of those bitter ironies of history, it happened to be on 29 March 1944, the anniversary of his death, that the family house suffered a direct hit by an Allied bombing raid and was completely destroyed. Inevitably there was a long and occasionally fractious debate about how and whether it, or at least the memorial, should be restored or reconstituted. The single consolation was that early in the war the house's contents had been put in safe storage. In the end, due in no small part to the backing of another Nobel laureate and Goethe fan, the poet Hermann Hesse, the decision was taken to rebuild the house and restock it with the stored items. The result today, nearly 70 years after its rebuilding, is a house that feels as if it could be original, with the original décor, paintings and furniture in place, and, happily, not the slightest feel of Disneyfication about it, no attempt to present it as other than it is: an extraordinary museum to one of the leading figures in European literature.

The concept of German unification was still a pipe dream in Goethe's early years, but the catastrophic change brought about on the old order in Europe by the French Revolutionary and Napoleonic Wars in his mid-life suddenly made anything and everything possible. Serious agitation for a pan-German state only came to the fore after Goethe's death, but the subject was in the air enough for him to give a considered answer when quizzed about it in an interview in 1828: 'I couldn't care less if Germany doesn't become united:

our good roads and our future good railways will do their bit. We just need to like one another... We are united as long as the German Thaler and Grosschen have the same value everywhere and my suitcase doesn't have to be opened by all 36 states... and for us not to talk about home and abroad any more.' It could have come straight from the mouths of one of the European Union's founding fathers or indeed one of those politicians today – still common in Germany but all but non-existent in the United Kingdom – who believe that the nation-state is an abstraction and what matters is a community of nations with commonly shared standards and values, common currency and open borders.

Goethe was dismissive of the need for one dominant capital city. But his aspirations for the residents of the greater part of the Central European land mass went even further: 'A German should learn all languages so no foreigner should feel uncomfortable and so that he should feel at home wherever he is.'

E Pluribus Unum

Already by the end of Goethe's life the subject of at least a common German identity and polity had been raised in earnest and was gathering support. The end of the Napoleonic Wars did not restore the old regimes quite the way the monarchies and aristocracy of the conservative coalition had wished. The wave of revolutions which swept Europe in 1830, starting in France and spreading out in ripples that were felt more in some regions than others, led inexorably to a resumption of popular revolt on an altogether wider scale in 1848. In France the restored post-Napoleonic monarchy was toppled in favour of a republic, which Napoleon's nephew, elected as president, soon turned back into an empire, which ironically would lead to a war that saw the French empire destroyed and a German one created.

In the German states, loosely lumped together into a

'German confederation' which now included the two 'big boys' – Austria and Prussia – which Napoleon had excluded from his vassal 'Confederation of the Rhine', there was growing dissatisfaction at the return to conservative rule by unelected aristocrats. There was a widespread desire for higher wages and better living standards. In 1833 an attempted putsch led by students in Frankfurt was put down violently. There was also a desire for an end to the nonsense, described by Goethe, where travellers across often relatively short distances – so small were some of the princes' and dukes' 'sovereign' domains that they were no bigger than a few English aristocratic country estates cobbled together under one ruler but often separate from one another – could be required to have their luggage checked and possibly pay duty, which applied in one state but not another. The result of the antipathy to this ridiculous state of affairs was the growth of pan-German sentiment and a feeling that the rulers of the 39 states in the confederation were more concerned with their own interests than those of their subjects. Which was by and large true.

⋐⋑

Once again events in Paris had a domino effect across the continent. Following what was known in France as the 'February Revolution', King Louis Philippe abandoned his throne and fled into exile in Britain. This evoked what would become known across the Rhine as the 'March Revolution'. It kicked off in the most important German-speaking city, Vienna. On 13 March street protests led to the resignation of Metternich, the conservative chancellor who had effectively wielded power in Central Europe for the past 30 years. His order to troops to fire on students in the street inspired the city's working class to join their protest. The contagion spread. The example of Louis Philippe's fate proved warning enough for some of the minor German rulers to listen to the protesters' demands. They were then met with greater demands. On the shopping list were things we now consider the basis of democratic states: freedom of the press, freedom of assembly and parliamentary representation.

Similar street protests in the capital of the other big German state, Prussia, led to conflict between the army and demonstrators on the streets of Berlin in which several were killed. King Friedrich Wilhelm IV promised take account of the people's views, and even work towards a united German state, but the clashes got worse, leading to barricades on the streets and a major clash with the army in which 254 civilians died.

The feeling on the streets throughout the German lands was that for too long the people had been ruled by a vast aristocratic–ecclesiastical oligarchy which had excelled in the art of divide and rule. There were no longer countless hundreds of petty princedoms, archbishoprics, duchies, margravates and supposedly 'free' cities, but the principle remained. In 1848 the German-speaking parts of Europe (excluding the German cantons of Switzerland) still numbered 39 different entities, from the vast territories of Austria and its new rival Prussia to tiny patches of land, sometimes not even contiguous, such as the Duchy of Saxe-Coburg-Gotha, from which Britain's Queen Victoria had plucked her husband Albert.

The French Revolution and Napoleon had swept away the old blind allegiances to royalty and aristocracy. In Bavaria King Ludwig I, having already lost face because of his romantic dalliance with the phoney Spanish dancer Lola Montez, abdicated in favour of his son, who promised greater reform. The story was much the same in nearly all the German states. In Heidelberg, capital of Baden, a group of liberals proposed an elected popular assembly representing the citizens of all the 39 states, rather than their rulers' chosen minions. In the hope of putting an end to the protests (and saving their positions), the rulers gave at least token agreement. Elections were set to be held in April and May in all the German states.

The rules were that one deputy would be chosen for every 70,000 men (a figure reduced to 50,000 when it was pointed out that some states had fewer than 70,000 inhabitants). Only those in the German-speaking parts of the Austrian Empire were eligible, a detail that presaged obvious problems to come. The same in theory should have applied to Prussia, which had absorbed a large chunk of 18th-century Poland, but, to Prussia's advantage, this was overlooked. The franchise was open to all males 'of age' (generally 25 and above) who were *selbstständig*, which literally meant 'self-sufficient', but this was interpreted differently in different states. In some, adult males still resident in their parents' homes were not allowed to vote. Women had no vote, nor did the working classes in some states. In theory this should have produced a 'national' assembly of some 649 representatives, but because constituencies in part of the Austrian realm designated as German but with a majority of Czech speakers, boycotted the elections, the final number was 586.

Frankfurt was chosen as the venue for the assembly partly because of its ancient role as the coronation place of the 'emperors' but also because as a 'free city' it was not under the jurisdiction of any of the princes. The assembly would meet in the Church of St Paul, the Paulskirche. Begun in 1789 by an architect heavily inspired by the ideals of the French Revolution but with construction delayed by the Napoleonic Wars, it had only been finished a few years previously in 1833. Designed as a Lutheran Protestant church, where the sermon was the main part of the service, the architect's prime aim was to make sure that everyone could hear the preacher. It was therefore designed in a circular form, which made it ideal, according to contemporary thinking, for a parliamentary assembly. There was also the advantage that it was large, with a maximum capacity of 2,000. The organisers of the election used it as their headquarters and in May 1848 the new assembly moved in and adopted a black, red and gold banner as the flag of the new state they hoped to create.

Almost all of them were professional people, including judges, lawyers, shopkeepers, but the vast majority were either university lecturers or teachers, with the result that it became known as the 'professors' parliament'. There were many men of principle, mostly socially liberal, but few experienced politicians. They chose a leading local liberal as president and set themselves the task of determining a central authority for 'all of Germany'. This embryonic parliament of amateurs met for four hours each day in well-meaning debates, but few of them led to any sort of conclusion.

To the assembly in Frankfurt even the idea of a 'German Union' without the largest and most powerful German state seemed nonsense. For more than four centuries the Habsburgs or their close relatives had, as Holy Roman Emperors, dominated the only (increasingly remotely) serious attempt to create a semblance of a pan-German state. In acknowledgement of this, the assembly almost automatically chose a member of the Austrian ruling family – albeit a socially liberal one – as *Reichsverweser*, a token interim head of a state that had yet to come into existence.

The problem was that through their skilful and prodigious match-making the Habsburg family's imperial adventure over the centuries had taken them further than ever expected: beyond Europe to the shores of the Pacific, the islands of southeast Asia. Even after the loss of the Spanish connection and Napoleon's removal of the 'Holy Roman' title, the renamed Austrian Empire was still rivalled only by European Russia as the continent's largest realm.

Yet out of its vast population, for the day, of 51 million, only 24 per cent spoke German, mostly living in the areas abutting the other German-speaking states (albeit with substantial minorities in Transylvania). This led to a suggestion in Frankfurt that maybe only those areas should be included in the proposed new nation-state. Unsurprisingly this was treated in Vienna as preposterous, apparently implying some sort of partition, at least in constitutional terms, of the empire.

In reality the empire was slowly running into trouble, as the 'power-sharing' agreement with the Hungarians less than 20 years later would show. But as so often with fading empires, there was a reluctance on the home front to recognise this. In other circumstances Vienna might well have ended up as capital of the coming new German Reich rather than Berlin.

The Austrians, however, made it quite clear that amalgamation of any of their territory into this new-fangled idea of a 'nation-state' was simply not on the cards. If there was to be some sort of pan-German 'union' it would be a loose confederation in which they played the leading role. To the would-be nation-makers in Frankfurt this sounded more like business as usual than a Central European constitutional revolution. The *Grossdeutschland* ('big Germany') – the *e pluribus unum*, to borrow a phrase from the United States, a union of the multiple states into one country, including the vast majority of Europe's German-speakers, seemed to be falling apart. The term is scarcely used these days because of the unwelcome echoes of its revival by Adolf Hitler. The only feasible alternative seemed to be what, to make the contrast, was described as *Kleindeutschland* ('little Germany') in which the largest element by far would be Prussia. Unsurprisingly, the Prussian delegates began to promote this idea and gradually it began to gain traction. Meanwhile, behind the scenes the old order was reasserting itself.

The assembly held admirable, even noble, views best expressed in a speech delivered to the assembly in July 1848 by Leipzig deputy Robert Blum, which might have been made in the European Parliament in Strasbourg in the spring of 1989: 'I offer my voice to the goal of fraternal relationships between the free people of the West and those fighting for their freedom. When we achieve this goal, we will have achieved both peace and freedom for Europe.' When fighting broke out again in Vienna that autumn he joined the revolutionaries, was arrested and – despite his claim of parliamentary immunity – was executed.

While the talking shop in the Paulskirche was still debating the forms of their new constitution for 'all of Germany', Berlin pushed through a new constitution for Prussia, without reference to Frankfurt, making quite clear that in all issues, ultimate authority lay with the king. The new constitution instituted a bicameral parliament, in which representation was split into three voting categories, heavily weighted towards landowners, the establishment and the wealthy; the rest of the adult male population were given the vote, but with far fewer representatives per head of the electorate.

Eventually the assembly in Frankfurt did agree on a serious and well thought-through constitution, passed on 28 March 1849, and supposed to come into immediate effect in all the states of the confederation. It proposed that the new country be a constitutional monarchy presided over by a hereditary Kaiser or emperor, a title which allowed all the kings, princes and dukes to retain their own status. Of the 39 members of the confederation 28 automatically accepted it. Fatally, those that did not included the biggest and most important: Austria, Prussia and Bavaria, along with the next two, Saxony and Hanover. That effectively meant that, despite the much higher number of states that accepted it, substantially less than half their combined territory was included.

The Prussian parliament accepted Frankfurt's proposed constitution, but the king did not, which under the Prussian constitution invalidated their acceptance. Nor was Friedrich Wilhelm IV impressed when Frankfurt offered him the imperial crown at the end of March 1849. Publicly the king declared himself 'honoured', but insisted he could not accept primacy over his peers in the confederation unless they themselves rather than an elected assembly offered it to him. Privately he wrote that he had never had any intention of accepting a crown 'disgraced by the stink of revolution, defiled by dirt and mud'.

The conservative faction in Prussia, including the young Otto von Bismarck, had regained the upper hand and made it clear that if it was going to take part in any form of German union, it would be on Prussia's terms. In May both Austria and Prussia declared that their delegates' mandate to the assembly had expired and forbade them from attending assembly sessions or taking part in further debate. Others opposed to the constitution did likewise, rapidly reducing the number of deputies and diminishing accordingly the assembly's claim to a popular mandate.

It was the end of the dream. Prussia and Austria led a campaign against any reforms other than those they had already instigated separately. The rump would-be parliament was now dominated by primarily left-wing factions increasingly threatened by repression. It abandoned Frankfurt at the end of May and reconvened in Stuttgart in Württemberg, briefly and with no claim to widespread public representation. The Württemberg militia was sent in to close it down. Many of those on the left fled abroad. Those on the centre-right got together in an assembly in Gotha at the end of June, but by then it was little more than a private gathering.

The constitution of 1849 did not completely die with the erosion of the revolution and the dissolution of the Frankfurt proto-parliament. Both that of the Weimar Republic, which came into force in 1919, and that of the Federal Republic of Germany (West), which was hammered out in 1948–9, took serious note of their forefathers' first attempt to create a unified, liberal Germany under the rule of law.

Back to Porridge and a Hope Dashed

Frankfurt's day in the sun was over. This was made palpable by the fact that with the outbreak in 1866 of the long inevitable war between Austria and Prussia that would eventually settle the question of supremacy in the German lands, the city was annexed by Prussia, its 'free city' status gone forever. The loss of status was, however, recompensed by a vast spurt in economic growth and rapid expansion of the city's population and boundaries, to the extent that for a brief period at the beginning of the 20th century it was by area the largest city in Germany. A new harbour on the Main encouraged growth and the city quickly became a centre of new modern industries from chemicals to electro-engineering, and eventually in 1914 a university was established.

Frankfurt too suffered from heavy bombing during World War II, although the casualties were not on the scale of those suffered in Dresden, Königsberg, Berlin or Hamburg. Some 5,500 people were killed in raids which saw the US and British air forces drop some 27,000 tonnes of bombs on the city, mostly in a series of raids carried out during 1944. The greatest loss, however, was that of the most complete and largest mediaeval city centre in Germany; in architectural if not human terms it was a far greater loss than those of Hamburg, Cologne, Königsberg or Dresden. The extent of this cultural and historical tragedy was aggravated by the fact that Frankfurt's city centre had been so well preserved that the vast majority of the buildings were timber-framed and went up in flames like a tinderbox when hit by incendiary bombs. One raid, on 22 March 1944, basically levelled 80 per cent of the historic Altstadt (old town), leaving only those few buildings made of stone – the Römer, St Bartholomäus church and a few others – as burnt-out shells. Altogether one-quarter of the city, a total of 12,148 buildings, was totally destroyed.

Despite the destruction, the second time that Frankfurt came close to being the capital of a large German state was in the years immediately after World War II. There was an almost inevitable logic to the idea that, with Berlin in the heart of the Soviet zone of occupation, and the Russians unlikely to permit German reunification on any other than their own terms, the old site of 'imperial' coronations, home to the first pan-German parliament, stock exchange and a famous and ancient trade fair should become capital of a new West German state, if, as it seemed, Germany's destiny was to be divided. The discussion became a concrete rather than abstract issue in 1949 when the three Western zones issued their own currency – a long overdue measure required to create economic stability – and in return the Soviet-occupied zone issued an alternative. There were now two new German Marks, and that effectively mean two new German states.

The 'Frankfurt Solution' seemed obvious to the locals and to the occupying Allies: Frankfurt was the base for the US occupying forces and the Americans initially had the idea of turning the former 'free city' (now endowed with a greatly enlarged urban area to better facilitate rebuilding of much needed accommodation) into an entity in its own right. The idea was based on the District of Columbia (DC), the autonomous region surrounding the US capital Washington. If one capital of the new, divided Germany was going to be in the Russian zone of occupation, why should the other not be in the American one?

One of the main proponents of the 'capital of the US zone' as capital of West Germany was its commander, US General Walter M. Robertson. The British, however, put up a rival candidate in their own zone: the little university city of Bonn, which had been twinned with Oxford during the war, with the consequence that neither had been bombed. As a result there were enough surviving buildings of sufficient status and size to house the new parliamentary bodies at least temporarily. The British trumped the American 'DC' idea by immediately offering to withdraw their forces from the city, which would then become an 'occupation-free' seat of government for a new democratic German state. The Americans had no intention of withdrawing their troops from Frankfurt, even if their proposal was adopted.

This British proposal had the immense advantage that Konrad Adenauer, who that summer had been elected as chancellor of the new country at the head of his equally new Christian Democratic Union party, favoured Bonn.

Adenauer's preference was twofold: partly because he himself was a Rhinelander, a former mayor of nearby Cologne, but also because as a fervent believer in eventual German reunification he thought that the little university town was a plausible temporary capital – even if it was long-term – while Frankfurt with its greater size and historical claims to the title, might come to be seen as permanent. That, he almost certainly rightly feared, could lead to the as yet unencircled western half of Berlin being seen as a meaningless anomaly and the entire city eventually falling into Soviet hands as capital of their puppet state.

The competition for the honour of becoming capital of this new German state was not just a two-way contest. Kassel and Stuttgart were also put forward, as was the suggestion that the parliament of the new republic should imitate the ancient court of the Holy Roman Emperors and migrate from city to city: the possibility that this might – as it had done in history – prevent the development of one central powerful state was not seen as necessarily a bad thing in the circumstances.

The issue was not settled until 3 November 1949, at a meeting of the new Bundestag, which had been elected in the summer and had already been meeting in Bonn since September. The vote to stay where they were was 200 against 176 for Frankfurt with just three abstentions. But despite his delight at winning the vote for Bonn, effectively a home win for the new chancellor, Adenauer also got his way on pledging devotion to Berlin as a symbol of hoped-for unity. The same session also produced a formal statement passed with an overwhelming majority that 'the chief organs of power will transfer their seat to the federal capital, Berlin, as soon as a general, free, secret ballot can be carried out in all of Berlin and the Soviet occupation zone'.

There were bitter arguments and afterwards even allegations of bribery. Frankfurt Mayor Walter Kolb was so certain of success he had already had a plenary chamber built for the new parliament and left the local radio station a recording of his speech of thanks to the new parliament for the decision. Ironically that radio station, Hessische Rundfunk, is now housed in that very building. Frankfurt itself was brought within the adjusted boundaries of the state of Hessen.

The runner-up prize proved not to be too bad. Bonn was too small to be a serious candidate for new corporate headquarters for companies that didn't want to be stuck in isolated West Berlin, which was already haemorrhaging population and businesses because of travel difficulties through the Soviet zone and its uncertain future. Frankfurt, in the middle of the new country, and its rapidly expanding airport supported by the Americans, was the obvious choice. Increasingly major concerns, federal industrial institutions and banks relocated to Frankfurt.

And with them came a new vision of the decimated city centre. The Americans had taken over a whole swathe of the northern part of the centre around a former factory transformed into a military headquarters and an occupation government for virtually the whole of southern Germany: the British, who controlled the north, and the Americans had each allocated a small area of their occupied lands to the French; the Russians had refused, insisting that France had lost the war. The American control centre was fenced off and marked as out of bounds to all Germans.

With initially no central civilian authority in control of the city, various organisations sprang up to deal with the mess. The most important was the *Trümmerverwaltungsgesellschaft* (another of those German words that looks impossibly long until you take into account that Germans mentally split it up automatically and it becomes 'Ruins Management Company'). Working mostly by hand, those set to the task managed to remove 1,500 tonnes of rubble daily. Much of it had to be simply disposed of in landfills, or in *Trümmerberg* (rubble mountains), given the state of the German economy with almost anything of use removed by the victors as reparation, there was a major effort to recycle as much as possible. The estimate at the time was that it would take nearly 40 years to completely clear the city centre of approximately 18 million tonnes of rubble. In the end they managed it in just 20 years; the last rubble recycling plant was finally shut down in 1964.

Mayor Walter Kolb made a public call for the first priority on the city's restoration list to be the Paulskirche, not out of any religious sentiment, but because of its historic role as scene of the first democratically elected German parliament. The building had been gutted in the firestorm, but its shell still stood. Interestingly, for those who have only ever seen Communism as a force for dictatorship rather than the democracy it affected to champion, the single greatest contribution, in material terms, came from the Soviet-occupied zone, which sent building materials, nails and the bells for the rebuilt church. Such was the enthusiasm for recreating a symbol of optimism in the aftermath of darkness that the church was ready to be reopened by 1948. It stands today as a monument to German democracy and serves as an exhibition centre for cultural events.

The other major priority for the rebuilders, as elsewhere in German's bomb-devastated cities, was providing housing and with it commercial premises, shops and factories, to enable the resumption of relatively normal life. The result, all across the country, but somehow particularly in Frankfurt, was endless rows of functional but unattractive four-storey blocks, fitted out as apartments, often with commercial premises on the ground floor. I remember on my earliest visits to Germany in the mid-1970s being profoundly depressed by most city centres, which seemed uniformly bland apart from the occasional church or sole surviving timber building, ornate and beautiful amid a landscape of bland functionality. The villages by contrast were beautiful, romantic and full of charm. Rather naively – I was a teenager at the time – it never occurred to me to wonder why.

Much effort was spent on the restoration of the Römer,

the great mediaeval building on the city's main square which had served as town hall for more than half a millennium and was one of the city's best-known landmarks. Its name comes not from the Romans, though they did in fact have a settlement nearby, but from early mediaeval Italian merchants, who congregated in the square when they came to Frankfurt to trade.

The basic layout of the building was created in 1405 by knocking together three houses on the site, hence its distinctive triple façade with stepped gables. The buildings were gutted and redesigned for their new purpose, but almost immediately after completion most of the new structure collapsed. The builder was sacked and his replacement obviously did a substantially better job because most of the external walls – if almost nothing else – were still standing at the end of World War II. Happily, it had been recognised at the beginning of the war that Frankfurt was an obvious target for air raids, and all the Römer's internal treasures, including portraits and wooden carvings, had been taken into storage, while the internal frescoes were photographed in detail, a cynical and pessimistic, if nonetheless wise precaution. After the war these were used to recreate the interior, to which the preserved mediaeval artefacts were returned, so that the present-day Römer is very close to what it looked like prior to the bombings.

The same can be said of St Bartholomäus, the great 14th-century church behind it, where the emperors were crowned, which survived the war with its structure almost totally intact. Unfortunately when it came to the rest of the buildings around the Römer, into which the town hall and other city services had expanded over the centuries, Coventry syndrome set in. The burnt-out houses behind the Römer were torn down, as scandalously were three mediaeval timber-framed houses that had survived the bombing intact, and replaced by what, in the awful modernist jargon of the time, was called the Technisches Rathaus, a 'technical town hall'.

Finished in 1970, it was a classic product of its age, a close cousin of the brutalist architecture at London's Elephant and Castle, and as bad as anything wrought by British architects on unlovely Coventry: lumpen, squared and downright ugly cubes of concrete piled one on top of another like something built with a set of children's building blocks. It was hailed, as these things often are, as a masterpiece of modern architecture, but roundly disliked by most of those who worked in it and all who saw it. I remember on an early visit to Frankfurt wondering how, when and why it was built; but then I was wondering that about a lot of the city at the time. It took 40 years for the civic authorities to see the light: the unloved structure was pulled down in 2010. Since then the authorities have begun work on rebuilding from scratch the three untouched ancient houses they pulled down in the 1960s, working from photographs and historical plans. The remainder of the large site occupied by the unloved Rathaus is being turned into apartments and offices, modern in construction and interior, but loosely modelled on the ancient architectural style so that they will at least look in keeping with the restored buildings around them rather than an insult to them. There are, of course, those who say that they are replacing tat with kitsch, but each generation takes its own decisions, even if it is often the next that has to live with them.

The other great cock-up of the post-war rebuilding was the decision by the postal service to pull down the Palais Thurn und Taxis, a beautiful petite baroque palace that had been badly damaged but by no means beyond repair, chiefly because it was in the way of what they considered necessary electrical work. Again it took decades before the mistake was realised. It has today been rebuilt and serves as an elegant restaurant, conference and concert venue on its original site, though that means it now sits in the shadow of the great glass bulk of the Jumeirah Hotel.

Frankfurt may not be the prettiest of German cities most of the year, but there is one time when the entire Altstadt is transformed. For the whole month of December, Frankfurt hosts Germany's biggest Christmas Market. It is as if overnight – in reality it takes some three weeks of setting up – the devastation of 1945 were undone, and the mediaeval wattle and timber cityscape reconstituted for a single magical month.

Unlike the Goethe house museum, this of course is overlaid with the 'Disney' touch, complete with *Weihnachtsmann* (the 'Christmas Man', which is what Germans call Santa Claus, to distinguish the ubiquitous import from the original Saint Nicklaus). It may be kitsch (the Germans did after all give us the word), but sip a *Glühwein* and wander round the artificial wonderland with its cornucopia of traditional crafts, from handblown Christmas tree baubles to wafer-thin wooden tree decorations displaying ridiculous intricately carved scenes, and it's probably as near as the 21st century wants to get to the original.

Even as the restoration and rebuilding was taking place, Frankfurt's development as the business and banking centre of the new Federal Republic was beginning to make its mark. The *Wirtschaftswunder* (economic miracle) was turning this new Germany, stripped of military muscle, into an economic powerhouse, with Frankfurt at its centre. Ever since at least the 12th century Frankfurt's central position in Europe on a major waterway had made it one of the continent's great trading centres. Merchants from the Mediterranean sold silks and spices from the Orient via Venice and Alexandria, and bought furs and metals from their counterparts from the Baltic and the Hanseatic League. When in 1454 a certain Johannes Gutenberg from nearby Mainz, with the backing of a financial loan from moneylender Johann Fust, had finally produced the first printed edition of the Bible, it was hardly surprising that they should choose Frankfurt at which to showcase it. By chance one of the visitors to the autumn trade fair that year was the bishop of Siena, one Aeneas Sylvius Piccolomini. He had heard rumours about a remarkable man with copies of a new type of Bible printed by a machine rather than hand-copied by a scribe, reputedly 'absolutely free from error and printed with extreme elegance'.

The man (whether it was Gutenberg himself or his backer Johann Fust is uncertain) was taking orders for finished copies, of which a promised total of 180 were available. Buyers were reputedly lining up, even though the printed versions would be unbound and needed some finishing touches such as highlighting in red ink at the beginning of each chapter. Piccolomini wrote to his Spanish friend Cardinal Caravajal that although he had not seen a complete finished copy, the script was 'very neat and legible', adding 'your Grace would be able to read it without effort and indeed without glasses'. Piccolomini, whose enthusiasm for this new-fangled printing business was not to be dismissed lightly, given that he would later become Pope Pius II, apologised for not having ordered one, but promised to try and see if there were any still to be had.

Private buyers were snapping up the new printed Bibles as fast as they came off Gutenberg's press, personalising them with their own lavish leather-bound covers and more often than not donating them to monasteries in the hope of enhancing their chances of reaching heaven. Understandably, by the time the next trade fair came around, printed works were one of the hottest commodities on sale. These included copies of 'indulgences' sold by the Vatican to lessen sinners' time in purgatory after their death – a custom that would anger a certain Martin Luther a century later – intended to be sold on to the masses of pilgrims who flocked to see the relics of the magi in the great cathedral being built in Cologne.

Before long, as the business of printing caught on across Europe, there were enough booksellers turning up at Frankfurt each year to organise a 'book fair' of their own. It rapidly became a huge success, attracting printers, and then the new trade of publishers, from all across the continent. Frankfurt was to dominate the bookselling world until the middle of the 17th century, when it was eclipsed by Leipzig. After World War II, with Leipzig on the wrong side of the Iron Curtain, Frankfurt quickly resumed its prominence, with the first post-war fair held in the newly restored Paulskirche in 1949. Today Frankfurt Book Fair, held every autumn, is the largest in the world in terms of the number of publishing houses represented, with some 7,000 from more than 100 countries – and is a major market for internationalising authors' fame.

Given Frankfurt's success in disseminating the printed word in the modern world, it was perhaps unsurprising that it has also became a major feature in showcasing another of German industry's greatest success stories: the motor car. Initially held in Berlin, the International Automobile Association's motor show switched to Frankfurt in 1951 and quickly became the world's biggest car launch event, where not just the German giants such as BMW, Audi, VW and Porsche, but major manufacturers from around the world show off their latest models and futuristic concept cars.

Reach for the Sky

With Frankfurt's commercial and business roles putting the city back on the international map from the 1950s onwards, the task of restoring the city soon switched to giving it new buildings to suit its new status. It was German national institutions which began the reach for the sky that over the decades would turn a low-level city on the banks of the Main, whose sole significant high-rise had been its 14th century 'cathedral', into continental Europe's mini-Manhattan. The 13-storey offices of the federal bank, the Bundesbank, finished in 1972, reached 54 metres, matching the Frankfurter Sparkasse. This was just the beginning of a surge in skyscraper-building that would see this pair dwarfed and would reach a pinnacle in the mid-1990s. But it is by no means over yet. Among the smaller contenders are the Eurotheum, a 31-storey 1999 mixed office and residential building that reaches 110 m and, similar in height, the 1996 Japan-Center (114 m), particularly notable because it was built with a pagoda-style roof and intended to resemble an ancient Japanese traditional lantern. More prosaic but equally notable are the twin Kastor and Pollux towers, built in 1997 with one at 97 m and the other at 130 m.

The real surge skyward began as early as 1980 with the 166 m Dresdner Bank tower followed by the 155 m Deutsche Bank tower. I remember sitting in one of the offices more than 49 storeys up interviewing a banker for the *Sunday Telegraph* in 1986, wondering how many more of these would be built and how high they might go. The answer to the first question was 'lots' and the second remains to be seen: the Main Tower (named after the river and pronounced accordingly: 'mine' rather than 'main'), finished in 1999 and housing the offices of Merrill Lynch and Standard & Poor's as well as a German regional bank and television studios, reaches 200 m (240 m if you include its aerial spire). The record was briefly held by the 1991 Messeturm (Trade Fair Tower), which topped out at 256 m but was just pipped in 1997 by Norman Foster's headquarters for Germany's biggest bank, Commerzbank, at 258 m.

To be fair, height isn't the only thing to impress. The Commerzbank in particular feels like an adjunct to the city rather than an alien spacecraft landed in it: the public can wander freely through its ground floor atrium, use the café along with the staff (although not at the same discount prices), and visit regular art exhibitions on the upper floors.

The greatest shock to the growing capitalist system that was fast becoming Frankfurt's beating heart came on a summer afternoon in July 1977. Jürgen Ponto, the 53-year-old chairman of the board of directors of Deutsche Bank and his wife Ignes were packing in their villa at Oberursel just outside Frankfurt when the daughter of some friends turned up at their door with two acquaintances. The daughter, Susanne Albrecht, handed Ponto's wife a bouquet of red roses and she left them alone in the living room with her husband as she went to put them in water. Seconds later she heard loud voices followed by gunshots, dashed back to find her husband lying in a pool of blood on the floor as the three visitors fled the house, climbing into a getaway car with waiting driver parked outside the door. It appeared they had tried to kidnap Ponto and when he fought back they shot him five times. He later died of his wounds.

Albrecht, who had called the man to whose murder she was an accomplice 'Uncle Jürgen', was, unbeknown to her parents and their friends, a member of the anti-capitalist terrorist gang which called itself the Red Army Faction, yet another reason for the initials RAF to have bitter connotations for Germans as late as the 1970s and 80s. She released a statement that said, 'It had not been clear to us that these people, who start wars in the Third World and destroy entire populations, are dumbfounded when violence faces them in their own house.'

She subsequently fled to Yemen, where she trained in guerrilla warfare in a Palestinian camp. She returned to Europe in 1979 and took part in a failed attempt to assassinate Nato commander Alexander Haig by planting a bomb near his car at the organisation's headquarters near Mons in Belgium. Haig was not near his car when the bomb exploded. The following year Albrecht fled to the Communist East, where she was given protection by the Stasi, took the new name of Ingrid Jäger, was given a job as an English translator, married a man who knew nothing of her past and had a son with him. In 1986 she was recognised in her local community of Köthen from West German television reportage on the RAF. She moved to East Berlin to recover her anonymity but after the Wall came down she was discovered living under the name 'Becker' and arrested. Sentenced to twelve years imprisonment in 1990, she was released on parole in

1996 and has since worked as a German language teacher to immigrant children.

The Ponto assassination came as a traumatic shock to the still relatively embryonic business growth in Frankfurt. The RAF, who had started out as the Baader-Meinhof gang, would terrorise Germany for nearly two decades. After the Ponto killing, they successfully kidnapped Hans Martin Schleyer, a senior German industrialist (who had previously been a member of the Nazi party and the SS), and demanded the release of 11 RAF prisoners in jail. When the government tried delaying tactics, the group coordinated the hijack of a Lufthansa flight from Majorca to Frankfurt by Palestinian terrorists demanding the release of the same German prisoners, plus two Palestinians and $15m in ransom. The incident dominated global news as the plane was flown via Larnaca in Cyprus to Dubai, then on to Aden – where the pilot was shot for his reluctance to cooperate – then eventually to Mogadishu in Somalia.

The German government decided on a high-risk rescue operation and sent in an elite police unit known as GSG-9, who stormed the aircraft on the runway. In a lightning strike the unit shot all four hijackers and took control of the plane without serious injury to any of the passengers. All 11 RAF prisoners, including Andreas Baader, immediately committed suicide in their cells. The kidnapped Schleyer was executed the next day and his body eventually found in the boot of a green Audi near Mulhouse in France.

As a 20-year old student I had the dubious honour to have stood in the dock of a British court at the same time as a member of the Baader-Meinhof gang, Astrid Proll. It was only a magistrate's court, albeit one of the country's most famous, in Bow Street. She was fighting extradition from London to Germany on charges of murder and bank robbery; I was accused of being drunk in charge of a bicycle. I got off (the magistrate threw the police evidence out) while Proll was remanded in custody pending a further hearing.

On her eventual extradition she was acquitted of murder but convicted of robbery and sentenced to five years, though as she had already served two-thirds of that time in British or German jails she was released immediately. I later came across her working as a picture editor for a magazine in Hamburg. She didn't remember our shared day in court.

The Bankenviertel, or 'bank district' as it is unofficially known, stands (the word 'lies' hardly seems appropriate for an area so dominated by the vertical) between Frankfurt station and what is now the centre of the city – the area beyond the Römer and around the old Rossplatz. The latter, which was once a horse market and the scene of public executions, is now dominated by hotels and shopping streets. Whereas most Frankfurters, unless they work in the sector, rarely pass through the skittle field of skyscrapers, many tourists do, not just to admire the architecture, but, particularly in the case of the Chinese and Japanese, to have their photograph taken next to one of the city's least likely landmarks. Standing some four metres high next to an unremarkable 40-storey, 148 m tower, on Willy-Brandt-Platz, named after the former chancellor and Frankfurt's public transport nexus, is a big blue €, the symbol for the euro, the European Union's common currency, used by 19 of the 28 member states, as well as non-EU Montenegro. First introduced as a non-tangible currency in the form of a fixed exchange rate in 1999, the euro took on physical form in the shape of notes and coins on 1 January 2002. Not without its troubles, particularly since the banking crisis of 2008, Greece's threatened default on the debt mountain acquired by successive governments piggybacking on a low interest rate they would not have had access to with a currency of their own, and perpetually scorned by British conservative governments, the euro remains the world's second reserve currency after the US dollar. It is used daily by nearly 340 million people while another 220 million use currencies pegged to it. And on almost any day in the tourist season it is common to see Asian tourists happily embracing the big blue €, if only for a souvenir photograph.

The building behind it, originally occupied by a German domestic bank, was taken over by the European Monetary Institute, the organisation responsible for preparing the ground for the common currency, and then, from 1998 onwards, by the new European Central Bank. Inevitably, with the passage of time, the building became too small for its tenant, which spread out into office space rented in other skyscrapers round about. Eventually a decision was taken to erect a new purpose-built headquarters, away from the downtown skyscraper cluster some two kilometres away on the other side of the river in Sachsenhausen. The new building, on the site of Frankfurt's former wholesale market hall, consists of two 'twinned' skyscrapers, 165 m and 185 m tall, linked by an atrium building. Designed by a Vienna architect, it was due to begin construction but had to be held up because of the financial crisis. The one advantage was that, when construction finally began in 2012, costs had fallen considerably.

The building was finished in the autumn of 2014, and staff began moving in immediately, although it was not formally opened until March 2015. The ceremony was marked by a three-day protest by left-wing groups, supported by, among others, Greece's governing party Syriza, angry at the €1.4bn spent on the building while member countries were being forced to enact austerity policies. Again almost certainly inevitably, it was discovered that with the bank's growing responsibilities as it works towards greater fiscal integration between the member states, they needed to keep some staff in the original tower on Willy-Brandt-Platz.

While there are still sceptics about the long-term future of the common currency, for the foreseeable future the euro and Frankfurt are all but synonymous. Once again Frankfurt is at the symbolic centre of a project for European union. Just how far that union proceeds and how long it lasts is, as ever, the stuff of history as yet unwritten. But, despite recent setbacks from the ever-insular English, the goal that Robert Blum pronounced on the floor of the assembly in 1848 is still in sight.

The Germans and Money

It was 1 July 1990 and I was sitting, as I have sat so many times on occasions historic and mundane, around the *Stammtisch* in Metzer Eck in East Berlin, my long-standing local corner bar that was then still – but for just three more months – in the capital of the German Democratic Republic, a country about to vote itself out of existence.

On the table in front of us were the usual glasses of Berliner Pilsner, but more importantly, in front of each person a small pile of crisp new banknotes in a currency that had been in circulation for years, though not officially: Deutsche Marks – in everyday language D-Marks. The shocking thing was: we now had to pay for our beer with them in the East, and everyone was happy about it.

Money: proverbially the root of all evil, but unfortunately also the root of all prosperity. But what matters is not just how much of it you have, but what it consists of: who or what guarantees that those little pieces of metal or paper, or nowadays the electronic digits that represent them, will be accepted in return for bread and circuses, goods and services. Germans know a lot about money. That might sound a pretty banal comment, true of almost any nation, but that would be to forget that Germans and Italians between them effectively invented the mediaeval banking system that is the origin of the capitalist system that fuels the City of London, its continental rival, Frankfurt, and global trade in general. But perhaps even more significantly, Germans of the early 1920s experienced at first hand what happens if the guarantee behind those pieces of paper is no longer trusted, when the price of a loaf of bread could more than double in a day. Hyperinflation has become a race memory in Germany and the reason why more than anything else government policy since 1949 has been to keep it in check.

In the few weeks before we sat down in Metzer Eck to

toast the death of one currency and the adoption of another, East Germans had seen the third radical change in what they accepted as money in little over a generation. Gone were those famous faces of German Communism's heroes, Karl Marx and Friedrich Engels, who had decorated the higher denomination notes of the old currency, the Mark of the German Democratic Republic. And nobody regretted their passing. In their place were D-Marks, the currency of the Federal Republic, big and brightly coloured with pictures of cultural figures, male and female, from German history, from the Brothers Grimm to writer Bettina von Arnim. East Germans had been familiar with D-Marks for years, as gifts from friends or relatives in the West, traded on the black market in the streets and hypocritically accepted in stores selling rare goods, run by their own government, which hankered after the D-Mark as much as its citizens did. The currencies had been the first step towards German partition. The D-Mark's introduction in June 1948 to replace the by then worthless Reichsmark, was effectively the foundation stone of the new West German federal republic. It was the last straw for the Russians, who had still dreamed of making all of Germany a demilitarised neutral buffer zone, and was a major factor in sparking the Berlin blockade, which eventually collapsed in the face of the Western Allies' airlift. In a reaction to the flood of now worthless Reichsmarks into the Soviet zone, where they were still legal tender, the Russians rapidly issued their own reformed currency a month later. The new Soviet zone notes were also labelled *Deutsche Mark*, but rapidly became known as the *Ostmark*.

The East German Mark was valid only in the Soviet zone, which produced few consumer goods the public wanted. In the West the *Wirtschaftswunder* (economic miracle) would soon make consumer goods – from cigarettes to imported goods and luxury cars – plentiful. While East Germans could still travel to the West, which became more and more difficult from 1952, as barbed wires fences went up and armed guards began patrolling the border, the value of the D-Mark rocketed against its Eastern equivalent, with the standard black market price at least 4–1, and even as high as 10–1. During the long years of partition, a new social division grew up in the supposedly classless DDR between those who had Western relatives who would send them money, and those who did not. Even with the border hermetically sealed, the East German state exploited its own people's longing for consumer goods by selling them itself in special stores called Intershop, which accepted only foreign currency – in practice the D-Mark.

In that heady summer of 1990, with a motion on German reunification shortly due to go before the *Volkskammer*, the 'People's Chamber', which had been the DDR's rubber-stamp parliament until free elections that spring, a currency union was a necessary prerequisite. But the question was: how to make it work? East German marks had become virtually valueless: the Communist economy, such as it was, had collapsed; farms and factories were in disarray, being privatised or put on sale; the market was swamped by the products flowing over the now open border. Nobody wanted them but everybody had them, and only a few had any serious quantity of 'West marks'. The solution had been one of the most daring, and generous, moves ever implemented by one nominally independent state towards the citizens of what was still theoretically another. The conservative Christian Democrat government of Helmut Kohl took a giant bet. There was no accepted rate of exchange, and if it were known the Ostmark was to be abolished it would literally have no value at all. Despite reservations of the Bundesbank, the government simply decided to place political unity ahead of economic risk. After long and detailed calculations, it was decided to offer a one-to-one exchange rate for a limited amount of cash per person, according to age. Those under 25 could exchange 2,000 East marks for West marks, those between 25 and 60, 4,000, and those over 60, 6,000. It was, in effect, a huge gift by the people of western Germany to their new compatriots.

That morning everyone around the table in Metzer Eck, apart from me, had spent hours queuing to withdraw funds from their bank accounts in the shiny new notes. And now they were celebrating in the only way they had ever known how in Metzer Eck: by drinking them. Bärbel, the landlady, reflected that since her grandmother Clara had bought the pub in 1913 after a lottery win, at least four currencies had passed over the counter: the original Mark of the old Kaiserreich (arguably the *Papiermark* introduced after abandoning the gold standard in 1914, though they were supposed to be the same), the *Rentenmark* which replaced it after the hyperinflation of 1921–3, the new *Reichsmark*, which was introduced after stability was restored in 1924, although notes of both continued to circulate until 1948, then the *Mark der DDR*, and now the D-Mark.

The currency union was both a success and a disaster. It caused rampant inflation in the East, and was a heavy burden on the economy of the West, necessitating an unpopular 'solidarity tax' on Western earners, which added to the undercurrent of envy, resentment and nostalgia on both sides that rapidly came to replace the initial euphoria of reunification. It also saw many state-owned industries which could have been sold off to workers or small investors quickly swallowed up and often asset-stripped by West German corporations, despite the existence of a government-supervised body known as the *Treuhand*, intended to make sure the privatisations were carried out fairly and legally, but instead turned into a mishandled travesty.

The 1990s was not the first decade in which the Germans had tried to find a common currency. It started before there even was a Germany. A multiplicity of spendthrift princes, who often envied titles and courts far beyond the means of their petty principalities, archbishoprics or duchies, had long needed to borrow money from elsewhere. It was out of their greed and financial incompetence that the first big German banks grew up in the early modern age. Most significant of all were the Bavarian Fugger family, who specialised in lending money to the Habsburgs to allow them to maintain their imperial ambitions, handing out loans which often took a century or more to pay back.

The multiplicity of different statelets also meant different tariffs on imported items and different coinages to pay for them. Discussions about some form of German unification followed the collapse of Napoleon's attempt to make the western areas French fiefdoms. These led to the creation in 1834 of the Zollverein, or customs union, an early precursor of modern Europe's 'single market'. This was led by Prussia, which had a particular interest because much of its territory was still a patchwork quilt, often surrounded by other states. As we have seen, Prussia's machinations to unify its territory were instrumental in leading to the clash with Austria and eventual German unification under a government in Berlin. For a while several of the southern states, notably Baden, Bavaria and Württemberg experimented with customs unions of their own, and at one stage several of these co-existed and competed against one another. But over the course of the mid-19th century more and more acceded to the Prussian *Zollverein*. By 1867, after the Prussian defeat of Austria and effective dominance of German Central Europe, the Prussian union was joined by all except Austria and a few other small exceptions, notably the Hansa trading cities of Hamburg and Bremen which, although members of the new German Reich brought into being in 1871, remained outside the customs union until 1888.

In the same way as the modern European single market suggested the creation of a single currency, the 19th-century German customs union also called for some form of unification of means of payment. For centuries there had been different coins with different values and weights, each bearing the head of their own ruler or arms of their city-state. But gradually a broad pattern had emerged; south of the Main river, most of the states – whatever image was on the coin – had used the *Gulden*, or guilder, as their main coin while to the north most used the taler, as did Austria.Gradually, and not without difficulties and arguments, a form of union emerged, initially by making the taler and guilder of equal weight in silver.

Mid-19th century Austria-Hungary, coping badly with rampant inflation throughout a vast, multicultural empire, had for some time increasingly relied on paper money. Banknotes rather than coins were essential for large sums and the development of commerce. Banks, almost all privately owned, were allowed to issue their own notes, provided these 'promissory notes' genuinely were convertible into silver on demand. Increasingly, the currency of Prussia became that most readily accepted. With an eye to the future, Prussia had in 1847 set up the Preussische Bank, half-owned by the state and with a government minister as its president, which issued its own taler banknotes and coins. After the creation of the Prussian-dominated Deutsches Reich in 1871, the constituent states agreed to adopt a new single currency to be issued by the Preussische Bank, which from 1876 onwards changed its name to Reichsbank. After some deliberation the name they chose for the new currency was that of an old coin which had been used in Cologne as far back as the eleventh century and continued to be issued among the Hansa states of Hamburg, Bremen and Lübeck, as well as being an accepted currency unit (though never an actual coin) in Anglo-Saxon and Danish-dominated England: the Mark.

The darkest days of the Mark were to come in the early 1920s, when it was overtaken by hyperinflation on an almost unprecedented scale. Having borrowed heavily to pay for World War I, its loss and the absurdly exaggerated reparations imposed by the peace treaties, meant that a Reichsmark, which had traded at approximately four to the US dollar in 1914, was trading at 8:1 in 1918 and 48:1 a little over a year later, by which time it was becoming rapidly clear that the ravaged German economy could not remotely enable the government to repay its debts. An ultimatum by the victorious wartime Allies issued in 1921, demanding that Germany pay reparations in hard currency, met with the absurd but only possible response that the government printed more money, which it traded on the foreign currency market, thereby only pushing down the value of the currency they were printing.

It was a ridiculous downward spiral which in the end would benefit nobody, not even the creditor nations. The country quite soon could not afford to buy any gold or foreign currency and so reparations were demanded in goods: the French occupied the Ruhr district, thereby reducing German industrial output even further, a situation which only worsened when the workers went on strike in protest at the occupation. The cost of living began rapidly to spiral out of control. In 1922 alone the exchange rate against the US dollar went from 320:1 to 7,400:1. By the end of the following year to buy one US dollar you would have needed to be able to lay your hands on over four *billion* Reichsmarks. The bank could no longer print them fast enough and resorted to reissuing used notes with stamps on them, turning thousands into millions, then billions. Some 130 subsidiary printers were hired to print banknotes. The price of a loaf of bread would soar while it was in the oven and be unaffordable by most people by the time it got onto the shelf. People were carrying banknotes around in wheelbarrows and shopping baskets, though a basket full of notes was not enough to buy a basket full of goods. The contemporary historian Golo Mann described it as a 'second revolution', and commented: 'the old trust was replaced with fear and cynicism ... what can anyone rely on, what can anyone plan if something like this is possible? Faith in democracy and the republic was wiped out overnight.' It was no coincidence that a group of populist fanatics calling themselves the National Socialist German Workers Party attempted a coup in Munich in November 1923.

By the time Adolf Hitler was released from jail in 1924, ironically, things were coming back under control. A new finance minister was appointed and notes in a new currency – *Rentenmarks* – began to be issued. Theoretically valued against land and industrial production, the new notes were effectively just another con trick and would only work if people believed in them. 'If it had come down to the knuckle,' the Hamburg news magazine *Der Spiegel* reflected in an article commemorating the hyperinflation crisis, 'nobody would have given up their property or their land for cash.' By then everyone was desperate enough to believe in anything that might just possibly end the chaos. One new *Rentenmark* was worth one *trillion* of the old Reichsmarks. The middle classes, those who had had savings, had effectively been wiped out; farmers and those with businesses or properties did best and those who had had nothing much in the first place still had nothing much. All anyone wanted was a strong man with strong opinions and determination to see them through.

Unfortunately, there was one to hand.

∈∋

Despite the chaos of the years 1923–45, the most remarkable thing that remains a constant in German society today is precisely that element of trust that Golo Mann regarded as lost forever in the hyperinflation crisis. German society is pervaded by a general atmosphere of trust and honesty that is almost unique.

Before I get a hail of derisive laughter and rage in the wake of the 2014 Volkswagen emissions scandal, I should point out that nobody in the world was more horrified than the Germans themselves to learn that software engineers at one of the country's most famous and celebrated institutions had created a cheating programme to falsify results.

Let's get one thing straight right at the beginning: the

Germans have as many thieves, fraudsters, cheats, liars, dodgy dealers, conmen and downright crooks as any other nation. And they know it. They were governed by a murderous bunch of them for twelve years.

But there is huge national pride in the reputation they have achieved over the last 70 years for quality and reliability in their industry. The VW scandal sent a shockwave through the country, a fear that the reputation of *Deutsche Wertarbeit* – German quality workmanship – had been irretrievably damaged. The idea that they had shamed not just their own brand, but possibly by inference dented the reputation of such global household names as Miele, Neff, Braun, Siemens, Bosch, Adidas, Sennheiser – the list is almost endless – was simply unthinkable. That is why the surviving VW bosses came out with a full and public apology and agreement to pay damages: they were afraid not only of losing a large share of their global market, but their domestic one as well.

There is a form of unwritten contract that runs throughout German society, but exists primarily at the level of the relationship between the state – including large public bodies – and the citizen: that each trusts the other to be honest, or to be more precise, to honour their side of the deal. The most ready example, and where the difference from other European countries, is most evident, is public transport. In Germany, there are no barriers, no entry or exit gates on any form of urban transport from the U-bahn underground and S-bahn overground city railways to trams and buses. You buy a pass for a specific period, or a ticket for a single journey – in which case you are expected to validate it yourself by clicking it in a machine – but there is nobody watching to make sure you have done so, no turnstile, or electronic barrier to be negotiated, either in or out. No bus or tram driver will ask to see your ticket. The assumption is that you have one. Unlike London, where there are formidable heavy gates which need presentation of your ticket to both leave and enter the Underground, or Paris, where at the Sorbonne station it can at rush hour resemble an Olympic hurdles competition as the city's brazenly ticketless students vault the barriers.

That is not to say that nobody cheats and travels without a ticket, or that there are no ticket inspectors. There are both; humanity is what it is. But in Germany things are done differently. On the London Underground and buses, signs proclaim: 'It's easy to spot a ticket inspector, they look just like you', a piece of Orwellian Newspeak designed to suggest that anyone around you might be really working for 'Big Brother', and that you are untrustworthy unless kept in check by a climate of suspicion.

In Munich, Berlin, or any other German city, the signs proclaim: *Sie fahren schwarz, und wir sehen rot!* ('You travel black [without a ticket] and we see red, and you pay €60!') It is a penalty strictly enforced by ticket inspectors who do not look 'just like you' at all. Instead of a plainclothes secret service travelling alone and with only a badge and the threat of 'calling the police' to enforce their diktat, German ticket inspectors are uniformed, carry truncheons and handcuffs and travel in pairs at least, empowered to escort any fare dodger to the nearest cash machine if he or she does not have the requisite cash to pay the spot fine. If they have no means of payment, the armed inspectors have the power (in every sense) of arrest without calling for auxiliary support. For most Germans, however, the ultimate penalty would be the shocked and disgusted stares of their fellow passengers.

Both methods rely on psychology, but in very different ways. The 'invisible inspector' suggests a general assumption of mistrust; the belief that if there wasn't the possibility of some secret spy sitting next to you, you wouldn't pay. The German system assumes you wouldn't think of not paying, thereby cheating on your fellow citizens, and that by not paying you risk public exposure as a fare dodger, and therefore not a responsible member of society. Unfortunately, following the massive migration of asylum seekers in 2016, some cities have experimented with a more 'British' approach. On the S-bahn overground railway from Munich airport into the city in April 2017, two ticket inspectors were dressed as backpackers.

Nonetheless, a basic assumption of honesty, lightly monitored, is equally apparent in bars, pubs, where the suggestion that a customer might pay per drink at the moment of service (as is customary in the UK and US) is regarded – except at large events with flowing custom – as mildly insulting to the customer: as if you were expected to pay the bill in a restaurant the moment your food is served.

The traditional way of keeping track of a drinker's consumption is to put a tick to represent each drink on the customer's beermat – and beer is *never* served without a beermat beneath the glass. This system has endured in German lands for centuries, to the extent that in many German *Länder*, the beermat has the legal status of a contractual document. Beermats are not optional, they are *Pflicht*, a public duty.

This can be hard for foreigners to understand; beermats are not something to be tossed off the corner of the bar with one hand and caught by the other, nor something to be used like a frisbee to attract the attention (or animosity) of a distant fellow drinker. A beermat is *ein Dokument!* These days of course, the ticked beermat is more a residual custom than an actual instrument of financial record; in almost all cases your waiter/barman has also automatically got an exact tally of your consumption on his or her computer tablet. When it comes to paying the bill, some will still go through the polite ritual of asking and letting you tell them what you have had in terms of food and drink and trusting your honesty, but make no mistake, they are checking it against their electronic tally.

The other point to make about this is that the English concept of 'round' buying with its rituals and its 'swings and roundabouts' assumptions, usually cannily overlaid with 'who hasn't bought theirs then?', doesn't exist. Each person's beermat – or electronic tally – is theirs and theirs only: if you feel flush and want to buy a round, the total number of drinks will be added to your tally. Reciprocation is fine, but the idea of everyone taking turns to 'treat' everyone else is unknown. You pay your share at the end, and 'round up' the bill as a tip to your server.

Some of this 'everyday honesty' social attitude has rubbed off on international affairs. When Greece proved incapable of paying back its debts to the 'troika' and its international creditors in 2013–15, there was a genuine element of shock among most Germans. Surely a loan was a 'debt of honour', was it not? Similarly when the Greeks – with some moral if not legal justification – suggested the Germans had never properly compensated them for the ravages of wartime occupation or paid back loans forced on them by the Wehrmacht, they were referred, legally correctly, to their signature of the 1953 London Agreement whereby a figure was agreed for German war debts including those reparations that went unpaid in the inflation crisis of the 1920s, to be repaid over the following 30 years by a West German economy that was at the beginning of an economic miracle. The payments were made. An extra payment included in the treaty 'in the event of German reunification', thought highly unlikely at the time, was paid in 1990. Reopening a closed case, was, in the minds of most Germans, 'moving the goalposts'. The deal had already been done, the debt settled.

If anyone had told us sitting around the Metzer Eck *Stammtisch* back in 1990 that the new currency the citizens of East Germany were at last getting their hands on would within a dozen years be gone, replaced by the euro, I doubt any of us would have believed it, but then again, we might well have done: after four currencies in under 80 years, what was wrong with one more? As it happened, negotiations within the EU, and particularly between Germany and France, were already under way. What matters with any currency is not its name or the pictures on the notes, but the validity of the guarantee behind it. In the early decades of the 21st century that remains a big question for Germany, and Europe. The Greek debt crisis raised grim spectres of the past not just in the German Bundesbank but in the folk memories of the population at large. The value of money is whatever enough people believe it is. As long as they do.

8

Cologne

From the days of the Romans through the Thirty Years War to today's party city and the problems of multiculturalism

Fancy Dress Anyone?

Thursday 4 February 2016: grey skies over the fast-flowing muddy waters of the Rhine, cold wind and a relentless drizzle dank enough to dampen the spirits of anyone in the world. Except, of course, the people of Cologne, *die Kölsche*, as they call themselves, from the enduring German name for the country's oldest major city, consider themselves the party animals of the German world. And that is probably an understatement.

Cologne's pre-Lenten *Karneval* is without a doubt Europe's prime street festival, a genuine local party open to everyone for four to five days of riotous partying on a totally different scale to the relatively formal Carnival event in Venice and even the vast party in Rio de Janeiro (much of which these days is held in a giant stadium). Cologne's street party is Europe's answer to Rio and a pretty impressive one it is too, particularly given that it takes place in a cold northern climate on the windy banks of one of the continent's greatest rivers.

In 2016, however, there was more than the usual apprehension about Germany's greatest street party. On New Year's

Eve, another occasion when the people of Cologne take to the streets, to let off fireworks and drink sparkling wine, there were sexual assaults on hundreds of young women, nearly all of them carried out by migrants from the Islamic world who had entered Germany in their hundreds of thousands as refugees and asylum-seekers.

The failure of the police to anticipate or cope with the problems saw the city's police chief sacked, and created a swell of outrage that threatened to turn on its head the general good-natured welcome provided to the migrants by most Germans. There was talk of vigilante groups, of reprisals, shops sold out of pepper spray and other 'female self-defence' items. It was only to be expected therefore that on the first night of the major *Karneval* celebrations – *Weiberfastnacht,* often translated into English as 'Ladies' Night' ('Girls' Party' would be more accurate, using the word 'girls' to mean attitude rather than age) – there were major concerns that there might be a repetition, or worse. Was it possible for the nearly one million migrants who entered Germany in 2015, most of them from conservative Muslim countries where most women were subject to strict patriarchal authority, went veiled and covered to the ankles, to come to terms with an alcohol-fuelled street party in a liberal society on a day when women traditionally rule the roost?

Happily, the fears were unfounded. There was only one sexual assault by a migrant reported and that had to be taken in context of an entire day given over to alcohol-fuelled and often ribald singing, dancing and general close-contact socialising, including with strangers. The tradition of *Weiberfastnacht* (confusingly known in the Cologne dialect as *Wieverfastelovend*) is that it was the day when women were briefly in charge, entitled to go around with scissors cutting off the ends of men's ties, compensating (or rewarding) them with a peck on the cheek. The *Butzchen* (or carnival kiss) is considered part of the event, usually (though not exclusively) initiated by the women, as a gesture of goodwill and cheer, but without any sexual connotation (although inevitably there are cases where things develop otherwise). In short, it is a day of almost mediaeval-style revels in which what modern parlance might call 'inappropriate touching' is omnipresent, if only by mutual consent. It is easy to see why there were fears that newly arrived migrants from conservative Islamic countries might easily get the wrong end of the stick.

The good women of Cologne, however, were not to be repressed, turning out in anything from micro-mini ballet skirts, to revealingly slashed, tight-fitting cat suits (with pro-vocative tails) – to give just a few examples. Bobsie and Emma in their late 30s had travelled up from Wuppertal in bee cos-tumes, short skirts, black tights, fuzzy wigs with black and yellow antennae bobbing on their heads, matching striped black and yellow handbags. Some of the more conservative opted for full-body pink panther suits, as all-covering as a burkha, save that faces are visible so you can admire exag-gerated pink false eyelashes and tips of noses made up black with added drawn-on whiskers.

For safety's sake the police were much in evidence; the difficulty lay in telling which were the real ones. If you relied on your eyes alone, the city had drafted in not just the local state police but several dozen Swat teams, the FBI, one London bobby and two East German *Volkspolizei*, presum-ably brought out of retirement, as well as random groups of blokes in peaked caps and leather jackets saucily bran-dishing plastic handcuffs. Happily the real police could be identified by the letters 'NRW' (for the state of Nordrhein-Westfalen), their prominently displayed numbers, copious equipment and the fact that in each group of eight, at least three were women. Easy enough to identify amid the array of Supermen, Spidermen, Batmen, clowns and authentically equipped Napoleonic guards, some of them actually official: the *Rote Funken* ('red sparks') descended from the city's own military force set up in the 17th century are now official 'carnival guards', whose main role is to prevent public urination near the cathedral.

The event passed peacefully, with only a tiny handful of reported gropings, which, given the number of drunk people carousing on the streets and in the alleyways, could only be considered a success. Not that it was hard for those tasked with security to spot anyone who was not one of the usual partygoers: the sure way to appear suspicious was not to be dressed ludicrously. Among the more extravagant costumes was an entire gaggle of middle-aged men joined together in a lime green multi-person caterpillar outfit. Then there were the lads dressed in beer barrel costumes, the tap placed strategically, the man in a petrol pump outfit, with the hose equally obviously situated, or the variations on suits bulging at the waist that gave the impression the wearer was being carried on the shoulders of some long-suffering dwarf.

Over the last half-dozen days before Lent, and particularly on the three big days of *Weiberfastnacht*, *Rosenmontag* and *Fasching Dienstag* (respectively the Thursday, Monday and Tuesday before Ash Wednesday), Cologne is in fancy dress and on the streets, singing, dancing, drinking and eating. Bars are packed to overflowing, *Kölsch*, the city's unique and traditional beer served in tiny 0.2 l glasses, their small size compensated by a 'carousel' delivery system – flows not quite from dawn but nearly to it. And everywhere the crowds sing the ever-growing repertoire of rowdy *Karneval* classics, performed on stage by live bands and in the back streets by sozzled choirs of revellers who know them by heart, from Gottlieb Wendehals's vintage early 1980s conga classic 'Polonäse Blankenese' – impromptu congas are an unavoidable part of *Karneval* – to the 2003 'Viva Kolonia', which is better known throughout Germany than the national anthem.

Some of these can even be used to express local rivalries, notably one by the typical *Karneval* ensemble Paraplüs entitled 'Über Köln da lacht die Sonne, über Düsseldorf die Welt'

(The sun smiles on Cologne, the whole world laughs at Düsseldorf). Nobody has ever forgiven their near rivals on the Rhine for being chosen by the British occupation forces in 1946 as capital city of Nordrhein-Westfalen, despite it being little over half the size and lacking Cologne's illustrious and ancient history. A common piece of graffiti is '*Besser a jeck als a D'dorfer*' – 'Better a carnival clown than a 'D'dorfer' – just in case you missed the fact that *Dorf* is German for 'village'.

Just how many of even the devout Catholic Rhinelanders – including the citizens of Düsseldorf – really do take to heart the literal meaning of *Karneval* (*carne-vale* is Latin for 'farewell to meat'), giving up their sausages and infamous but delicious *Mett* raw pork for the duration of Lent, is an open question. Today *Karneval* is a party for everyone who cares to join in rather than a particularly religious Roman Catholic celebration.

The fears that preceded the 2016 festival may have been primarily about social order and immigration, but anything that evokes 'wars of religion' has more than a nasty aftertaste in Cologne, where people still remember the Thirty Years War, the great 17th-century conflict between Protestantism and Catholicism, which devastated Europe and saw the population of the German-speaking lands fall by around one-third. But we are not quite there yet.

Unearthing the Distant Past

If more is known about the origins of Cologne as a city than almost any other in today's Germany, it is chiefly because of its antiquity, and the fact that it began life as a military outpost, guarding against the Germans themselves on the far limits of the Roman empire. It is often taken for granted that the Roman presence in Germany was slight, and it is true that the Rhine would prove a barrier they eventually decided was better as a border, as were the dense forests beyond.

But things were different in the south: much of Bavaria was Romanised – the city today known as Augsburg was founded as *Augusta Vindelicorum*. I have seen carvings referring to legionaries from Bavaria as far away as the town of Volubilia in Morocco, at the empire's southernmost frontier.

Rome's clashes with the barbarians to the immediate north would be a major factor in the empire's military expansion from the time of Julius Caesar, the first Roman general to make a major expedition across the Rhine. Eventually the German tribes would play a major role in Rome's downfall, but at the same time be so fascinated by the empire that its legacy would play a major role in their history for the next 2,000 years.

Hamburg has its two-letter acronym 'HH' (for *Hansestadt Hamburg*), but Cologne has a four-letter one, with an even older pedigree. CCAA stands for *Colonia Claudia Ara Agrippinensium*, once inscribed above the main city gate, meaning 'colony and place of worship founded by Claudius on the initiative of Agrippina', the name it bore from AD 50 onwards. The first recorded settlement goes back over half a century earlier to 19 BC when the Romans forcibly resettled a group of Germanic tribespeople from the right bank of the Rhine to a low hill on the left bank, still just about recognisable today west of the city centre Alter Markt (Old Market) square. The new town was given a high altar (*ara* in the city's Latin name) intended as a focal point for the inhabitants and the German tribes beyond the Rhine, whose conquest was at the time high on the Roman agenda.

That agenda was dramatically changed almost overnight barely a decade later, in 9 BC, when the general Publius Quintus Varus was ambushed by an unknown number of tribesmen in the Teutoburg Forest, and two entire legions wiped out, a disaster that drove the first Roman Emperor Augustus to distraction that 'savages' could have inflicted such a defeat on the pride of Rome's military power. Augustus reputedly never quite recovered from the defeat and for years afterwards would call out, 'Varus, where are my eagles?', in reference to the legions' lost golden standards. Varus himself, of course, was not available to answer. For the next four decades the future Cologne, instead of being the centre of a new and expanding imperial province, would become a garrison city, a 'Watch on the Rhine' albeit facing in the wrong direction for the minds of generations in the distant future for whom that phrase would mean a guardian against French incursion.

Two legions were stationed in or near the city, including the one commanded by the great general Tiberius Claudius Nero 'Germanicus', the sobriquet given for his achievements, as much for stopping the German tribes crossing the river as for his victories in punitive campaigns on the other side. Germanicus, recalled to Rome in AD 16, had been destined to succeed Augustus's adopted heir Tiberius, whose name he had been given, but he died and his half-insane son Caligula became emperor in his stead.

It was Caligula's successor, after his murder in Rome and the praetorian guard's choice of his uncle Claudius to replace him, who would elevate the status of this little frontier post on the far northern fringes of the empire (Britain had not yet been invaded). Claudius married Germanicus' younger daughter Agrippina, who had been born there, and his new wife persuaded him to give her birthplace the title of 'colony'. This was hugely important, for it gave the citizens of the city the equivalent of Roman citizenship, encouraging both trade and settlement, particularly by retired legionaries. As a result the city quickly developed. It became the port for the Roman fleet on the river Rhine and had a substantial brick-built city wall nearly four kilometres in length, small stretches of which can still be seen.

The fortifications were needed. After the death of the Emperor Nero in AD 68, civil war again broke out in the empire over the succession. The legions based in the colony on the Rhine spontaneously declared their commander

Aulus Vitellius emperor. With support from troops in the
Iberian peninsula, Gaul and the recently conquered province
of Britannia, Vitellius took his own army and marched on
Rome, leaving the Rhine frontier relatively undefended. The
inevitable result was an invasion by Germanic tribes, who
initially managed to persuade the townspeople to side with
them, until they demanded the dismantlement of the walls
at which point the citizens decided to stick with the Roman
garrison. Vitellius hung on to the vestiges of power in Rome
for barely eight months until he was defeated and killed by
troops from the eastern part of the empire, who had proclaimed their own general, Vespasian, emperor.

Safely back in the bosom of the empire, the city had
grown to such an extent that it merited an aqueduct of its
own, bringing water down from the Eifel hills, one of the
longest the Romans ever built. The Emperor Domitian (AD
85–90), obviously convinced that the region had settled
down, changed the status of the Rhineland from an area
under military occupation into that of an official Roman
province, made the city capital of what was now known as
Germania Inferior (Lower Germany, as it lay in the direction
the Rhine flowed), and its military commander governor of
the province. An extended period of peace on the border,
and an ideal location for river trade between the empire and
the regions beyond, meant that over the next two centuries
the population of the city and surrounding district grew to
reach some 20,000 in the late second century AD. For more
than two centuries there were also good connections by road
– arguably as good as they would ever be until the building of the autobahns in the 1930s – with a main route that
led via the settlement of Beda Vicus (today's Bitburg, mostly
known for its beer) and Augusta Trevorum (today's Trier), all
the way south to Lugdunum (today's Lyon in France), where
it melded into the great pan-European network of Roman
highways, originally military, but for most of the lengthy
Pax Romana major trade arteries. For much of the second

and third centuries, CCAA was undoubtedly a city of note throughout the Roman empire and easily the greatest city north of the Alps.

It may have been the presence on German soil of one of the great cities of ancient Rome that inspired the German archaeologists who in the late 19th and early 20th centuries did so much to expand our knowledge of the classical world. Many of them were self-taught, notably Heinrich Schliemann and Robert Koldewey, who between them reacquainted the world with the sites of Mycenae, Troy and Babylon.

Schliemann, born in 1822, was a businessman and talented linguist who had lived and traded in both Russia and California, acquiring US citizenship when the state joined the USA. His great passion in life was the study of ancient Greece and he used a fortune amassed in banking and the dye industry to finance his interest, in particular his determination to prove the accuracy of Homer's *Iliad* by discovering the locations of Troy and Mycenae. In a series of digs in Turkey and the Peloponnese, he discovered both, although neither would later turn out to be exactly what he had been looking for. There was, and still is, much controversy over Schliemann's research, methods and reputation: to what extent was he a serious archaeologist rather than a rich playboy indulging a hobby?

He confirmed a hill in modern Turkey owned by an English diplomat and amateur archaeologist – like Schliemann himself – as that of ancient Troy, and began digging there in 1871. In his hurried excavations it is now believed Schliemann's workers dug down beneath the city of Homer's tale, damaging the remains of the city he was looking for. But what he did discover in the ruins of a city up to a thousand years older was a remarkable hoard of gold and jewellery, which he quickly named 'Priam's Treasure', after Troy's fabled king. Most striking among what he called the 'Jewels of Helen of Troy' was a golden headdress in which Schliemann famously dressed his second wife,

Sophia, a young Greek woman 30 years his junior, whom he had found by advertising in a newspaper.

Within three years he had moved to Greece and began excavating at a site on the Peloponnese believed to be Mycenae, home to Agamemnon, the great general of the Greek army during the Trojan war. Again he came across a remarkable treasure hoard, although again it later proved to be much older than the historically accepted date for the war. Chief among these finds was a golden funerary mask found on a body, which Schliemann declared to be that of Agamemnon himself (he named his son after him, for which the boy may not have thanked him). I vividly remember as a schoolboy, fascinated by Greek myths and the story of the Trojan war, standing at the entrance to what Schliemann had proclaimed in 1879 to have been the Tomb of Agamemnon. I have ever since wondered if Schliemann or the classical historians were right, and whether the remarkable items he found at both Troy and Mycenae did not indeed belong to Priam and Agamemnon: and that the legendary war took place far longer ago than anyone imagines.

Apart from that school trip to Mycenae, my later discovery of the achievements of German archaeologists came as one of the most remarkable surprises in my first months in Communist East Germany in 1981. I had never expected the Cold War capital to be home to some of the finest monuments of antiquity. Along with the British Museum in London, the Pergamon Museum in Berlin is one of the world's greatest treasure troves of material from the ancient world. During World War II, thankfully, most of its prime exhibits had been relocated to storage and could be reinstated after 1945. The East German government returned them all to a restored museum, save for Schliemann's 'Jewels of Helen', which were taken from Berlin to Moscow and to this day are on display there in the Pushkin Museum.

The exhibit which gave the museum its name is the second-century BC Altar of Pergamon, discovered on the site of the ancient city, again in modern Turkey, by a German engineer called Carl Humann shortly after Schliemann's discoveries at Mycenae and Troy. Humann, in the manner of Lord Elgin in Athens, had his find shipped stone by stone back to Berlin and reassembled in a purpose-built museum (rebuilt to accommodate more treasures a dozen years later). As monuments of antiquity removed from their original site to Europe, the Pergamon Altar is on a scale with the so-called Elgin Marbles in the British Museum. Almost equally imposing in the same museum is the Market Gate of Miletus built 400 years later, in the second century AD, excavated by Theodor Wiegand, actually a trained archaeologist who had studied in Berlin, Freiburg and Munich. This was 20 years after Schliemann had excited the world and created a global vogue for archaeology.

But for me on that first visit to the Pergamon back in 1981, the most remarkable thing in the whole museum, so unexpected, so radically different to any of the other marvels of the relatively familiar classical world, was the Ishtar Gate of Babylon. Coming in out of the dull grey skies and dull grey streets of East Berlin into a world of ancient Greek and Roman classical splendour was magical enough, but nothing like the shock of turning a corner to face a soaring gateway, 14 metres high, of shining deep blue lapis lazuli, decorated with yellow and black depictions of gods and goddesses, opening into a corridor of the same, bearing images of dragons and bulls. I had, quite literally, not only seen nothing like it in my life, but had no idea it even existed. Yet here it was, an explosion of bright colour and craftsmanship from the sixth century BC, tucked away in a museum on the wrong side of the Berlin Wall, in one of the world's less accessible countries, seen by few tourists other than an occasional group of Communist Party apparatchiks from Moscow. It was not only that the structure itself was awe-inspiring, it was the resonance of the names associated with it: the goddess Ishtar and the word 'Babylon' itself, which I had first come across as a child in the mouth of Ulster Protestant firebrand Ian Paisley, accusing the Pope of being the 'Whore of Babylon', causing me to ask awkward questions as a six-year-old. What made the impact complete was the appearance of one of those Biblical references that seems more to do with religious legend than historical reality: the inscribed name of the man who had it built, King Nebuchadnezzar.

Its presence in Berlin is down to one man, Robert Koldewey, a self-trained archaeologist from Braunschweig, who spent most of the first two decades of the 20th century probing the remains of Babylon, confirming that the legendary Hanging Gardens had actually existed, and uncovering the remnants of the gate. What Koldewey and his team dug up were primarily fragments of the tiles, but in exactly where it had long been predicted the ancient Processional Way of Nebuchadnezzar's Babylon lay. Over the years they retrieved more and more, including foundation remnants which gave a clear scale of the structure. The tiles were shipped to Berlin, where copies were made as close as possible to fill in gaps, and applied to the walls within the Pergamon, to recreate as much as possible of the original gate in its new home. It remains, in my mind, one of the most remarkable finds, the most remarkable rebuild, in the history of archaeology.

Those who doubt the wisdom and morality of such finds being taken to a new location on a different continent, might first reflect on the fact that in 2003–4, during the US occupation of Baghdad, a helicopter pad was built on the site where the Ishtar Gate had been found, and tanks drove over the remains of the Processional Way, shattering numerous tiles. Nebuchadnezzar's armies would have treated the cities they conquered with similar disdain. Today we are supposed to know better.

A little way up the Rhine from Cologne, the little city of Trier, founded by Celts in the fourth century BC, is today the best place in which to see the remains of Roman civilisation in the German-speaking world. The subsequent growth of Cologne and Augsburg in the Middle Ages and beyond covered over most remnants of the Roman cities. Trier, by contrast, reached the high point of its fame and importance during the Roman period, then gradually declined to today's provincial status.

As in the case of many cities of renown whose economic fate declined swiftly – the most notable example is Venice – the result has been the preservation of sites and buildings that would otherwise have been built over or demolished. Trier's largely intact huge Porta Nigra (Black Gate), built at the height of the city's importance around AD 175 during the reigns of Marcus Aurelius and Commodus, is still one of the most impressive Roman remains anywhere in the world. By the beginning of the fourth century AD, when the empire was briefly recovering from crisis and before another was about to strike it, Trier was at the height of its glory, home for several years to the Emperor Constantine the Great, whose father the tetrarch Constantius Chlorus had spent time there, and his son Constantine II, and likely to have been substantially larger than Cologne. It was during their time that Trier's other great surviving Roman monument, the Imperial Baths, were built. The city was also home to a massive amphitheatre.

Cologne's Roman heritage was mostly built over as the city expanded through the mediaeval period. Ironically it was the blackest moment in its history that helped throw light on its early glories: clearing the rubble of World War II bombing uncovered numerous relics from the Roman age as well as allowing archaeologists to get a better idea of ancient street plans, nearly all of which were destroyed during the higgledy-piggledy building of the Middle Ages. The city's Römisch-Germanisches Museum (Roman–German museum) next to the cathedral, contains the best of these, includ-ing gravestones, oil lamps with erotic designs, glassware, mosaics and gladiator helmets, evidence that the city had at least one amphitheatre (most experts believe there may have been more than one), even though no definitive remnants of such a structure have as yet been uncovered. One of the most impressive remnants is the Römerturm, sole survivor of the 19 defensive towers that encircled the city in the third century. With its crenellations and mosaic, it has remained in good condition down the centuries, largely because it spent the Middle Ages within a Franciscan monastery, where it was used as a toilet.

The Pax Romana did not last forever, and fell apart fastest for those colonies furthest from the heart. In the third century the empire began to come under increasing pressure on all sides, particularly in Persia, but also from the German tribes on the other side of the Rhine. There was a brief respite under Constantine the Great, but by the middle of the fourth century the legions were pulling back all over, and their colony on the Rhine was left to the tender mercies of waves of invaders, chief of whom was a Germanic tribe from the lower Rhine that would make almost as great a mark on European history as the Romans: the Franks.

Precisely what ordinary folk in the first three to four centuries of Cologne's existence called the city in everyday terms – in written form it survives only as CCAA – we do not know. There were other *coloniae* across the empire and although *Colonia Agrippina* was a shorter way of putting the full name, it was still unlikely to catch on with common folk. Clearly simply *colonia* became the routine way of referring to it. Over the centuries this was warped by the vernacular to produce *Coellen*, which evolved via *Cöllen, Cölln,* and *Cöln* to the modern Köln, although not without complications in the 19th century, when it went from being an independent 'free' city, under an archbishop, to being part of first France and then Prussia. Ask most inhabitants of the city today what they call it and they will use two syllables: *Koelle.*

Cologne's founding location on the western rather than eastern bank of the Rhine was to determine its history, and become a defining feature in relations between what – in a far distant future – would become France and Germany. Initially a base for further Roman expansion across the Rhine, when that became more daunting than had been imagined, it became the opposite: a bulwark against aggression from the other bank. Its success in this role was to become historically limited, particularly from the end of the fifth century, when it finally fell to the native tribes living by the banks and estuary of the Rhine. These tribes spoke similar Germanic languages, which today we might consider dialects, although at those times there were as many drifting apart as coming together. The English word for Netherlanders – Dutch – comes from the German word for German – *deutsch* – a linguistic grouping the Netherlanders belonged to (and up to a point still do) until they started deliberately creating differences in a campaign to define a distinct identity. The 21st-century concept of a 'national language' distorts or ignores the history of linguistic evolution whereby streams of linguistic forms spread apart from basic Indo-European origins and went in different directions (it is an interesting exercise to go through which modern European and Indian languages have mutual Sanskrit-derived roots for specific words, and where these words have been lost in others).

Each tribe had its own name – probably derived from ancient paternal figures – but they became collectively known as the Franks. It remains disputed whether that name derived from an old Germanic term for a javelin, or from some concept of 'freedom' or 'entitlement', which many scholars today consider a retrospective definition based on the societies the Franks created, and the word's later use in the Middle East for all Western Europeans. Another possibility is that it has roots similar to the North American Cheyenne, considered to be a corruption of their native language for 'people like us', or Cherokee, apparently meaning 'main people', both not dissimilar to the origins of the common southern European name for Germany – Allemagne, Alemania – derived from the most southerly Germanic tribes they encountered, who considered themselves to be the only real human beings, in their terms 'all the men' (in modern German: *alle Männer*). It is one of history's ironies that these Germanic tribes, whose name would give us the ultra-modern economic term of 'franchise' – an extension of a corporate name and personality to a small business – would be adopted by an area of Europe that strongly retained its Romanised status, language and customs: France. The northern Bavarian province of Franken has, beyond modern Germany's borders, largely been forgotten as having the same derivation. But the fact that the biggest Roman city north of the Alps lay on a river that had once been seen as a potential bridgehead was to have a legacy that would rattle down the centuries.

Money for Old Bones

The collapse of the Roman empire was far from the end for the growth of Cologne. What turned out to be the Romans' greatest legacy to their colony on the Rhine was the religion adopted by one-time resident Constantine: Christianity. The Romanised citizenry did not flee the Frankish takeover of their city: instead they gradually assimilated with their new masters, and the city's bishop, later archbishop, who would become one of the leading figures in the realm. Despite Viking raids down the Rhine in the ninth century, the city's position as a trading centre ensured it continued to grow. But perhaps the greatest boost to its status was a box of some old bones brought from Milan.

The origin of Cologne's great leap forward in the 12th century went back to the Emperor Constantine's mother Helena (255–330) who, either out of devout faith, a determination to make the religion her son had chosen stick with the public, or just possibly sheer gullibility in the face of some smooth-talking Jewish or Arab tradesman, had brought back what she claimed to be the bones of the Three Wise

Men from a pilgrimage to the Holy Land (she also picked up fragments of Jesus's tunic and the rope with which he had been tied to the cross – no mention of nails – along with some pieces of wood described as fragments of the 'true cross'). In fact, the Bible makes very little mention of the so-called 'wise men' – of the gospel writers only Matthew mentions them, as 'magi from the east' , and there is not the slightest indication of why they would not have returned home, or where, why and when a collective act of 'regicide' might have occurred, allowing Helena to have acquired all three skeletons as a job lot. Despite their minimal mention in Christian scripture, they had in Christian legend been elevated to 'three kings of Orient', particularly celebrated in Catholic Germany, where children dressed in oriental garb visit local homes on Twelfth Night and the letters C+M+B for Caspar, Melchior and Balthazar – names which only appeared for the first time in the sixth century – are chalked over every door.

The bones Helena brought back to Rome ended up installed in a church in Milan as sacred relics to be worshipped by the faithful. After a rebellious Milan was conquered in 1162 by Friedrich Barbarossa, the contemporary claimant of the imperial title, his chancellor Rainald von Dassel, who happened to be archbishop of what was then called Cöllen, decided that the earthly remains of the magi had to go back with him. Von Dassel knew what he was doing: on his long journey back to the Rhineland, he held solemn and well-attended masses on every stop along his route, so that by the time the bones – long neglected in Milan – finally got to their new home, their fame had spread far and wide. In 1164 they arrived in a triumphal procession through the city to the old cathedral building, already nearly 300 years old. The city on the Rhine was well on the way to being one of the most important pilgrimage sites in the Christian world, ranking alongside Rome, the less accessible Jerusalem, and Santiago de Compostela, which allegedly housed the bones of the apostle James. The arrival of the relics in Cologne allowed the city to claim the title *sancta* (holy) in its name, an appellation otherwise granted only to Rome, Constantinople and Jerusalem. Its full title in Latin was Sancta Colonia Dei Gratiae Romanae Ecclesiae Fidelis Filia (Holy Cologne, by the Grace of God, faithful Daughter of the Roman Church).

By now the former Roman colony was the largest German-speaking city in the world, with a population of some 40,000, a city wall as long as that of Paris (7.5 kilometres, with a dozen towers). The good citizens, realising the sanctity of the relics entrusted to their care – not to mention a nice little earner for the innkeepers, alehouses and victuallers of the city over the next few centuries – commissioned one of the age's most famous goldsmiths, Nicholas of Verdun, to make a golden triple coffin to house them. The job took him over 40 years to produce the spectacular masterpiece that – with some major alterations and repairs over the centuries – lies behind the altar in the cathedral today. Or, put the other way around, it is substantially because of the relics in their golden casket, that the tallest Catholic cathedral in Europe exists in anything like its current form. The decision to build a new cathedral in honour of the relics was taken in 1225, and work, according to plans drawn up by master builder Gerhard von Rile, using the cathedral of Amiens in northern France as his model, began in 1248.

Inevitably, it wasn't a quick job: in fact it would take more than 600 years for it to be completed. Not that that stopped the flow of pilgrims. By 1322, less than 60 years after starting work, the choir was complete, allowing the holy relics to be installed, while building work continued. Towards the end of the century, the building was big enough for a mass to be said there to celebrate the foundation of the city's first university. The southern tower reached its second storey early in the 15th century and by 1437 it was high enough, at 59 metres, for two bells to be hung in it. That, it would appear to have been decided at the time, would do for now. A foundation stone for the planned northern tower was laid in 1500, but that was as far as it got. Whether or not the numbers of pilgrims had tailed off is unclear, but there was apparently no consensus that it was worth the expenditure to continue the work. For much of the next 300 years the wise men's bones lay in their golden catafalque in a magnificent specimen of late mediaeval Gothic architecture that had nonetheless been left half-finished. Cologne's position on the Rhine, along with the Elbe a chief artery for bringing the products of the Hanseatic League into the heart of the continent, gave it the status of a *Hansestadt* in its own right, on a par with those on the Baltic coast, and ensured continuing economic success with or without the pilgrims.

For all that the Kölner Dom remains the greatest symbol of Catholicism in Germany and one of the country's most popular tourist attractions with some six million people a year passing beneath the great spires, it is also a reminder of how a religious revolution with much of its origins in the German lands came to decimate them and spark a war that would eventually draw in most of Europe.

The suspension of the building of the cathedral did not represent a decline in interest in religion in the German-speaking countries of Central Europe. Far from it. Perhaps it was the cost of pilgrimages, the number of relics of various saints appearing all across Christendom to the lucrative benefit of the churches or monasteries that housed them, but there was a growing restlessness among the common people that as far as the Catholic – 'universal' – Church was concerned, saving souls wasn't a 'not for profit' business. Questioning the way the Vatican ran its supposedly universal church was not new. There had been criticism from the wings going on for several centuries. John Wycliffe in 14th-century England had produced a translation of the Bible and argued that it and it alone, rather than edicts from Rome, should be the basis of Christian faith. Jan Hus in Bohemia in the early 15th century had done much the same and even translated some of Wycliffe's writing into his native Czech. The church did not take criticism kindly. At the Council of Constance in 1415, Wycliffe, who had died of a stroke in 1384 before he could feel the Vatican's full wrath, was posthumously declared a heretic, his body removed from consecrated ground (whether that meant his soul was unceremoniously expelled from heaven is not clear) and his writings collected and burned. His body was dug up from his grave in Lutterworth, Leicestershire, in 1428, burnt, and his ashes thrown into the River Swift. Hus, who was unlucky enough still to be alive, was summoned to attend the same council, and did so voluntarily, only to be tried for heresy and burnt alive at the stake. His ashes were thrown into the Rhine.

But memory of their ideas lived on, and came to the fore again in the early 16th century when an emissary was sent from the Vatican to collect money for the rebuilding of St Paul's in Rome by selling 'indulgences', a great many of them to the pilgrims visiting Cologne. These indulgences were effectively promissory notes that supposedly guaranteed the purchaser's soul would spend less time being purged of sin in purgatory before being admitted to heaven. Not everybody believed they would work, and even among those who did, there was a feeling that it offered an unfair fast track to the rich, which was hardly what Jesus Christ seemed to have been preaching when he talked about it being 'easier for a camel to pass through the eye of the needle than for a rich man to enter the Kingdom of God'. The whole business brought a particularly bad taste to the mouth of an Augustinian monk who was doctor of theology at the University of Wittenberg. His name was Martin Luther and he particularly questioned the theological basis of such a deal: surely the Bible made it quite clear that only faith and piety guaranteed entrance to heaven? He sent his queries, set out in 95 theses, to his bishop in Mainz, not in anger but as a basis for further discussion as to the legitimacy of the practice.

Legend has it that he defiantly nailed them to the door of

Wittenberg Castle church in October 1517, but there is no evidence to back it up, although it is possible that he might have posted a copy of his letter in the church to encourage the discussion he wanted. In any case it was not until 1518, when the theses were translated from Latin into German, that the ideas came to wider attention, largely thanks to the relatively recent invention and spread of the printing press. By 1519 copies were being passed around not just throughout the German lands but also in France and England. Luther never got a reply from his bishop, almost certainly because he needed the pope's sanction for him to hold two bishoprics, in Magdeburg as well as Mainz. Instead he sent them straight to Rome as suspected heresy.

Luther had lit a spark that would not die out; instead it would fire a conflagration. Those influenced by him would include the radical Thomas Müntzer, who seized on Luther's ideas as the basis for an overall attack on the wealthy (who could afford indulgences while the poor could not), which fuelled a rebellion by peasants in 1524–5. Luther, however, failed to support the rebellion, seeing it as little more than an excuse for theft of land and property. His lack of endorsement disheartened many of the rebels, who laid down their arms. One decisive battle, at Frankenhausen in May 1525, saw the rebellion defeated. Müntzer was captured and executed, though he would achieve posthumous fame by featuring on East German banknotes as a sort of proto-Marxist. Luther instead focused his energies on getting married and organising a new church, which he claimed would be more closely linked to the word of the Bible. Other reformers too were playing their part: Ulrich Zwingli in Zurich had already been calling for an end to Lenten fasting, pictures of saints and clerical celibacy. The Frenchman Jean Calvin, a lawyer and zealous polemicist, fled to Geneva and so won over the population to the need for reform that the city threw off the influence of Catholicism. By the mid-16th century, the schism had become irrevocable. The reformers had created the Reformation: the protesters became Protestants.

As so often, religion carried over into politics. By the mid-1560s the inhabitants of the Habsburg provinces on the North Sea, known as the Spanish Netherlands (including most of present-day Belgium as well as the modern Netherlands), ruled from Madrid since the division of the Habsburg empire after the abdication of Charles V, had mostly adopted the new Protestant form of worship, and rebelled against their staunchly Catholic Spanish overlords. Although ostensibly about freedom of worship, the rebellion was also an attempt to gain political independence from Spain. Despite early setbacks, the northern area managed to rebuff Spanish attempts at reconquest, and from around 1581 was nominally independent (although not legally so until 1648). Initially the rebels chose to follow contemporary European practice and appoint a monarch. There were two obvious candidates from neighbouring states: Philip of Anjou, younger brother of the King of France, and Elizabeth I of England. Anjou was eventually rejected because he was a Catholic. Elizabeth refused, unwilling to antagonise the husband of her late elder half-sister Mary Tudor, Philip II of Spain, who still maintained he had a rightful claim to the throne of England. The rebels in response declared themselves a republic and took the name of the United Provinces.

Meanwhile next door in Cöllen, the Archbishop-Prince-Elector Gebhard Truchsess von Waldburg stunned the Catholic church and his subjects in 1582 by announcing that he was converting to Protestantism. The established rule, set out in the 1555 Peace of Augsburg, which ended the first attempt by the Catholic Habsburgs to suppress the growth of Protestantism, was described in Latin as *cuius regio, eius religio*: 'the religion of the people should be that of their ruler'. Given that in the 1550s there were more than 200 independent or semi-independent German states, this did not exactly simplify the religious map of Europe. A clause called the Ecclesiastical Reservation was supposed to ensure that this only worked in one direction: the people were supposed to follow the religion of the ruler, not he follow theirs, and were given a grace period to convert or emigrate. In the case of a Catholic ruler converting to Protestantism, the rule did not apply, and instead he was supposed to step down. Unsurprisingly the Protestants thought this unfair.

Almost immediately the Catholic Cathedral Chapter declared Waldburg deposed and named Ernst of Bavaria, who had been a canon at the cathedral since 1570, as his successor. There were now two archbishops at war with one another. Gebhard got the support of rebellious Netherlanders, plus some Scottish and English mercenaries, while his rival had the enthusiastic support of the Spanish determined to quash their rebel possession. England's Robert Dudley, Earl of Leicester, had been sent by Elizabeth I to support the rebellious Dutch, while mercenaries on the other side came from Bavaria paid from the papal coffers. The result was a series of devastating sieges throughout the disparate and unconnected patches of land included in the Cologne electorate on either side of the Rhine.

A Spanish and Italian army laid siege to the city of Neuss, north of Cologne, eventually capturing it, slaughtering the garrison and burning the city to the ground. When Rheinberg in the north also fell, the scale of the defeat left Gebhard with little choice but to give in and accept the offer of asylum in the free city of Strassburg, the other predominately German-speaking city on the western bank of the Rhine. This 'Cologne War' was but an inkling of the chaos to come. The Protestant states, mostly in the northern German lands, at the instigation of Elector Friedrich IV of the Palatinate, yet another disparate collection of territories cobbled together as a result of various inheritances, formed themselves into an 'Evangelical Union'. This in turn prompted the southern states led by Bavaria, to form a Catholic League. This schism in Christianity was to lead to a religious war on a par with anything seen in the schism between Sunni and Shia Islam, and become – as that conflict has done – as much about power and politics as about faith.

A Plague upon All Your Houses

In 1618, the now accepted if rather arbitrary date for the beginning of what has come to be known as the Thirty Years War, the Protestant inhabitants of Habsburg-ruled Bohemia, who had already flirted with reformed religion under the influence of Jan Hus, by then revered as one of the earliest Protestant martyrs, rebelled against their Catholic overlords in spectacular manner. On 23 May, a delegation of some 200 eminent Protestant citizens of Prague marched to the castle, accusing the Austrian emperor of going back on a letter assuring their religious freedom. Their talks with the governor and other imperial officials did not go well. After several hours, the unhappy citizens took the law into their own hands and threw the three officials out of a window 17 metres above the ground. Incredibly, all three survived, though injured, and fled as well as they were able. The incident became known as the Defenestration of Prague.

Spectacular as it may have been, it was never going to work. Bohemia abjured allegiance to the Austrian emperor and instead chose as king the son of the man who had created the 'Evangelical Union', now Friedrich V of the Palatinate. He accepted, without consulting his fellow princes and electors, and travelled to Prague, where he was crowned in November 1619. Unsurprisingly, the rebels felt the full force of Habsburg displeasure. The rebellion was quickly crushed by imperial forces in alliance with the army of Bavaria equally determined not to see a 'legitimate' monarch ousted by Protestant rebels. Friedrich, who would be known in Czech history as the 'Winter King' for his short spell on the throne, was roundly defeated by an army three times the size of his at White Mountain outside Prague and fled, first north to Breslau in Silesia, then eventually to the Netherlands. He had won no sympathy from anyone for stirring up the seeds of wider conflict. By 1622 Spanish troops had completed his humiliation by capturing his homeland's two major cities, Heidelberg and Mannheim, and the Palatinate was awarded to Maximilian of Bavaria, who had led the Bavarian–Austrian forces at White Mountain, creating yet another two-part German state which would survive at least theoretically until after World War II, and is today chiefly commemorated by the Pfälzer Weinstube in Munich's Residenz palace which serves Rhineland wine to those looking for a change from ubiquitous Bavarian beer.

There was, however, no halting the spread of the war, which took on a new dimension, more to do with dynastic power than religion, when largely Catholic France improbably took the side of the mostly Protestant states in the expanding conflict, fearing encirclement by the Habsburgs should the revolt in the Spanish Netherlands fail. In the east a Protestant prince of Transylvania rebelled against his Catholic Habsburg overlords, winning over opportunistic support from the Muslim Ottoman Empire, which had offered troops to Friedrich of Bohemia and as a result ended up in a brief war with Habsburg-supporting Poland, mostly fought in what is now Moldova. Like toppling dominoes, the conflicts multiplied across the continent, with dynastic struggles and regional disturbances adding to a climate of almost constant warfare, rebellion and destruction.

In France the Protestant Huguenots rebelled, as their wide freedoms embodied in the 1598 Edict of Nantes passed by Henri IV were being constrained by his son, Louis XIII, with the result that the French army laid siege to La Rochelle, the coastal city that was a centre of Protestantism. This led to yet another English intervention on the side of the Huguenots. King Charles I sent a fleet of 80 ships under the command of his father's old favourite (and possibly lover) George Villiers, Duke of Buckingham, which landed a small army on the nearby Île de Ré, only to be forced out after three months. A second fleet sent to relieve the siege of La Rochelle also failed. The English support was remembered though and when Louis XIV finally repealed the last of the Huguenots' freedoms in 1685, many fled to England. Some settled in the East End of London, but more were delighted to take up the offer of 'free land' (usually seized from Catholic rebels) in the north of Ireland, bringing their linen-making skills with them.

The growing complexity of this multi-sided conflict was exemplified by the fact that the French, busily repressing their own Protestants at home, were allies of most of the other Protestant states in Europe because of their fear of Habsburg domination of the continent. In the midst of a war about religious faith and commitment, hypocrisy was rife, and at times almost ludicrous. For example, the Protestant Dutch were happy to rent ships to the Catholic French, their allies against the Catholic Habsburgs, to use against their own Protestant citizens; but they banned them from saying Catholic mass on deck.

Few of the leading figures in the war that lasted a generation came out of it alive with great successes to chalk up. The luckless Friedrich V's fate for having accepted a crown offered him by the people rather than his peers, was exile and ignominy. He died in 1635 of a 'pestilential fever' in Mainz. Even the last resting place of his bones is unknown. Yet he was to leave a lasting legacy in European history through his daughter Sophia. Friedrich's wife, Elizabeth Stuart, was the daughter of King James VI of Scotland and I of England and sister of his successor, Charles I. Primarily on Friedrich's daughter's account, an Anglo-Dutch regiment sided with his forces against the invading Spanish in the Palatinate and a Scottish–Dutch regiment took his side in Bohemia, albeit in both cases in vain.

Traditional schoolbook British history (which in effect has mostly meant English history), particularly among those who from the imperial heyday onwards have propagated the myth of 'British exceptionalism', tends to suggest 'Great Britain' (which did not legally exist until the 1707 Act of Union) played little part in the Thirty Years War, treating it as a 'continental affair'. Yet not only had James's predecessor Elizabeth I sent troops to La Rochelle to support the Huguenots, his son and heir, Charles I, did likewise, the defeat leading to Charles having to petition the English parliament for funds which led to his personal rule for 11 years and eventually civil war. Long referred to as just the 'English Civil War', it has of late (arguably more correctly given how the conflict impinged on Ireland and Scotland) also been labelled the 'War of the Three Kingdoms'. This conflict between a Puritan parliament and a king who, despite being nominally Protestant, was widely and justifiably suspected of being a closet Catholic, was effectively a peripheral offshoot of the Thirty Years War, Charles's execution in January 1649 coming just months after the general cessation of hostilities on the mainland.

Charles's niece Sophia, daughter of the unfortunate Friedrich V, outlived it all and was to prove progenitor of the long-term survival of the British monarchy. With the Stuart dynasty on the verge of extinction by the time Queen Anne reached middle age childless, Sophia, now married to the Elector of Hanover, became heir to what, after the 1707 Act of Union between England and Scotland, was now officially called Great Britain. Despite living to the ripe old age of 83, Sophia herself did not directly benefit, having died just two months before Anne (at the, even then, relatively young age of 49). As a result it was Sophia's 54-year-old eldest son and Elector of Hanover, Georg Ludwig (George Louis in the English version), who found himself overnight handed the combined English and Scottish throne.

∈∋

Meanwhile the religious fever generated by the extended conflict in Europe gave rise to accusations of heresy flung in all directions, as were charges of witchcraft. In the circumstances it was no surprise that unsupported allegations could be used to settle disputes that were on the face of it more mundane, because they were linked to the real world, such as a row over the post office. One notorious incident includes one of the most important and enduring German noble houses, the Thurn und Taxis family, whose wealthy and glamorous descendants still make headlines today: Gloria Thurn und Taxis was one of Europe's most celebrated party animals throughout the 1980s, only to turn arch-conservative in her later years, opposing liberal abortion laws and criticising the presence of condom machines in schools.

But back in the early 17th century, the main thing on the mind of her husband's ancestor, Leonhard II von Taxis, was keeping the lucrative business of running postal services in Europe in the family hands. Like most things at the time, this came down to relations with the Habsburgs, who happened to own most of Europe. His grandfather had already secured the right to run the post office in what was still for the moment the Spanish Netherlands, and the family were determined to extend it throughout the Habsburg realms. But there was an argument over just how independent local post masters could be. In particular the office of chief postmaster for Cöllen caused problems when he and his father fell out over who should occupy it. Jacob Henot in Cologne thought he should have the right to keep the regional office in the family. When he died, his daughter Katharina took over. Leonhard insisted he had the power to appoint whoever he wanted and when he tried to impose it, Katharina and her brother took him to court.

All of a sudden, and happily for the Taxis family, out of nowhere a nun turned up accusing the postmistress of witchcraft in the midst of a rash of such allegations, at a time when it seemed all Europe was at war over religion. She accused Katharina of causing a plague in her convent and the deaths of several people. Despite her pleas of innocence and refusal to confess even under torture, which legally ought to have required her to be set free, she was quickly declared guilty and burnt alive at the stake. In June 2012 Katharina Henot and the other victims of the witch-hunts were officially exonerated by the city council. I am sure it was a great comfort to them.

Meanwhile, the spread of the war continued. Protestant Denmark, frightened by Catholic successes to the south, took up arms against a Habsburg army marching north. King Christian IV sent a Danish army to meet them, backed up by 20,000 mercenaries plus some 13,000 Scots, and eventually 6,000 English, sent by his nephew Charles I. Rather than the glorious victory such reinforcements might have been expected to bring, the result was catastrophic defeat at the hands of the inspired Habsburg general Albrecht von Wallenstein, who came close to conquering the whole of Denmark. Worried that he might lose other gains, in the end he settled for a peace treaty if the Danes pledged to keep their forces within their own borders. The Danes did.

The Swedes didn't. Under their charismatic and militarily gifted king, Gustavus Adolphus, a Swedish army also backed by mercenaries (virtually the only profession to do well out of the war) – mostly German but again with more than 25,000 Scots – took up arms on behalf of the Protestants, taking on first the Catholic Polish–Lithuanian Commonwealth and enlisting Russian help to do so. They then took on the Habsburg armies, provided with financial help from France as long as they promised to keep an army on German soil. For a time it seemed the Swedes were unstoppable, even though Gustavus Adolphus died in 1632 at the Battle of Lützen, when he got caught behind enemy lines. He was just 37. The Protestants had won the battle but lost one of their most important leaders. Far from retreating, the Swedes intensified their war effort after a brief interlude of mourning and despite a few setbacks, eventually reached as far south as Vienna, though they failed to take the city. By now not only the Swedes were getting war-weary, all of Europe was exhausted.

Cöllen itself, despite the events there that had foreshadowed the wars to come, survived remarkably well, declaring itself officially neutral and becoming a place of sanctuary for nobles on both sides of the religious divide, not least because the city's merchants and bankers had realised they were on to a good thing. They paid bribes to generals of passing armies to leave the city alone, in the meantime working out how to make money from the war. Over the three decades of conflict, the city had become one of Europe's leading centres of arms manufacturing, an industry which had grown exponentially, enthusiastically backed by the city's moneylenders. Financial credit was afforded only to Catholic powers, but the weapons the city produced were sold to both sides. The greatest inconvenience came when the Dutch rebels in their fight against their Habsburg overlords erected fortifications on an island in the Rhine south of the city giving them control over river trade. The Swedes at one stage considered attacking and taking the city and on 22 December 1632 seized what is today the suburb of Deutz on the right bank of the Rhine, only to be repulsed by gunfire from the city walls across the river and three companies of troops who crossed it. The main casualty was a church, blown up when shots hit the gunpowder reserves stored inside.

The extended warfare had never been clear-cut between two sides. There had been bilateral conflicts, trilateral conflicts, multilateral conflicts. Three decades of constant warfare could be divided up into any number of 'wars' between particular states, in the case of England, a civil war; there had been any number of truces, negotiations and peace treaties. The so-called Peace of Westphalia was itself not one peace treaty but a series of them signed between May and

October 1648, chiefly but not only, in the Westphalian cities of Munster and Osnabrück. The chief political result was the weakening of the 'imperial' title that the Habsburgs had passed down from generation to generation: the power of the princelings over their own dominions was confirmed.

The pre-eminence of Austria among the German states had been diminished, which effectively cleared the way for the emergence of one of the statelets to eventually rival it. At the time, however, it would still have been considered wildly improbable that the state which would do so, and eventually succeed in turning the German lands into a major European power, would be two widely separated but dynastically linked chunks of land known as Brandenburg-Prussia. Its lands in the west had been devastated, not least because their ruler changed sides three times; population loss had averaged 50 per cent, and in a few areas 70–90 per cent. But the peace treaties added a few formerly independent bishoprics to a growing patchwork of dependent territories to create a territorially absurd polity – the antithesis of the modern concept of a nation-state – comprised in 1618 of nine unconnected patches of land, differing hugely in size and distance from one another. But what made it different, what made it matter, was that in the wake of the war, in 1653 this disparate grouping of territories formed a single standing army, which would play an increasingly important role in European history over the centuries to come.

The other relatively minor player on the wider European stage to emerge with a greater presence was the new kingdom of Great Britain. Still very much in the throes of trying to forge itself into a nation-state, despite repeated rebellions by Scots opposed to the union and the Irish who perpetually refused to accept their position as a conquered colony, now demanded a greater say in the power play on the European mainland. But the clear winners in the war were the Dutch, who after 80 years of warfare had finally gained independence from Spain and rapidly began to expand via maritime trade from a colony to masters of a colonial empire of their own, quickly coming into conflict with the British, who had similar ambitions.

By 1648, Central Europe in particular was exhausted. The immediate and horribly visible result of 30 years of unceasing warfare had been the enormous devastation of land and loss of life, not just among soldiers, unprecedented and as yet – proportional to the populations of the time – never repeated in European history, including during the two world wars of the 20th century. Not just war took its toll, but starvation and illness as well. Fighting between Spanish and French forces in northern Italy took place against an outbreak of bubonic plague. Typhus was rampant and the lack of vegetable crops in the burnt fields led to widespread outbreaks of scurvy. Dysentery was endemic. In parts of Central Europe almost two-thirds of the population died.

From the contemporary point of view, the most significant factor was that France was now clearly the strongest power on the European mainland. Having escaped the worst of the fighting, its population by the middle of the century was some 21 million, roughly equivalent to one-fifth of all of Europe including the British Isles and Scandinavia. Significantly, on a continent where most states were still dynastic rather than 'national', France was a well-established nation-state, a fact made only too apparent to the others in the revolutions of 1789–93 when it abolished the monarchy, executed the king and declared a national republic. That would rapidly result in further consequences for the continent as a whole and the German lands in particular.

The French Revolutionary – subsequently Napoleonic – wars changed the status of Cöllen as dramatically as they changed most of continental Europe. From the point of view of the rapidly expanding French empire, Cöllen was situated on 'their' side of the Rhine. After French troops marched in on 6 October 1794, it ceased to be a 'free city', and indeed ceased to be German even if the population

remained largely the same. Yet again states were not synonymous with nations. The city, like everything on the left
bank of the Rhine, was assimilated into a greater revolutionary France. The occupation was not as regretted as much as
might be imagined today. There was still no strong concept
in the German-speaking lands of a nation-state or even of
nationality. Napoleon was welcomed as a liberator when he
visited the city in 1804. What he had brought to it was a
greater degree of religious tolerance, particularly welcomed
by the city's Jewish and Protestant populations. Cöllen, now
renamed as Cologne – the name that would endure in the
French and English-speaking worlds – was integrated into
the new 'greater France' in 1801 and subsequently declared
a *Bonne Ville de l'Empire Française*, a title that at the height
of the Napoleonic empire's extent it shared not only with
Marseille, Paris, Bordeaux and Toulouse, but also Hamburg,
Antwerp, Amsterdam, Florence and Turin.

The area just to the north of Cologne, around the Ruhr
river, one of the most important tributaries of the Rhine, had
become a centre of industrial production due to its iron and
coal reserves. Places which in early mediaeval times had been
villages in awe of the ancient city to the south grew into towns
and eventually the large cities we know today, including Dortmund, Essen, Duisburg and Düsseldorf. The name of the river
would rapidly evolve into that of the whole urban agglomeration which would grow up over the next two centuries.

Already by the time of Napoleon's arrival, the lands
around the Ruhr were known for their resources of coal and
iron, which by then were being increasingly exploited for
the production of steel, the essential ingredient in modern
warfare. The area became the French *Département de la
Roer*, the capital of which was not the Rhine metropolis but,
for reasons which we will see in the following chapter, the
relatively small nearby city of Aachen, known in France as
Aix-la-Chapelle, where the man the French and English (with
the latter's curious proclivity for adopting French historical

names) call Charlemagne and the Germans call Karl der Grosse, died, exactly a millennium before Napoleon's defeat.

The Completion of the Cathedral and Sweet Smell of Success

However much some of the population of Cologne might have welcomed elements of French Revolutionary and Napoleonic rule, it brought no joy whatsoever to the Catholic hierarchy, particularly those still dreaming that one day construction of their great cathedral might resume. The newly atheist French troops who arrived in 1794 ordered an end to religious services. They used the cathedral as a military storeroom and as a stable for their horses. The three kings' bones had been evacuated just in time. Napoleon's 1801 concordat with the papacy, which once again permitted Catholic worship, allowed the relics to come back again ahead of his own visit in 1804, when he was greeted enthusiastically by a population that cared more about 'liberté, égalité, fraternité' than any vague concept of nationality.

It was only in 1814 that, with Napoleon defeated, there was again mention of resuming the long-suspended work on the cathedral. The formerly free city which had been integrated into the French empire was annexed by a much-expanded Prussia and its name re-Germanified as Cöln (now with just one 'l'). In November that year a journalist writing in the *Rheinisches Merkur* suggested it was time to finish the project once and for all. By chance, it was that very year that half of the original four square metre mediaeval plan for the cathedral's façade had been discovered in Darmstadt. The blueprint dated back to the era of the original architect Gerhard's successor. Then, in an almost incredible stroke of luck, the other half turned up two years later in Paris. With the blossoming Romantic movement's enthusiasm for all things mediaeval (or at least a fairytale version of them), and growing discussion about the eventual possibility of some form of German unification, enthusiasm for completing the most spectacular and only truly Gothic stone cathedral grew rapidly.

Restoration work and internal finishing touches began in the 1820s along with architectural plans for the few parts of the building for which original mediaeval documents were lacking. Eventually in 1842 Friedrich Wilhelm IV of Prussia laid a foundation stone to mark the resumption of building work: the fact that a Protestant monarch would initiate the completion of Germany's greatest symbol of Catholicism indicated how much things had changed. In August 1848, with the foundations of a democratic German union supposedly being laid in the Frankfurt assembly, a great celebration was held to mark the 600th anniversary of the laying of the cathedral's first foundation stone. Unfortunately it was marred by the fall of a stone from one of the rising new towers, which hit a woman in the crowd, killing her outright.

By the mid-1860s much of the internal work on the choir and nave were completed and the great towers continued to rise. The architects confessed to cheating slightly by using some modern technology such as steel girders. Eventually, on 15 October 1880, the vast cathedral was completed, externally at least, almost exactly according to the plans laid down 600 years earlier. And there to celebrate this great achievement of German art and technology was Wilhelm I, no longer just a king but an emperor: it was as if everything in the Germanic world's dream was coming together at once. Unless, of course, you were an Austrian. The great twin spires soaring into the sky above the Rhine reached an unprecedented height of 157.38 metres, making the cathedral the tallest building in the world. It was a record that would last only four years, however, until the construction of the Washington Monument, which would cap it by 12 metres.

One of the ironies of the cathedral's completion was that it pleased and impressed almost everyone save the man who could become one of the city's most famous sons: the 20th-century Nobel Literature Prize laureate Heinrich Böll. A staunchly devout Catholic, he loved his city and hated the Nazis in every way, not least their decoration of his beloved city with swastika banners. Conscripted into the Wehrmacht, he served in France and Romania as well as on the Eastern Front, was captured by the Americans in 1945, then returned to Cologne, where he took up writing, initially, like Borchert in Hamburg, as a cathartic process to overcome the trauma of war, although later he turned to more contemporary themes, notably *The Lost Honour of Katharina Blum* in 1974. He died in 1985. Böll's Catholicism informed nearly all his work, leading to comparisons with the English writer Graham Greene. He had been particularly devastated by the bomb damage in his much-loved home city, which included the total destruction of 17 churches. The remarkable survival of the cathedral despite numerous hits did not particularly impress him. He would later say, 'I love the interior of the cathedral, but I don't like the outside much.' He made clear he would have preferred it to have been left as it had stood until 1848, with a wooden 14th-century crane on the top where the spires were to have been built.

One small but significant remnant of the Napoleonic conquest and Köln's time as a French city called Cologne, lingers still. In the early 18th century a Germanised Italian living in this greatest of Catholic cities north of the Alps had the idea of creating a 'fragrance that reminds me of an Italian spring morning, of mountain daffodils and orange blossoms just after the rain'. Using essential oils of lemon, orange, mandarin, lime, grapefruit, cedar, bergamot and local herbs, Johanne Maria Farina created the perfume he desired. Initially sold only locally, then at the trade fair in Frankfurt under the description Aqua Mirabilis (miracle water), it quickly attracted fans all across Europe. Farina stepped up production and was soon sending his product in its distinctive elongated green bottles to shopkeepers from Vienna to Paris. In particular French army officers took a fancy to it to complement the dandy style they affected of wearing face powder and wigs. In a city where nobody had yet come up with the idea of street numbers, his manufactory was known simply as 'Johann Maria Farina opposite Jülichs Square'.

Farina died in 1766 and there follows a confusion of stories as to what happened to his original fragrance, save that from 1797, with the city firmly in French hands, it was being made and marketed by one Wilhelm Mühlens under the name Eau de Cologne, translated back into German as Kölnisches Wasser. Whether or not it was the same as the original recipe is disputed; all that is clear is that Mühlens hired several members of the original creator's family – or at least people with the surname Farina – in an attempt to claim authenticity. Mühlens faced charges of brand infringement from those still manufacturing at the original site, and so decided to market his version using the number of his house on Glockengasse in the city centre.

This in itself was a daring novelty. Up until the French occupation, Köln had never considered street numbers a necessity. As with 'opposite Jülichs Square', Mühlens' manufactory had been designated as 'opposite the horse carriage station'. The mistrustful French, unsure of the loyalty of their new subjects and unfamiliar with the city layout, decided these 'locals only' addresses simply weren't good enough. Cologne's city councillors were individually ordered to provide an inventory of everyone living in their part of town within 48 hours, not least because in the interests of public safety (and that of their own troops) the French were intending to install lighting. To keep the job under control, each house was issued a number: but instead of differentiating between the various streets and alleyways, the French just started with the first house on their list and carried on. By the time they got to Glockengasse they had reached just over 4,700. Mühlens' house, manufactory and shop therefore acquired the number 4711, the four-thousand-seven-hundred-and-eleventh house listed in Cologne. It wasn't until 1811, by which time Cologne was no longer an occupied city but integrated into the French empire (a situation radically to change with Napoleon's defeat three years later), that the order was given to reclassify the house numbers by street.

The original 4711 house was torn down in the mid-19th century and the street was heavily damaged by bombing in 1943. It was only in 1963 that it was replaced by the neo-baroque building which today houses a shop selling its perfume, believed to be the oldest continuously produced perfume in the world. There is another side to the argument, however, in that Köln is also home to a Fragrance Museum, run by descendants, so they claim, of the original Johann Maria Farina, who also produce their own version, which they claim to be the real thing.

In reality it hardly matters, there are few fashionistas today who would admit that they regularly wore *eau de cologne* in the modern world of a million designer fragrances. Perhaps the greatest legacy is the fact that, particularly in the USA, the term 'cologne' is still used, as a synonym for scent, in particular men's. There is an apocryphal anecdote that it also has a legacy in Russia, as a cheaper alternative to vodka. As a former inhabitant of the Soviet Union, I doubt this: there were cheaper, if even more dangerous, alternatives.

Not that I never came across it. When we lived in the Soviet Union in the early to mid-1980s, I was puzzled by a word I came across that not only did I not know but didn't look or feel very Russian. I tried in vain to break it down into any constituent Slavic elements. The word was 'одиколон'. In the end I gave up and looked it up in a dictionary only to feel the biggest fool in the world: if only I had said it out loud! But then how was I to guess I was looking at a transliteration into Cyrillic script of a phonetic rendering of an English pronunciation of a French term for a German perfume created by an Italian: Odikolon.

In the context of Cöllen/Köln/Cologne's role in European history, it made a strange sort of sense.

The Germans and Football

Despite the many British myths about England being Germany's greatest rival – as we have seen, that honour is disputed between Russia and France – there is one field of conflict in which it undoubtedly rings true: football.

'Two World Wars and one World Cup,' the crusader-clad England fans sing loudly at every meeting. It is more than a little distasteful to associate mass slaughter with a game of football (played genially between British and German soldiers in the trenches during the Christmas truce of 1914), but then one may perhaps excuse the England fans, given that the football statistics are so stacked against them. German fans could, if they were so inclined, chant in reply: 'Four World Cups, four times runners-up.' It is a matter of some national trauma in England that the legendary 1966 World Cup win was their team's one and only appearance in a final. They may have 'three lions' on their shirts, but only one star against the Germans' four. To that impressive total the German team can add three European Champions titles. There is common acknowledgement in Germany that England invented the 'beautiful game' and that Germany only reluctantly adopted it at first, but they are quite clear who has the better claim to being *Weltmeister*.

German football is actually proud of its British origins, celebrated for having changed social attitudes particularly in authoritarian Prussia where the favoured sport was team gymnastics intended to promote discipline and order. Football was seen as counter-productive to this social aim and widely branded the 'English disease'. It was an English and Classics teacher called Konrad Koch who, with a colleague, brought a genuine leather football from England, and, defying official opprobrium, introduced the game to his pupils at the Martino-Katherineum school in Braunschweig back in 1873, 20 years after the foundation of England's Football League.

Koch is credited with organising the first ever game to be played in Germany, although there are sources which say there was a game in Dresden around the same time. But it was unquestionably Koch who first formulated the German version of the rules, even if at that early stage they still incorporated elements that would only survive in rugby football.

The traditional version of the story is brought to life in the extremely anglophile movie, *Der Ganz Grosse Traum* (2011), despite a somewhat inappropriate fondness for that most Scottish of songs, 'Auld Lang Syne', which suggests the author was clearly confused about Anglo-Scottish rivalry and the passionate Scotland fan's desire for a tournament to be won by anyone but England. Written and directed by Sebastian Drobler, literally translated as *The Great Big Dream*, it was curiously translated into English as *Lessons of a Dream* (best watched with subtitles if you don't speak German).

Despite doubts amid Prussian officialdom, the popularity of this new sport grew as rapidly as it had done in its motherland. The first clubs were founded in Berlin, Hamburg and Karlsruhe, but it was in the capital particularly that it took off with a 'federation of German football players' founded in 1890. The oldest surviving German club is BFC (Berliner Fussballclub) Germania, which dates from 1888, even if nowadays it has long been confined to the lower leagues. The Deutsche Fussball-Bund, the equivalent of England's Football League, was founded in 1890 in a pub in Leipzig, and, significantly to the leitmotiv of this book in which 'Germany' and 'Germans' have rarely been synonymous, its first president came from Prague.

I have a dim childhood black-and-white television memory of watching England win that long ago World Cup final, and a colour television memory decades later with my own children watching an England team beat Germany 5–1, and the Germans walking out of the stadium in disgust at their own team. But more vivid than both was watching the hordes of ecstatic supporters in the summer of 1990 singing in the streets of Berlin, now reunited, celebrating a World Cup win with only one German flag flying, although in theory for a few months longer East Germany and its own football team still existed. United Germany's most impressive match win came during the World Cup competition in Brazil in 2014, which they went on to win, when they beat the hosts —- the only team to have won the title more times, with possibly the world's most fanatical football fans – by a hugely embarrassing 7–1. German Chancellor Angela Merkel was ecstatic when her team went into the lead, happier still when another two goals almost certainly confirmed their victory, but almost squirming in embarrassment after the fifth, and looked mortified by the sixth. A consolation goal for Brazil in the final minute did little more than accentuate the embarrassment. To everyone's surprise, despite deep disappointment and soul searching afterwards, the Brazilian hosts took it remarkably well.

Germany's top league – Bundesliga 1 – is one of the most competitive and thrilling in the world, with huge global TV audiences, on a par with the Spanish and Italian leagues, all of them, however, trailing England's Premier League, and even its second tier Championship. The Bundesliga, however, has as much premier talent as its English equivalent. It even has its behemoth clubs: Bayern München, for example, the Manchester United of Germany, the country's most successful team, and by association the team most hated by almost all the rest of the country's football fans. Founded by a group of just 11 lads at the turn of the last century, at a time when the remnants of resistance by sporting authorities who thought football a 'degenerate' game, as opposed to the classic German devotion to athletics, were finally fading, Bayern München is a legend in German football history.

Their rise to success was originally orchestrated by club president and coach Kurt Landauer in the 1920s, but the fact that he was Jewish led to discrimination against the team during the Nazi period, and his own incarceration in

Dachau. His service as a soldier in World War I, however, earned him early release and he emigrated to Switzerland, returning to Munich in 1947 to be elected club president for another four-year term.

When the new West German Bundesliga was founded in 1963, Bayern were not selected as members for the first year while their old rivals TSV 1860, who had won their own league the previous year, were. It was a situation soon to be reversed. Bayern forced the door open by way of promotion two years later (1860 were relegated in 1970 and have only been intermittent visitors to the top flight ever since). Bayern's promotion began what would be a golden age in the club's history. Their new success was built on a trio of young stars, who would go on to be football legends: Franz Beckenbauer, Gerd Müller and Sepp Maier. The club would in quick succession win the national title three times and then go on to stun European football by winning the European Cup (equivalent of the Champions League today) three times in a row in 1974, 1975 and 1976.

A relatively fallow period followed, in international terms, but Bayern still regularly triumphed in the Bundesliga, which, at the time of writing they have won 24 times in the 50 years since they became members, but Bayern returned to European prominence with Champions League wins in 2001 and 2013, and as runners-up in 2010 and 2012. In stark contrast, their old rivals TSV 1860 have suffered serious ups and downs and since 2004 have been resigned to mid-table in the national second tier, the Bundesliga 2. Both teams have shared the imposing 75,000-seater Allianz Arena in northern Munich, since it was completed ahead of the 2006 World Cup. Looking somewhat like a squashed globe paper lantern, it is the only stadium in the world that can completely change its external colour, from red when Bayern are playing to blue when 1860 take the stage.

But unquestionably the most remarkable football stadium is that in Berlin, since its total renovation – effectively rebuilding – for the 2006 World Cup. When I first lived in Berlin in 1981 the venue was still occupied by the British army, a source of minor embarrassment, having been purpose-built for the notorious 1936 Olympics, used as a propaganda showcase by Adolf Hitler, and where the British athletes – for fear of causing offence – gave the dictator the stiff-armed *Hitlergruss* as they marched around the arena in the opening ceremony. After the war, when that part of western Berlin became the headquarters for the occupying troops, knowing what to do with the stadium was awkward. Despite its history, it was a spectacular building: built of massive granite in the austere spartan neo-classical style that was a hallmark of 1930s architecture, even if the holders for flaming torches on the outside walls evoked unpleasant memories for some. By the mid-1980s the British primarily used it, and the surround-ing greenfield area, as a helicopter landing site.

Its conversion for the 2006 World Cup was a masterpiece of vision as well as architecture. Having been an Olympic stadium complete with running tracks, football fans would have been too far from the pitch to create the game's tradi-tional atmosphere. The stadium's capacity was also far too small for a big national team these days, let along a World Cup final. The solution was inspired: the imposing outside of the stadium was left untouched, but the interior was gutted, stone benches replaced with more comfortable plastic seats, but most crucially, the whole arena was excavated downward, as far as necessary to leave just the space for a football pitch, with seating installed in the excavated area. The result was a striking, original, old yet new stadium, with the odd feature that the highest seats were actually closest to 'ground level'.

The most significant difference, however, between German football and most other countries', in particular the UK, is the rules on ownership. Over the years the word football 'club' in English has lost most of its original meaning: the word 'corporation' would nowadays be more accurate. When fans of my own south London club, Charlton Athletic, demonstrated in 2015–16 about the way the club was being run, the Belgian Chief Executive Officer Katrien Meire completely failed to understand: 'The fans think they have some sort of ownership,' she complained. 'Who do they think pays the bills?' She went on to compare the attitude of thousands of loyal supporters to 'people complaining at a restaurant or theatre', thereby demonstrating a complete misunderstanding of the game and its relationship to local identity and fan loyalty. The villains in all this are the 'big' clubs and the globalisation of the game through television rights: the result being that the majority of their followers may be thousands of miles away on other continents, never see a game other than on TV and their main relationship with 'their' club is buying overpriced replica shirts. This is football as an industry, not a local sport, caused and fuelled by allowing rich individuals or corporations to buy up teams and make money primarily from marketing and merchandising, as well as the vast sums now brought in by television rights.

It is this attitude to the 'beautiful game' that has led legions of German fans to protest at proposed changes to their own system, chanting and holding up placards reading '*Nein zum englischen Modell*' (No to the English model). The development of ownership in German football clubs has historically been very different. Traditionally German football teams were run and owned exactly as it says on the tin: by 'clubs', sometimes employees at a particular factory but usually just groups of fans who banded together and put money in to run the grounds and pay the wages. In other words, the clubs were run by their fans. And, most importantly of all – almost hard to believe in the modern world of commercialised football – they were run as not-for-profit organisations.

All of this changed in 1998, when, in response to the soaring costs of running a football club and the need to maintain solvency, which meant allowing a profit, the national association (*Deutsche Fussballbund*) changed the rules to allow teams to be converted into public or private limited companies. So much for that, you might think, but the new rules contained one very important stipulation, known as the 50+1 rule, that at least 50 per cent of the shares, *plus one*, had to remain in the hands of the original clubs, i.e. in most cases, the fans. This has meant that it is impossible for an 'owner' to flout club traditions – such as when a Thai businessman bought Cardiff City, who traditionally played in pale blue strips and were known as the Bluebirds, and forced them to change to red, and put a dragon instead of a bird on their crest to make them more appealing to Asian fans. (Only mass protests by their native supporters, and the odd sight of a team playing in red while all their fans in the stands wore blue, eventually forced him to relent.) Such a thing could never, in theory, happen in Germany. Nor could the price of tickets rise exponentially as they have done at some English clubs, notably Arsenal and Chelsea, with profit for the owners taking precedence over affordability for supporters.

The German regulations, however, are not perfect. For a start there are some exceptions, notably when a person, company or organisation has for over 20 years made long-term investments in a club, the 50+1 rule in favour of the fans is dropped. The main examples of this are two clubs in particular which were originally set up and maintained by local industries to provide exercise and entertainment for their workers: Bayer Leverkusen and Vfl Wolfsburg, which are owned respectively by the Bayer pharmaceuticals company and automobile giant Volkswagen, in both cases the main local employer. This is seen by most German fans as a fair exception to the rule. More worrying by far is when companies operate by stealth and manipulate the cost of 'club membership': this has been notably the case in one or two clubs in the former East Germany, which had to be totally funded anew after reunification. In particular Leipzig, rebranded as RB Leipzig, which was financed by Red Bull, which set an exorbitant 'membership fee' for the club, and reserved the right to turn down new members. As a result it obeys the 50+1 rule, but as the 'members' are nearly all connected with the company, it is effectively a corporate institution, run with marketing in mind.

German teams are also no more immune to the profits and enthusiasm to be garnered from fans at the opposite ends of the earth. Although they may have fewer foreign fans than Man U, Arsenal or Chelsea, and these days also Man City, the big German names also have their far-flung followers, Bayern München as well as Borussia Dortmund and even Wolfsburg, a relative newcomer to the big league, sell replica shirts and attract fans across the planet.

Meanwhile, back home, German fans are among the most fervent in the world, and they often have quite a lot to sing about.

9

Strasbourg

The beginning of the continental divide – and the end?

Alsace-Lorraine, or Elsass-Lothringen

The first taste of something new and wonderful is invariably forever linked with the circumstances and the place, at least in my experience. For instance, the Dutch city of Maastricht in which the treaty which renamed the European Communities as the European Union was signed, will always be linked for me to a particular snack lunch in a local restaurant. I was introduced to it by a French fellow journalist also there to cover the event. But it was the meal that has remained more vividly in my memory: a crispy fresh baguette spread with a particularly pungent cheese from Romadour-du-Hervé, a little village on the already non-existent Belgian–German border, topped with strawberry jam and washed down with fresh, raw Beaujolais Nouveau. It was an amalgam that should have been disgusting, but was in fact delicious, the stinking but rich and creamy cheese offset perfectly by the sweetness of the jam and the rough fruitiness of the wine, given texture by the crunchy crust and soft interior of the bread. One of those experiences that is unrepeatable. No matter how hard you try it is never possible to recreate the exact circumstances, a second taste is never the same as the first.

It was in Strasbourg – another crucially important city in the history of the European Union, Germany, France, and Europe in the widest sense – that 15 years earlier I had first tasted another, less challenging, combination that has also stayed with me forever but never matched that magical first time. It was 1977 and I was a trainee reporter for Reuters news agency, based in Brussels, and had driven (been driven by a colleague actually, I would not pass a driving test until four years later in East Berlin) down to Strasbourg to cover a meeting of the European Parliament. On the evening of the first day of the session, the city's mayor Pierre Pflimlin, who had run the city for nearly 20 years and was determined to stifle any ideas about ending the parliament's inefficient but symbolically important regular commute between Brussels and Strasbourg, astutely invited the entire European press corps to dinner.

This was no small matter: we were loaded onto coaches and driven to one of Alsace's largest and most beautifully situated restaurants set among green fields outside the city. There we were served a remarkably simple meal which for the first time introduced me to three new things – remember I was still young and had grown up in Northern Ireland where 'culinary delights' would probably have been banned by the Presbyterian Church on instinct – succulent *petits poussins* (baby chickens), freshly picked and steamed green asparagus and chilled, exotic, spicy Alsace Gewürztraminer wine. It was a threesome made in heaven, fittingly including one of the most quirkily unusual German grape varieties (the name means literally 'spicy grape') that perversely only reaches its apogee when grown and made into wine by the French.

For me that experience forever encapsulates Strasbourg, a city that for most of its history was German-speaking and known to most if its inhabitants as Strassburg. The original means 'city of streets' and its origins go back to a Roman fort built to protect the gateway to its province of Germania Inferior, the road to Colonia Agrippinensium, modern Cologne.

In recent centuries, since the concept of nation-states began to evolve, Strasbourg has been the most significant city to change hands repeatedly between the French and Germans. But more importantly, as this chapter will explain, that dispute goes back to the origins of both nations and, indirectly, the political shape of Europe itself. All those reasons lie behind the choice of Strasbourg as a seat of the post-1945 European institutions designed to consign such conflicts to the past. It is the permanent home of the Council of Europe and the European Court of Human Rights, the two most inclusive pan-European bodies, which include Russia, Ukraine, Serbia and other states and have nothing to do with the European Union, a fact widely misunderstood.

Strasbourg's signature dish is also one that is a fine example of what we would nowadays call 'fusion food'. *Choucroute* is, on the face of it, about as Germanic as you could imagine: a vast array of meat – primarily sausages, and boiled, smoked pork belly – piled up on a mountain of cooked pickled cabbage: what you might be tempted to call *Sauerkraut*. And you would not be wrong. Indeed, it is one of those nice little ironies that while it is perfectly obvious to anyone with a bit of linguistic instinct that '*choucroute*' is simply a francification of '*Sauerkraut*', you should try not to tell that to any patriotic Frenchman. He is likely to point out that '*chou*' is the French for cabbage, whereas '*croûte*' is also a French word, although the fact that it means 'crust', which has no part in the dish, is gracefully overlooked.

Like 'Cologne' – as they definitely call it here – Strasbourg also boasts its own great Gothic cathedral, implausibly built of dark red sandstone, which has made the base of its great tower famed, alongside its architectural magnificence, for the dozens of names carved into it by soldiers of occupying armies, usually alternating French or German, through history. Even those carved names are now caged in with wire to prevent armies of modern tourists being tempted into copycat behaviour. Its principal architect was the

German-speaking Erwin von Steinbach, who worked on its impressive soaring west façade from 1277 until his death in 1318. By far the most disconcerting thing about Strasbourg cathedral, though, is that although its architects succeeded in their aim by creating what was then the second tallest spire in the word, finished in 1439 (after that in the German city of Stralsund on the Baltic fell down, Strasbourg would be the tallest in the world for several centuries), they only completed one of the two planned spires, making it the most lopsided building in Europe. The experience of standing on the roof at the spire's base was responsible for my first attack of the vertigo which has dogged me ever since. Where the other spire should be is a little pink bungalow used for selling postcards.

∈∋

For centuries even after the cathedral's completion, Strasbourg was a primarily German-speaking 'free city' within the increasingly loose bounds of the Holy Roman Empire. But it was the man who more than any other epitomised the consolidation and expansionist nationalism of the modern nation-state, France's 'Sun King' Louis XIV, whose reign saw the end of that status. Louis was still only ten years old when his mother Anne, acting as regent with her highly skilled adviser Cardinal Mazarin, helped dictate the terms which ended the Thirty Years War in 1648. Strasbourg and the border territories of Alsace and Lorraine, which had appealed for French help during the war, got more than they bargained for: they were declared a French protectorate and in 1681 the whole province and Strasbourg itself with its strategic bridge across the Rhine, were annexed and made part of France. The locals, however, were given a degree of autonomy, including in their use of language, and many German-speakers in this age of only nascent nationalism were relatively happy to stay where they were.

Before Louis, France had been virtually a mirror image of the German world, with nobles vying with one another for power in their own fiefdoms and the king little more than a figurehead to whom they paid nominal obeisance. The Fronde rebellion of 1648–53 was an attempt by the provincial nobility to usurp most of the crown's prerogatives. Louis stamped down on the rebels, building his vast palace at Versailles with rooms enough to accommodate most of his court, requiring the nobles to come to him, and making their ranks and titles dependent on royal whim. Europe was entering a new order of absolute monarchy and nation-states. The Germans would be the last to follow suit, but when they did, following France's comprehensive defeat by Prussia in 1870, the new German empire would take revenge by repossessing Alsace and neighbouring Lorraine. German defeat in 1918 meant Alsace-Lorraine and Strasbourg returning to France, only to be reincorporated into Hitler's Reich in 1940, then return to France again five years later.

In November 1987 I reported on the first ever joint military exercises between the French and German armies, practising defence against a Warsaw Pact that within three years would no longer exist. A memorable cartoon in the German newspaper *Westdeutsche Allgemeine Zeitung* showed French President François Mitterrand and West German Chancellor Helmut Kohl in modern military dress toasting one another beneath paintings of their ancestors killing each other. But it was the cartoon on the front page of the French daily, *Libération*, which caught the wry tone of the occasion: commanders of two tanks, one French, the other German, embracing one another from their turrets, the Frenchman declaring, '*Cher camarade, avec vous, on n'aurait jamais perdu l'Algérie ni l'Indochine*' ('Dear comrade, with you we would never have lost Algeria or Indochina.') to which the German replies, '*Ni l'Alsace, ni la Lorraine!*' ('Nor Alsace or Lorraine!')

Until 1945 the switch of 'nationalities' had not been as confusing as it might seem to us in the modern world of instant communication. The dialect spoken in Strassburg and the surrounding region was Elsässisch, from the German name for Alsace: Elsass. This was a form of Low German including older tribal dialects such as Frankish and Alemannisch, but riddled with Romance influences. It was, as so many regional languages were before the modern age, a language for locals, who rarely travelled further than the nearest town.

Since 1945 the French government's attitude to Elsässisch was at first to ignore its existence, insisting that all teaching was done in French. Having lost the city in 1870 and again in 1939, there was a determination to define once and for all the French identity of the city where, back in 1792, Claude Joseph Rouget de Lisle had composed 'La Marseillaise', one of Europe's finest, but most bloodthirsty national anthems. By the early 1990s travelling through Alsace in search of some fine Gewürztraminer, I stayed in the charming ancient village of Eguisheim, where I lucked upon Bruno Sorg, who makes one of the most excellent examples I have yet come across. Over a tasting glass or two, which soon became a bottle or two, we chatted about Alsace's complex history. He admitted that he himself had been educated wholly in French and had no more than a few basic words of Elsässisch, which he almost never used, yet he said his father still had some and he definitely remembered that his grandfather had been fluent.

Charles, Great Caesar

For the origins of the conflict that saw the language of Strasbourg change so many times, we must go to a small city several hundred kilometres to the north, closer to the Belgian border than the French, in the administrative district of Cologne. Very definitely German in character, it is still known to much of the world by its French name, Aix-la-Chapelle: Aachen. The *Chapelle* in Aachen is not just any chapel, it is one of the most remarkable buildings in Europe. This is a building with as much, if not significantly more, standing in European history as the cathedral of St Mark in Venice, with which its shares its architectural style.

At the heart of the mediaeval cathedral, an impressive building in its own right, lies an octagonal chapel dating from the eighth century that is the only major structure in Byzantine style north of the Alps. It is Byzantine in structure deliberately, politically, to make the point that the man who ordered its construction was on a par with the emperors in Byzantium – Constantinople – as heir to the Roman caesars, the man who had restored the Western Roman Empire as a parallel to the Eastern Roman Empire. A tenth-century inscription bears witness to his claims with reference to the architect Odo and the man himself *Karolus caesar magnus*, Charles Great Caesar: who as we have seen is known to the Germans as Karl der Grosse, to the Dutch as Karel de Grote, to the Spanish as Carlomagno and to French- and English-speakers as Charlemagne. The chapel itself is the only remaining section of what was once Charlemagne's imperial palace, from where a new empire was to be ruled, an empire that began with the ambitions of a Germanic tribe, before declaring itself – and being accepted as – the heir to Rome, and the salvation of the Western world. It didn't quite work out like that.

It was Julius Caesar, the man whose name would become synonymous with 'emperor', who introduced the Germans to recorded history. The first Caesar expanded the frontiers of the Roman empire as much as any of his successors, moving north from its Mediterranean power base to the conquest of Gaul, including all of modern France and Belgium, even crossing the sea to the distant island of Britannia, but most importantly for the future of Europe, making the first forays across the Rhine. Caesar's own accounts of his wars were well written but more concerned with his victories than any account of the people he faced. It took the historian Tacitus to pull together from various sources an account of the people beyond the great river, finding praise for their virtues and their habit of making decisions by communal agreement as well as their valour and drinking capacity.

There are hints in Tacitus that these were a people Rome might do best to leave alone, as Publius Quintus Varus had discovered nearly a century earlier in AD 9 when he lost three legions to an ambush in the Teutoburg Forest, leading the great Augustus ever after to lament the loss of his 'eagles'. Although the Romans ventured north of the Danube and up the west bank of the Rhine, they were quickly persuaded that to the north and east the existing borders of the empire along the two rivers were easier to defend. That did not mean a lack of contact, however: apart from fending off occasional raids from the 'barbarians', there was also trade and cultural exchange, and more than a few of these 'excellent warriors' found lucrative jobs as mercenaries in the legions, even in Rome itself.

It was probably obvious even to a few Romans that if and when Rome ever fell it might be to these people. As the tribes of Central Europe first felt themselves under pressure from the armies of the Huns pressing west from the steppes, the people of Central Europe – or at least some of them – set out on their own wars of conquest into the heart of the rich empire lying, increasingly prostrate, at their doorstep. Even though the empire had long been split into eastern and western halves and the capital of the western empire moved to Ravenna, it still came as a shock to the world when the German-speaking barbarian we know as Alaric, king of the Visigoths, sacked the 'eternal city' of Rome in AD 410. Because so much of our history of the ancient world – including northern and Central Europe – comes from Greek or Latin sources, rather than the largely lost languages of the native people, we tend to see them through Latin-tinted glasses. Alaric the Visigoth and Theodoric the Ostrogoth sound a lot more Germanic if we update them to their modern equivalents: Ulrich the West German and Dietrich the East German – *Wessies* and *Ossies* of their day. (As we have already noted, Arminius, the name by which we know the general who defeated Varus, is in Germany referred to as Hermann.)

The Visigoths did not stay in Rome. While a few settled in Italy, the bulk of their armies moved west and south into the Iberian peninsula, where they would put their towels on the beaches, or more precisely build their castles on the mountains, conquering and ruling over the native Romano-Iberians in a Visigothic kingdom that would last nearly 400 years until the jihadi waves of Arabs and Berbers would eliminate their leaders and their kingdom and pose a challenge to the whole of Western Europe. It would take Charlemagne, the man seen as the heir to the Caesars, to definitively block their progress, though his grandfather, Charles Martel, dealt them the first real blow, earning his nickname 'the hammer' (*martel* in old French).

The exact origins of the north and Central European tribes which from the Roman period onward were loosely referred to as Germani are not precisely known nor to what extent they were related to each other, apart from the fact that they spoke related languages or at least what seemed such to the ancient classical historians and ethnographers whose records we rely on. There are literally dozens of tribes recorded, though as few of the ancient ethnographers ever did anything as dangerous as venture out there to meet any of them we can have little idea how many might overlap. The most significant included the Alemani (meaning 'all men' to all who spoke their tongue), the Goths (divided by later historians into Visi- and Ostro-), the Suebi, the Vandals (arguably 'from the valley' – *van/von dem Thal* – but also arguably not), the Langobardi (quite clearly from the fact that they boasted 'long beards' and who would go on to conquer and settle in the part of northern Italy we still call Lombardy).

It is the Franks who would come to matter most in the period long called the 'Dark Ages' but which we now refer to as Late Antiquity, as it began to morph into what we call the Middle Ages. The Franks had straddled the *limes,* the imperial Roman frontier, and had both fought them and joined their legions as mercenaries. The later perception that their name had anything to do with 'freedom' is a myth, but they certainly seemed free enough in choosing sides. As the power of the empire weakened and its hold on the frontier provinces declined, Frankish commanders in Roman service increasingly saw the opportunity to set themselves up as local rulers, eventually leading to the emergence of small kingdoms. The most important was that of Clovis. Towards the end of the fifth century he founded a dynasty known to history as the Merovingians, which established its rule over a substantial part of Western Europe, roughly equivalent to all of today's France, Belgium, Flanders, southern and western Germany. The Merovingians, though, were subject to the Frankish curse, in terms of empire building, by routinely dividing their realms equally among male children. Over time this led to the diminishment of their empire and endless family squabbles. By the mid-eighth century the pope stepped in to divert heaven's seal of approval to another Frankish family, one which had promised to put military protection of the papacy first.

The lands that Clovis and his descendants ruled were known to their contemporaries in Latin as Francia, and in Frankish (there are no records – all official documents were kept in Latin) as something between Frankreich and Frankrijk, the latter two being respectively the German and Dutch words for modern France, while the first is the term used in Spanish and Italian. The language spoken by the ruling class in Francia however was an early dialect of German, even if the mass of the people spoke something that had evolved from Latin. Like the Visigoths in Spain, the Franks ruled the native Romanised population but did not outnumber them and over the centuries melded into them. Their territory on the other side of the Rhine, the far east of their domains in what is today Northern Bavaria is still called Franken, and I have met people in the great beer-brewing town of Bamberg who claim their dialect is the closest thing to what Karl der Grosse might have spoken.

That we will never know. Karl, great-grandson of the first of his line to inherit the Frankish crown, and which came to be known as the Carolingians, spoke decent Latin as well as his native Frankish and a few words of Greek, but he struggled with reading and writing. We know a considerable amount about him, thanks to the extensive biography written by Einhard, a courtier and servant to both him and his son. Einhard's *Vita Karoli Magni* is a superb piece of biographical writing, at least in tone apparently remarkably honest. I bought my own copy of this treasured survival from the early Middle Ages from the bookstore in Aachen cathedral, with parallel versions in the original Latin and modern German. He paints a candid picture of his lord and master:

> He was well-built, and of impressive stature, although not excessive, his height being seven times the length of his foot. He had a round head, large and lively eyes, a rather large nose and white hair, which still looked good, a fat, short neck. He enjoyed good health at least until struck by fevers in his later years. Towards the end he dragged one leg, but insisted on doing whatever he wanted and refused to listen to doctors whom he hated, not least because they insisted he eat only boiled and not roasted meat, which he loved.

Hunting, eating and making war were not the only things he loved. We know of at least ten wives or concubines, and he sired 18 children in all. Although he himself struggled with literacy, he was a great believer in education. He built up a huge library and gathered around him a large group of scholars, chief among whom, according to Einhard, was a Yorkshireman called Alcuin whom he had encountered in the Italian city of Parma, who flourished in the united European culture that Karl created, reorganising the palace school in

Aachen, managing the sensitivities of the Italians who had run it previously, writing regular letters to the archbishop of Canterbury as well as copious correspondence with Arno, the bishop of Salzburg. He was eventually given an abbey in retirement and is buried in the cathedral of St Martin in Tours. Einhard also tells us how the emperor dressed: a far cry from the imperial toga of old. Karl preferred traditional Frankish style: 'a linen shirt and linen trousers, a silk-fringed tunic, leggings and shoes, and to keep warm in winter a close-fitting coat of otter or pine marten skins.' Only twice, we are told, did he ever don traditional Roman dress, both times on significant occasions.

By the end of the eighth century, the Franks under 'Great Karl' had not only pushed across the Pyrenees to create the Spanish Marche, a border region either side of the mountains free of Muslim control, but also expanded their conquests into what is now northern and southeastern Germany, Switzerland, Austria, Slovenia, the Netherlands and north-ern-central Italy, including Rome itself, suppressing on the way the Lombards, who had invaded the territory of Pope Hadrian I, land given to the papacy by Charles's own father. It was in the presence of a grateful pope in Rome that Karl first symbolically put on the toga.

The second time was the more important. Hadrian's suc-cessor Leo III, who had fled a mob intent on blinding him and tearing out his tongue, reached Karl in Paderborn on the northern Rhine, and begged for the Frankish king's help. The army descended on Rome in early December, Leo's enemies were exiled and in a move that, according to Einhard, Karl himself had no suspicion of, while the Frankish ruler knelt at the altar to pray, the pope placed on his head an imperial crown and declared him Imperator Romanorum, Emperor of the Romans. It seems improbable that Karl did not know of Leo's plans in advance and despite his later protestations that he would not have entered the old St Paul's basilica if he had, the new emperor did not lose time in making use of the title. In his own official documents from then on he would style himself *Karolus Serenissumus Augustus a Deo coronatus magnus pacificus imperator Romanorum gubernans imperium* (Karl, most supreme Augustus crowned by God, great and peaceful master of the Romans ruling the empire). Whether or not there was a serious intention to challenge for the throne of the eastern empire as well is disputed (it was at the time ruled by a woman, a situation which the Westerners considered not to be valid). The Byzantine style of the chapel in Aachen hints it might have been in tribute to the style of the Roman legacy to the East. What mattered was that the de facto ruler of most of Western Europe had claimed the mantel of Caesar Augustus. The empire had struck back.

Charlemagne made it quite clear that he regarded himself as by far the most important figure, reminding the new pope that his job was to defend the church and the realm, while the pope's was to pray for it and for the victory of his armies. It was the first shot across the bows in a what would eventually become a bitter battle for supremacy between the spiritual and secular powers. This impromptu restoration of a 'Roman' Empire was doomed to speedy disintegration – like that of the Merovingians – through the traditional Frankish custom of dividing up inheritances. The fact that it grabbed a toehold on future history was due to the fact that by 813 when Karl (now undisputedly 'the Great', translated for his Romance-speaking subjects as *Charles le magne,* a version that only came to England with the Norman Conquest more than two centuries later) was seriously ill, he had only one legitimate surviving son. He summoned him to Aachen and with his own hand crowned him co-emperor, so that when he died in January 814, at the grand age of 72, his succession to the imperial throne was already enacted.

His son is known to history as Louis, as he had already been 'king' of Aquitaine, and as such had necessarily learnt the Romance language of his local subjects, which we now call Old French. Having managed to inherit the empire on his own, he quickly sent his unmarried sisters to nunneries to eliminate the possibility of acquiring ambitious brothers-in-law. He nonetheless faced rebellions from within the family, from a nephew who had been left in charge of northern Italy and even from his own sons. Following Louis's death in 840, aged 62, the inevitable partition took place. The sons fought each other for greater shares of the Frankish conquests for three years until finally a treaty was signed between them in AD 843 at Verdun, the site of one of the greatest battles between their distant heirs nearly 1,100 years later. The emperor's oldest son, Lothar, was given what at the time must have appeared the chief prize, the imperial title, the two capitals of Aachen and Rome and all the territories between them. His younger brother Karl was given the western territories (west Francia) and would be remembered by later generations as the first king of France, Charles the Bald. The third brother received east Francia (including today's German province of Franken), and the historical nickname (bestowed much later) of Louis the German. It was the decisive moment that set in motion the division between what would gradually become a nation-state called France and what it would take nearly a millennium to turn into a nation-state called Germany, and create the late 20th- and early 21st-century desire to end the strife between them for good.

What must have seemed like a smart choice to Lothar – getting the title of emperor and the two imperial capital cities – proved disastrous. Trapped between his rival brothers and with the pope to cope with south of the Alps, his heirs proved incapable of holding any of it together for very long. His chief legacy to history (other than briefly preserving the imperial title for a new dynasty to take up) was in his own name: the lands he ruled became known as Lothari Regnum (the kingdom of Lothar), bastardised into German as Lothringen, and even further in French as Lorraine. The trouble was that with the man called 'emperor' ruling the most fractious portion of the 'empire' with no easy means of expansion other than by challenging his brothers, the inevitable strife over the next few generations effectively put an end to the title and the territory.

The rebirth of the concept of a West European 'empire' began with the choice as king of East Francia of an ambitious duke of Saxony, known to history as Heinrich der Vogler (Henry the Fowler in English), the nickname coming from the fact that as a dedicated hunter he was setting traps for birds when he was told he had been elected. Inevitably his territories were almost immediately invaded by his cousin Karl, Charles the Simple in French history, though we must remember that neither ruler thought of their domain as anything but east or west Francia. Heinrich marched back against him and took the eastern part of Lorraine.

It was neither Heinrich nor Charles/Karl who would truly revive the Frankish claim to have inherited the empire of Rome, but Heinrich's son, Otto. Already nominated and confirmed in childhood as his father's successor to the East Frankish realm, Otto made a point of having himself crowned (by the archbishop of Mainz) in Charlemagne's palace in Aachen. He then went ahead to prove his right to the throne by military means, roundly defeating the pagan Hungarians, who had been ravaging his territories and threatening further western expansion. His achievements earned him the popular title of 'saviour of Christendom'. When Pope John XII, the son of a rich Italian noble, who was more famous for corruption and fornication than holiness, appealed for help against rival Italian families eager to depose him, Otto hastened to his rescue, but only at the price of being crowned in 962 by the desperate pope as heir to Charlemagne and the caesars.

Otto then solved the previously unanswered question about relations with the Roman empire of the east in Constantinople by marrying his son to the eastern emperor's daughter, Theophano, implying equality rather than rivalry between the two. Whereas Charlemagne's empire had been Frankish in essence, Otto's was to be known as the Holy Roman Empire, with Rome itself its proclaimed capital, insofar as any city could be called its capital when the emperor was forever on the move, pacifying his many domains. His grandson Otto III briefly did make Rome a functioning capital, styled himself 'consul', raised the role of the senate and built himself a palace on the Palatine Hill. To emphasise that this 'new' empire was both a Mediterranean and a European one, the Ottos saw to it that the passes through the Alps were made easier to negotiate. This would be carried on by his successors over the coming generations with the development of the St Gotthard Pass and the building of bridges, including one widely believed to have been the world's earliest suspended bridge, over the river Reuss where it flows through the chasm of the Schöllenen Gorge.

Unsurprisingly, given the means by which he acquired the imperial title, Otto I, and his son and grandson (both named Otto) naturally assumed they had the right to choose and depose popes at will. Constantine the Great, the first Roman emperor to become a Christian, had retained to the last his title of *pontifex maximus* (chief priest) pertaining to the old pagan deities. Being in charge of religion went a long way towards being in control of the state. The title had been acquired by Julius Caesar before he was declared 'dictator'. Constantine I, who clearly found the feuds within warring Christian sects confusing and wanted to know what it was he was supposed to be sponsoring, had convened the congress of Nicaea in 325 to get the bishops to establish the official dogma of Christianity. In 380 the Emperor Theodosius I, while not totally outlawing paganism, declared Nicene Christianity to be the official religion of the empire.

To a large extent the custom of the emperor being supreme head of the church had, as Constantine had always intended, continued in the eastern empire. In the West, where the secular imperial power had vacated the stage until restored by papal help or conspiracy, the continuum of the two offices had been broken. The bishops of Rome had assumed superiority and whoever held the position had been considered de facto head of the church. The bishop of Rome took over the old title of *pontifex maximus* (anglicised as 'pontiff' and used to this day) but by claiming the right to choose new emperors – or at the very least agreeing to those chosen – they had created an unintentional rivalry.

Render unto Caesar the things that are Caesar's?

It remains a matter of dispute whether Leo III, placing an imperial crown on the head of the Frankish King Karl in Rome on Christmas Day 800, intended to bestow on him supreme power or proclaim his own right to decide who wielded secular power. The issue could apparently be summed up in the words of Jesus Christ: 'Render unto Caesar the things that are Caesar's and unto God the things that are God's'. Christ was, we assume, talking about taxes versus the soul; the popes were of the opinion that as God had created the world, there was nothing that wasn't God's, and therefore, as God's representative on Earth, theirs. But did the pope have the power to veto an elected emperor, or did the emperor have the power to veto an elected pope, or depose him and name his own? The successors of both inevitably interpreted the quandary in their own favour. God, as usual, failed to intervene.

By the early 11th century the Ottonian Franks had managed to make the imperial title hereditary, much as the Habsburgs would do with greater and more lasting success half a millennium later. When Heinrich III, who had spent much of his life fighting to maintain the empire as a political entity both north and south of the Alps, died aged just 39, Pope Victor II, his own appointee and guardian of his son, immediately crowned his six-year-old son Heinrich IV – who had been crowned as 'King of Hungary' at the age of three – as 'King of the Romans', the title bestowed on prospective emperors before they could be formally given the imperial crown by the pope in Rome.

Heinrich's lengthy reign – he held the title for almost half a century – would see one of the biggest theoretical conflicts on the nature of power between the emperor and the pope, one that would briefly raise its head again 800 years later. The child ruler – still not crowned in Rome – with his mother acting as regent, was considered easy prey for a religious hierarchy determined to assert its primacy over their military protectors. To understand the passions – and the weapons – it is not wrong to draw parallels with the Muslim world even today, in which religion matters more than 'nationality', and being declared an apostate by religious authorities could bring down a president or a king. In a world where the concept of nation-state was all but unknown, and what we today call Europe was loosely known as Christendom, it seemed logical to the pope, as head of Christianity, that he should wield ultimate power, including that to appoint or dismiss the emperor, who ought to be little more than the protector of Christendom, the church's empire. To the emperors, Christendom only survived because their armies held up the Muslim steamroller from both east and west, and therefore it should be up to them to choose which of a host of frequently bickering clergymen should be appointed chief among them. In short, both sides saw the other as subordinate.

The argument between spiritual and secular power has persisted beyond the Muslim world. Soviet dictator Josef Stalin would ask mockingly: 'The Pope? How many divisions does he have?' His successors found out when the charismatic Polish pope John Paul II's pilgrimages back to his homeland drew crowds of millions and fostered support for the free trade union Solidarity, two factors that together would spark the movements in Eastern Europe that ended with the demise of Stalin's empire. The outcome back in the 11th century was not dissimilar. The Investiture Crisis, as it came to be known, was to set the popes and their protectors at each other's throats for a generation.

Our modern concepts of nationality could hardly be better confounded by the name and origins of the pope who successfully called the emperor's bluff. The pope elected in 1073 came from a small town in southern Tuscany, today's central Italy: we cannot be sure today what his native language was as anything that remains is in Latin, but the fact that he is known to history almost universally as Hildebrand (Ildebrando in Italian, which has never been a common name) strongly suggests that German was at least one of them. As I have repeatedly stressed, in this world where power was wielded by families, the memory of multicultural Rome was strong, large scale movements of people recent, and the concept of nationality little more than tribal, a man's native language only rarely gave a clue to his loyalty to any person or institution.

Hildebrand, who took the papal name Gregory VII, certainly had no 'national' agenda in launching his campaign against the German-speaking emperor. As far as Pope Gregory was concerned, the whole of the human race were 'God's children' and therefore all under his charge, as God's chief representative on earth. Gregory was the first pontiff to claim responsibility for – and rule over – the morality, and therefore the lives, of all humanity (or at least those who had seen the light and accepted universal Christianity). In this he was – if you'll pardon the phrase – hell-bent on a course of confrontation with the secular emperor, who claimed to be the guarantor of believers' security on earth if not necessarily in heaven. There was a lot at stake, not just the title of pope or emperor, but the right to appoint and remove bishops and archbishops, who in many cases were not just spiritual but also secular leaders with their own lands or cities which they had ruled since the collapse of the original Roman empire when the people often opted for religious rulers over the 'dukes' and 'princes', who were usually little more than warlords. Being able to appoint or dismiss a bishop therefore was a key weapon in a ruler's armoury, as much for the pope as for the emperor.

Heinrich's own father had offhandedly deposed three popes whose opinions he disliked. His son aspired to follow his example. Heinrich declared the pope deposed in a letter which called him 'Hildebrand, no longer pope but false monk', affirming his own legitimacy as 'by the Grace of God' and claiming the support of 'all my bishops'. In response the pope used his own nuclear weapon: he declared Heinrich excommunicated, cut off from God, in effect no longer a Christian and therefore no longer fit to be ruler of a Christian people: 'I relieve the son of the Emperor Heinrich, who has with unheard of arrogance risen against the Church, of his rule over the Germans and over Italy and release Christians everywhere from any oath they may have sworn to him or might swear to him in future.'

It was a 'this life or the afterlife' contest, and with 'this life' pretty miserable for most people in 11th-century Europe, many of them were tempted to go for the 'afterlife' they had been promised. Religion was woven into the fabric of both power and society, and for a ruler to be excluded was a threat to not just his credibility but any claim to rule. The 'divine right of kings' meant they were given their thrones by God, but in the pre-Reformation world, where the pope was God's unchallenged chief representative on earth, excommunication meant he was effectively withdrawing 'divine right'.

Heinrich's authority – he was still a young man in his 20s – was weakened catastrophically by his excommunication. He faced renewed, widespread rebellion, including a conspiracy to accept the pope's decision and elect a new emperor in his place, in particular from the aristocracy in Saxony, who backed a rival for the imperial title. Heinrich decided there was no alternative and set out with his wife, child and small band of followers for Italy, crossing the Alps in early winter and going to meet the pope at the pontiff's winter retreat at Canossa. More out of pragmatism than contrition, he begged the pope to reverse his excommunication, standing barefoot outside Canossa Castle in January 1077 allegedly for three days and nights without sustenance. It worked: the pope granted him absolution. It would turn out to be a temporary reprieve, but enough to calm revolts against him.

Before the end of either's life, Gregory would again excommunicate him, while Heinrich would again depose him as pope, choosing a successor who finally bestowed the imperial crown on him in Rome. Even that did not last long. Popes even then tended often to be old men with not long to reign. Within two decades a new pope had again excommunicated Heinrich (now for the third time). This time it gave his son, Conrad, tired of waiting for the throne, an excuse to challenge his own father and declare him deposed. His father in return declared Conrad deposed in favour of his other son, Heinrich, on promise he would not follow suit. But after Conrad's death he could not resist and also rebelled against his father, forcing him to abdicate and declaring himself Heinrich V.

The Investiture Crisis finally petered out in a series of agreements that began with the Concordat of Westminster in London in 1107 and ended with the Concordat of Worms in 1122. The end was officially a score draw, but in effect the papacy had won the right to confirm candidates for ecclesiastical positions. Heinrich IV's concession by kneeling before the pope and asking for atonement has gone down in German history as a humiliation of the secular power by the religious. 'Canossa' had become, in German secular consciousness, a euphemism for capitulation.

Following the creation of the first relatively unified German state (albeit without Austria) in 1871, the relationship between secular and religious power again became contentious, largely because most of the southerly states that joined the Reich created by Protestant Prussia were devoutly

Roman Catholic. In 1872 the Vatican refused to accept the ambassador sent by Otto von Bismarck, Chancellor of the newly created German Reich, because he had expressed scepticism towards the doctrine of papal infallibility. The dispute centred on the accession of the mainly Catholic southern German states (notably Bavaria) to the new Reich. The Jesuits in particular preached what the new Reich's Chancellor saw as supremacy of the church over the state. The result was a suspension of relations between the new Germany and the Vatican. The affair led to a dramatic and passionate debate in the new country's parliament, the Reichstag, in which Bismarck made a powerful speech that rang down the centuries evoking old memories: 'Have no fear, we will not be going to Canossa, either in person or in spirit.'

The struggle, which lasted six years, became known as the *Kulturkampf*, and Bismarck gained a major triumph in making state rather than religious marriage obligatory throughout the country, but he eventually backed down on major restrictions on Catholic influence in all education. That, and the elevation of a new pope, meant that once again the conflict had effectively ended in a score draw.

When is a Nation not a Nation?

It is important to pay some attention to the matter of the titles held by the rulers of the empire that still purported to be heir to Rome, including in its territory much of Northern Italy and regions that would eventually fall to France. Most history written in English uses the title 'German King' to refer to emperors or their chosen successors prior to their actual coronation in Rome. This is a classic anachronism, which views the early mediaeval world through the lens of our latter-day concept of nation-states as being somehow eternal. It presupposes that there was at the time an agreed German nation and that therefore it must have had, or strove to have, a 'king'. There was no such thing. As Herbert

Schutz, the distinguished Canadian historian of the period, has rightly noted, 'At the beginning of the tenth century, Central Europe was a a generally amorphous assembly of peoples without definable identity coloured only by the Frankish veneer borne by its leading group.'

There were good historical reasons for this. In AD 212 the Roman Emperor Caracalla had extended citizenship to all free men in the empire, with the result that the key factor in defining identity was the label 'Roman'. This was then followed from the fourth century onwards by the vast migrations known as the *Völkerwanderung*, which saw Germanic tribes move from north and Central Europe to Italy, Spain and North Africa. With 'Roman' by then of increasingly little practical meaning, the definition of identity became little more than tribal or, at its most extended, linguistic. Nor was there any concept of 'homeland' that was more than transient. To quote Schutz again, 'At all times the frontiers were in a state of flux. The concept of borders defining areas of sovereignty had not yet been invented.'

The idea of an overall 'German King' is one largely invented by later historians, mainly in the English-speaking world, to reinforce the misleading idea of a 'German Kingdom' that even remotely resembled a nation-state in the modern sense. The one significant contemporary use of the term was in Latin *rex teutonicorum*, made by Pope Gregory VII, who in his battle with Emperor Heinrich IV used it to pointedly insist he had by his excommunication been stripped of the Roman title. The reaction of Heinrich and his successors was an equally deliberate insistence that the term 'King of the Romans' be used at their 'first coronation' in Aachen rather than left to be handed to them by the papacy. They were thereby reinforcing their claim to represent the legacy of the Caesars, an overlordship of the 'imperial' territory in Italy, including the papal states, which as far as they were concerned were leased rather than given to the popes.

The importance of the title King of the Romans as

something with more than just German significance was most clearly recognised – and almost reinstated – by the man who brought the long, and by then tired, legacy of Charlemagne's empire to an end and tried, unsuccessfully, to create its successor. Anglophone history in particular tends to refer to Napoleon's empire as French and skips over the wider historical perspective. That is again a way of thinking which reflects the result from a later post-Napoleonic viewpoint, a product of the eventual victory of the *anciens régimes* and their national aristocracies, rather than the revolutionary aims of their erstwhile enemy.

There is no question that Napoleon was an advocate of French supremacy in Europe, but he also had his eye on an older aim: to recast the succession to Charlemagne but this time in favour of West Francia rather than East Francia, France instead of Germany. He was not so much destroying the empire that had succeeded that of Rome – which by the time he buried it in 1806 had in any case long effectively lost its lifeblood – but recreating it, with a French rather than German flavour. We know that the love of his life was his first wife, Joséphine de Beauharnais, and not his second. But with Joséphine by that stage no longer fertile, Napoleon's dynastic ambitions required a new marriage with a princess of childbearing age. None could have been better than the daughter of the last Holy Roman Emperor, Marie-Louise, duchess of Parma (the title inherited by the last Habsburg empress, Zita). Perhaps unsurprisingly, his marriage to a pretty 19-year-old worked out better than anticipated. Napoleon became devoted to her.

To understand not only his dynastic ambition but claim to the throne of the Caesars (most of whom in the latter days of empire were, like himself, generals who had taken the throne), we need only look at the names given his son born in 1811. The son of Napoleon Bonaparte, Napoleon François Charles Joseph, had his father's first name followed by the French forms of those of his maternal grandfather, Franz

Joseph Karl, the Austrian and last Holy Roman Emperor, whose imperial title Napoleon had in theory abolished, but in reality intended to replace. The newborn baby would be the first to succeed to the new dynasty. Nor could there be any mistaking the title bestowed on the child at birth: King of the Romans. Born in the Tuileries Palace in Paris, seat of French kings and now his emperor father, he nominally inherited the title of emperor at age four, for just a few days after his father was deposed, but was not allowed by the victors to retain it. He died of tuberculosis at just 21 in Schönbrunn Palace in Vienna, residence of the Habsburgs, whose dynasty he had been supposed to supersede. Not that they were not kind to him. His grandfather gave him the title Duke of Reichstadt, a little fortress now in the Czech Republic. The family called him Franz rather than Napoleon, and he at first showed military prowess as an officer in the Habsburg army, a matter of no minor concern among his father's former foes. One of the more touching exhibits in the Hofburg, the former royal palace in Vienna, is his crib, with an imperial canopy over where his head would have lain and a golden eagle at its foot.

Napoleon's determination to replace the line of German-speaking heirs to the Caesars with his own, francophone family line, with himself as the Augustus of the modern age, is evident in almost everything he did. It is in that light that what is often interpreted as a fateful aberration and 'betrayal' of the French Revolution by turning it into a hereditary monarchical empire should be seen. In one way, that is exactly what Napoleon did, initially by effectively copying the tactics of Augustus Caesar when he ended Rome's civil wars by assuming total power for himself but claiming to be no more than 'first citizen' (*princeps* in Latin, the origin of our word 'prince', showing how easily words can change to fit the circumstances).

Napoleon took the opportunity of civil strife and his own military victories to overthrow the Directoire government and set up new institutions that mirrored those of ancient

Rome, with tribunes and a senate. Napoleon himself took the old Roman title of consul, along with two allies, but made it quite clear that he was 'First Consul', organising a public call for him to be given the office for life, exactly as Augustus had done. He would reinforce the imagery further when he captured Venice and removed from the roof of St Mark's the four great bronze horses which had originally graced the podium of the hippodrome in Constantinople until they were looted by the Venetians helping the notorious fourth crusade, which rather than regaining Jerusalem sacked Christianity's second holiest city. Venetian booty became French booty; yet another symbol of Roman power moved to Paris.

Having already absorbed German lands on the west bank of the Rhine, it took only his colossal victory at Austerlitz to humble the Austrians and that at Jena to cow the Prussians. His armies occupied both Berlin and Vienna. He declared the old 'Holy Roman Empire of the German nation' dead and buried. The new 'Roman Empire' would be that which revolved around the French nation. The vast number – some 300 – of tiny Germanic statelets was radically reduced, though there were still around 100 of them, and nearly all became French vassals, something, as we have seen in the case of Cologne, far from all their citizens resented. Already in 1804 Napoleon had melded the role model of Augustus with that of Charlemagne, implying that he had restored the 'western empire', this time for that branch of the ancient Franks who had become *Français* rather than *Franken*. His evocation of the empire of the early Middle Ages was reinforced by having his robes embroidered with gold bees copied from those on regalia found in the tomb of one of the even earlier Merovingians. He had summoned the pope from Rome to Notre-Dame in Paris, but no doubt with a mind to the Investiture Crisis, placed the crown on his own head to make clear he owed it to no man but himself. The sceptre he held had belonged to Charles V of Spain and

Austria. At his coronation he initially placed on his own head a golden laurel wreath in the manner of the ancient Roman emperors, then with a crown he had designed and commissioned himself in a mediaeval style. Eschewing the diamonds and other sparklers preferred by later European monarchs, the Napoleonic crown was made simply of gold with shell cameos on carnelian stones. He called it, predictably enough, the Charlemagne Crown.

Two other crowns have historically claimed that title, though neither ever sat on the head of Charlemagne. One of them had been used since the 13th century for the coronation of kings of France, and had only recently been destroyed in the French Revolution. The other is officially known as the Imperial Crown of the Holy Roman Empire, a splendid, unconventional structure of eight hinged golden plates held together by two strips of iron, topped with a cross and encrusted with pearls and precious stones. It was probably made for Otto I in the tenth century or for one of his early successors. It is first referred to in the 12th century. For a century it resided in Carlstein Castle in what is today the Czech Republic, and then for a further 300 years in Nürnberg, in the Franken province of Bavaria. Today there are identical replicas in Carlstein and, unsurprisingly, in the chapel in Aachen. The original is on display in the Habsburgs' Hofburg Palace in Vienna where it can be seen today, not far from the cradle of the last King of the Romans, Napoleon II.

The kings and emperors had failed. It was time for their successors to take up the task.

Conclusion

This book began in Berlin, but quickly moved to a historically German city no longer in Germany, Königsberg, today's Russian Kaliningrad, where the *Drang nach Osten,* the great Germanic push eastwards, began with the Teutonic Knights in the 12th century. That long period of conquest and settlement would end in the 20th century in total collapse, a withdrawal westwards of millions of people and near destruction of a nation-state which had taken nearly a millennium to create. We have come to a close in another historically German city no longer in Germany, today's French Strasbourg, in the lands of Alsace-Lorraine, the former 'Realm of Lothar', Charlemagne's grandson, disputed by his heirs, and the beginning of a simmering conflict that would endure more than a thousand years.

The 19th-century English novelist Samuel Butler, whose best known work *Erewhon* ('nowhere' read backwards) is a satire on utopian dreams, is credited with coining the phrase 'God tolerates historians because they can do the one thing that he cannot; change the past'. That does not make the profession immune to surprises. Quite the contrary. In Britain's 2016 referendum on membership of the European Union, amid a torrent of misinformation from politicians on both sides, one that stood out was leading 'Leave' campaigner Boris Johnson, the former London mayor and subsequently UK Foreign Secretary, implicitly comparing the EU with what he claimed were attempts by past powers from the Romans via Charlemagne, Napoleon and Hitler to create a super-state ruled by one power. It was a statement which, particularly with the reference to Hitler, sparked a wave of disbelief and disgust. The biggest problem was that it appeared broadly right to those with a schoolchild's acquaintance with history, while in fact it was very wrong in detail.

'Charlemagne's was the first of a string of failed attempts to construct a Europe dominated by one people or one empire. The Europes of Charles V, Napoleon and Hitler were in fact anti-Europes,' French historian Jacques Le Goff has pointed out. Charlemagne had always intended his empire to be a Frankish-dominated realm rather than a grouping of like-minded polities. The crown thrust on his head by the pope on Christmas Day AD 800 may not have been unwelcome but it was never part of the original plan. His was an empire in the traditional form, intended for rule to be handed down through one family in one tribe, but the Frankish tradition of partitioning kingdoms between male offspring doomed it from the start to fragmentation or internecine warfare. The Ottonian empire which succeeded it was little different, although the Carolingian precedent meant it had from the outset a wider aspiration to recreate the Pax Romana. At one stage it even relocated the capital back to Rome. This mediaeval Holy Roman Empire was hindered by two things in particular: the conflict between the popes and emperors, fighting over the right to ratify the other's election by his peers, and the rivalries between the princes, dukes, counts, bishops and archbishops all competing for the extension of their own power and territory, largely ignoring the emperor in the process.

By the time of Charles V, whose empire was arguably the greatest multinational realm ever, the concept of the nation-state was entirely alien to it. Charles was brought up speaking French, learned German at a relatively early age, but only later came to terms with the language of the greater part of his empire, Castilian Spanish. The Habsburg empire was first and foremost a family affair, and the family would over the generations sprout many branches and speak many languages, down to the dozen or so spoken by the late Otto Habsburg, born in 1913 to what was still a ruling family.

The greatest outbursts of nationalism in the Habsburg empire came relatively late, when the concept of the nation-state as the natural order was reaching its peak: first in the early 19th century when Joseph II abortively tried to make German the sole legal and official language of the empire, and then the 1867 *Ausgleich/Kiegyezés* (in German and Hungarian) compromise, which ended a nationalist revolt in Budapest by giving Hungary equal status with Austria. Even at that stage the official languages of the empire included – alongside German and Hungarian – Czech, Slovak, Polish, Serbian, Croatian, Slovene, Italian, Romanian and Ukrainian. The collapse of the empire was the product of bungling administration, a failure to recognise and placate the 19th century's growing nationalist fever, topped by a blunt and incoherent decision that war was the way to solve all problems.

Napoleon's enthusiasm for emulating the Holy Roman Emperors was based on French domination (as Charlemagne's had been based on that of the Franks). The Conservative British nationalist trick of comparing him to Hitler is not only historically absurd but morally offensive (diminishing as it does the outright evil of Nazism). It is also plain wrong. One of the prime reasons – apart from generalship – of Napoleon's early successes was that he and the French troops who marched at his command were spreading a revolutionary liberalisation of the masses from the aristocratic control of the *anciens régimes* across Europe. For all that he was a dictator, he was also a lawmaker and a leveller regularly welcomed by citizens of the territories he conquered (as we have seen was the case in Cologne). That is why he was feared by the rulers of hidebound states such as Russia and the Habsburg empire. Napoleon sowed a seed of popular dissatisfaction with *anciens régimes* all over Europe which would come to fruition in the revolutions of 1848. The British ruling class portrayed him as a monster to neutralise the degree of support they suspected he would receive from the British working classes, if he ever set foot in England, which they specifically ruled against even after his defeat in 1815.

Most importantly, the comparison of Adolf Hitler to any of the others is an absurdity. Hitler never remotely had a vision of a 'united Europe': he had a vision of a racially pure Germanic empire stretching from the French border to the Urals, on land seized from the 'inferior' Slavs, as laid out clearly from the outset in *Mein Kampf*. His was an empire of aggressive, racist nationalism. He would have been apoplectic at the very concept of multiculturalism. He saw war as necessary, even welcome, but almost certainly regretted the extent to which it spread, which robbed him of leaving to posterity the totalitarian society he dreamed of. The victory over France delighted him as revenge for the humiliation of 1918, but it was never part of his original plan; nor was the invasion and occupation of Belgium, the Netherlands, Denmark or Norway, Greece or Yugoslavia. And he certainly did not want to fight the United Kingdom, which he had hoped would be neutral or even, encouraged by some words in his ear by members of the English aristocracy, an ally.

The English and French declarations of war following his invasion of Poland called his bluff; they had not intervened over the deconstruction of Czechoslovakia. Belgium and the Netherlands were 'collateral damage' in the defeat of France, Denmark and Norway: 'necessary distractions' in securing a western front while he dealt with Russia (and of course acquiring the Norwegian 'hard water' needed for the development of an atomic weapon), while the interventions in Greece, the Balkans and North Africa were primarily brought about by the bungling incompetence of his Italian allies in their attempts to recreate a Mediterranean Roman empire by expanding from their colonial bases in Albania and Libya. Without so many unwanted distractions, the steamroller against Russia might – just might – have worked. We have a few things to thank Mussolini for.

Hitler's absurd claim that Germany needed 'Lebensraum' backfired spectacularly. His war of aggression did indeed expand Germany's presence on the map of Europe from some 541,000 square kilometres, to nearly 700,000 square kilometres at its peak, and included nearly all native German speakers (the exceptions were those in the territory of his Italian ally, and the Swiss Germans). In this the original *Grossdeutschland* vision of the democratic assembly of 1848 in Frankfurt had been realised, but with a very different flavour. The implosion of 1944–5 saw that vast expanse radically reduced to the extent that even the unified Germany of 2017, with a higher population, is substantially smaller than it was a century earlier (357,000 square kilometres), and little more than half what it had been at the Nazis' expansionist peak.

The original rift between the sons of Charlemagne and the division of the empire he cobbled together has been at the heart of conflict in Western Europe for more than a millennium, yet it is a mistake to see it purely as a conflict between France and Germany. For most of that period 'Germany' as a nation-state simply did not exist. The disputes over the divided territory of Lotharingen involved popes, monarchs and would-be monarchs and worse, down to the genocidal wars of the 20th century. The first attempt to heal the wound forever was the European Coal and Steel Community, proposed in 1950 by a French foreign minister, born in Luxembourg to a German father, who in turn had been born French: Robert Schuman. Instituted the following year, the ECSC was intended to neutralise competition over access to the two commodities then still considered essential to warfare. This was most pertinent in the area around the Ruhr, the resource-rich economic powerhouse coveted by Napoleon. But the organisation quickly took in the other

European power wounded by World War II and which had been the emotional heart of the Holy Roman Empire, as well as actual heart of its predecessor: Italy. Thrown into the mix were the three modern countries of the Netherlands, Belgium and Luxembourg, which over the centuries had been ruled by the Spanish, French and Austrian Burgundians, while the House of Luxembourg itself had provided mediaeval Holy Roman Emperors before the Habsburgs made the title their own.

As World War II began to hurtle towards a by now inevitable end, it was the outstanding European leader on the side of democracy who proposed a new pan-European institution to ensure the human rights of all the continent's citizens, not least against their own government. British Prime Minister Winston Churchill had first referred to the idea of a Council of Europe as early as 1943 and it was formally founded by the Treaty of London in May, 1949. The choice of Strasbourg as the home of the new institution was well considered, a city on the Rhine which had for so long been the border between French and German speakers, the fault line which had caused so many geopolitical earthquakes down the centuries. Its greatest achievement, and the one of which Churchill was most proud, remains the European Convention on Human Rights, signed in 1950 and subsequently adopted by 47 European countries (including all the members of the European Union – a wholly separate and quite different organisation, albeit one with its roots in the Council of Europe), among them Russia, Turkey, Serbia and Albania. Indeed, apart from a few disputed territories and the anomaly which is the Vatican City, every state in the largest possible definition of the term 'Europe' is a signatory, save for the post-Soviet dictatorship of Belarus. It is hard to imagine what its founding father, Winston Churchill, would have thought of the idea that the only state considering secession nearly 70 years later would be the one with his face on its banknotes: Great Britain.

What later, through the 1957 Treaty of Rome, became the

European Communities and eventually the European Union, expanded from the six states of Benelux, France, Germany and Italy, over the decades, first to nine, with the addition of Britain, Ireland and Denmark then 12, then 15 members and following the end of the Cold War a rapid expansion to 28 with the 2013 accession of Croatia. Free trade, free movement and erosion of frontier controls prevented some unpleasant settling of old scores, notably between Hungary and the surrounding states of Romania, Serbia and Slovakia, which all seized territories and chunks of population from the historical lands 'belonging' to the Hungarian crown. The implosion of Yugoslavia – the bloodiest war in post-1945 Europe before the Russian–Ukrainian conflict over the old internal Soviet borders – might have been averted if the nationalisms that erupted after Josip Tito's death had been mollified by inclusion in a greater and more affluent union. Slovenia and Croatia have since joined the European Union, while their former mortal enemy, Serbia, has arrested and handed over war criminals from the conflict in an attempt to follow suit. Nato's guarantee in times of war notwithstanding, it has been the European Union's achievements in bringing countries together in time of peace that has been the greatest guarantor of that peace in European history without a single conflict between member states in the 60 years since the Treaty of Rome was signed in 1957.

But history is nothing if not fluid. From the long-term viewpoint, the matter of Europe remains in the balance. The creation of the euro as the single currency of, at time of writing, 19 countries, was a bold and brave step, avowedly taken for political rather than economic reasons. It has put stress on the economies of some states, but it is significant that even the country which has suffered most, Greece, refused to consider abandoning it. Those who dislike and disparage the idea of the European Union regularly predict the euro's collapse, but so far it has become the second largest global reserve currency after the US dollar. Most of the stress on the euro came in the wake of the 2008 global financial crisis. Since then, moves to integrate and streamline the banking systems within the eurozone have moved apace. Whether the euro survives and/or expands may yet be the biggest deciding factor as to what form the future of Europe will take.

The risk for Germany and the Germans is that, as the largest state and the largest linguistic grouping, the Germans can easily be seen as overwhelmingly dominant. As with other languages, German has many accents and dialects, but these are stronger by far than they are in, say, France, England or Russia. The situation in Germany has always been closer to that in Italy, the other great nation-state compilation of the 19th century, where the Piedmontese statesman Massimo d'Azeglio famously declared: 'We have made Italy, now we must make Italians,' a task which required subsuming the multiple dialects – in reality written as well as spoken linguistic variations – of Sicily, Venice, Tuscany, etc. into an accepted common tongue. The same has been true of German, with Hochdeutsch (literally 'High German') more accepted than used. In most regions – formerly independent states in some cases – and notably in Bavaria, Saxony, the Rhineland and Berlin, the language on the streets can seem far removed from Hochdeutsch. Yet it remains the great common denominator. As well as in Germany and Austria, it is also an official language in Switzerland, Belgium and Luxembourg, and is widely understood in southern Denmark, whereas the Plattdeutsch dialect can be as close to Dutch as to be indistinguishable, although the Dutch will never admit it. There is no political desire for dominance in the Germany of the early 21st century, more of a latent dread, yet strongly laced with the hope that their modern vision of a post-conflict Europe with common ideals and values will flourish, overcoming the narrow nationalism which has wrought so much havoc in favour of a shared respect for diversity.

With the possible exception of Spain, Germany is the least

centralised country in Europe, with many powers and laws decided at the level of the *Länder* (the plural of *Land*), the identical word used for other countries as it is not that long since they themselves were 'other countries'. It would be the supreme irony in German history if, after taking a millennium to invent and establish a country called Germany – albeit not containing all Germans – its eventual destiny lay in absorption in a united, federal Europe. The political structure of such a European confederation need not be radically different from that of the federated Germany that exists today, or indeed the United States of America, in which the individual states still have very substantial autonomy in law-making and taxation. As citizens of a federal state, Germans understand this instinctively and are bemused that Britain, which over the past 30 years has also become more of a confederation, does not see things the same way and faces growing centrifugal forces as a result.

For the moment at least, a closer European confederation does not seem to be on the cards. Nationalism remains a powerful force at grass roots level, the United Kingdom's narrow popular vote to leave the EU is proof of this, but by no means proof that the project is doomed. Indeed it is equally possible, given the larger votes in favour of the European Union in Scotland and Northern Ireland, that the most significant casualty could yet be the United Kingdom itself.

This is no time to be complacent about Europe or the relations between its peoples. The flood of migrants from Africa and the Middle East has caused immense pressures and a resurrection of far-right politics in Germany and Austria as well as in France, Hungary, the Netherlands and the United Kingdom. A reversion to competing rival nation-states may be treated as a great game by some politicians but the consequences for their people can be grim, as Europe's bloody history has shown only too well. It is the job of the journalist to report the present, ideally (if all too rarely) with a grasp of historical context, that of the historian to understand the past in its own terms and attempt to relate it to the present. It is the job of neither, but the hobby of both, to predict the future. Journalists report trends. Historians identify patterns. Events often ignore both of them.

It remains to be seen whether the resurgence of nationalism following the near collapse of global capitalism in the first decade of the 21st century, like a malignant cancer returning after a long and unexpected remission, will be a short-term phenomenon or lead to a return to the 'patriotic' tribalism that inevitably leads to war. Europe was extraordinarily lucky to survive the series of cataclysms that made up most of the 20th century. Whether or not the patient – the human race in any civilised form – could survive another outbreak is very much in doubt. At least this time the Germans, with full awareness of their own long and strife-ridden history, are – for the moment at least – on the side of the cure rather than the cancer.

Timeline of German History

55 BC	Julius Caesar crosses Rhine, in show of force against 'barbarians', then retreats.
AD 9	Battle of the Teutoberger Forest. Three Roman legions massacred by Germans. Rome ends plans to extend empire east of Rhine.
AD 50	Cologne founded. Small Roman Settlement on left bank of Rhine expanded to become garrison city.
410	Sack of Rome. Alaric/Ulrich shocks civilisation by capturing the 'eternal city', turning point in decline of the Roman empire.
c.450–750	Major migration of Germanic-speaking tribes south of the Alps, to Italy, Spain, North Africa and Balkans.
800	Frankish King Karl der Grosse (Charlemagne) crowned by the pope as heir to the Caesars. His palace chapel and eventual burial site in Aachen (Aix-la-Chapelle) becomes secondary site, after Rome, for coronations.
840	Charlemagne's empire split between grandsons, basis of a millennium of conflict between future France and future Germany.
962	Otto I, Duke of Saxony, claims Charlemagne's legacy, revives imperial title, crowned by pope as Holy Roman Emperor.
1040	Bavarian monks found Weihenstephan brewery, world's oldest still functioning.
1072–85	Investiture Crisis: power play between pope and emperor. Emperor little more than titular overlord of 1,600 different statelets.
1152	Emperor Friedrich 'Barbarossa' reinstates Roman law, tries to restore central imperial authority but with limited success. Opts for Frankfurt as coronation site for 'King of the Romans', designated heir to Holy Roman Emperor.

1248	Foundation of new Cologne Cathedral around relics of Three Kings donated by Barbarossa.
1255	Königsberg founded by Teutonic Knights on shores of the Baltic. Beginning of Germanic expansion east.
1356	First sitting of the *Hansetag*, Baltic trading league's assembly.
1439	Gutenberg develops movable type printing press.
1452	Friedrich III first Habsburg elected Holy Roman Emperor.
1493	Election of Maximilian I confirms hereditary Habsburg hold on Empire. Dynastic marriages extend family territory west of German-speaking world.
1516	*Reinheitsgebot*: Bavaria passes law on ingredients for beer.
1517	Martin Luther's Ninety-five Theses against church corruption. Beginning of Protestant Reformation.
1516–19	Maximilian I's grandson, Charles V, born in Ghent, Flanders, inherits most of Central Europe, the imperial title and, via his mother, the new nation-state of Spain, plus its New World colonies. Phrase 'empire on which the sun never sets' coined.
1529	Charles V's combined armies see off Ottoman siege of Vienna.
1543	Copernicus's work showing Earth revolves around Sun published.
1618	Defenestration of Prague. Beginning of religious Thirty Years War. German lands devastated. Sweden becomes military power.
1648	Treaty of Westphalia ends Thirty Years War.
1683	Second siege of Vienna ends Ottoman incursions into Habsburg lands.
1701	Friedrich, Elector of Brandenburg, declares himself 'King in Prussia', crowned in Königsberg.
1714	Georg, Elector of Hanover, inherits English throne as George I.
1764	Mozart completes first symphony, aged eight.
1774	Johann Wolfgang von Goethe publishes *The Sorrows of Young Werther*.
1781	Immanuel Kant publishes *A Critique of Pure Reason*.
1791	Mozart conducts premiere of *The Magic Flute* in Vienna.
1804	Beethoven writes 'Eroica' symphony dedicated to Napoleon, but later excises the dedication.
1805	Napoleon occupies Vienna.

1806	Napoleon abolishes Holy Roman Empire. Habsburgs rename their lands Austrian Empire. Napoleon defeats Prussia, occupies Berlin. Napoleon forms Confederation of the Rhine, a grouping of western German states which he intended to become French vassals.
1810	Ludwig I of Bavaria marries Thérèse of Hildburgshausen, wedding party outside Munich becomes first Oktoberfest. Napoleon marries Marie-Louise of Austria, their son proclaimed King of Rome, echoing Holy Roman Emperor heir designate title.
1810–12	Napoleon annexes Hamburg, Bremen, Cologne and Lübeck to French Empire.
1815	Defeat of Napoleon. Confederation of the Rhine merged into new German Confederation, now including Prussia and Austria.
1824	Beethoven conducts premiere of his Ninth Symphony in Vienna.
1848–9	Revolutions throughout Europe. First pan-German assembly meets in Frankfurt as provisional parliament. Squabbles between 'big two', Prussia and Austria, block progress.
1857	*Weisswurst*, Munich's idiosyncratic white sausage invented.
1866	Austro-Prussian war. Battle of Königgrätz seals Prussia's supremacy among German-speaking nations.
1869	Premiere of *Rheingold*, first in Richard Wagner's *Ring* cycle.
1870–1	Franco-Prussian War. Decisive victory for Prussia and allies. German princes acclaim Prussian King Wilhelm I Emperor (Kaiser) of *Deutsches Reich* first pan-German 'nation-state, ('Kleindeutschland' solution excluding Austria).
1886	Karl Benz puts first Patent Motor Car on sale (25 available). Two years later his wife Bertha undertakes world's first distance motor car journey, to visit her mother.
1914	Assassination of heir to Austrian throne in Sarajevo leads to outbreak of World War I.
1918–19	German military reverses, mutiny in army, revolution at home. German Kaiser Wilhelm II abdicates. Armistice declared. Austrian Emperor Karl goes into exile. Versailles treaty blames Germany, demands huge reparations.

Austrian empire dismembered. Rump German-speaking lands demand to join Germany, but vetoed by France and Britain.

German Republic declared in Weimar, Thuringia.

National Socialist German Workers' Party (NSDAP) founded.

1921–4   Hyperinflation caused by reparations.

1923   NSDAP (Nazi) Beer Hall Putsch in Munich.

Adolf Hitler jailed for five years, but released after nine months.

1930–32   NSDAP gains votes in wake of Great Depression.

1932–3   NSDAP largest party in November election with 33 per cent of vote.

January: Hitler asked to form coalition government.

February: Reichstag fire leads to suspension of basic rights.

March: elections give Nazis 43.9 per cent of vote. Communist deputies arrested.

'Enabling Act': Hitler's cabinet to rule without parliament.

New elections held in November with Nazis as sole legal party.

1937   Volkswagen founded by Nazi-run German Labour Front.

1938   March: *Anschluss* – Germany annexes Austria.

September: Munich agreement – French and British prime ministers agree to German annexation of Sudetenland.

1939   German attack on Poland 1 September. Start of World War II.

1941   Hitler attacks Russia in Operation Barbarossa.

1942–3   Defeat at Stalingrad crushes German Eastern Front.

1944   Stauffenberg plot to kill Hitler at Wolf's Lair in East Prussia.

D-Day invasion of occupied Normandy.

1945   January: Soviet troops enter East Prussia.

April: Soviet troops launch assault on Berlin.

Hitler commits suicide.

May 8: German forces surrender unconditionally.

July–August: Potsdam Conference. Germany and Berlin divided into occupation zones. Austria re-established with Vienna as capital, also divided into occupation zones.

German border pushed west to Oder–Neisse line. Eastern territories ceded to Russia and Poland.

Czechoslovakia re-established.

1945–50   Some 12 million German-speakers expelled from 'lost lands', flee to western Germany and Austria.

1948   Currency reform in Western occupation zones creates new Deutsche Mark. Russian zone responds by issuing own currency.

1948–9 Berlin blockade: Russian attempt to block supplies to West Berlin foiled by British–American airlift.

1949   New Federal Republic of Germany comes into existence after signing of constitution agreed with Western occupying powers. 'Provisional' capital set up in Bonn.
German Democratic Republic declared in Soviet zone, claims East Berlin as capital.

1957   Treaty of Rome. West Germany joins with France, Italy, Belgium the Netherlands and Luxembourg to create the European Economic Community, predecessor of today's European Union.

1961   Berlin Wall erected around West Berlin, cutting off access for East German citizens to West.

1969–72 *Ostpolitik*. West German Chancellor Willy Brandt's policy of reconciliation with Eastern Europe peaks in mutual diplomatic recognition by East and West Germany.

1973   Both German states join the United Nations.

1989   Protest movements throughout Eastern Europe. East Germans flee west via Czechoslovakia and Poland. Demonstrations in Leipzig and Berlin.
October: East Germany celebrates 40th anniversary. Demonstrations in East Berlin.
9 November: opening of Berlin Wall. East Germans pour west.

1990   Free elections in East Germany produce coalition in favour of unity with West. 'Two-plus-Four' treaty between both German states and WWII allies formally ends occupation, acknowledging sovereignty of united Germany.
1 July: *Mark der DDR* abolished.
4 October: German reunification marked with ceremony at Brandenburg Gate. Berlin declared capital. Institutions remain provisionally in Bonn.

1999   Chancellery and Bundestag (parliament) of unified Germany move to Berlin

2002   Deutsche Mark abolished. Germany leads adoption of the euro, intended to become common currency for all EU members.

2017   25 March: celebrations of 60th anniversary of Treaty of Rome.

Bibliography and Sources

All publications London, unless otherwise stated.

Stefan Aust, *Der Baader-Meinhof Komplex* (Hoffmann und Kampe, Hamburg, 1985)

Geoffrey Barraclough, *The Making of Modern Germany* (Blackwell, Oxford, 1946)

Christabel Bielenberg, *The Past is Myself* (Chatto & Windus, 1968)

Pater Anselm Bilgri, Peter Köhler and Birgt Adam, *Geheimnisse der Klosterbraurerei* (Sankt Ulrich Verlag, Augsburg, 1998)

Peter Brown, *The World of Late Antiquity* (Thames & Hudson, 1971)

James Bryce, *The Holy Roman Empire* (MacMillan and Co., 1864)

J. B. Bury (ed.), Cambridge Medieval History, vol. 3, *Germany and the Western Empire* (Cambridge University Press, 1922)

Thomas Carlyle, *History of Friedrich II of Prussia* (1858, now available from Project Gutenberg)

Norman Davies, *Europe: A History* (Oxford University Press, 1996)

Len Deighton, *Blood, Tears and Folly* (William Collins, 1993)

Einhard, *Vita Karoli Magni: Das Leben Karls des Großen* (Reclam, Ditzingen, 1996)

Ernst Engelberg, *Bismarck: Das Reich in der Mitte Europas* (Siedler, Munich, 1990)

Mary Fulbrook, *The Divided Nation: Germany 1918–1990* (Fontana, 1991)

Kurt Gayer, *Das deutsche Bierlexikon* (Stern, Hamburg, 1985)

Jürgen Gehl, *Austria, Germany and the Anschluss* (Oxford University Press, 1963)

Martin Gilbert, *A History of the 20th Century: Challenge to Civilisation 1952–1999* (Harper Collins, 1999)

Andrei Gromyko, *Memories* (Hutchinson, 1989)

Sebastian Haffner, *Preussen: Versuch einer Bilanz* (Rowohlt, Reinbek, 1981)

Adolf Hitler, *Mein Kampf* (Eher Verlag, Munich, 1925)

Peter Hoffman, *German Resistance to Hitler* (Harvard University Press, 1988)

Helmut Kohl, *Ich wollte Deutschlands Einheit* (Propyläen, Berlin, 1996)

Walter Laqueur, *Europe since Hitler* (Penguin, 1982)

Jacques Le Goff, *The Birth of Europe: 400–1500* (Blackwell, Oxford, 2005)

Elizabeth Levett, *Europe since Napoleon* (Blackie & Son, second edition, 1925)

Margaret McMillan, *The War that Ended Peace* (Random House, 2014)

Franz von Papen, *Memoirs* (André Deutsch, 1952)

Ronald Payne, Chris Dobson and John Miller, *The Cruellest Night* (Hodder and Stoughton, 1979)

M. E. Pelly and H. J. Yasamee (Eds.), *Documents on British Policy Overseas*, Series 1, vol. v: Germany and Western Europe, 11 August–31 December 1945 (HMSO, 1990)

Bernhard Pollmann (ed.), *Lesebuch zur Deutschen Geschichte, Texte und Dokumente aus zwei Jahrtausende* (Harenberg, Dortmund, 1989)

Alexandra Richie, *Faust's Metropolis: A History of Berlin* (Harper Collins, 1999)

Willam L. Shirer, *The Rise and Fall of the Third Reich* (Simon and Schuster, NYC, 1960)

Helmut Schmidt, *Die Deutschen und Ihre Nachbarn* (Siedler, Munich, 1990)

Helmut Schmitz, *Spray-Athen: Graffiti in Berlin* (Rixdorfer, Berlin, 1982)

Wolfgang Schneider, *Berlin* (Gustav Kiepenheuer, Cologne, 1980)

Jonathan Steinberg, *Bismarck: A Life* (Oxford University Press, 2011)

Hester Vaizey, *Born in the GDR* (Oxford University Press, 2014)

W. Volk, *Berlin, Hauptstadt der DDR* (Verlag für Bauwesen, Berlin, 1980)

And, of course:

Peter Millar, *1989 – The Berlin Wall: My Part in its Downfall* (Arcadia, 2009)

Acknowledgements

A book like this obviously involves a lot of debts to a lot of people, far beyond the bibliography. My interest in Germany and German goes back a long way to my earliest schooldays in Northern Ireland and to oblique family connections.

My uncle Stanley, who had served in the British Parachute Regiment in World War II and been involved in the Normandy landings, went on to become a chaplain in the US army and at the time of my birth, in 1955, was stationed in Garmisch-Partenkirchen in southern Bavaria, not far from where I am as I write this. The earliest present I recall was a teddy bear brought back by my grandparents after visiting him. I much later learned that he was a Horst model by Hermann, the second-oldest German manufacture of toy bears. To me he became 'Deutscher Ted', and he remains so to this day.

Stanley returned to Germany on several occasions with my by then American cousins Brian and Marnie and I would visit the family in both Stuttgart and Heidelberg over the years. By then, in my late teens, I was a more than competent German speaker, something I owe in large part to Bruce Greenfield, my inspired and slightly mad German and Russian teacher at Bangor Grammar School in the 1970s. Bruce made it abundantly clear that learning languages was not a chore but a delight, a way to open windows other people could only peer through, and doors which for them were locked. It has been a great gift.

I also owe a debt to the late Oxford Professor Geoffrey

Barraclough, who had left the university before I arrived, and died in 1984, shortly before I came across his inspirational book, *The Making of Modern Germany*, published in 1946, which demonstrated that to see beyond recent reality you have to delve deep into the past at a time when it seemed the country known as Germany had committed murderous suicide on the world stage.

Thanks are particularly due to Manfred Pagel, then editor of Reuters, who saw fit to send me at the tender age of 26 to be the only non-German correspondent in East Berlin, if only because he thought nothing much was likely to happen there.

The friends and sources I owe a debt to in German-speaking Europe are innumerable, but I will seek to name at least a few, some of whom – given the time scale I have sought to cover – are sadly no longer with us: in roughly chronological order of our acquaintance: Alex Margan, Bärbel Falkner, Dieter and Hannelore Kahnitz, Erdmute Greis-Behrendt, Jochen Kaske, Hartmut Jennerjahn, Karl-Heinz Baum, Uli Joerges, Günther Tzschäckl, Rainer Eppelmann, Volker Scharnewski, Karin Beutler, Horst and Sylvia Falkner, Marion Gräfin Dönhoff, Tatjana Dönhoff, Manica Golob, Vasile Popp, Helga and Gerhard Leitner.

I should also mention the wonderful people at Frankfurt's Institut für Stadtgeschichte, who let me plunder their archives. Also my old school friend, fellow linguist and pupil of Bruce Greenfield, Stephen Conn, and his partner Reinhold Kratz, who first introduced me to the culinary curiosity that is *Grüne Sosse*.

I owe enormous thanks to my editor George Miller, who did such a wonderful job of weeding out my innumerable repetitions, tweaking overly wordy passages and making suggestions of omissions. A non-linear history is an ambitious project and therefore always risked being confusing. George did his level best to make it less so. I shall leave it to the reader to decide to what extent we have succeeded. I thank Piers

Russell-Cobb and Joe Harper of Arcadia Books for having faith in the project and bearing with the repeated delays. Also James Nunn, who has done a great job with the covers of so many of my books and showed great patience in my temperamental attitude towards both front and back covers on this one. Also many thanks to my son Oscar Millar for his draftsmanship in helping with adaptation of maps from Wikimedia Commons.

Last but very far from least, my long-suffering wife Jackie, who has shared so much of the journey from our first marital home in a Stasi-monitored flat in East Berlin to my late-night meandering musings in Liebighof, near her firm's apartment in Munich's salubrious Lehel district, which has been our surrogate home in Germany for some 25 years.

They have been good years.

Peter Millar
Munich, 3 March 2017